ENGLISH

COMMUNICATION SKILLS IN THE NEW MILLENNIUM

LANGUAGE HANDBOOK

J.A. Senn
Carol Ann Skinner

PERFECTION LEARNING® CORPORATION

CRITICAL READERS

Sarah Barlow
Little Red Schoolhouse
New York, NY

Renn Edenfield
Cobb Middle School
Tallahassee, FL

David Thompson
O'Henry Middle School
Austin, TX

Jason Davis
First Avenue Middle
School
Sierra Madre, CA

Kara Mowrey
Bradley Middle School
San Antonio, TX

PROJECT MANAGER
Sandra Stucker Blevins

EDITORIAL DIRECTOR
Sandra Mangurian

EDITORIAL STAFF
Marianne Murphy
Marlene Greil
Donna Laughlin
Susan Sandoval
Vicki Tyler
Catherine Foy
Michelle Quijano
Elizabeth Wenning
Cheryl Duksta
Margaret Rickard

PRODUCTION DIRECTORS
Gene Allen, Pun Nio

PHOTO RESEARCH AND
PERMISSIONS
Laurie O'Meara

ART AND DESIGN
Pun Nio
Leslie Kell
Rhonda Warwick

PRODUCTION
Bethany Powell
Isabel Garza
Rhonda Warwick

COVER
Leslie Kell Designs
Pun Nio
Images © Photodiscs, Inc.

EDITORIAL AND PRODUCTION
SERVICES
Book Builders, Inc.
Gryphon Graphics
Inkwell Publishing
Solutions, Inc.
NETS

Printed in the United States of America.

For information, contact Perfection Learning® Corporation
1000 North Second Avenue, P.O. Box 500
Logan, Iowa 51546-0500.
Phone: 1-800-831-4190 • Fax: 1-800-543-2745
perfectionlearning.com

ISBN-10: 1-58079-397-5
ISBN-13: 978-1-58079-397-1

ISBN-10: 0-7569-7997-8
ISBN-13: 978-0-7569-7997-3

3 4 5 6 RRD 12 11 10 09

Senior Consultants

Tommy Boley, Ph.D.
Director of English Education
The University of Texas at El Paso
El Paso, TX

Deborah Cooper, M.Ed.
Coordinating Director of PK-12
    Curriculum
Charlotte-Mecklenburg Public Schools
Charlotte, NC

Susan Marie Harrington, Ph.D.
Associate Professor of English,
    Director of Writing, Director of
    Placement and Assessment, and
    Adjunct Assistant Professor
    of Women's Studies
Indiana University-Purdue University,
    Indianapolis
Indianapolis, IN

Carol Pope, Ed.D.
Associate Professor of Curriculum
    and Instruction
North Carolina State University
Raleigh, NC

Rebecca Rickly, Ph.D.
Department of English
Texas Tech University
Lubbock, TX

John Simmons, Ph.D.
Professor of English Education and
    Reading
Florida State University
Tallahassee, FL

John Trimble, Ph.D.
University Distinguished Teaching
    Professor of English
The University of Texas
Austin, TX

Contributing Writers

Jeannie Ball

Grace Bultman

Richard Cohen

Elizabeth Egan-Rivera

Laurie Hopkins Etzel

Bobbi Fagone

Lesli Favor

Nancy-Jo Hereford

Susan Maxey

Linda Mazumdar

Elizabeth McGuire

Shannon Murphy

Carole Osterink

Michael Raymond

Duncan Searl

Jocelyn Sigue

Lorraine Sintetos

James Strickler

Diane Zahler

Kathy Zahler

LANGUAGE

Grammar

CHAPTER 6 Complements

CHAPTER 7 Phrases

CHAPTER 8 Verbals and Verbal Phrases

Usage

Mechanics

Spelling

CHAPTER 19 **Spelling Correctly**

Study and Test-Taking Skills Resource

LANGUAGE

firs
nd almo
oped for so
hless. The ho
miraculo
fe

CHAPTER 1

The Sentence

Directions
Write the letter of the term that correctly identifies the
underlined word or words in each sentence.

EXAMPLE   **1.** <u>My family</u> and <u>I</u> drove across the
                     country last summer.
                 1 A simple subject
                     B compound subject
                     C simple predicate
                     D complete predicate

ANSWER   **1 B**

1. We <u>headed south to the Grand Canyon</u>.

2. <u>Have you seen this incredible sight</u>?

3. <u>Incredible walls of red rock</u>.

4. <u>A group of girl scouts,</u> <u>a pair of teachers from Ohio,</u>
     and <u>my family</u> rode down the canyon on donkeys.

5. I <u>could</u> not <u>believe</u> the bumpiness of the ride.

6. <u>Down the canyon we went</u>!

7. The quiet in the canyon <u>was</u> eerie.

8. We <u>could see a hawk circling lazily far above us</u>.

9. The only sound <u>was the roar of the river below</u>.

10. <u>There were beautiful colors in the rock formations</u>
      <u>around us</u>.

1	**A**	simple subject	**6**	**A**	inverted order
	B	simple predicate		**B**	sentence fragment
	C	compound subject		**C**	complete subject
	D	complete predicate		**D**	complete predicate
2	**A**	inverted order	**7**	**A**	complete predicate
	B	compound subject		**B**	simple predicate
	C	simple subject		**C**	simple subject
	D	complete predicate		**D**	inverted order
3	**A**	simple predicate	**8**	**A**	compound subject
	B	complete predicate		**B**	verb phrase
	C	sentence fragment		**C**	complete predicate
	D	simple subject		**D**	complete subject
4	**A**	simple subject	**9**	**A**	simple predicate
	B	compound subject		**B**	compound subject
	C	sentence fragment		**C**	verb phrase
	D	complete predicate		**D**	complete predicate
5	**A**	simple subject	**10**	**A**	sentence fragment
	B	complete predicate		**B**	inverted order
	C	verb phrase		**C**	verb phrase
	D	sentence fragment		**D**	complete subject

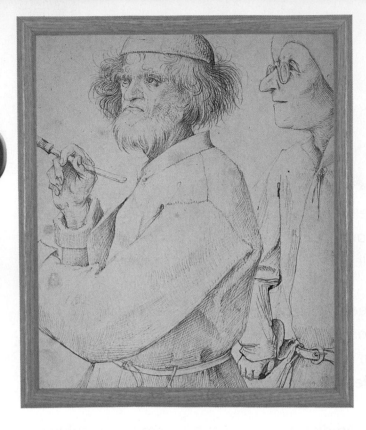

Pieter Brueghel, the Elder. *Painter and the Patron (with Brueghel's self-portrait)*, ca. 1566.
Pen and ink drawing, 8⅔ by 10¼ inches.

Describe What do you think is happening in the drawing? What are the figures holding?

Analyze How do you think each figure in the drawing is feeling? What do you suppose they are thinking?

Interpret What do you think Brueghel is trying to say about the role of patrons in artists' lives?

Judge Which figure seems more interesting to you? Why?

At the end of this chapter, you will use the artwork to stimulate ideas for writing.

A Sentence

One of the most important keys to good speaking and writing is understanding what a complete sentence is.

A **sentence** is a group of words that expresses a complete thought.

To express a complete thought, a sentence must have two parts. The first part, the **subject,** names the person, place, thing, or idea that the sentence is about. The second part, the **predicate,** tells what the subject is or does.

SUBJECT	(names whom or what the sentence is about)
	My brother's friend
	The waffles for breakfast
PREDICATE	(tells what the subject is or does)
	eats a big breakfast every day.
	smell delicious.

From time to time, everyone accidentally includes a group of words without a subject or predicate in writing or conversation. The result is an incomplete thought called a **sentence fragment.**

You can learn more about sentence fragments on pages L283–L292.

CONNECT TO SPEAKING AND WRITING

When you write, your words alone communicate your thoughts and feelings. Organize your words in complete sentences to make your meanings clear. In speaking, you can also use facial expressions, body language, and tone of voice.

PRACTICE YOUR SKILLS

● Check Your Understanding
Combining Subjects and Predicates

 Health Topic **Match a subject in column A with a predicate in column B. Then combine them to form a sentence that makes sense. Begin each sentence with a capital letter and end each one with a period.**

A	B
1. orange juice	cooks breakfast every day
2. the eggs	looks delicious
3. my mom	belongs to my brother
4. many good mornings	is my favorite meal
5. breakfast at our house	starts with a glass of milk
6. the food on the table	cook in the pan
7. the task of cleaning up	provides calcium
8. bacon	begin with breakfast
9. a glass of milk	sizzles on the stove
10. breakfast	contains vitamin C

● Connect to the Writing Process: Drafting
Completing Sentences

Complete each of the sentence fragments below by adding either a subject or a predicate.

11. Every morning my mother

12. A bowl of cereal

13. wants us to eat a good breakfast

14. spilled all over the new carpet

15. My sister

APPLY TO WRITING

E-mail Message: *Subjects and Predicates*

Your cousin is going to be spending a week with you while her parents are away. Because you want her to feel at home, you decide to send her an E-mail message that describes what mornings are like at your house. Be sure that each sentence includes both a subject and a predicate.

Complete Subjects

Some of the subjects in the previous exercises—such as *a glass of milk*—have more than one word. They have more than one word because they are complete subjects.

A **complete subject** includes all the words used to identify the person, place, thing, or idea that the sentence is about.

To find a complete subject, ask yourself either *Who or what is doing something?* or *About whom or what is some statement being made?*

---complete subject---

The heavy fish on the end of my line does not want to be caught.

(Who or what does not want to be caught? *The heavy fish on the end of my line* is the complete subject.)

---complete subject---

The turtle at the bottom of the pond is huge.

(What is huge? *The turtle at the bottom of the pond* is the complete subject.)

PRACTICE YOUR SKILLS

● Check Your Understanding
Finding Complete Subjects

Science Topic **Write each complete subject.**

1. Schools of fish stay together for protection.

2. An average goldfish lives four years.

3. The horseshoe crab existed in its current form 500 million years ago.

4. A small trout swims faster than a person.

5. The upside-down catfish floats on its back.

6. The huge whale shark eats only small plants and small water animals, not people.

7. The world's smallest frog fits inside a thimble.

8. The common sponge is a sea animal with a soft skeleton.

9. The basket starfish has more than eighty thousand arms up to fifteen inches long.

10. Scientists around the world have identified about 21,000 different kinds of fish.

▶ Simple Subjects

As you have seen, a complete subject often includes several words. Within each complete subject, however, there is one main word. This one main word is called the simple subject. It most clearly answers either the question *Who or what is doing something?* or *About whom or what is some statement being made?*

A **simple subject** is the main word in the complete subject.

The complete subject is in bold type, and the simple subject is underlined.

> **That big black <u>cloud</u> on the horizon** means rain.
>
> (What is the main word in the complete subject? Who or what is doing something in this sentence? The simple subject is *cloud*.)

Sometimes the simple subject can have more than one word. Usually these subjects are the names of persons or places.

> **<u>Sports Plus</u> in the mall** has a sale on umbrellas.

Sometimes a complete subject and a simple subject are the same word.

> **<u>Marianna</u>** danced in the rain.

Throughout the rest of this book, the simple subject will be called the subject.

PRACTICE YOUR SKILLS

● Check Your Understanding

Finding Complete and Simple Subjects

Contemporary Life **Write each complete subject. Then underline each simple subject.**

1. A heavy shower ended the monthlong drought.

2. The cotton in the fields needed the rain.

3. Texas receives little rainfall in July.

4. The local farmers welcomed the heavy rain with huge grins.

5. Doppler radar tracked the active storm system across the county.

6. The large trees next door survived the storm.

7. My younger brother danced joyfully in the rain.

8. Many people enjoyed the summer storm.

9. Corn in the fields began to ripen.

10. The TV meteorologist predicted the arrival of the violent storm.

● Check Your Understanding
Finding Complete and Simple Subjects

General Interest **Write each complete subject. Then underline each simple subject.**

11. China is the third-largest country in the world.

12. *Viking I* took pictures of the surface of Mars.

13. A healthy person can take twelve to eighteen breaths per minute.

14. Hair on your head grows daily about 1/100 of an inch.

15. Robert Fulton built the first successful steamboat.

16. The Statue of Liberty is almost 152 feet high.

17. Chinese inventors of the twelfth century created the compass.

18. The first transatlantic journey in a hot-air balloon was in 1978.

19. Ancient Egyptians were the first to develop a calendar year that included 365 days.

20. Elephants reach old age at about sixty-five.

● Connect to the Writing Process: Drafting
Using Complete or Simple Subjects

Follow the directions to write complete sentences.

21. Use the word *boy* as a simple subject.

22. Use the word *teacher* as part of a complete subject.

23. Use the word *cat* as part of a complete subject.

24. Use the word *students* as a simple subject.

25. Use any two-word noun as a simple subject.

Communicate Your Ideas

APPLY TO WRITING

Postcard: *Simple and Complete Subjects*

Grandma Moses. *Moving Day on the Farm,* 1951.
Oil on pressed wood, 17 by 22 inches. Copyright © 1951 (renewed 1979), Grandma Moses Properties Co., New York.

After a trip to the country, you plan to send a postcard to your parents describing a scene similar to the one shown in the painting above. Brainstorm responses to the following questions before writing.

- Which country scene was your favorite? Why?
- Which specific items in the scene were interesting?
- How did items in your scene look, feel, or smell?

Be sure to include complete and simple subjects in your description.

▶ Complete Predicates

In addition to a subject, every sentence must have a predicate.

> A **complete predicate** includes all the words that tell what the subject is doing or that tell something about the subject.

To find a complete predicate, first find the subject. Then ask yourself either *What is the subject doing?* or *What is being said about the subject?*

⌐———————— complete predicate ————————⌐
The cat **purred loudly in the quiet room.**

(The subject is *cat*. What did the cat do? *Purred loudly in the quiet room* is the complete predicate.)

⌐———— complete predicate ————⌐
Our dog **has a brand-new collar.**

(The subject is *dog*. What is being said about the dog? *Has a brand-new collar* is the complete predicate.)

PRACTICE YOUR SKILLS

● Check Your Understanding
Finding Complete Predicates

General Interest **Write each complete predicate.**

1. That zany zebra plays the zither.
2. A big bear with a balloon bolted through the barn.
3. Furry foxes fought fiercely for food.
4. The giant giraffes greeted me graciously.
5. Lazy llamas from Liberia licked the lemons.

6. Chilly chipmunks chattered cheerfully.

7. The brown baboons banged on the bongo drums.

8. The round raccoons raced the reindeer.

9. The timid tiger tripped on a torn tuxedo.

10. Pudgy pandas played the piano with precision.

11. Giant gorillas gathered guavas for guests.

12. Kangaroos kept kiwis in their kitchens.

13. Worms wrestled with weary wasps in watermelons.

14. Capable cheetahs challenged customers to chess.

15. Slippery seals sounded the shiny saxophones.

Simple Predicates, or Verbs

Each complete predicate has one main word or phrase that tells what the subject is doing or that tells something about the subject. This main word or phrase is called a simple predicate, or verb.

A **simple predicate,** or **verb,** is the main word or phrase in the complete predicate.

In the following sentences, the complete predicate is in bold type and the simple predicate, or verb, is underlined twice.

My father **cooked Italian food last night.**

(What is the main word in the complete predicate? What did the subject do? The verb is *cooked.*)

Jody **wants a trip to Mexico for her birthday.**

Some verbs tell what the subject is doing. These are action verbs. Some action verbs—such as *run, talk,* and *drive*—show physical action. Other action verbs—such as *dream, think,* and *worry*—show mental action.

Sometimes verbs do not show action. These verbs tell something about a subject. The following is a list of some common verb forms that are used to make a statement about a subject.

COMMON VERBS THAT MAKE STATEMENTS				
am	is	are	was	were

My map **is in the trunk of your car.**

The geography test **was unusually long yesterday.**

A complete predicate and a simple predicate can be the same.

The happy child **giggled.**

You can learn about subject-verb agreement on pages L393–L429.

PRACTICE YOUR SKILLS

 Check Your Understanding
Finding Complete Predicates and Verbs

Geography Topic **Write each complete predicate. Then underline each verb.**

1. The largest state in the United States is Alaska.

2. The Alaskan pipeline transports crude oil over land.

3. The Underground is the name of London's busy subway system.

4. Christopher Columbus's discoveries in 1492 led to the European settlement of the Americas.

5. The Pyrenees Mountains separate France from Spain.

6. Lafayette sailed from France to America on March 26, 1777.

7. The Black Sea is along the northern coast of Turkey and below the southern coast of Ukraine.

8. The Mississippi River divides the eastern United States from the western United States.

9. The Rio Grande borders Mexico and Texas.

10. California's coastline runs along the Pacific Ocean.

● Check Your Understanding
Finding Verbs

Sports Topic **Write each verb.**

11. The infielder caught the ball for an out.

12. Their brothers are the umpires for tonight's game.

13. Paul worries about his batting average.

14. I thought about your suggestion for a new coach.

15. Dad was a coach for my team last year.

16. The pitcher threw the ball quickly to second base.

17. Jerry played on Sue's team.

18. Kyle dreamed of home runs.

19. The coach yelled at the players.

20. The most popular team sport in our small town is baseball.

● Connect to the Writing Process: Revising
Expanding Sentences

Revise the following sentences, which do not contain enough information, by adding information to the simple predicate.

21. The catcher missed.

22. John hit.

23. Myra batted.

24. The shortstop tagged.

25. I play.

26. Samantha pitched.

APPLY TO WRITING

News Story: *Predicates and Verbs*

The editor of your school newspaper has asked you to write a news story about tonight's baseball game. Be sure to include information in your story that answers the questions *Who? What? Where?* and *When?* Don't forget to tell which team won the game! When you have finished, underline the complete predicates and circle the verbs in your story.

▶ Verb Phrases

The verb of a sentence sometimes needs help to make a statement or to tell what action is taking place. Words that help a verb are called **helping verbs,** or auxiliary verbs.

The main verb and any helping verbs make up a **verb phrase.**

The following is a list of common helping verbs.

COMMON HELPING VERBS	
be	am, is, are, was, were, be, being, been
have	has, have, had
do	do, does, did
OTHER VERBS	may, might, must, can, could, shall, should, will, would

The verb phrases in the following examples are underlined twice, and the helping verbs are in **bold** type.

The cast **is** practicing hard for next week's play.

John **has been** acting for years.

The Baldwins **must have** seen a different play.

You can learn about subject-verb agreement with verb phrases on pages L400–L401.

PRACTICE YOUR SKILLS

● Check Your Understanding
Finding Verb Phrases

Contemporary Life | **Write each verb phrase.**

1. Drew might audition for a part in the school play.

2. Sarah may be singing in the talent show tomorrow.

3. Karen can memorize almost anything.

4. Next month I will volunteer as a set painter.

5. The drama club does practice an hour every afternoon after school.

6. The director should have warned us about the trap door on the set.

7. By the end of Saturday's rehearsal, the cast had blocked the entire first act of the play.

8. Susan did get the lead in the play.

9. My brother has forgotten his lines in the second act again this afternoon.

10. My family has invited the cast to a party after the performance.

Interrupted Verb Phrases

A verb phrase is often interrupted by one or more words. The verb phrases below are in bold type.

> A compass **can** easily **locate** true north.
>
> I **have** never **hiked** this canyon before.

Not and its contraction *n't* are never part of a verb phrase.

> Pearl **is** not **going** with us.
>
> Paulo **did**n't **hear** the weather report.

In some questions the subject comes in the middle of a verb phrase. To find the verb phrase in a question like this, turn the question around to make a statement.

> **Does** Terry **know** the date of his trip?
>
> (Terry *does know* the date of his trip.)

Throughout the rest of this book, a verb phrase will be called a verb.

When you read a question aloud, your voice usually changes at the end of the sentence. This change in pitch signals to the listener that you are asking a question.

PRACTICE YOUR SKILLS

● Check Your Understanding
Finding Verb Phrases

Contemporary Life   **Write each verb phrase.**

1. We couldn't find the tent.
2. Will your brother drive us to the campground in Sumter County?
3. Does the campfire begin at sunset?
4. My sister can easily cook over an open fire.
5. Campers will often toast marshmallows.
6. Does Gina like camp life?
7. I have never been to this campground before.
8. Sabrina wouldn't help with the extra gear.
9. Would you swim in this lake?
10. Tom could easily bring his canoe along with us.
11. The boys can't forget their warm jackets.
12. Did you pack the lantern?
13. Molly has only brought enough food for dinner tonight and breakfast tomorrow.
14. What will she eat for breakfast?
15. Our parents are not going to the grocery store.

Writing Sentences Using Helping Verbs

Write a sentence for each verb. Include the helping verb *has* or *have* in at least two of your sentences. Then underline each subject once and each verb twice.

16. paddled   **19.** waded

17. tumbled   **20.** sank

18. raced   **21.** sailed

Communicate Your Ideas

APPLY TO WRITING

Letter of Application: *Interrupted Verb Phrases*

Your scout leader has recommended you to serve as an assistant day camp counselor for first- and second-grade children. Think about the situation illustrated in the photograph. Write a letter to the head counselor, explaining why you are interested in the job. Use verb phrases and interrupted verb phrases in your letter. Be prepared to identify all the verbs you used.

Sports Topic **Write the subject and verb in each sentence.**

1. Without William Webb Ellis, people wouldn't enjoy football today.

2. This little-known athlete of long ago scored football's first touchdown.

3. In 1823, Ellis was eagerly playing a game of soccer at Rugby School in England.

4. Soccer players could move the ball only with their feet and their heads.

5. Team members couldn't touch the ball with their hands in that game.

6. All of a sudden, Ellis grabbed the ball.

7. Ellis ran toward the goal line at the opposite end of the field.

8. The strange new play gave the game many more exciting possibilities.

9. A new game had just begun.

10. American football definitely was on its way.

11. Several teams organized the first American professional team in 1895.

12. In the early days of football, players didn't wear any equipment, not even helmets.

13. In the last seventy-five years, many changes have occurred in football.

14. For example, coaches developed the forward pass in 1906.

15. Now football captures the attention of millions of spectators.

⏵ Different Positions of Subjects

When the subject comes before the verb, a sentence is in its **natural order.** In the following examples, each subject is underlined once, and each verb is underlined twice.

> The audience cheered as the show began.
>
> In April the teachers stage a show.

When the verb comes before the subject, the sentence is in **inverted order.** To find the subject in such a sentence, turn the sentence around to its natural order.

> INVERTED ORDER   Over the noise sang Mr. Davis.
>
> NATURAL ORDER   Mr. Davis sang over the noise.

Questions are usually written in inverted order. To find the subject easily in a question, change the question into a statement.

> QUESTION   Has Roberta operated these lights before?
>
> STATEMENT   Roberta has operated these lights before.
>
> QUESTION   Did you finish your costume?
>
> STATEMENT   You did finish your costume.

Sentences beginning with *there* or *here* are also in inverted order. To find the subject in such a sentence, turn it around to its natural order.

> INVERTED ORDER   There are some mittens in the chest.
>
> NATURAL ORDER   Some mittens are in the chest.
>
>   (Sometimes *there* must be dropped for the sentence to make sense.)

INVERTED ORDER	Here is the script.
NATURAL ORDER	The script is here.

You can learn about subject-verb agreement with inverted order on page L407.

CONNECT TO WRITER'S CRAFT

One way that writers create variety with their sentence structure is to use sentences with inverted order from time to time. This variety in structure helps the writer present images in an order that can be visualized smoothly and realistically by the reader. Notice that the second sentence in the following passage is in inverted order.

> This old man wore a blue denim coat buttoned to the throat with brass buttons, as all men do who wear no shirts. Out of the sleeves came strong bony wrists and hands gnarled and knotted and hard as peach branches. The nails were flat and blunt and shiny.
>
> —*John Steinbeck,* The Red Pony

Understood Subjects

Subjects sometimes do not even appear in a sentence. In a command or a request, the subject *you* is not stated. That use of the word *you* is called an **understood subject,** because the subject is understood to be in the sentence.

COMMAND OR REQUEST	(you) Wait for me!
	(you) Smile for the camera.
	(you) Enjoy the show.

PRACTICE YOUR SKILLS

● Check Your Understanding
Finding Subjects and Verbs

Contemporary Life **Write the subject and verb in each sentence.**

1. Is the faculty rehearsing the skits with the seventh graders for the comedy hour tonight?

2. There are not many tickets available anymore.

3. From the auditorium came a boisterous cheer during rehearsal today.

4. Did Allison finish her work on the set?

5. There are three door prizes for the students.

6. Can the teachers actually be funny?

7. Here is Ms. Barton in the center of the stage.

8. With a timid grin, she greeted the rowdy audience.

9. Over the P.A. system came the music for her song, "Yankee Doodle Dandy."

10. Through the auditorium ran Mr. Helms.

● Check Your Understanding
Finding Subjects and Verbs

Science Topic **Write the subject and verb in each sentence. If the subject is an understood *you*, write *you* in parentheses.**

11. Did Nathan see a snowflake under his microscope during lab period today?

12. Write an entry in your journal every day this week about your science experiments.

13. During third period today, Mr. Brown will invite a guest speaker to our science class.

14. Along the edge of the glass beaker were dozens of tiny crystals.

15. Deliver my journal of experiments to Mr. Brown.

16. Read to the class your journal entry about our experiment with the hamster.

17. At the end of the class period, I will ask Mr. Brown about sound waves.

18. Is Dennis taking life science again this year?

19. Answer the question quickly.

20. Will salt dissolve in our solution?

● Connect to the Writing Process: Revising
Using Different Positions of Subjects

21.–25. Rewrite any five of the preceding sentences so that they are in natural order.

Communicate Your Ideas

APPLY TO WRITING

Friendly Letter: *Different Positions of Subjects*

The teachers at your school put on a talent show to help raise money for a local charity. Your best friend was unable to attend, because he had the flu. Write him a friendly letter. Include details about some of the funniest moments from the show. Before writing, brainstorm answers to the following questions.

- Who gave a creative performance? What did he or she do?
- What was the best presentation? Why?
- What did you learn about the teachers?

Be sure to use subjects in different positions.

QuickCheck   Mixed Practice

Write the subject and verb in each sentence. If the subject is an understood *you*, write *you* in parentheses.

1. Do you know the poems of Edgar Allan Poe?
2. Have you ever read any of his short stories?
3. You can discover more about his personality.
4. There are many fans of his detective stories.
5. Didn't the Allans adopt him at the age of three?
6. Into schoolwork plunged young Poe.
7. At the beginning of his writing career were hundreds of publishing opportunities for his poetry.
8. Write an essay about "The Raven."
9. After the poems came fiction.
10. Did you ever read "The Masque of the Red Death"?
11. Here are some of his first detective stories.
12. To many literary publications, Poe contributed articles.
13. On your paper, write a description of C. Auguste Dupin, the main character in Poe's detective stories.
14. Poe worked as an editor throughout his life.
15. Does Poe have an effect on world literature?
16. Listen to a reading of "The Tell-Tale Heart."
17. The suspense builds constantly in the story.
18. Does Susan enjoy the poem "Annabel Lee"?
19. Its rhythm is eerie.
20. She was overcome by the loneliness in the poem.

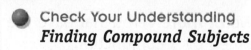

► Compound Subjects

Some sentences have two or more subjects joined by the conjunction *and* or *or*. These subjects together are called a compound subject.

A **compound subject** is two or more subjects in one sentence that have the same verb and are joined by a conjunction.

Notice that each subject in the following examples shares the same verb—*attended*.

ONE SUBJECT	The <u>children</u> <u>attended</u> the performance.
COMPOUND SUBJECT	The <u>children</u> and their <u>parents</u> <u>attended</u> the performance.
COMPOUND SUBJECT	The <u>children</u>, their <u>parents</u>, and the <u>mayor</u> <u>attended</u> the performance.

You can learn about subject-verb agreement of compound subjects on pages L411–L412.

PRACTICE YOUR SKILLS

● Check Your Understanding
Finding Compound Subjects

General Interest **Write each compound subject.** Remember that *and* and *or* are not considered part of the subject.

1. At the circus, clowns and acrobats will be featured.

2. Lions and elephants do not often appear in the same act.

3. Dancers and jugglers were photographed during the parade to center ring.

4. Popcorn and cotton candy taste good at the circus.

5. Did horses, dogs, or lions perform in the show?

6. Only dedicated performers and gifted artists work for the circus.

7. A trapeze performance and a clown act are scheduled.

8. The ringmaster and the bandleader have arrived.

9. A tiger and a lion will perform tricks.

10. At today's circus were clowns, lions, and horses.

11. The dogs and the silly seals barked to the audience.

12. A magician and a bunny entertained the crowd.

13. A clown on stilts and a clown on a unicycle crashed.

14. Motorcycles and baby carriages were clown vehicles.

15. The elephants and the horses performed in different rings.

▶ Compound Verbs

Some sentences have two or more verbs joined by the conjunction *and, or,* or *but.* These verbs together are called a compound verb.

A **compound verb** is two or more verbs that have the same subject and are joined by a conjunction.

Notice that each verb in the following examples shares the same subject—*Patty.*

| ONE VERB | Patty is sunning herself. |
| COMPOUND VERB | Patty is sunning herself and will swim in the ocean later. |

A sentence can include both a compound subject and a compound verb.

> The <u>parents</u> and their <u>children</u> <u>talked</u> with the lifeguards and <u>toured</u> the beach.

PRACTICE YOUR SKILLS

● Check Your Understanding
Finding Compound Verbs

Contemporary Life **Write each compound verb.**

1. Janet has packed a lunch and will spend the day at the beach.
2. She will take pictures and develop them quickly.
3. Guy played in the sand and built a sand castle.
4. Mark walked the beach and looked for shells.
5. Brian fished for bait and caught a turtle.
6. Jean will run and swim at the beach.
7. Shirley caught the beach ball and threw it back.
8. Mark will take the boat to the repair shop or will fix it himself.
9. Cherri took a soda from the ice chest and drank it.
10. Mia applied sunscreen and removed her sunglasses.

● Connect to the Writing Process: Revising
Using Compound Subjects and Verbs

11.–15. Choose five sentences from the two previous exercises, and write them so that they include both a compound subject and a compound verb.

APPLY TO WRITING

Persuasive Paragraph: *Compound Subjects and Verbs*

Your parents are in charge of choosing a location for the family reunion this year. You would like for it to be at the same place it was last year, because you and your cousins really enjoyed yourselves. Prepare a persuasive paragraph for your parents in which you state that you would like to return to the same place for the reunion.

- Brainstorm a few good reasons why the reunion should be held at the same place.
- Consider details about the location, shelter, facilities, and your family's needs.
- Give examples of activities you and your cousins enjoyed to support your choice.

Use compound subjects, compound verbs, and a combination of the two in your sentences.

Science Topic **Write the subject and verb in each sentence.**

1. In 1951, a powerful hurricane and heavy winds were heading for Bermuda.

2. Weather forecasters and the people of the island were waiting for the hurricane with fear.

3. By noon the storm had almost reached the coast and caused much damage.

4. Trees and poles were swaying in the fierce wind.

5. Then a weather forecaster stopped and noticed something very strange.

6. A second hurricane was also traveling and blowing toward the island.

7. Eventually the second storm reached the first storm and smashed into it.

8. The collision weakened both hurricanes and threw them off course!

9. The storms changed course and headed toward the ocean.

10. The buildings and the people of the island survived both hurricanes.

11. The natives and tourists on the island were very happy and grateful.

12. The winds and water from the storm had caused much fear.

13. Water flooded buildings and eroded the beach.

14. Scientists and weather observers seldom have witnessed anything like those two hurricanes.

15. Wind and rain can cause a great deal of damage.

Kinds of Sentences

A sentence has one of four purposes. A sentence can make a statement, ask a question, give a command, or express strong feeling. The purpose of a particular sentence determines which end mark will go at the end of that sentence.

A **declarative sentence** makes a statement or expresses an opinion and ends with a period.

> The California Gold Rush occurred in 1849. (statement)
>
> Gold makes people greedy. (opinion)

An **interrogative sentence** asks a question and ends with a question mark.

> Do you like gold?
>
> How many people traveled to California for the gold?

An **imperative sentence** makes a request or gives a command and ends with either a period or an exclamation point.

> Follow me along Route 6 to the gold museum.
>
> (This imperative sentence ends with a period because it is a mild request.)
>
> Catch that gold nugget!
>
> (This imperative sentence ends with an exclamation point because it is a strong command.)

An **exclamatory sentence** expresses strong feeling and ends with an exclamation point.

That's the biggest piece of gold I have ever seen!

What a thrilling discovery that was!

Professional writers use a variety of types of sentences when they write. This keeps their writing interesting. Notice the different types of sentences used in the following dialogue:

"She'll make you miss the parade," said Odett.

"Oh, no!" cried Sally, who was only six.

"Don't worry," said Billy, holding her hand as they crossed the street on the brick walkway. "I'll see you get to the parade—if there is one."

"Why shouldn't there be?" Odett tilted her head back to examine the white clouds overhead.

—*Peni R. Griffin*, Switching Well

PRACTICE YOUR SKILLS

● Check Your Understanding
Classifying Sentences

General Interest **Using the following abbreviations, label each sentence.**

declarative = *d.*   imperative = *imp.*
interrogative = *int.*   exclamatory = *ex.*

1. What an amazing place gold has had in legend and history

2. It was partly responsible for the rapid settlement of the West

3. Do you know when the Gold Rush started

4. Is gold still mined in the United States

5. Gold is a metal that never rusts or tarnishes

6. Read the story about Croesus

7. Wasn't he a wealthy ruler in ancient times

8. Yes, gold filled every room in the house

9. How proud he was of his golden throne

10. At the library look for pictures of his house

● **Connect to the Writing Process: Editing**
Using Different Kinds of Sentences

11.–20. Write the sentences from the preceding exercise, adding the correct end punctuation for each sentence.

Communicate Your Ideas

APPLY TO WRITING
Descriptive Note: *Kinds of Sentences*

Your class has taken a trip to a local museum to see a gem collection like the one in the picture. Write a note to your mother that describes what you have seen on the field trip. Use declarative, interrogative, imperative, and exclamatory sentences in your note.

✓ QuickCheck Mixed Practice

Science Topic **Using the following abbreviations, label each sentence.**

declarative = *d.*   imperative = *imp.*
interrogative = *int.*   exclamatory = *ex.*

1. Diamonds are the hardest natural stones on Earth
2. Are they used to cut gemstones
3. Where can you find diamonds
4. Most diamonds are mined in Africa
5. How beautiful they are
6. Diamonds are cut into many different shapes
7. Do you see the marquis-shaped stone
8. The brilliant, or round, cut is the most popular
9. Many diamonds have flaws
10. These flaws might make them look cloudy
11. A diamond's color is graded from yellow to white
12. Look at that white diamond
13. Carbon is under pressure for millions of years
14. Are there blue diamonds
15. You can buy irradiated diamonds of other colors

Diagraming Subjects and Verbs

A diagram to a buried treasure would show you where the roads and landmarks that lead to the treasure are. A **sentence diagram** is very similar. It uses lines and words to help you find and identify all the parts of a sentence.

Subjects and Verbs All sentence diagrams begin with a baseline. A straight, vertical line then separates the subject (or subjects) on the left from the verb (or verbs) on the right. Capital letters are included in a diagram, but punctuation is not. In the second example that follows, notice that the whole verb phrase is written on the baseline.

Flies buzzed.

Flies	buzzed

John had been winning.

John	had been winning

Questions A question is diagramed as if it were a statement.

Was Donna listening? (Donna was listening.)

Donna	Was listening

Understood Subjects When the subject of a sentence is an understood *you,* as in a command or a request, place *you* in parentheses in the subject position.

Listen.

(you)	Listen

Compound Subjects and Verbs Place the parts of a compound subject or a compound verb on parallel horizontal lines. Then put the conjunction connecting each part on a broken line between them.

Canoes and kayaks were drifting.　　　　Lee hums or whistles.

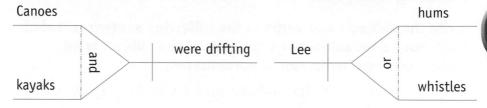

Maria and Rita studied and read.

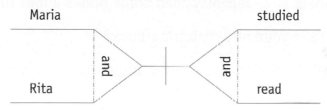

PRACTICE YOUR SKILLS

Diagraming Subjects and Verbs

Diagram the following sentences or copy them. If you copy them, draw one line under each subject and two lines under each verb. If the subject is an understood *you,* write *you* in parentheses.

1. Weeds grow.
2. Shutters are banging.
3. Are you looking?
4. Stop!
5. Raul and Martin are coming.
6. We are shaking!
7. Martin tripped and stumbled.
8. Are you staying?
9. Doors and windows creaked and rattled.
10. Everyone ran and ran!

Finding Subjects and Verb Phrases

Write the subjects and verbs in the following sentences. Label each word _S_ for subject or _V_ for verb. If the subject is an understood _you_, write _you_ in parentheses.

1. The science club has chosen bird study for its summer project this year.

2. The members have recently read some books about birds.

3. Has Jeff read your bird-watching book?

4. Kele has started a collection of stamps with bird pictures on them.

5. Other members are now constructing a simple ceramic birdbath.

6. We don't need a fancy concrete one.

7. A garbage can cover on a wooden post would work just as nicely.

8. We will always have water in it for the birds.

9. Many different birds will use the birdbath.

10. The members have also planned some food stations.

11. Our teacher gave several pairs of binoculars to the club.

12. Look at that beautiful bluebird!

13. Through his binoculars Andy spotted a warbler.

14. There is a raven at the birdbath now.

15. A bird sanctuary has always been a joy to both birds and people.

Understanding Kinds of Sentences

Write each sentence, using the correct end mark. Then label each sentence *declarative, interrogative, imperative,* or *exclamatory.*

1. Some people research their family history
2. What do they do with the information
3. They chart a family tree
4. Look at my family tree
5. At the top are my great-grandparents
6. That chart is very impressive
7. Where is your name
8. Be patient
9. I haven't gotten that far yet
10. I can hardly wait to start my family tree

Using Subjects and Verbs

Write ten sentences that follow the directions below. (The sentences may come in any order.) Write about one of the following topics or a topic of your choice: Little League baseball, girls in sports, or a new sport.

1. Write a declarative sentence.
2. Write an interrogative sentence.
3. Write an imperative sentence.
4. Write an exclamatory sentence.
5. Write a sentence with a verb phrase.
6. Write a sentence with an interrupted verb phrase.
7. Write a sentence with a compound subject.
8. Write a sentence with a compound verb.
9. Write a sentence with a compound subject and a compound verb.
10. Write a sentence that starts with the word *there.*

Underline each subject once and each verb twice. Then check for capital letters and end punctuation.

Language and *Self-Expression*

Pieter Brueghel (1525?–1569) was a Flemish artist who worked as an engraver, illustrator, printer, and painter. He is best known for his landscapes and his depiction of peasant life.

This self-portrait reveals Brueghel's attitude toward the role of patrons in painters' lives. A self-portrait is similar to an autobiography in the way it reveals something about the artist through its details. Write a brief autobiographical sketch. Choose an event from your life that reveals something important about your attitudes or feelings. Use varied sentences in your sketch.

Prewriting Make a cluster diagram for your autobiographical sketch. In the center, write the event you will describe. Radiating from the center, write the details you will include. Write down what the details reveal about you.

Drafting Write a first draft. In it describe the event you have chosen and use the details from your cluster diagram.

Revising Reread your sketch. Be sure you have used different kinds of sentences to keep your writing interesting. Does your sketch reveal something about your attitudes or feelings? Make any changes necessary to help readers learn something about you from the sketch.

Editing Check for errors in spelling and punctuation. Be sure you have used appropriate end marks for each type of sentence in your sketch.

Publishing Make a final copy of your autobiographical sketch. Share it with family members, and compare memories of the event you have described.

Another Look

A **sentence** is a group of words that expresses a complete thought.

A group of words that expresses an incomplete thought is called a **sentence fragment**.

Subjects and Predicates
A **complete subject** includes all the words used to identify the person, place, thing, or idea that the sentence is about. *(page L7)*

A **simple subject** is the main word in the complete subject. *(pages L8–L9)*

A **compound subject** is two or more subjects in one sentence that have the same verb and are joined by a conjunction. *(page L27)*

A **complete predicate** includes all the words that tell what the subject is doing or that tell something about the subject. *(page L12)*

A **simple predicate,** or **verb,** is the main word or phrase in the complete predicate. *(pages L13–L14)*

The main verb and any helping verbs make up a **verb phrase.** A verb phrase is often interrupted by one or more words. *(pages L16–L18)*

A **compound verb** is two or more verbs that have the same subject and are joined by a conjunction. *(pages L28–L29)*

Other Information about Subjects and Verbs
Recognizing sentences in **natural order** *(page L22)*

Recognizing sentences in **inverted order** *(page L22)*

Identifying an **understood subject** *(page L23)*

Kinds of Sentences
A **declarative sentence** makes a statement or expresses an opinion and ends with a period. *(page L32)*

An **interrogative sentence** asks a question and ends with a question mark. *(page L32)*

An **imperative sentence** makes a request or gives a command and ends with either a period or an exclamation point. *(page L32)*

An **exclamatory sentence** expresses strong feeling and ends with an exclamation point. *(pages L32–L33)*

 **Posttest**

Directions
Write the letter of the term that correctly identifies the underlined word or words in each sentence.

EXAMPLE   **1.** Carlotta, Lucy, and I <u>entered</u> the science fair.

      1 A simple subject
        B compound subject
        C simple predicate
        D complete predicate

ANSWER   **1 C**

1. Our <u>entry</u> in our class's science fair was a model of a volcano.

2. <u>Carlotta</u> and <u>I</u> built the volcano.

3. <u>Was tall and colorful</u>.

4. Lucy <u>mixed the chemicals for a grand eruption</u>.

5. The exhibit <u>looked great</u>.

6. <u>All the other contestants</u> admired our life-like miniature volcano.

7. <u>There were some other really amazing entries, too</u>.

8. <u>One of the other entries</u> was an interesting homemade barometer.

9. <u>Could</u> we <u>beat</u> such a great project?

10. <u>All three of us</u>.

1 A simple subject
   B simple predicate
   C compound subject
   D complete predicate

2 A inverted order
   B compound subject
   C simple subject
   D complete predicate

3 A simple predicate
   B complete predicate
   C sentence fragment
   D simple subject

4 A simple subject
   B compound subject
   C sentence fragment
   D complete predicate

5 A simple subject
   B complete predicate
   C verb phrase
   D sentence fragment

6 A inverted order
   B sentence fragment
   C complete subject
   D complete predicate

7 A complete predicate
   B simple predicate
   C sentence fragment
   D inverted order

8 A compound subject
   B verb phrase
   C complete predicate
   D complete subject

9 A simple subject
   B compound subject
   C verb phrase
   D complete predicate

10 A sentence fragment
    B inverted order
    C verb phrase
    D complete subject

CHAPTER 2

Nouns and Pronouns

 **Pretest**

Directions
Write the letter of the term that correctly identifies the underlined word or words in each sentence.

EXAMPLE
1. My father and I went on <u>our</u> yearly camping trip last week.
   1 A common noun
     B reflexive pronoun
     C personal pronoun
     D indefinite pronoun

ANSWER   **1 C**

1. We each carried a <u>backpack</u> and a water bottle.
2. We started hiking at the foot of <u>Hunter Mountain</u>.
3. For hours, we pushed <u>ourselves</u> to hike uphill.
4. <u>Several</u> of the climbs required crawling over rocks.
5. After a long period of continuous hiking, <u>we</u> sat down for a rest.
6. Later we climbed the <u>foothills</u> of the Berkshires.
7. <u>Everyone</u> we passed looked exhausted.
8. We <u>ourselves</u> were getting pretty tired, too.
9. <u>Those</u> were the highest mountains I'd ever climbed.
10. When we stopped to rest again, we found we had left our <u>canteens</u> at our last rest stop.

1   **A** proper noun
    B compound noun
    C personal pronoun
    D intensive pronoun

2   **A** common noun
    B personal pronoun
    C intensive pronoun
    D proper noun

3   **A** personal pronoun
    B intensive pronoun
    C reflexive pronoun
    D demonstrative pronoun

4   **A** indefinite pronoun
    B interrogative pronoun
    C intensive pronoun
    D reflexive pronoun

5   **A** intensive pronoun
    B personal pronoun
    C common noun
    D demonstrative pronoun

6   **A** proper noun
    B personal pronoun
    C common noun
    D reflexive pronoun

7   **A** intensive pronoun
    B reflexive pronoun
    C demonstrative pronoun
    D indefinite pronoun

8   **A** personal pronoun
    B intensive pronoun
    C reflexive pronoun
    D demonstrative pronoun

9   **A** reflexive pronoun
    B proper noun
    C demonstrative pronoun
    D interrogative pronoun

10 **A** proper noun
    B personal pronoun
    C compound noun
    D common noun

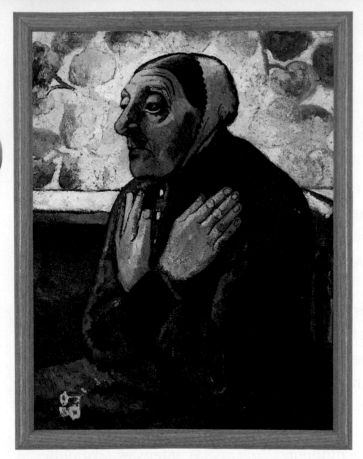

Paula Modersohn-Becker. *Old Peasant Woman,* 1905.
Oil on canvas, 30¼ by 23⅛ inches. The Detroit Institute of Arts, Gift of Robert H. Tannahill. Photograph ©1996
The Detroit Institute of Arts.

Describe   What does the woman in the painting look like? What is she doing?

Analyze   What do you think the position of the woman's arms mean?

Interpret   Why do you think the artist chose to position the woman's arms as he did? What is he saying about society?

Judge   How does this painting make you feel? Why?

At the end of this chapter, you will use the artwork to stimulate ideas for writing.

Nouns

The thousands of words in the English language can be divided into eight groups called the **parts of speech.** Each part of speech does a different job in a sentence.

THE EIGHT PARTS OF SPEECH	
noun (names)	**preposition** (relates)
pronoun (replaces)	**conjunction** (connects)
verb (states action or being)	**interjection** (expresses strong feeling)
adjective (describes, limits)	**adverb** (describes, limits)

The most common part of speech is the noun. Nouns are sometimes called naming words, because they name people, places, things, and ideas.

A **noun** is a word that names a person, a place, a thing, or an idea.

NOUNS	
PEOPLE	boy, pilot, family, Mr. Jenkins, Pamela
PLACES	classrooms, park, theater, Arizona, lake
THINGS	bells, water, Mars, oxygen, memory
IDEAS AND QUALITIES	honesty, kindness, peace, truth, wisdom hope, independence, freedom, loyalty

Some of the nouns in the preceding lists can be seen or touched. They are nouns such as *boy, classrooms,* and *bells.* These nouns are called **concrete nouns.** Other nouns, called **abstract nouns,** cannot be seen or touched. They are nouns such as *memory, honesty,* and *hope.*

Many times a writer will try to use a very specific, concrete noun to help create a vivid picture or scene. Notice the underlined specific nouns in the following passage. Think about the items they name.

> He stood his <u>hoe</u> against the split-rail fence. He walked down the <u>cornfield</u> until he was out of sight of the <u>cabin</u>. He swung himself over the fence on his two hands. Old Julia the <u>hound</u> had followed his father in the wagon to <u>Grahamsville</u>, but <u>Rip</u> the <u>bull-dog</u> and <u>Perk</u> the new <u>feist</u> saw the form clear the fence and ran toward him. <u>Rip</u> barked deeply but the voice of the small <u>mongrel</u> was high and shrill.
>
> —Marjorie Kinnan Rawlings, The Yearling

PRACTICE YOUR SKILLS

Check Your Understanding
Finding Nouns

Science Topic **Write each noun.** (There are fifty-three nouns.)

1. At one time dinosaurs were rulers of the earth.

2. Some of these creatures were as big as houses.

3. Other dinosaurs were as small as turkeys.

4. Many of these animals walked on two legs and used their hands to hold things.

5. Their brains were tiny—no bigger than a walnut.

6. We know about these reptiles from footprints and from fossils such as eggs, bones, and teeth.

7. Some bones have been formed into whole skeletons.

8. Experts can tell from fossils whether dinosaurs ate plants or meat.

9. Many questions, however, still have no answers.

10. One mystery is that we have no knowledge of what color these ancient creatures were.

11. Scientists guess that their colors might have been similar to those of living reptiles.

12. Another unsolved mystery concerns what caused dinosaurs to become extinct.

13. One popular theory is that Earth was struck by a large asteroid.

14. The impact would have sent a thick cloud of dust into the atmosphere.

15. Sunlight might have been blocked by the dust, and supplies of food would have decreased.

16. Dinosaurs and other species would have suffered because of changes in temperature, too.

Connect to the Writing Process: Revising
Using Specific Nouns

Rewrite each sentence, replacing the underlined word or words with a more specific noun.

17. The big lizards are a very popular attraction at the museum.

18. Small humans seem to enjoy lizards and snakes the most.

19. My science teacher is an expert on dinosaurs.

20. Even my best friend likes learning about them.

21. Do you believe that a dinosaur could be the size of a small dog?

22. Would it be an interesting thought to keep a brachiosaurus for a protector?

APPLY TO WRITING
Descriptive Writing: *Nouns*

A local museum is creating a new display, and your science teacher wants you to help put it together. Your job is to write a descriptive paragraph about the *Tyrannosaurus rex*. The paragraph will be used as a script to narrate an interactive computer display about dinosaurs for young children. Write your description for first or second graders, and use a variety of concrete, abstract, and specific nouns.

▶ Compound Nouns

A noun that includes more than one word is called a **compound noun.**

For example, *city* is one noun, but *city hall* is also one noun because it names one place. All compound nouns do not look alike, because they can take one of three different forms. If you are unsure of the form of any compound noun, you should check a dictionary.

COMPOUND NOUNS	
SEPARATE WORDS	compact disc, fire truck
HYPHENATED WORDS	father-in-law, great-grandmother
COMBINED	carpool, notebook, sidewalk

PRACTICE YOUR SKILLS

● Check Your Understanding
Finding Compound Nouns

 Write the compound noun or nouns in each sentence.

1. The police officer directed us to the picnic area.

2. Finally my great-grandfather was able to attend the family reunion.

3. My aunt brought her golden retriever.

4. Some of my cousins played on the sidewalk.

5. A cloudburst made all of us run for shelter.

6. Susie, my older sister, volunteered to be a baby-sitter while my aunts prepared the food.

7. My uncles played football.

8. After lunch we all watched the sailboats.

9. Fire ants ruined part of the picnic.

10. My cousin Katelyn asked me to be the maid of honor at her wedding next year.

Writing Compound Nouns

Write correctly the underlined compound noun in each sentence. If the noun is correct, write C. Use a dictionary to check your spelling.

11. My Aunt Sally used to be a <u>cheer-leader</u>.

12. Uncle Tom has been promoted to <u>firechief</u>.

13. By the next family reunion, I will have a new <u>brother in law</u>.

14. My dad got hurt sliding into <u>home plate</u>.

15. Mom attached the <u>fish-hook</u> to the end of the line.

▶ Common and Proper Nouns

A **common noun** names any person, place, or thing.

A **proper noun** names a particular person, place, or thing.

Because proper nouns begin with a capital letter, they generally are easy to recognize.

COMMON AND PROPER NOUNS	
Common Nouns	**Proper Nouns**
teacher	Mrs. Gray
lake	Lake Erie
country	Canada
dog	Buck

Notice that some proper nouns such as *Lake Erie* are more than one word. *Lake Erie* is still considered one noun because it is the name of one place.

PRACTICE YOUR SKILLS

● Check Your Understanding
Finding Common and Proper Nouns

Literature Topic **Make two columns on your paper. Write the common nouns in one column and the proper nouns in the other column.**

1. Buck did not read the newspapers, or he would have known about the problem in California.

2. When gold was found, prospectors rushed to the area.

3. They needed strong dogs with warm coats.

4. Buck was the son of a huge Saint Bernard.

5. He lived in a house owned by Judge Miller.

6. On the night that Buck was kidnapped, the judge was at a meeting of the Raisin Growers' Association.

7. The stolen dog would never return to his home.

8. He was sold to several different people.

9. Once he even pulled a sled that delivered mail between the towns of Dawson and Skagway.

10. After his last master died, he joined several wolves and roamed freely throughout the wilderness.

● Connect to the Writing Process: Editing
Capitalizing Nouns

Write the following sentences, using capital letters for nouns correctly. If a sentence is correct, write C.

11. Jack London wrote the novel *The Call of the Wild*.

12. Buck's story takes place in california and alaska.

13. My favorite part of the Book was when buck joined the wolves and roamed the frozen Wilderness.

14. In one Part of the story, buck had to pull a sled with a tremendous Weight on it.

15. The whole story is told from the Dog's point of view.

Communicate Your Ideas

APPLY TO WRITING

Business Letter: *Common and Proper Nouns*

Because your class is reading *The Call of the Wild,* you decide to find out more about Alaska. Write a business letter to the Chamber of Commerce in Fairbanks, Alaska. Request information about the history and climate of the area. Be sure to use common and proper nouns correctly in your letter.

✓ QuickCheck Mixed Practice

General Interest **Write each noun and label it *common* or *proper.* (A date is considered a noun.)**

1. In 1785, Thomas Pool presented the first circus in the United States.

2. It is not popcorn or elephants that have made circuses last all these years.

3. The excitement has come from original acts and unusual performers.

4. Five brothers once gathered some entertainers and traveled by wagons to various cities.

5. Their name was Ringling.

6. Later P. T. Barnum offered three shows at the same time in different rings.

7. Americans always loved Emmett Kelly, a clown with a sad face.

8. Miguel Vazquez first performed four somersaults through the air to a catcher.

9. Tom Thumb was less than a yard tall.

10. President Lincoln invited him to the White House.

Pronouns

Notice the differences between these sentences.

> Rafael asked Jill if Jill would help Rafael with Rafael's soccer techniques.

> Rafael asked Jill if **she** would help **him** with **his** soccer techniques.

The second sentence is shorter and clearer because pronouns have been substituted for nouns.

A **pronoun** is a word that takes the place of one or more nouns.

Pronoun Antecedents

In the preceding example about Rafael and Jill, the pronoun *she* replaces *Jill,* and the pronouns *him* and *his* replace *Rafael.*

The noun that a pronoun replaces, or refers to, is called its **antecedent.**

An antecedent usually comes before the pronoun. It may be in the same sentence as the pronoun or in another sentence. In the following examples, arrows point from the pronouns to their antecedents.

> Rosalie dribbled the **ball** and kicked **it.**

> **Tim** made a nice score. **He** saved the game.

> **Kara** played **her** best game yet.

Sometimes a pronoun will have more than one antecedent.

Mary and **Dan** timed **their** defense perfectly.

You can learn more about pronouns and antecedents on pages L376–L381.

PRACTICE YOUR SKILLS

● Check Your Understanding
Finding Antecedents

Sports Topic **Write the antecedent of each underlined pronoun.**

1. Michelle Akers, a star soccer player, is never sure how <u>she</u> will feel each day.

2. Michelle knows that <u>she</u> suffers from chronic fatigue syndrome.

3. The disease literally steals energy from <u>its</u> hosts.

4. Her coach, Tony DiCicco, says <u>he</u> is never sure how long Michelle will be able to <u>play</u>.

5. Michelle's family members say <u>they</u> worry about her health.

6. Still, Michelle is able to overcome <u>her</u> challenge and play great soccer for the U.S. women's team.

7. "<u>We</u> are a better team when Michelle is playing for <u>us</u>," says the coach.

8. In the 1996 Olympics, Michelle helped <u>her</u> team win the gold medal.

9. Michelle loves the sport, but <u>it</u> is a constant challenge for <u>her</u>.

10. "<u>I</u> don't know how long I'll be able to train or play in a match," says Michelle.

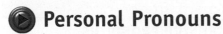

Personal Pronouns

There are several different kinds of pronouns. **Personal pronouns** are the kind used most often.

PERSONAL PRONOUNS		
	Singular	**Plural**
FIRST PERSON (speaker)	I, me, my, mine	we, us, our, ours
SECOND PERSON (person spoken to)	you, your, yours	you, your, yours
THIRD PERSON (person or thing spoken about)	he, him, his, she, her, hers, it, its	they, them, their, theirs

FIRST PERSON PRONOUNS	I have **my** butterfly net with **me.** **We** left **ours** at the cottage.
SECOND PERSON PRONOUNS	Did **you** take **your** hat with you? These boots must be **yours.**
THIRD PERSON PRONOUNS	**She** finished **her** hike first. **They** put **their** backpacks by the door.

Reflexive and Intensive Pronouns

Reflexive and **intensive pronouns** refer to or emphasize a noun or another pronoun.

These pronouns are formed by adding *-self* or *-selves* to certain personal pronouns.

REFLEXIVE AND INTENSIVE PRONOUNS	
SINGULAR	myself, yourself, himself, herself, itself
PLURAL	ourselves, yourselves, themselves

Megan taught **herself** to identify different kinds of butterflies and cocoons.

(The reflexive pronoun *herself* tells who Megan taught.)

Gardeners **themselves** supported the new butterfly exhibit at the park.

(The intensive pronoun *themselves* emphasizes who supported the idea.)

It is important to remember that you should never use reflexive or intensive pronouns by themselves. They must always have an antecedent to refer to. Also, never use *hisself* or *theirselves*.

PRACTICE YOUR SKILLS

● Check Your Understanding
Finding Personal, Reflexive, and Intensive Pronouns

General Interest **Write each personal, reflexive, and intensive pronoun. Label each one *P* for personal, *R* for reflexive, or *I* for intensive.**

1. Our class has enjoyed itself learning about butterflies and moths in science.

2. I am writing a report about monarch butterflies.

3. I looked up their migration information on the Internet myself.

4. Did you know that butterflies touch plants with their feet because they have taste sensors in their feet?

5. When you see a butterfly hop from plant to plant, it is searching for a host plant for its eggs.

6. David Millard studies the habitats of butterflies and their predators.

7. Millard himself gave me much information for my science report.

8. Of all the reports about butterflies, I liked yours the best.

9. We want to plan and build a butterfly garden at our school.

10. Please be sure to share your drawings for the garden with me.

● Connect to the Writing Process: Revising
Replacing Nouns with Pronouns

Rewrite the following sentences, replacing some of the nouns with pronouns. Add reflexive or intensive pronouns wherever possible.

11. Mary said that Mary would help Charlotte hatch some butterfly eggs.

12. The students are going to present Mary with a special award for Mary's careful, accurate work with the butterflies.

13. David said that David would like to be able to present the special award to Mary.

14. Charlotte will take a picture of David and Mary in the new butterfly garden.

15. Will the students be able to enjoy the garden that the students helped to create?

APPLY TO WRITING

Proposal: *Pronouns*

For your class to build a new butterfly garden on the school grounds, you must first present your plan to the school principal. Write a plan for the project for the principal. Explain the garden's purpose. Give details about the plants you want to grow in the garden and about the butterflies you hope to attract. Include convincing reasons for building such a garden. Be prepared to identify the pronouns and antecedents you used.

▶ Indefinite Pronouns

The indefinite pronouns are another group of pronouns.

Indefinite pronouns refer to unnamed people, places, things, or ideas.

COMMON INDEFINITE PRONOUNS			
all	both	few	nothing
another	each	many	one
any	either	most	several
anybody	everybody	neither	some
anyone	everyone	none	someone
anything	everything	no one	something

No one knew how to fold the flag.

Everything I know about the flag I learned in Boy Scouts.

There must be **something** we can do to help.

Few wanted to take the first step.

You can learn about indefinite pronouns used as adjectives on page L109.

PRACTICE YOUR SKILLS

● Check Your Understanding
Finding Indefinite Pronouns

Social Studies **Write each indefinite pronoun.**

1. Few know that flags first appeared in ancient China.

2. Most of the flags before then were actually poles with carved symbols on top.

3. Each of the units in the Roman army had a flag.

4. Someone discovered an Aztec flag made from feathers.

5. Many of the flags have important symbols on them.

6. All of the sailors learn the meaning of the flags.

7. Everyone has seen flags in sports.

8. Anyone who sees the red flag must stop immediately.

9. Most know a white flag means a single lap is left.

10. Anyone in the stands can see the checkered flag for the winner.

11. One of our legends states that Betsy Ross made the first American flag.

12. Everybody should stand when the flag passes by.

▶ Demonstrative and Interrogative Pronouns

Demonstrative pronouns point out a specific person, place, thing, or idea.

DEMONSTRATIVE PRONOUNS			
this	that	these	those

The pronouns *this* and *these* are used to point out people or things that are close by. *That* and *those* are used to point out items in the distance.

This is my best speech so far.

I want to buy **these** for the rally.

That is the place for the debate.

Those are the buses at the top of the hill.

Interrogative pronouns are used to ask questions.

INTERROGATIVE PRONOUNS				
what	which	who	whom	whose

What did you do then?

Who was at the rally?

One other kind of pronoun, called a relative pronoun, *will be covered in on pages L255–L256.*

PRACTICE YOUR SKILLS

● Check Your Understanding
Finding Pronouns

 Write each pronoun.

1. Either of the candidates will make a good class president for seventh grade.

2. What has Rebecca said about the campaign speech?

3. Who is running for treasurer?

4. All of the students are voting today.

5. These were found in the voting area.

6. Many voted for class historian.

7. What did Mrs. Thompson do with the extra ballots?

8. A campaign promise like this will be hard to keep.

9. Which is the ballot for the seventh-grade officers?

10. Whom did David tell about the new voting rules?

● Connect to the Writing Process: Drafting
Writing Sentences

Write a sentence that follows each direction. Underline the pronoun you use in each sentence.

11. Use an interrogative pronoun to ask a question about an important election.

12. Use a demonstrative pronoun to point out the voting booth.

13. Use an indefinite pronoun to explain who is allowed to vote.

14. Use an interrogative pronoun to find out the time that the winners will be announced.

15. Use a demonstrative pronoun to point out the winner of the election.

Communicate Your Ideas

APPLY TO WRITING
Radio Advertisement: *Pronouns*

As your best friend's campaign manager, you have to write a radio ad for the student election. The ad will be read over the morning announcements. Consider the preceding photograph. What would you share with your class about your friend's abilities to be a good class officer? Introduce your candidate and provide details that will interest your classmates. As you write your ad, be sure to use indefinite, demonstrative, and interrogative pronouns. When you finish, underline all the pronouns you used.

 **Mixed Practice**

Write each pronoun.

1. No germs from the moon were found on *Apollo 11* or its astronauts.
2. The doctors examined each of the astronauts.
3. This was the moment everyone had waited for.
4. They landed their spacecraft in the Pacific Ocean on July 24, 1969.
5. Which was the first astronaut to walk on the moon?
6. It was Neil Armstrong.
7. He said, "That's one small step for man, one giant leap for mankind."
8. The *Apollo 11* mission to the moon was one of the greatest human achievements.
9. Who did not land on the moon?
10. That was Michael Collins in orbit around the moon.
11. All of the astronauts made important discoveries.
12. These came from their mission.
13. A few of the discoveries included evidence of "moonquakes."
14. All of the data they collected was helpful to scientists.
15. Everybody was proud of the astronauts' success.
16. The astronauts left their country's flag on the moon.
17. Many wanted to see the moon rocks.
18. None looked like green cheese.
19. Who is your favorite astronaut?
20. This is a picture of her.

Finding Nouns

Make two columns on your paper. Then write the common nouns in one column and the proper nouns in the other column. (There are 40 nouns.)

1. The Army once recruited some kids at Fort Belvoir in Virginia.
2. These kids were actually goats, and their job was to eat the grass and weeds.
3. Officers preferred them to lawn mowers because goats didn't give off sparks that start fires.
4. That was important, because at that time Fort Belvoir stored ammunition.
5. These helpful animals worked hard at this military base for many years.
6. Starting with only a few goats, they quickly multiplied into a large herd.
7. Neither sunshine nor snowfall seemed to bother them, and they never had a single complaint.
8. During the winter a person from a nearby town would feed them, and a veterinarian would give them regular check-ups.
9. The goats were always treated with respect and appreciation.
10. The Army had many requests from other branches of the Armed Services—from Alaska to Germany—for these hard workers.

Finding Pronouns and Their Antecedents

Write each pronoun. Then beside each one, write its antecedent.

1. Are Andrew and Emily visiting their cousin?

2. Emma's parents can't see the play because they will be out of town.

3. No United States coin shows its denomination in numbers.

4. Are Cora and Lily still good friends? Lately they don't spend much time together.

5. The players themselves were the happiest about the championship.

6. Jonathan said that he won't be taking the bus tomorrow.

7. Fleas don't have wings; they have powerful legs.

8. On Saturday Tara will fly her kite in the park.

9. Kevin kept telling himself that he could make the team.

10. Dawn waited until she heard the school bell.

Using Nouns and Pronouns

Write five sentences that follow the directions below. (The sentences may come in any order.) Write about one of the following topics or a topic of your own choice: an interesting story about a brother, sister, or friend.

1. Write a sentence that includes nouns that name a person, a place, and a thing.

2. Write a sentence that includes a proper noun that names a place.

3. Write a sentence that includes an indefinite pronoun.

4. Write a sentence that includes several personal pronouns.

5. Write a sentence that includes a reflexive pronoun.

Put an N over each noun and P over each pronoun.

Language and *Self-Expression*

Paula Modersohn-Becker was a member of the German Expressionist school of painting. Her goal in painting was to express her personal convictions about the human condition. What convictions do you think she is trying to express in this painting?

The portrait depicts a woman whom many people might pass by without noticing. Think of a person you pass frequently. It could be a neighborhood police officer or crossing guard, or a cafeteria worker. Write a description of the person. Include physical details in your word portrait, but also try to reveal something important about your subject. Use vivid, concrete nouns and a variety of pronouns in your description.

Prewriting Make a character-traits chart for your subject. Include details of your subject's physical traits. Try to write down details that reveal your subject's dreams, thoughts, or feelings.

Drafting Use your chart to write a description of your subject. Use details to reveal as many facets of your subject as possible.

Revising Read your description to a classmate. Ask your partner to comment on how well you have captured the physical traits and personality of your subject. Make any changes necessary to make your word portrait more vivid and interesting.

Editing Review your description for errors in spelling and punctuation. Be sure proper nouns are capitalized, and make sure your pronouns have clear antecedents.

Publishing Collect your description together with your classmates' descriptions in a booklet titled "People We Pass By."

 **Another Look**

A **noun** is a word that names a person, place, thing, or idea.

Kinds of Nouns

A **concrete noun** names people, places, or things you can see or touch. *(pages L47–L48)*
An **abstract noun** names ideas or qualities. *(page L47)*
A **common noun** names any person, place, or thing. *(page L52)*
A **proper noun** names a particular person, place, or thing. *(page L52)*
A **compound noun** includes more than one word. *(pages L50–L51)*

A **pronoun** is a word that takes the place of one or more nouns.

PERSONAL PRONOUNS		
	Singular	**Plural**
FIRST PERSON (speaker)	I, me, my, mine	we, us, our, ours
SECOND PERSON (person spoken to)	you, your, yours	you, your, yours
THIRD PERSON (person or thing spoken about)	he, him, his, she, her, hers, it, its	they, them, their, theirs,

The suffix *–self* or *–selves* can be added to some personal pronouns. These **reflexive pronouns** and **intensive pronouns** refer to or emphasize another noun or pronoun. *(pages L57–L58)*
Indefinite pronouns refer to unnamed people or things. *(pages L60–L61)*
Demonstrative pronouns point out certain people or things. *(page L62)*
Interrogative pronouns are used to ask questions. *(pages L62–L63)*

Other Information About Pronouns

The word or group of words that a pronoun refers to or replaces is called its **antecedent.** *(pages L55–L56)*

 **Posttest**

Directions
Write the letter of the term that correctly identifies the underlined word or words in each sentence.

EXAMPLE

1. <u>This</u> is the most beautiful autumn I can remember.

  1 A personal pronoun
    B intensive pronoun
    C demonstrative pronoun
    D common noun

ANSWER   **1 C**

1. In the Northeast where <u>I</u> live, fall is always a wonderful season.

2. This year there was a wet <u>spring</u> and dry summer with a lot of sunshine.

3. Scientists <u>themselves</u> admit they can't predict the fall colors perfectly.

4. <u>Many</u> think that a wet spring and dry summer produce the best effects.

5. Whatever the reason, the <u>leaves</u> are spectacular now.

6. Tourists flock to the <u>Green Mountains</u> to see the colorful foliage.

7. Almost <u>everyone</u> in our area makes a living from tourism.

8. <u>My</u> parents run a bed-and-breakfast.

9. <u>Which</u> is their best season?

10. For <u>them</u>, as for many others, it is the autumn.

1 **A** proper noun
  B compound noun
  C personal pronoun
  D intensive pronoun

2 **A** common noun
  B personal pronoun
  C compound noun
  D proper noun

3 **A** personal pronoun
  B intensive pronoun
  C reflexive pronoun
  D demonstrative pronoun

4 **A** indefinite pronoun
  B interrogative pronoun
  C intensive pronoun
  D reflexive pronoun

5 **A** intensive pronoun
  B personal pronoun
  C common noun
  D demonstrative pronoun

6 **A** proper noun
  B personal pronoun
  C compound noun
  D reflexive pronoun

7 **A** intensive pronoun
  B reflexive pronoun
  C demonstrative pronoun
  D indefinite pronoun

8 **A** personal pronoun
  B intensive pronoun
  C reflexive pronoun
  D demonstrative pronoun

9 **A** reflexive pronoun
  B proper noun
  C demonstrative pronoun
  D interrogative pronoun

10 **A** proper noun
   B personal pronoun
   C compound noun
   D common noun

CHAPTER 3

Verbs

 **Pretest**

Directions
Write the letter of the term that correctly identifies the underlined word or words in each sentence.

EXAMPLE   **1.** Every year we <u>visit</u> a lake in the Adirondacks.

     1 **A** action verb
        B helping verb
        C verb phrase
        D linking verb

ANSWER   **1** **A**

1. The lake <u>has</u> always <u>been</u> quiet and peaceful.

2. The loudest sound <u>is</u> the call of the loons.

3. This year, jet skis <u>came</u> to the lake.

4. Their loud roar <u>echoed</u> from the mountain peaks.

5. At first, I <u>liked</u> the jet skis.

6. The jet skis <u>seemed</u> fun and exciting.

7. Soon, though, they <u>had</u> chased away the loons.

8. The moose <u>were</u> no longer <u>coming</u> around in the early mornings.

9. People along the lake also <u>became</u> angry about the noise.

10. They <u>wrote</u> letters to the local newspaper and argued in the stores and on the street.

1	A	helping verb	6	A	helping verb
	B	action verb		B	action verb
	C	verb phrase		C	linking verb
	D	linking verb		D	verb phrase
2	A	transitive verb	7	A	helping verb
	B	intransitive verb		B	action verb
	C	helping verb		C	linking verb
	D	linking verb		D	verb phrase
3	A	transitive verb	8	A	transitive verb
	B	intransitive verb		B	linking verb
	C	helping verb		C	helping verb
	D	linking verb		D	verb phrase
4	A	verb phrase	9	A	helping verb
	B	helping verb		B	action verb
	C	linking verb		C	linking verb
	D	action verb		D	verb phrase
5	A	verb phrase	10	A	helping verb
	B	intransitive verb		B	transitive verb
	C	transitive verb		C	intransitive verb
	D	helping verb		D	linking verb

Andy Goldsworthy. *Sand Brought to an Edge to Catch the Light,* August, 1991.
Shore of Lake Michigan. © Andy Goldsworthy. Photograph courtesy of the artist.

Describe How would you describe this sculpture?
How does it "catch the light"?

Analyze Why do you think the artist was inspired
to work with sand?

Interpret What statement do you think the artist
was trying to make with this sculpture?
Why do you think that?

Judge Do you consider a sculpture made in sand
to be art? Explain.

At the end of this chapter, you will use the artwork to
stimulate ideas for writing.

Action Verbs

Without a verb, a group of words cannot be a sentence.

> A **verb** is a word used to express an action or a state of being.

One kind of verb is called an action verb. Action verbs are easy to recognize because they show action or movement.

> An **action verb** tells what action a subject is performing.

To find an action verb, first find the subject of the sentence. Then ask yourself, *What is the subject doing?*

> Carl **drove** the dogsled fast.
>
> (The subject is *Carl*. What did Carl do? *Drove* is the action verb.)

Some action verbs show physical action. Others show mental action.

PHYSICAL ACTION	Sandy **pulled** the team to a stop. The large sled **toppled** over.
MENTAL ACTION	Belinda always **thinks** positively before a race. We **believed** in her team.

Other action verbs, such as *have* and *own*, show ownership or possession.

OWNERSHIP	Lilly **has** two tickets to the race. The Russos **own** a dogsled. The huskies **belong** to Peyton.

You can learn more about regular and irregular verbs on pages L307–L325.

Writers often use vivid action verbs to help create a picture of a character's actions. Notice the action verbs—in bold type—in the following passage.

> The car **churned** off into the dust. The boy **rose** and **cupped** his hands to his mouth and **shouted** one last time at Teece: "Mr. Teece, Mr. Teece, what *you* goin' to do nights from now on? What you goin' to *do* nights, Mr. Teece?"
>
> —*Ray Bradbury,* The Martian Chronicles

PRACTICE YOUR SKILLS

● Check Your Understanding
Finding Action Verbs

General Interest **Write each action verb.**

1. Every year dogsled drivers race across the frozen landscape of Alaska.

2. The course stretches more than a thousand miles from Anchorage to Nome.

3. Weather conditions often create severe hazards for the racers.

4. Snow and storms sometimes hide the trails.

5. Each driver carries snowshoes, a sleeping bag, and food for the dogs.

6. Drivers even take boots for the dogs' feet.

7. Veterinarians examine the dogs at checkpoints along the route.

8. Host families welcome the racers into their homes.

9. They feed the drivers and their dogs.

10. Most competitors complete the race within twelve or thirteen days.

11. A serious racer usually owns two or three different teams of dogs.

12. Some racers train all year long for the Iditarod.

13. Most teams enjoy the challenge of a good race.

14. A good "musher" has several strategies for the race.

15. People cheer for the victorious team.

● Connect to the Writing Process: Revising
Revising with More Specific Verbs

For each sentence, replace the underlined verb with a more specific verb.

16. The sleds slid across the frozen ground.

17. The dogs walked past the spectators.

18. The injured dog walked to the rest station.

19. With plenty of time to spare, the winning team crossed over the finish line.

20. The weary sled dogs walked into camp.

Communicate Your Ideas

APPLY TO WRITING
E-mail Message: *Action Verbs*

Through your social studies class, you have been keeping up with an Iditarod racer over the Internet. You send her an E-mail message asking about a particular part of the race. Be sure to use vivid action verbs in your E-mail message.

⏵ Transitive and Intransitive Verbs

All action verbs can be either transitive or intransitive. They are **transitive** if the action they express is directed at a person or thing. However, they are **intransitive** if the action they express is not directed at a person or thing.

To decide whether an action verb is transitive or intransitive, say the subject and verb. Then ask the question *What?* or *Whom?* A word that answers either question is called an **object.** An action verb that has an object is transitive. An action verb that does not have an object is intransitive.

TRANSITIVE	Kevin **answered** the difficult history question.
	(Kevin answered what? *Question* is the object. Therefore, *answered* is a transitive verb.)
	Granddad **took** us to the Alamo.
	(Granddad took whom? *Us* is the object. Therefore, *took* is a transitive verb.)
INTRANSITIVE	Jim Bowie **died** at the Alamo.
	(Jim Bowie died what? Jim Bowie died whom? Because there is no object, *died* is an intransitive verb.)

Notice that some verbs can be transitive in one sentence and intransitive in another sentence.

TRANSITIVE	Jim Bowie **explored** parts of Texas.
	(Jim Bowie explored what? *Parts* is the object.)

INTRANSITIVE	Jim Bowie **explored** often.
	(Jim Bowie explored what or whom? There is no object.)

You can learn more about objects on pages L157–L162.

PRACTICE YOUR SKILLS

● Check Your Understanding

Understanding Transitive and Intransitive Verbs

History Topic **Write the verb in each sentence. Label the verb *T* for transitive or *I* for intransitive.**

1. Jim Bowie lived in Tennessee and Louisiana during his childhood.
2. He inherited his parents' adventurous spirit.
3. During his childhood, he rode alligators.
4. Bowie learned from his mother.
5. He learned French and Spanish.
6. At the age of eighteen, Bowie sought his fortune.
7. He worked hard.
8. He made a profit from the work on his farm.
9. Jim Bowie received recognition as a frontiersman.
10. He arrived in Texas in 1828.
11. He searched Texas for silver.
12. He searched throughout Bexar County in Texas.
13. He led American settlers against the Mexican government.
14. Bowie's courage prevailed throughout the revolution.
15. Bowie defended the Alamo.

▶ Helping Verbs

Helping verbs, or auxiliary verbs, are used with a main verb to form a verb phrase.

A **verb phrase** is a main verb plus one or more helping verbs.

The following is a list of common helping verbs.

COMMON HELPING VERBS	
be	am, is, are, was, were, be, being, been
have	has, have, had
do	do, does, did
OTHERS	may, might, must, can, could, shall, should, will, would

A verb phrase may have one or more helping verbs.

> Birds **have** flown north for the spring.
>
> The flower baskets **will be** hanging on the front porch.

Sometimes a verb phrase is interrupted by other words.

> Julio **must** not **be** coming to the spring dance.
>
> I **have**n't heard any birds yet.

You can learn about contractions on pages L605–L606.

To find the verb phrase in a question, turn the question around to make a statement.

> QUESTION   **Have** they joined the garden club?
>
> STATEMENT   They **have** joined the garden club.

Remember that a verb phrase is called a verb.

PRACTICE YOUR SKILLS

● Check Your Understanding
Finding Verb Phrases

Contemporary Life **Write each verb phrase. Remember that a verb phrase may be interrupted by one or more words.**

1. This rain shower should stop in a few minutes.

2. We will not go on a picnic in the rain.

3. Flowers have been appearing early this year.

4. The weather has not turned cooler today.

5. Rachel is planting her garden.

6. Have you seen any robins yet?

7. My parents will be cleaning the whole house soon.

8. We were planning a party this afternoon.

9. I haven't seen any dogwoods in bloom yet.

10. Will Kara be happy with the warmer weather?

● Connect to the Writing Process: Revising
Using Verb Phrases in Sentences

General Interest **Write the following sentences. Add a different helping verb to each one.**

11. The dogwoods bloom in April in New Jersey.

12. Florida strawberries turn red in February.

13. Washington apples blush in the fall.

14. Peonies burst into bloom in May in Indiana.

15. Oranges sweeten in the frost.

16. Texas bluebonnets appear in the spring.

17. Potatoes grow underground.

18. The corn plants seem short.

Science Topic **Write each verb.**

1. The average tiger weighs between 396 and 583 pounds.

2. Do tigers live in Africa?

3. Tigers have lived in Asia for centuries.

4. Tigers are related to lions, leopards, and jaguars.

5. The tiger's distinctive black stripes provide excellent camouflage.

6. White tigers are not seen often.

7. The Bengal tiger is smaller than other tigers.

8. The male grows to an adult weight of 400 pounds.

9. Tiger babies are called *cubs.*

10. Cubs might stay with their parents for two years.

11. The father tiger does not help with the care of the cubs.

12. The Bengal tiger combines great power with lethal slyness.

13. A tiger can kill a water buffalo nearly four times its own weight.

14. They eat deer, wild pigs, and even monkeys.

15. Tigers have become a group in danger.

16. In 1972, the World Wide Fund for Nature launched Project Tiger.

17. More than forty tiger reserves were created.

18. Tigers are still killed in Asia.

19. Many people fear tigers.

20. Their survival depends on our cooperation.

Linking Verbs

Some verbs show *being* instead of *action*.

> Theresa and Jeff **are** on the sailboat.
>
> The sails **were** full of wind.
>
> The breeze **is** constant.
>
> I **am** crazy about the sport of sailing!
>
> The sailboat ride **was** over too soon.

Some being verbs, called linking verbs, link the subject with another word in the sentence.

A **linking verb** links the subject with another word that renames or describes the subject.

> Joan **was** captain of our sailboat.
>
> (*Was* links *captain* with *Joan*. *Captain* renames the subject.)
>
> The wind **will be** strong tomorrow.
>
> (*Will be* links *strong* to *wind*. *Strong* describes the wind.)

COMMON FORMS OF *BE* USED AS LINKING VERBS			
be	was	could be	have been
is	were	should be	has been
am	shall be	may be	could have been
are	will be	might be	must have been

PRACTICE YOUR SKILLS

● Check Your Understanding
Finding Linking Verbs

 Write each linking verb.
General
Interest

1. Ships have been useful throughout history.
2. They might be the oldest form of transportation.
3. They are certainly popular today.
4. Lakes and rivers are home to many small boats.
5. A catamaran is a sailboat with twin hulls.
6. That boat can be fast.
7. The USS *Constitution* is a very old ship.
8. Steamships were the main form of transportation in the 1800s.
9. Could the lights on the cruise ship in the harbor be any brighter?
10. The largest ship is the oil tanker.

● Check Your Understanding
Finding Linking Verbs

Science
Topic
Write each linking verb. Then write the words that the verb links.

11. The giraffe is the world's tallest animal.
12. Earth's first space traveler was a dog.
13. In some parts of the world, cattle are still wild.
14. The whale is a mammal, not a fish.
15. Will snakes be warm in the winter?
16. Wild horses may be dangerous.
17. Most animals in Australia are unusual.
18. Dinosaurs must have been huge.

19. Birds could be descendants of dinosaurs.

20. The first horses were small.

 Additional Linking Verbs

Forms of the verb *be* are not the only linking verbs. The following words can also be used as linking verbs.

ADDITIONAL LINKING VERBS					
appear	feel	look	seem	sound	taste
become	grow	remain	smell	stay	turn

Lucy **became** the new conductor.

(*Became* links *conductor* and *Lucy*. *Conductor* renames the subject.)

The old sheet music **smelled** musty.

(*Smelled* links *musty* and *music*. *Musty* describes the subject.)

Like action verbs, these linking verbs can also have helping verbs.

My flute **did sound** a little flat.

It **may have sounded** flat because of our long practice session.

Did your flute **stay** warm for too long?

In the preceding sentences, flat *and* warm *are subject complements. You can learn more about subject complements on pages L165–L170.*

PRACTICE YOUR SKILLS

● Check Your Understanding
Finding Linking Verbs

Music Topic **Write each linking verb. Then write the words that the verb links.**

1. Mozart's music appears difficult.
2. He became famous throughout Europe at a very young age.
3. His music does sound wonderful.
4. After the death of his father, Mozart's music turned darker.
5. *Don Giovanni* must have seemed scary to his audiences.
6. Mozart's music grew more complex.
7. His musical scores look perfect.
8. Did he ever feel successful?
9. Mozart did become ill toward the end of his life.
10. He and Haydn remained friends for many years.

● Connect to the Writing Process: Revising
Changing Sentences with Linking Verbs

Rewrite each sentence, replacing the verb *was* with a different linking verb. In some sentences you will have to supply a helping verb.

11. Sherman was upset at the new score.
12. The music was difficult.
13. The conductor was firm about the selection.
14. Our first practice was awful.
15. Sherman was doubtful.
16. The selection was easier with each practice.

Linking Verb or Action Verb?

Some of the linking verbs listed on page L85 can also be action verbs. If the verb links two words, it is a linking verb. If the verb shows action, it is an action verb.

LINKING VERB   The research boat **looked** new.
                (*Looked* links *new* and *boat*. *New* describes the boat.)

ACTION VERB   Angie **looked** for the whales.
                (*Looked* shows action. It tells what Angie did.)

PRACTICE YOUR SKILLS

 Check Your Understanding
Distinguishing Between Linking Verbs and Action Verbs

Science Topic **Write each verb. Then label each one A for *action* or L for *linking*.**

1. The biggest dinosaur on Earth appeared smaller than a blue whale.

2. Blue whales stay calm in most situations.

3. Blue whales appeared after dinosaurs.

4. These huge animals stay underwater for periods as long as twenty minutes.

5. During the summer blue whales remain in arctic and antarctic waters.

6. In winter the blue whales migrate to subtropical waters.

7. Blue whales seem very intelligent.

8. Unfortunately, blue whales became an endangered species some time ago.

9. Many people look for a change in this situation.

10. What will become of the blue whale?

Connect to the Writing Process: Drafting

Writing Sentences with Linking and Action Verbs

Write two sentences for each of the following verbs. First use the verb as a linking verb. Then use it as an action verb. Label each verb _L_ for _linking_ or _A_ for _action_.

11. look   **13.** taste   **15.** sound

12. feel   **14.** smell   **16.** stay

Communicate Your Ideas

APPLY TO WRITING

Persuasive Letter: *Action and Linking Verbs*

Your local zoo has decided not to open a new aquarium exhibit because the director believes that sea animals would not be interesting enough to draw large crowds. Write a letter to the director of the zoo explaining how interesting sea animals are. Be prepared to identify the linking and action verbs in your letter.

General Interest **Write each verb. Then label each one *A* for *action* or *L* for *linking*.**

1. Many people had not heard about El Niño before 1998.

2. El Niño means "the boy" in Spanish.

3. El Niño has been responsible for unusual weather conditions around the world.

4. Florida was one state with problems from El Niño.

5. In the winter months, the ground in Florida normally becomes dry.

6. The ground does not remain dry for long, though.

7. In May and June, the afternoon showers begin.

8. In 1998, the afternoon showers stayed away.

9. People looked for rain.

10. The ground grew drier.

11. By the end of June, the air smelled smoky.

12. Wildfires spread through grass and trees and across highways.

13. The situation was a dangerous one.

14. Some people lost their homes to the flames.

15. Finally, El Niño turned away.

16. The afternoon showers had become a reality again.

17. The loud thunder sounded wonderful to everyone.

18. The sky looked clear and blue once more.

19. People could stay outdoors for their activities.

20. The only reminders of El Niño were the bare black trees along the roads.

Finding Verbs

Write each verb. Then label each one *action* or *linking*.

1. For millions of years, dinosaurs ruled the land.
2. The apatosaurus was a huge animal.
3. This dinosaur reached a weight of thirty or forty tons!
4. Because of its size, it ate a tremendous amount.
5. Massive legs took the pressure of the animal's weight.
6. Its large tail was like an extra leg.
7. The large tail also protected it from its enemies.
8. The apatosaurus looked fierce and mean.
9. Actually, it was never a threat to other dinosaurs.
10. This huge animal ate only vegetation.

Finding Verb Phrases

Write the verb or verb phrase in each sentence.

1. My brother will be home by noon.
2. Because of the storm, we might not go to the concert.
3. During your lifetime your brain may store up to 100 million bits of information.
4. Cars with front-wheel drive are becoming very popular.
5. At sunset the fire was still burning out of control.
6. The first public railroad was not built until 1825.
7. Robins have been appearing early this spring.
8. Haven't they become friends quickly?
9. Don't these lilies smell wonderful?
10. People have been wearing glasses for over seven hundred years.

Finding Verbs

Write each verb or verb phrase. Then label each one *action* or *linking*.

1. Have you ever heard this story about a dog with ESP?
2. Jim was a black-and-white setter.
3. He apparently could guess the thoughts in people's minds.
4. Experts at a college in Missouri tested the dog.
5. At first the experts didn't believe the incredible stories about Jim.
6. One professor told Jim in French the number on a license plate.
7. Instantly Jim was standing beside the license plate.
8. The tests then grew harder.
9. The results, nevertheless, were always exactly the same.
10. By the end of the session, the professors had become believers in Jim's unusual ability.

Writing Sentences

Write five sentences that follow the directions below. (The sentences may come in any order.) Write about one of the following topics or a topic of your own choice: the funniest or scariest situation you have ever been in.

Write a sentence that...

1. includes an action verb.
2. includes a linking verb.
3. includes an action verb with one or more helping verbs.
4. includes a linking verb with one or more helping verbs.
5. includes an interrupted verb phrase.

After writing the sentences, underline each verb or verb phrase.

Language and *Self-Expression*

British artist Andy Goldsworthy created this sand sculpture on the shores of Lake Michigan. He has also made sculptures out of ice, grass, thorns, twigs, mud, and water. Few of his sculptures last long; he records them in photographs.

Goldsworthy's sculpture takes advantage of the beauty of its natural setting—the shore of a lake. Think of a natural setting that you find especially beautiful or moving. Write a description of the place. Use action, helping, and linking verbs in your description.

Prewriting Make a sensory-details chart for your description. In columns labeled "Sight," "Sound," "Smell," "Taste," and "Touch," write details about the place you have chosen that appeal to those senses.

Drafting Write a first draft of your description. Try to create a vivid picture with words.

Revising Read your description aloud to a classmate. Ask your classmate if he or she has a vivid mental image of the place you have described. Add details to make your description clearer if necessary.

Editing Check your description for errors in spelling and punctuation. Be sure you have used verbs correctly.

Publishing To go with your description, draw a picture of the place you have described or bring in a photograph. Put your description with classmates' descriptions in a collection of "Places to Remember."

 **Another Look**

A **verb** is a word used to express an action or a state of being.

An **action verb** tells what action a subject is performing. *(page L75)*

Kinds of Action Verbs
A **transitive verb** is an action verb that directs its action at a person or thing. *(pages L78–L79)*

An **intransitive verb** does not direct its action at a person or thing. *(pages L78–L79)*

Helping Verbs and Linking Verbs
A **helping verb,** or an auxiliary verb, is used with a main verb to form a verb phrase. *(page L80)*

COMMON HELPING VERBS	
be	am, is, are, was, were, am, be, being, been
have	has, have, had
do	do, does, did
OTHERS	may, might, must, can, could, shall, should, will, would

A **verb phrase** is a main verb plus one or more helping verbs.

A **linking verb** links the subject with another word in the sentence that renames or describes the subject. *(page L83)*

Other Information About Verbs
Recognizing additional linking verbs *(page L85)*
Distinguishing between action verbs and linking verbs *(page L87)*

Posttest

Directions
Write the letter of the term that correctly identifies the
underlined word or words in each sentence.

EXAMPLE   **1.** Jenna <u>has been involved</u> in a local debate
             for the past year.
             1 A   transitive verb
                 B   helping verb
                 C   linking verb
                 D   verb phrase

ANSWER   **1 D**

1. A local company <u>wanted</u> to mine a mountainside near her
    house.

2. However, there <u>could</u> be a nest of rattlesnakes nearby.

3. The rattlesnakes <u>are</u> an endangered species.

4. Mining there <u>might destroy</u> the rattlesnake community.

5. The mining company <u>asked</u> the government for a permit
    to mine.

6. Jenna <u>was</u> writing letters and staging demonstrations by
    then.

7. She and some friends <u>organized</u> the local homeowners
    into a protest group.

8. The group <u>was</u> quick to contact their government
    representatives.

9. They <u>did</u> not <u>leave</u> anything to chance.

10. They <u>hired</u> a rattlesnake specialist.

1 **A** helping verb
   B action verb
   C verb phrase
   D linking verb

2 **A** transitive verb
   B intransitive verb
   C helping verb
   D linking verb

3 **A** transitive verb
   B intransitive verb
   C helping verb
   D linking verb

4 **A** verb phrase
   B helping verb
   C linking verb
   D intransitive verb

5 **A** verb phrase
   B intransitive verb
   C transitive verb
   D helping verb

6 **A** helping verb
   B action verb
   C linking verb
   D verb phrase

7 **A** helping verb
   B action verb
   C linking verb
   D verb phrase

8 **A** action verb
   B linking verb
   C helping verb
   D verb phrase

9 **A** helping verb
   B intransitive verb
   C linking verb
   D verb phrase

10 **A** helping verb
   B transitive verb
   C intransitive verb
   D linking verb

Adjectives and Adverbs

· ·

 **Pretest**

Directions
Write the letter of the term that correctly identifies the underlined word in each sentence.

EXAMPLE **1.** The seventh-grade class gave a <u>fashion</u> show last week.
1 A adjective
B pronoun
C adverb
D article

ANSWER **1 A**

1. All of <u>the</u> class had a hand in designing, sewing, or modeling the clothes.
2. <u>Some</u> of the clothes were truly amazing.
3. The colors were <u>bold</u> and unusual.
4. The models stepped <u>jauntily</u> onto the stage.
5. Dion Clemens designed a hat that looked like a <u>rain</u> forest.
6. <u>That</u> got the loudest applause from the audience.
7. He was <u>very</u> proud of his creation.
8. There was loud <u>African</u> music playing during the show.
9. A <u>local</u> newspaper took pictures and wrote up a story.
10. Kendra Sauer's velvet dresses hung <u>gorgeously</u> in thick folds.

1	A	noun	6	A	adjective
	B	article		B	article
	C	adverb		C	adverb
	D	pronoun		D	pronoun

2	A	adjective	7	A	adjective
	B	article		B	article
	C	adverb		C	adverb
	D	pronoun		D	pronoun

3	A	adjective	8	A	proper adjective
	B	article		B	article
	C	adverb		C	adverb
	D	pronoun		D	proper noun

4	A	proper adjective	9	A	adjective
	B	article		B	article
	C	adverb		C	adverb
	D	pronoun		D	pronoun

5	A	adjective	10	A	adjective
	B	verb		B	article
	C	adverb		C	adverb
	D	noun		D	pronoun

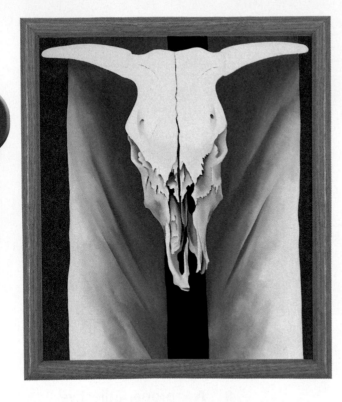

Georgia O'Keeffe. *Cow's Skull: Red, White, and Blue,* 1931.
Oil on canvas, 39⅞ by 35⅞ inches. The Metropolitan Museum of Art, New York.

Describe   What does this painting show? How does the artist use color in it?

Analyze   Why do you think the artist chose to paint a cow's skull? What do you think the skull represented to the artist?

Interpret   What do you think the use of red, white, and blue adds to the painting? What do those colors often symbolize?

Judge   What do you think of when you look at this painting? Why?

At the end of this chapter, you will use the artwork to stimulate ideas for writing.

Adjectives

Two of the eight parts of speech are called modifiers. A **modifier** makes the meaning of another word more precise. Modifiers are important because they add color and exactness to writing and speaking. One kind of modifier is an adjective.

An **adjective** is a word that modifies a noun or pronoun.

An adjective answers the question *What kind? Which one? How many?* or *How much?* about nouns and some pronouns. Adjectives in the following examples are in **bold** type. An arrow points to the noun or pronoun each adjective modifies.

ADJECTIVES		
WHAT KIND?	**famous** hurricane	**heavy** rainfall
WHICH ONE?	**these** boats	**those** few
HOW MANY?	**three** tornadoes	**several** records
HOW MUCH?	**little** damage	**much** work

CONNECT TO WRITER'S CRAFT

Writers know that choosing the right adjective can make a difference. In the following passage, notice how Mildred Taylor uses specific adjectives to help describe the scene the children are witnessing. (The adjectives are in **bold** type.)

Beyond the Avery house **bright** lights appeared far away on the road near the Granger mansion. For a **breathless** second they lingered there, then

plunged suddenly downward toward the Averys'.
The **first** set of lights was followed by a **second,**
then a **third,** until there were **half a dozen** sets of
headlights beaming over the trail.

"Wh-what's happening?" cried Christopher-John.
For what seemed an **interminable** wait, we
stood watching those lights drawing nearer and
nearer before Stacey clicked off the flashlight and
ordered us into the forest. Silently, we slipped into
the brush and fell flat to the ground. **Two** pickups
and **four** cars rattled into the yard, their lights
focused like spotlights on the Avery **front** porch.
Noisy, angry men leaped from the cars and surrounded the house.

Mildred Taylor, Roll of Thunder, Hear My Cry

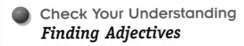

PRACTICE YOUR SKILLS

 Check Your Understanding
Finding Adjectives

> Science Topic · **Write each adjective. Beside each one, write the word it modifies.**

1. A fierce hurricane begins over the ocean in the hot parts of the world.

2. Strong winds come from opposite directions and smash together.

3. Then the wild winds move in a circular pattern.

4. The calm center of the hurricane is called the eye.

5. The eye has light breezes and puffy clouds.

6. If the mighty winds of a hurricane hit land, they can cause severe damage.

7. Sturdy buildings have collapsed because of the huge waves or terrible winds of a severe hurricane.

8. With a hurricane comes heavy rain that often causes additional damage to property.

9. The rains often cause many rivers to overflow.

10. The powerful storm may weaken after it hits land.

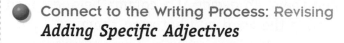 Connect to the Writing Process: Revising

Adding Specific Adjectives

Rewrite the following sentences, adding specific adjectives wherever possible.

11. The winds damaged the homes.

12. The boats rode out the storm on the ocean.

13. The storm ruined businesses.

14. People were without power for hours.

15. After the storm the winds calmed down.

▶ Different Positions of Adjectives

An adjective usually comes right in front of the word it modifies. Occasionally, however, an adjective will follow the word it modifies. An adjective can also follow a linking verb.

BEFORE A NOUN	A **huge, beautiful** flower was the subject of the painting.
AFTER A NOUN	A flower, **huge** and **beautiful,** was the subject of the painting.
AFTER A LINKING VERB	The flower was **huge** and **beautiful** in the painting.

Notice that more than one adjective can modify the same noun.

You can find lists of common linking verbs on pages L83–L85.

PUNCTUATION WITH TWO ADJECTIVES

Sometimes you will write two adjectives together before or after the noun they describe. If those two adjectives are not connected by *and* or *or,* you might need to put a comma between them. To decide if a comma belongs, read the adjectives with the word *and* between them.

- If the adjectives make sense, put a comma in to replace the word *and.*
- If the adjectives do not make sense with the word *and* between them, do not add a comma.

COMMA NEEDED	It was a long, hard day.
	(*It was a long and hard day* reads well.)
COMMA NOT NEEDED	It was a dry summer day.
	(*It was a dry and summer day* does not read well.)

Usually no comma is needed after a number or after an adjective that refers to size, shape, or age.

six blue flowers   a large sunny painting

You can learn more about commas before nouns on pages L532–L533.

Articles

The words *a, an,* and *the* form a special group of adjectives called **articles.** *A* comes before words that begin with a consonant sound. *An* comes before words that begin with a vowel sound.

Marcy wrote **a** report about **an** artist.

(*A* comes before a consonant sound such as the *r* in *report,* and *an* comes before a vowel sound such as the *a* in *artist.*)

You will not be asked to list articles in the exercises in this book.

PRACTICE YOUR SKILLS

● Check Your Understanding
Finding Adjectives

Art Topic **Write each adjective. Beside each one, write the word it modifies. (Do not include articles.)**

1. Georgia O'Keeffe was one of the most original artists of the early twentieth century.

2. Her famous flower paintings, large and colorful, appeared in the art scene of the mid-1920s.

3. She also painted precise and geometric city scenes.

4. In 1929, she moved to New Mexico, where she painted beautiful and unusual still lifes and landscapes.

5. Her paintings reflected the colorful desert of the Southwest.

6. A teacher once told Georgia that her drawings were small and dark.

7. As a result, she always painted everything large and bright.

8. Her unique style increased her popularity as an artist.

9. She enjoyed a long career.

10. Her bold, inspirational paintings are still popular today.

Write the following sentences, adding or removing a comma between adjectives if necessary. If a sentence is correct, write C.

11. Our favorite, art teacher took us to the museum today.

12. She wanted us to see the museum's famous new collection of Georgia O'Keeffe paintings.

13. At the entrance a large colorful poster of a poppy amazed us.

14. The bright, red flower dominated the exhibit.

15. I found O'Keeffe's bold unique paintings very beautiful.

Communicate Your Ideas

APPLY TO WRITING
Friendly Letter: *Adjectives*

Georgia O'Keeffe.
Red Poppy, 1927.
Oil on canvas, 7 by 9 inches.
Private collection.

You and your cousin who lives in the next town cannot decide how to spend Saturday. You want to go to see the new exhibit at the art museum. You decide to persuade your cousin by describing this painting, which is on display. Write a friendly letter that describes the painting so your cousin will be curious enough to want to go to the museum with you. Be sure to use adjectives in a variety of sentence positions.

Proper Adjectives

A proper noun is the name of a particular person, place, or thing. A **proper adjective** is formed from a proper noun. A proper adjective always begins with a capital letter.

PROPER NOUNS	China, Europe, Democrat, England, Switzerland
PROPER ADJECTIVES	**Chinese** history, **European** countries, **Democratic** candidate, **English** sheepdog, **Swiss** watch

You can learn more about capitalization of proper adjectives on page L504.

PRACTICE YOUR SKILLS

 Check Your Understanding
Finding Adjectives

Contemporary Life **Write each proper adjective. Beside each one, write the word it modifies.**

1. Mr. Taylor told us, in his best English accent, that we would be participating in the school's cultural fair.

2. Nancy Coleman brought a German clock for our booth.

3. I saw wonderful African masks at the booth next to ours.

4. We ate Greek food at the fair.

5. While at the festival, José bought a souvenir at the Italian booth.

6. The Chinese embroidery that Ming brought was very delicate.

7. The local Republican candidate helped us open the fair.

8. We could hear the Mexican musicians playing mariachi music.

9. A Congressional representative also came to the fair.

10. She was surprised to win a Hawaiian vacation at the raffle.

● Connect to the Writing Process: Editing
Capitalizing Proper Adjectives

Write the following sentences, capitalizing each proper adjective. If a sentence is correct, write C.

11. My mother can speak the french language very well.

12. Did you get to see the irish dancers?

13. My favorite part of the fair was the performance of the Scottish pipers.

14. John liked the spanish flamenco dancers.

15. Did Sara like the african storyteller?

APPLY TO WRITING

Advertisement: *Proper Adjectives*

Your class has been asked to make posters for the school's cultural fair, which will also be one of the school's largest fund-raisers for this year. Think about what kind of booths the fair will have. What types of activities will interest people of all ages? Then make a poster that will be placed in business windows throughout the community to advertise the fair. Be sure to use proper adjectives correctly in your advertisement.

▶ Adjective or Noun?

A word's part of speech depends on how it is used in a sentence. That is why the same word can be a noun in one sentence and an adjective in another sentence.

NOUN	Let's watch some **baseball** today.
ADJECTIVE	Did you lose your **baseball** bat?
NOUN	The coach caught my **cold.**
ADJECTIVE	I do not like **cold** weather during baseball season.
NOUN	The first game of the baseball season is always in the **spring.**
ADJECTIVE	Most professional baseball teams hold **spring** training in Arizona or Florida.

PRACTICE YOUR SKILLS

● Check Your Understanding
Distinguishing Between Adjectives and Nouns

Contemporary Life | **Write *adjective* or *noun* to identify each underlined word.**

1. How many gallons of <u>paint</u> will we need for the dugout?

2. I will need a new <u>spring</u> jacket before we start practice.

3. The <u>baseball</u> soared over center field and into the <u>bleachers</u>.

4. On which <u>train</u> car will the team eat?

5. Finding time to practice can be a <u>major</u> problem for me.

6. Can the <u>paint</u> stains be removed from the dugout floor?

7. The <u>train</u> was empty except for our team.

8. This <u>spring</u> we have had better practices.

9. Our coach was a <u>major</u> in the army.

10. Why did you join the <u>baseball</u> team this year?

● Connect to the Writing Process: Drafting
Writing Sentences with Nouns and Adjectives

Write two sentences for each of the following words. Use the word as an adjective in the first sentence. Use the word as a noun in the second sentence. Then label the use of each one.

11. radio

12. art

13. silver

14. city

15. apple

▶ Adjective or Pronoun?

Some words can be used as either pronouns or adjectives. A word such as *these* is a pronoun if it stands alone and takes the place of a noun. The same word can be an adjective if it modifies a noun or a pronoun.

ADJECTIVE	**That** plane belongs to Orville.
	(*That* modifies *plane.*)
PRONOUN	**That** belongs to Orville.
	(*That* takes the place of the noun *plane.*)
ADJECTIVE	**Which** plane do you want?
PRONOUN	**Which** do you want?
ADJECTIVE	**Many** onlookers stayed to congratulate Orville.
PRONOUN	**Many** stayed to congratulate Orville.

All of the following words can be used as pronouns or adjectives.

WORDS USED AS PRONOUNS OR ADJECTIVES			
Demonstrative	**Interrogative**	**Indefinite**	
that	what	all	many
these	which	another	more
this	whose	any	most
those		both	neither
		each	other
		either	several
		few	some

PRACTICE YOUR SKILLS

● Check Your Understanding
Distinguishing Between Adjectives and Pronouns

History Topic **Label each underlined word as an *adjective* or a *pronoun*.**

1. <u>Few</u> people realize that Wilbur and Orville Wright made bicycles before airplanes.

2. They experimented with <u>many</u> designs before their historic flight at Kitty Hawk.

3. <u>Which</u> brother made the first flight?

4. <u>Few</u> understand the dangers of the first flight.

5. <u>That</u> airplane of the Wright brothers began as a glider.

6. <u>What</u> challenges did they face in December 1903?

7. <u>Both</u> brothers continued to make airplanes.

8. <u>Many</u> wanted to fly after Wilbur and Orville's successful flight.

9. <u>What</u> did Wilbur do?

10. A <u>few</u> people helped the Wright brothers with their first flight on December 17, 1903.

● Connect to the Writing Process: Drafting
Drafting Sentences for Adjectives and Pronouns

Write two sentences for each of the following words. Use the word as an adjective in the first sentence. Use the word as a pronoun in the second sentence. Then label the use of each one.

11. some

12. this

13. which

14. these

15. all

APPLY TO WRITING
News Story: *Adjectives and Pronouns*

You have traveled back in time to Kitty Hawk, North Carolina, in 1903. The Wright brothers are about to make their first flight in their flying machine. As a reporter for the local newspaper, write a news story that describes this historic occasion. Use adjectives and pronouns correctly.

QuickCheck Mixed Practice

Science Topic **Write each adjective. Beside each one, write the word it modifies. Do not list articles. (There are thirty-five adjectives.)**

1. Gorillas, shy and gentle, are peaceful animals.
2. A gorilla may reach a height of six feet.

3. The arms, long and powerful, almost touch the ground.

4. Gorillas live in small family groups.

5. They roam many miles each day in search of food for their family group.

6. They eat fruits and green leafy plants.

7. Toward evening they construct several platforms for sleeping.

8. The male leader sleeps on the bottom platform of the structure.

9. The leader is the strongest and protects the other members of the group.

10. The females and the young gorillas sleep on the top platforms on high branches.

11. Every day gorillas build new shelters.

12. Gorillas with short hair live in the hot, damp areas of the Congo River valley.

13. The faces of these gorillas are hairless and shiny.

14. Gorillas with coarse hair live in the cool air of the African mountains.

15. Most gorillas live in and around the central part of Africa.

Adverbs

Another kind of modifier is an adverb. Adverbs make writing more precise. Notice in the following examples how the second sentence gives more information with the addition of two adverbs.

> Jonathan is running the marathon.
>
> Jonathan is **carefully** running the marathon **now.**

An **adverb** is a word that modifies a verb, an adjective, or another adverb.

Many adverbs are easy to recognize because they end in –*ly*.

> Run **quickly** and grasp the baton **firmly.**
>
> Did Ruth **finally** complete her training session **successfully?**

The following chart shows, however, that some common adverbs do not end in –*ly*.

COMMON ADVERBS			
again	far	never	soon
almost	fast	next	still
already	hard	not (n't)	then
also	here	now	there
always	just	often	too
down	late	quite	very
even	more	rather	well
ever	near	so	yet

Remember that *not* and its contraction *n't* are always adverbs.

> The stopwatch is **not** working.
>
> I have**n't** run the mile.

 ## Adverbs That Modify Verbs

Most adverbs modify verbs. To find these adverbs, first find each verb. Then ask yourself, *Where? When? How?* or *To what extent?* about each one. The answers to these questions will be adverbs. Notice that an adverb can appear anywhere in the sentence.

WHERE?	The old fence fell **down.**
WHEN?	**Then** the runners jumped.
HOW?	The track meet ended **abruptly.**
TO WHAT EXTENT?	Stacy **almost** won the race.

If the verb contains helping verbs, the adverb modifies the entire verb phrase.

> He has packed the equipment **carefully.**
>
> **Soon** the heavy rains will begin **again.**
>
> She can run **quickly.**
>
> Uncle Ray has **not** met my track coach.
>
> Does Jenny **often** compete at track?
>
> Don has **not yet** arrived for the meet.

Notice in the preceding examples that an adverb can interrupt a verb phrase.

PRACTICE YOUR SKILLS

● Check Your Understanding
Finding Adverbs

Contemporary Life

Write each adverb and the word or words it modifies.

1. Our track team rarely loses.
2. Stephanie rushed forward to the finish line.
3. Lately the team has been practicing in the morning.
4. Danny was quickly tying his shoes.
5. Did you really forget your discus?
6. Finally the meet has begun.
7. Mira is practicing the long jump again.
8. We have looked everywhere for a new stopwatch.
9. Ellis will never run there.
10. Don't stop now!
11. You should always stretch thoroughly.
12. Sometimes I also run hurdles.
13. We often run here.
14. Nancy always jumps superbly.
15. Franklin hasn't finished the shot put yet.

● Connect to the Writing Process: Drafting
Writing Sentences with Adverbs

Using adverbs, write sentences that follow each direction. Underline each adverb.

16. Describe how a friend talks.
17. Describe how a detective enters a dark, scary house.
18. Describe how a toddler walks.

19. Describe how you do your homework.

20. Describe how you eat spaghetti.

Adverbs That Modify Adjectives and Other Adverbs

An adverb can modify an adjective or another adverb. When it does, it usually comes before the word it modifies.

MODIFYING AN ADJECTIVE	Barry's compliments were **truly** sincere.
	(*Sincere* is an adjective. *Truly* tells how sincere Barry's compliments were.)
MODIFYING AN ADVERB	Ada finished her lines **very** quickly.
	(*Quickly* is an adverb. *Very* tells how quickly Ada finished.)

You can learn about using adjectives and adverbs for comparisons on pages L435–L440.

PRACTICE YOUR SKILLS

● Check Your Understanding
Finding Adverbs

Write each adverb. Beside each one, write the word it modifies.

1. The actors were extremely nervous.

2. You should whisper very quietly backstage.

3. It rained quite often during the month of outdoor performances.

4. The actors were truly responsible.

5. Rita arrived too early for her cue.

6. Rain fell quite heavily for an hour before the show.

7. Lenny has an unusually powerful voice.

8. The pace was moving rather slowly.

9. The music was exceptionally loud.

10. The play seemed somewhat long.

11. The audience is usually enthusiastic.

12. Joyce is often absent from practice.

13. The crowd grew curiously silent after the last act.

14. This play is strangely familiar.

15. Despite the problems the actors appeared totally calm.

Connect to the Writing Process: Drafting
Writing Sentences with Adverbs

Use each word as an adverb in a sentence. Then rewrite the sentence, putting the adverb in a different part of the sentence.

16. calmly	**18.** never	**20.** quickly
17. finally	**19.** soon	

Communicate Your Ideas

APPLY TO WRITING

Review: *Adverbs*

The adviser to the school newspaper has invited students to write reviews. Write a review for the school paper of a movie, television show, compact disc, concert, or play that interests you. Be sure to use adverbs to modify verbs, adjectives, and other adverbs.

QuickCheck · Mixed Practice

Write each adverb. Beside each one, write the word or words it modifies.

1. Giraffes glide gracefully and noiselessly across the plains of Kenya in Africa.

2. There they search hungrily and eagerly for the acacia tree.

3. A family of giraffes will often feed from the same tree.

4. Drinking water is the most difficult job for a giraffe.

5. This unusually tall animal drinks slowly and awkwardly.

6. Carefully it bends its knees and its neck and laps cautiously at the cool water.

7. The giraffe's very long neck contains the same number of bones as the neck of a guinea pig.

8. These neck bones are much longer in the giraffe than in the guinea pig.

9. The neck bones are also bigger in the giraffe.

10. The giraffe seldom uses its quite unusual voice.

11. Ordinarily, a giraffe will not attack other creatures.

12. Daily a giraffe will eat acacia leaves on the grassy plains.

13. Other animals rarely threaten the giraffe's survival.

14. Lions occasionally bother giraffes.

15. Sometimes visitors to Kenya's national parks see the giraffes.

General Interest **Write each adverb and adjective. Beside each one, write the word it modifies.**

1. Venus is often visible in the evening sky.

2. Some people worry about comets.

3. Several planets can be easily seen in the night sky.

4. Many objects in the night sky have been given Latin names from Roman myths.

5. Orion, the hunter, always chases his prey across the winter sky.

6. The earth spins slowly on its axis.

7. Suddenly the brilliant supernova disappeared.

8. The star Vega burns brightly in the constellation Lyra.

9. Usually the middle of August is a good time to see summer stars.

10. Summer is often the best time to see the Milky Way.

11. Many people mistake it for a weather cloud.

12. The Big Dipper is usually identifiable.

13. Pluto is a very cold, dark planet.

14. Frequently you can see Mars, Jupiter, or Saturn.

15. They look like bright stars, but they do not twinkle.

Diagraming Adjectives and Adverbs

In a sentence diagram, adjectives and adverbs are both diagramed on a slanted line below the words they modify.

Eventually the poor tree fell.

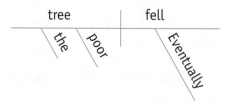

An Adverb That Modifies an Adjective or Another Adverb   This adverb is also connected to the word it modifies. It is written on a line parallel to the word it modifies.

Evening arrived very quickly.

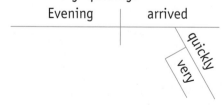

Frighteningly dark clouds floated by.

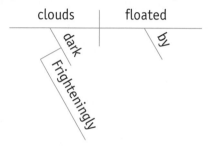

The unusually bright stars glittered quite intensely.

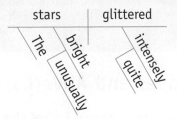

PRACTICE YOUR SKILLS

Diagraming Adjectives and Adverbs

Diagram the following sentences or copy them. If you copy them, draw one line under each subject and two lines under each verb. Then label each modifier *adjective* or *adverb*.

1. Three chickens have escaped.
2. Julia worked steadily.
3. Suddenly the brilliant sun disappeared.
4. Fierce winds blew daily.
5. An elephant can move noiselessly.
6. The strong batter grinned confidently.
7. The rather large ball bounced high.
8. She writes quite often.
9. Have the three workers finished so soon?
10. Very young kittens run quite awkwardly.
11. The proud horse flung its mane back and snorted loudly.
12. The Davis family moved recently.
13. We don't know the next winner yet.
14. Moviegoers were really frightened.
15. The antique cars moved very slowly.

Finding Adjectives and Adverbs

Make two columns on your paper. Label the first column *adjectives* and the second column *adverbs*. Then in the proper column, write each adjective and adverb.

1. Finally we finished the new doghouse for Tex.
2. The Irish soccer team has often won.
3. Lee spoke slowly and calmly.
4. A car skidded dangerously on the icy road.
5. The French diplomats were formally introduced.
6. The ride was too scary for me.
7. Did you bring that warm jacket?
8. They left the dance unusually early.
9. You should not drive the car through the deep water.
10. The English nurse is extremely thoughtful.

Identifying Adjectives and Adverbs

Write each adjective and adverb. Then beside each one, write the word or words each one describes.

1. Jody answered the first question correctly.
2. The spring concert will begin soon.
3. Slowly Jeff opened the old window.
4. Karen has never tasted a green apple.
5. Occasionally Mom does research for large companies.
6. I haven't seen that movie.
7. Muffy often eats small grasshoppers.
8. Now we should listen to the latest news.

Distinguishing Among Different Parts of Speech

Write each underlined word. Then label each one *noun*, *pronoun*, or *adjective*.

1. The words of <u>that</u> <u>song</u> are funny.
2. Use <u>these</u> to wash the <u>car</u> windows.
3. I always enjoy watching the <u>news</u> on <u>television</u>.
4. <u>Which</u> is the best buy for <u>each</u> of us?
5. <u>Several</u> of the musicians knew the <u>song</u> title.
6. We will need a <u>bicycle</u> rack for the <u>car</u>.
7. <u>These</u> <u>news</u> bulletins just arrived for the President.
8. <u>Which</u> <u>television</u> station do you watch?
9. <u>That</u> is the <u>bicycle</u> for me.
10. <u>Each</u> runner ate <u>several</u> bananas.

Writing Sentences

Write five sentences that follow the directions below. (The sentences may come in any order.) Write about one of the following topics or a topic of your choice: the best or the worst birthday present you ever received or gave.

Write a sentence that...

1. includes two adjectives before a noun.
2. includes an adjective after a linking verb.
3. includes two adjectives after a noun.
4. includes a proper adjective.
5. includes *that* as an adjective.

Language and *Self-Expression*

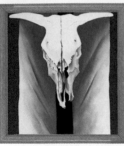

Georgia O'Keeffe (1887–1986) taught art in public schools after studying at the Art Institute of Chicago. A trip to New Mexico in 1931 inspired this painting and led to her eventual move to that state.

O'Keeffe considered this painting an "American painting," both for its use of color and for its subject. Think of an object that you consider especially American. Write a brief composition about the object and why you think of it as American in nature. Use adjectives and adverbs to make your writing more vivid and interesting.

Prewriting Make a main idea and details chart for your composition. Under the heading "Main Idea," describe the object you want to write about. Under "Details," explain what about the object you consider particularly American in nature.

Drafting Use your main idea and details chart as the basis for your first draft. Try to explain clearly why you consider the object you have chosen to be distinctly American.

Revising Reread your composition. Ask yourself if you have expressed your ideas clearly and concretely. Add adjectives and adverbs, if necessary, to make your writing more vivid.

Editing Check your composition for errors in spelling and punctuation. Be sure all proper adjectives begin with capital letters. Include commas between two or more adjectives, if appropriate.

Publishing Collect your composition with classmates' in an "American Objects" folder.

Another Look

An **adjective** is a word that modifies a noun or pronoun.

The words *a, an,* and *the* form a special group of adjectives called **articles**.

A **proper adjective** is formed from a proper noun and begins with a capital letter.

Using Adjectives

An adjective usually comes right in front of the word it modifies. However, an adjective can follow the word it modifies and can follow a linking verb. *(pages L101–L102)*

If the adjectives make sense with the word *and* between them replace the word *and* with a comma. *(page L102)*

If the adjectives do not make sense with the word *and* between them, do not add a comma. *(page L102)*

An **adverb** is a word that modifies a verb, an adjective, or another adverb.

Using Adverbs

To find an adverb that modifies a verb, find the verb and ask *Where? When? How?* or *To what extent?* about it. The answer will be an adverb. *(page L114)*

An adverb can modify an adjective or another adverb. When it does, it usually comes before the word it modifies. *(page L116)*

Other Information About Adjectives and Adverbs

Recognizing modifiers *(page L99)*

Distinguishing between adjectives and nouns *(page L107)*

Distinguishing between adjectives and pronouns *(page L109)*

Recognizing demonstrative, interrogative, and indefinite pronouns *(page L109)*

Directions
Write the letter of the term that correctly identifies the underlined word in each sentence.

EXAMPLE

1. <u>The</u> Finellis traveled to Iceland over the summer.

1 **A** noun
   B article
   C adverb
   D pronoun

ANSWER   1 **B**

1. It was a <u>strange</u> place.

2. There were <u>very</u> few trees, and the land was strewn with huge volcanic rocks.

3. In <u>many</u> places they could see steam escaping from the earth between rocks.

4. Iceland is full of <u>geothermic</u> springs.

5. <u>These</u> bring heat to most of the country without polluting the air.

6. The Finellis swam in one hot spring while sleet fell on their <u>chilly</u> heads.

7. Geysers spray hot water high into <u>the</u> sky.

8. The <u>Icelandic</u> language is ancient, and many great stories have been written in it.

9. Iceland is on a spot where two great <u>tectonic</u> plates meet.

10. The plates <u>often</u> rub against each other, causing earthquakes.

Adjectives and Adverbs

1	A	adjective		6	A	adjective
	B	article			B	article
	C	adverb			C	adverb
	D	pronoun			D	pronoun
2	A	proper adjective		7	A	noun
	B	article			B	article
	C	adverb			C	adverb
	D	pronoun			D	pronoun
3	A	adjective		8	A	proper adjective
	B	article			B	article
	C	adverb			C	adverb
	D	pronoun			D	proper noun
4	A	adjective		9	A	adjective
	B	article			B	article
	C	adverb			C	adverb
	D	pronoun			D	pronoun
5	A	adjective		10	A	adjective
	B	article			B	article
	C	adverb			C	adverb
	D	pronoun			D	pronoun

CHAPTER 5

Other Parts of Speech and Review

 **Pretest**

Directions
Write the letter of the term that correctly identifies the underlined word or words in each sentence.

EXAMPLE **1.** We hiked <u>to</u> the top of Mt. Greylock.
1 **A** preposition
   B adverb
   C conjunction
   D interjection

ANSWER 1 **A**

1. Mt. Greylock is a mountain <u>in</u> Massachusetts.
2. <u>Neither</u> Jayson <u>nor</u> I had ever climbed it before.
3. We climbed <u>upward</u> for hours.
4. <u>From a distance</u> Mt. Greylock looks like a whale.
5. <u>Well</u>, I heard that the mountain inspired Herman Melville to write *Moby-Dick*.
6. We climbed on the hottest day <u>of</u> summer.
7. Our legs were trembling <u>and</u> weak.
8. "<u>Hey!</u>" Jayson said. "I don't know if we can make it!"
9. I told him it wasn't <u>much</u> farther.
10. <u>Below us</u>, we could see for miles.

1	**A**	preposition	**6**	**A**	preposition
	B	adverb		**B**	adverb
	C	conjunction		**C**	conjunction
	D	interjection		**D**	interjection
2	**A**	prepositions	**7**	**A**	preposition
	B	adverbs		**B**	adverb
	C	conjunctions		**C**	conjunction
	D	interjections		**D**	interjection
3	**A**	preposition	**8**	**A**	preposition
	B	adverb		**B**	adverb
	C	conjunction		**C**	conjunction
	D	interjection		**D**	interjection
4	**A**	prepositional phrase	**9**	**A**	preposition
	B	adverb		**B**	adverb
	C	verb phrase		**C**	adjective
	D	interjection		**D**	noun
5	**A**	adjective	**10**	**A**	prepositional phrase
	B	adverb		**B**	adverb
	C	conjunction		**C**	conjunction
	D	interjection		**D**	verb phrase

Nam June Paik. *Family of Robot: Aunt and Uncle,* 1986.
Mixed media, 89½ by 45 by 25 inches. Courtesy Carl Solway Gallery.

Describe   What are the robots made of? What shapes does the artist include in the sculpture?

Analyze   How are the robots similar? How do they differ?

Interpret   Why do you think the artist included video images in the sculpture? What do you think he is trying to say about television?

Judge   Do you find the robots amusing or menacing? Explain your answer.

At the end of this chapter, you will use the artwork to stimulate ideas for writing.

Prepositions

Prepositions can change the entire meaning of a sentence.

> Please hand me the first-aid kit **on** the table.
> Please hand me the first-aid kit **near** the table.
> Please hand me the first-aid kit **under** the table.

A **preposition** is a word that shows the relationship between a noun or a pronoun and another word in the sentence.

The following is a list of common prepositions. Notice that some prepositions are more than one word.

COMMON PREPOSITIONS		
about	beyond	over
above	by	past
according to	down	since
across	during	through
after	except	throughout
against	for	to
along	from	toward
among	in	under
around	in front of	underneath
at	inside	until
because of	into	up
before	like	upon
behind	near	up to
below	of	with
beneath	off	within
beside	on	without
between	out of	

PRACTICE YOUR SKILLS

● Check Your Understanding
Supplying Prepositions

 Contemporary Life **Write two prepositions that could fill each blank in the following sentences.**

1. The narrow road ran ■ the cliffs.
2. A huge boulder was lying ■ the path.
3. The scouts camped ■ the lake.
4. I found my compass ■ the stream.
5. Kathleen found the missing backpack ■ the tent.
6. Our guide looked for a bear ■ the bushes.
7. A huge falcon flew ■ the clouds.
8. The hikers climbed ■ the rocks.
9. That tent was pitched ■ Shelly.
10. This trail leads ■ the river.

● Prepositional Phrases

A preposition is always the first word of a group of words called a prepositional phrase.

A **prepositional phrase** is a group of words made up of a preposition, its object, and any words that modify the object.

PREPOSITIONAL PHRASES   **In *July* the islands are often crowded.**

(*July* is the object of the preposition *in*.)

An iguana stood **in front of *us*.**

(The pronoun *us* is the object of the preposition *in front of*.)

Put the binoculars **inside** *the small backpack.*

(*Backpack* is the object of the preposition *inside. The* and *small* modify *backpack.*)

Sometimes a preposition has more than one object. Then the prepositional phrase has a **compound object of the preposition.**

| COMPOUND OBJECT OF A PREPOSITION | All the scientists **except** *Kevin* **and** *Brianna* have arrived. |

Some sentences may include more than one prepositional phrase.

The penguin eggs **on the islands** usually hatch **around May.**

After dinner we went **to the island.**

You can learn more about prepositional phrases on pages L189–L197.

PRACTICE YOUR SKILLS

 Check Your Understanding
Finding Prepositional Phrases

Geography Topic **Write each prepositional phrase.**

1. The Galapagos Islands are located near Ecuador.
2. They cover an area of 3,029 square miles.
3. The islands contain many animals of interest.
4. You can find turtles throughout the islands.
5. Marine iguanas are sometimes found in junkyards.

6. During his visit in 1835, Charles Darwin observed many interesting animals.

7. According to Darwin, each of the islands is inhabited by vastly different species.

8. Centuries before Darwin's famous visit, ancient people traveled to the islands.

9. Many tourists enjoy the Galapagos Islands for their different animals and plants.

10. Certain species of penguins live on one of the islands near the equator!

● Check Your Understanding
Finding Prepositional Phrases

Science Topic **Write each prepositional phrase. Underline the preposition and circle its object. (There are fifteen phrases.)**

11. The trunk of an elephant is like a hose.

12. Elephants inhale water through their trunks.

13. Then they curl their trunks and shoot the water into their mouths.

14. Elephants eat food in a similar way.

15. With their trunks elephants also spray water on their backs.

16. They like water and can swim for six hours.

17. During the hottest hours, elephants often huddle under trees.

18. Elephants also throw mud over their bodies.

19. With their trunks elephants can break large branches from trees.

20. In a wildlife park, an elephant can live for sixty-five years.

Connect to the Writing Process: Drafting
Writing Sentences

> **21.–25. Write five sentences about an animal that lives in the wild. Use at least one prepositional phrase in each sentence.**

Preposition or Adverb?

Certain words, such as *inside*, can be a preposition in one sentence and an adverb in another. Such a word is a preposition when it is part of a prepositional phrase. It is an adverb when it stands alone.

PREPOSITION	Carolyn and Jackie went **inside** *the hotel.*
	(*Inside the hotel* is a prepositional phrase.)
ADVERB	Carolyn and Jackie went **inside.**
	(*Inside* is an adverb that tells where Carolyn and Jackie went. It is not part of a prepositional phrase, and it has no object.)
PREPOSTITION	Climb **up** *the ladder* and check on the luggage.
ADVERB	Climb **up** and check on the luggage.
PREPOSITION	His very last quarter rolled **down** *the aisle.*
ADVERB	She rolled the window **down.**
PREPOSITION	She drove **past** *the house.*
ADVERB	She drove **past.**

PRACTICE YOUR SKILLS

● Check Your Understanding
Distinguishing Between Prepositions and Adverbs

Contemporary Life **Label each underlined word *P* for preposition or *A* for adverb.**

1. We drove <u>through</u> Chicago in less than an hour.

2. The mountains stood a long way <u>off</u>.

3. We ate our lunch <u>near</u> Lake Michigan.

4. Every morning Dad checked <u>around</u> the car.

5. Did you drive straight <u>through</u>?

6. Lisa left the tickets <u>behind</u>.

7. My suitcase rolled <u>off</u> the roof rack.

8. Don't come <u>near</u>, for I have to focus the camera.

9. Did you look <u>around</u>?

10. The spare tire may have rolled <u>behind</u> that bush.

● Connect to the Writing Process: Drafting
Drafting Sentences with Prepositional Phrases and Adverbs

Write two sentences for each of the following words. Use the word as a preposition in the first sentence and as an adverb in the second sentence. Then label the use of each one.

11. in

12. across

13. below

14. up

15. along

APPLY TO WRITING

Postcard: *Prepositions and Adverbs*

While driving with your family on vacation, you stop at the area shown above and purchase this postcard. Write a short message to your grandmother, telling her about your trip and the things you have been doing. Consider these questions before you write your message.

- What did you do yesterday?
- What do you plan to do today?
- What has made this trip special or fun?

Be sure to use prepositional phrases and some prepositions that can be adverbs to make your writing interesting.

General Interest **Write the prepositional phrases in the following paragraphs.**

Does a monster really hide in Loch Ness? For many centuries people have reportedly seen this strange creature. The Loch Ness monster first had its picture taken in 1934. Dr. R. K. Wilson was driving along the shore. Suddenly he saw movement in the water and grabbed his camera. The result is a very famous, very blurry photograph of a mysterious object. The fuzzy picture just *might* show a strange animal with an extremely long neck. Some people, however, are not convinced by this photograph.

With special underwater cameras, scientists have searched more recently for the Loch Ness monster. Unfortunately, the new pictures also show little except fuzzy shapes. Most scientists do not believe in the monster. Possible explanations for the monster include a large fish, an unusual wave, and a giant seal. Believers, though, think that a dinosaur may have survived from prehistoric times. Without better evidence the Loch Ness mystery will remain unsolved.

Conjunctions and Interjections

You have learned that prepositions show relationships between words. Conjunctions connect words.

A **conjunction** connects words or groups of words.

The following is a list of some **coordinating conjunctions.** These conjunctions connect single words and groups of words.

COORDINATING CONJUNCTIONS			
and	but	or	yet

CONNECTING WORDS	I have *rods* **and** *reels.* (connects nouns)
	He **or** *I* will meet Tim. (connects pronouns)
	The wind *blew* **and** *howled.* (connects verbs)
	Get *blue* **or** *green* worms. (connects adjectives)
	He spoke *firmly* **yet** *kindly* about my poor fishing skills. (connects adverbs)
CONNECTING GROUPS OF WORDS	Tad looked *in the boat* **and** *outside the boat.* (connects prepositional phrases)
	Everyone was here early for the fish fry, **but** *the special guest was late.* (connects sentences)

In addition to coordinating conjunctions, there are pairs of conjunctions called **correlative conjunctions.** Although they look different from coordinating conjunctions, they do the same job. They connect groups of words.

CORRELATIVE CONJUNCTIONS		
both/and	either/or	neither/nor

CONNECTING WORDS	**Both** *bass* **and** *catfish* are tender. (connects nouns)
	The two fish **neither** *look* alike **nor** *swim* alike. (connects verbs)
CONNECTING GROUPS OF WORDS	**Either** *Raymond will come here,* **or** *I will go to the pond.* (connects sentences)

The third kind of conjunction is a subordinating conjunction. *It will be covered on page L251.*

An interjection is unusual because it is always set off from the rest of the sentence by a mark of punctuation.

An **interjection** is a word that expresses strong feeling.

The following is a list of some common interjections.

COMMON INTERJECTIONS		
aha	oops	wow
goodness	ouch	yes
hooray	ugh	yikes
oh	well	yippee

An interjection at the beginning of a sentence is followed by an exclamation point or a comma.

> **Wow!** That was the best catch of the day.
>
> **Oh,** I forgot my tackle box!
>
> **Great!** We can leave now.

CONNECT TO SPEAKING AND WRITING

When you use an exclamation mark with an interjection, the volume of your voice will be louder than for the other parts of the sentence. The volume helps convey strong emotion.

It is important to remember not to use interjections too often, or they will lose their force.

PRACTICE YOUR SKILLS

Check Your Understanding
Finding Conjunctions and Interjections

Contemporary Life
Write and label each conjunction or interjection.

1. Either Sam or David will have to bait my hook.

2. You and I are responsible for the fish.

3. Wow! Did you see the size of the fish Susan caught?

4. Nani will bake or broil the fresh fish.

5. The fish were biting, but no one caught any.

6. Both bass and trout are tasty.

7. Ugh! Someone removed the fish from the cooler.

8. Lures and hooks are scattered everywhere.

9. Neither Tom nor Cherri could clean the fish.

10. Oh, you should have seen the big one that got away!

● Connect to the Writing Process: Revising
Revising Sentences with Conjunctions

Rewrite the following passage, removing any conjunctions. In some cases, you may have to write a new sentence altogether. Notice how different the passage is without conjunctions!

> Besides, he thought, next year he would be bigger and could walk faster and get to school before it started and wouldn't be laughed at. And when he wasn't dead-tired from walking home from school, his father would let him hunt with Sounder. Having both school and Sounder would be mighty good, but if he couldn't have school, he could always have Sounder.
>
> —*William Armstrong*, Sounder

Communicate Your Ideas

APPLY TO WRITING

Script: *Conjunctions and Interjections*

Your scout leader can't decide between taking your troop to the local museum or on a fishing trip this weekend. You and the other members of your troop decide to put on a skit to help your leader make a decision. Be sure to use conjunctions and prepositions in the script you write for your skit.

Parts of Speech Review

Along with the definitions of words, the dictionary includes abbreviations like *n., adj.,* and *v.* The word *work,* for example, would first be labeled *n.* for *noun.* This label, however, does not mean that *work* is always a noun. It means that *work* may be used as a noun. A word does not become a part of speech until it is used in a sentence. *Work,* as a matter of fact, can be used as three different parts of speech.

NOUN	Clara's success depended on hard **work.**
VERB	She **work**ed very hard.
ADJECTIVE	Her **work** schedule was tremendous.

To find a word's part of speech, ask yourself, *What is the word doing in this sentence?*

NOUN	Is the word naming a person, a place, a thing, or an idea?
	The **girl** who healed **pets** lives in **Massachusetts.**
	Compassion is important to all **nurses.**
PRONOUN	Is the word taking the place of a noun?
	That was the best job for **her.**
VERB	Is the word showing action? Does it link the subject with another word in the sentence?
	Everyone **read** about the Civil War.
	Clara Barton's life **was** very interesting.

ADJECTIVE	Is the word modifying a noun or pronoun? Does it answer the question *What kind? Which one? How many?* or *How much?*

The **gentle** girl became a **famous** nurse.

That flag has a **red** cross.

ADVERB	Is the word modifying a verb, an adjective, or another adverb? Does it answer the question *How? When? Where?* or *To what extent?*

Nurses work **quite calmly** in **unusually** difficult situations.

PREPOSITION	Is the word showing a relationship between a noun or pronoun and another word in the sentence? Is it a part of a phrase?

During the afternoon we watched a film *about* Clara Barton.

CONJUNCTION	Is the word connecting words or groups of words?

Go find the iodine **and** some clean bandages.

Clara had many brothers and sisters, **but** she was sometimes lonely.

INTERJECTION	Is the word expressing strong feeling?

Wow! I received my first-aid badge.

Hooray! I passed my first-aid test.

PRACTICE YOUR SKILLS

● Check Your Understanding
Determining Parts of Speech

History Topic **Write each underlined word. Then write its part of speech, using the following abbreviations:**

noun = *n.*   adverb = *adv.*
preposition = *prep.*   verb = *v.*
adjective = *adj.*   pronoun = *pro.*
conjunction = *conj.*   interjection = *inter.*

1. As a <u>young</u> child, Clara proved to be good <u>at</u> her studies.

2. <u>Everyone</u> loved her, <u>and</u> her family encouraged her many interests.

3. Her father <u>sometimes</u> told her exciting adventure stories.

4. <u>Oh</u>, did you know that she was born on Christmas day?

5. She owned <u>several</u> pets, including a turkey and a snapping turtle that <u>frequently</u> frightened the other children.

6. <u>Well</u>, one day her brother's dog <u>became</u> sick, and only Clara was able to heal it.

7. Soon children from other farms <u>brought</u> their cats <u>and</u> dogs to Clara.

8. As a <u>young</u> woman, she cared for wounded soldiers <u>during</u> the Civil War.

9. Many soldiers knew her <u>only</u> as "The Angel of the Battlefield" and a <u>gentle</u> voice.

10. In later years, <u>Clara</u> <u>founded</u> the American Red Cross.

Check Your Understanding
Determining Parts of Speech

General Interest **Write each underlined word. Then write its part of speech, using the following abbreviations:**

noun = *n.*   adverb = *adv.*   conjunction = *conj.*
preposition = *prep.*   verb = *v.*   interjection = *inter.*
adjective = *adj.*   pronoun = *pro.*

The study of names <u>is</u> <u>fun</u>. <u>During</u> the Middle Ages, <u>most</u> people <u>had</u> only a first name. <u>That</u> was <u>fine</u>, as long as <u>everyone</u> stayed in <u>his</u> or her village. Cities were <u>finally</u> formed, <u>and</u> people moved <u>from</u> place to place. Five Marys in the same place <u>became</u> confusing. The solution <u>was</u> easy. Most people added information to their names. <u>They</u> used one of four methods.

First, a <u>son</u> might take the <u>name</u> of his father. As a result, Henry would become Henry, son of John. <u>Through</u> time, this became Henry Johnson.

Second, <u>people</u> were named <u>for</u> some of their features. A strong person could be named Henry Strong or Henry Hardy. A person with <u>red</u> hair might take the last name of Reed or Reid. The names Wise, Grim, Moody, and Sharp came about <u>for</u> the same reason.

Third, people became identified with the place <u>of</u> their birth. The Woods <u>or</u> the Atwoods, for example,

L146 Other Parts of Speech and Review

lived near a forest. The Fairbanks family would have come from the edge of a lovely river or stream.

Fourth, people were named for their occupations. A town's blacksmith might be called Henry the Smith. Later this would become Henry Smith. The roofmaker would be called Henry Thatcher, but the village grain merchant would be Henry Miller.

● Connect to the Writing Process: Drafting
Drafting Sentences with Different Parts of Speech

Write sentences that follow the directions.

1. Use *baseball* as a noun and an adjective.
2. Use *this* as a pronoun and an adjective.
3. Use *one* as a pronoun and an adjective.
4. Use *outside* as a preposition and an adverb.
5. Use *watch* as a noun and a verb.

Communicate Your Ideas

APPLY TO WRITING
Proposal: *Different Parts of Speech*

The student council has asked for suggestions to improve the cafeteria. You and your friends would like to see a sound system installed so that you can listen to music at lunch. Write a proposal for the student council that lists the good and bad points of having a sound system installed. Use a variety of parts of speech, and be prepared to identify them.

Finding Prepositions, Conjunctions, Interjections, and Prepositional Phrases

Write each sentence. Label each preposition *(prep.)*, conjunction *(conj.)* and interjection *(interj.)*. Then underline each prepositional phrase.

1. Both pineapple and watermelon were served after dinner.
2. Underneath our car a small kitten was sleeping.
3. Congratulations! You won first prize for your sculpture.
4. Roberto will either sing or dance at the variety show.
5. All members were present, yet no vote was taken.
6. Ouch! A hornet just stung me on my arm and my hand.
7. On a long journey, wild geese often fly in a V-shaped formation.
8. Those strawberries were big but tasteless.
9. Within five minutes the firefighters had the fire under control.
10. Because of so much rain, neither the bananas nor the peaches were ripe.
11. Golf balls were once stuffed with feathers.
12. No! Don't lean against the wet paint.
13. We will get a ride or take the bus.
14. Within ten minutes I will be ready.
15. That box is large but light.
16. Hurray! We won the championship for the second year.
17. Pepper, nutmeg, and mustard are all made from seeds.
18. That wonderful story was written by Raymond.

Identifying Parts of Speech

Write each underlined word. Then beside each one, write its part of speech: *noun, pronoun, verb, adjective, adverb, preposition, conjunction,* **or** *interjection.*

1. Louis, a young boy <u>of</u> five, <u>became</u> the king of <u>France</u> in 1643.
2. He <u>was</u> the king, <u>but</u> he didn't rule.
3. <u>His</u> mother and <u>other</u> adults <u>made</u> the decisions.
4. During <u>much</u> of his <u>childhood</u>, his life was in <u>danger</u>.
5. A <u>group</u> of people <u>wanted</u> a change in the <u>government</u>.
6. <u>Once</u>, the <u>royal</u> family was trapped in the <u>palace</u>.
7. <u>Outside</u>, people <u>yelled</u> and threatened the young king <u>and</u> his family.
8. <u>At</u> sixteen Louis <u>finally</u> <u>became</u> king.
9. He was called the Sun King, and <u>his</u> court was <u>very</u> fancy.
10. <u>According to</u> history books, he acquired <u>much</u> land for France <u>during</u> his reign.

Writing Sentences

Write ten sentences that follow the directions below. Then label the use of each word in the sentence.

1. Use *television* as a noun and an adjective.
2. Use *glue* as a noun and a verb.
3. Use *all* as a pronoun and an adjective.
4. Use *over* as an adverb and a preposition.
5. Use *picture* as a noun and an adjective.
6. Use *one* as a pronoun and an adjective.
7. Use *inside* as an adverb and a preposition.
8. Use *these* as a pronoun and an adjective.
9. Use *well* as a noun, an adverb, and an interjection.
10. Use *paper* as a noun, a verb, and an adjective.

Language and *Self-Expression*

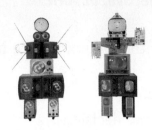

Nam June Paik is a visual artist, musician, scientist, and engineer. He is considered to be the father of video art. After he moved to the United States, he began using televised images in sculptures and musical performances, and he developed the video synthesizer, which enables artists to manipulate images.

Imagine that you could have a robot of your own. What would it look like? What would it be able to do? Describe your robot and its talents. Be sure to use a variety of parts of speech in your description.

Prewriting Make a details web to describe your robot. Include circles for physical characteristics, mental abilities, and talents. If your robot has any drawbacks or problems, include them in your web as well.

Drafting Use your web as the basis of a first draft of a description. Tell what your robot looks like, what it does, and any other details you think are interesting or important.

Revising Reread your description. Be sure you have used the parts of speech correctly.

Editing Go over your description for mistakes in spelling and punctuation. Be sure you have capitalized proper nouns and adjectives and placed a comma or exclamation point after any interjections.

Publishing Draw a picture of your robot, or follow Nam June Paik's example and create a sculpture of it. Display your creation along with your description.

Another Look

A **preposition** is a word that shows the relationship between a noun or a pronoun and another word in the sentence.

A **prepositional phrase** is a group of words made up of a preposition, its object, and any words that modify the object.

A **conjunction** connects words or groups of words.

An **interjection** is a word that expresses strong feeling.

Parts of Speech Review

To find a word's part of speech, ask yourself, *What is the word doing in this sentence? (pages L143–L144)*

NOUN	Is the word naming a person, place, thing, or idea?
PRONOUN	Is the word taking the place of a noun?
VERB	Is the word showing action or linking the subject with another word in the sentence?
ADJECTIVE	Is the word modifying a noun or pronoun?
ADVERB	Is the word modifying a verb, an adjective, or another adverb?
PREPOSITION	Is the word showing a relationship between a noun or pronoun and another word in the sentence? Is it part of a phrase?
CONJUNCTION	Is the word connecting words or groups of words?
INTERJECTION	Is the word expressing strong feeling?

Posttest

Directions

Write the letter of the term that correctly identifies the underlined word or words in each sentence.

EXAMPLE **1.** The Jarmans took a trip <u>to</u> Portugal.

    1 A preposition
       B adverb
       C conjunction
       D interjection

ANSWER   **1 A**

1. They loved the twisted cobblestone streets <u>and</u> whitewashed houses of Lisbon.

2. One evening, they listened to *fado*, a sad, haunting music that speaks <u>of</u> love and loss.

3. They had never heard anything like it <u>before</u>.

4. The next day, they drove <u>out of</u> the city and into the countryside.

5. <u>Well</u>, they had some adventures there!

6. First, their car broke down <u>outside the palaces of Sintra</u>.

7. The townspeople, <u>friendly</u> and concerned, helped them find a new rental car.

8. The Jarmans spoke no Portuguese and the townspeople spoke no English, <u>yet</u> they managed to communicate.

9. Finally, the Jarmans were <u>on their way</u> again.

10. They drove up a hill and <u>saw</u> acres of lemon trees below.

1 **A** preposition
 B adverb
 C conjunction
 D interjection

2 **A** preposition
 B adverb
 C conjunction
 D interjection

3 **A** preposition
 B adverb
 C conjunction
 D interjection

4 **A** preposition
 B adverb
 C conjunction
 D interjection

5 **A** preposition
 B adverb
 C conjunction
 D interjection

6 **A** prepositional phrase
 B adverb
 C conjunction
 D verb phrase

7 **A** preposition
 B adverb
 C adjective
 D noun

8 **A** preposition
 B adverb
 C conjunction
 D interjection

9 **A** prepositional phrase
 B adverb
 C verb phrase
 D interjection

10 **A** preposition
 B verb
 C noun
 D adjective

CHAPTER 6

Complements

Directions
**Write the letter of the term that correctly identifies the
underlined word in each sentence.**

EXAMPLE   **1.** One of the greatest ancient Greek
arts was <u>architecture</u>.

1 A direct object
   B indirect object
   C predicate nominative
   D predicate adjective

ANSWER   **1 C**

1. The Greeks built <u>Athena</u> a temple.
2. The Parthenon is the <u>name</u> of this temple.
3. The Parthenon is very <u>beautiful</u>.
4. The Greeks constructed the <u>Parthenon</u> between 447
and 432 B.C.
5. Much Greek art glorified <u>humans</u>.
6. It also gave the <u>gods</u> thanks for life and fortune.
7. Their sculptures showed the <u>perfection</u> of humans.
8. The ancient Greeks also produced great <u>thinkers</u>.
9. Socrates was a famous <u>philosopher</u>.
10. Plato may be even more <u>famous</u>.

1
A direct object
B indirect object
C predicate nominative
D predicate adjective

6
A direct object
B indirect object
C predicate nominative
D predicate adjective

2
A direct object
B indirect object
C predicate nominative
D predicate adjective

7
A direct object
B indirect object
C predicate nominative
D predicate adjective

3
A direct object
B indirect object
C predicate nominative
D predicate adjective

8
A direct object
B indirect object
C predicate nominative
D predicate adjective

4
A direct object
B indirect object
C predicate nominative
D predicate adjective

9
A direct object
B indirect object
C predicate nominative
D predicate adjective

5
A direct object
B indirect object
C predicate nominative
D predicate adjective

10
A direct object
B indirect object
C predicate nominative
D predicate adjective

Frida Kahlo. *Long Live Life*, 1954.
Oil on masonite, 20¼ by 28⅛ inches. National Institute of Fine Arts and Literature, Mexico City, Mexico.

Describe What does this painting portray? What colors does the artist use?

Analyze What do you think the title of the painting has to do with its content?

Interpret The artist died shortly after she completed this painting. How might her knowledge of her impending death have influenced the painting? How might a writer react to the knowledge of his or her impending death?

Judge Do you feel this painting portrays a life energy or force in any way? Explain your answer.

At the end of this chapter, you will use the artwork to stimulate ideas for writing.

A sentence must have a subject and a verb. Some sentences, however, need another word to complete the meaning of the sentence. By themselves, the following subjects and verbs are not complete statements.

> Birds build.
> Lions seem.

A **complement,** or completer, is necessary to complete the meaning of these statements.

> Birds build **nests.**
> Lions seem **hungry.**

There are four common kinds of complements. Direct objects and indirect objects follow action verbs. Predicate nominatives and predicate adjectives, called subject complements, follow linking verbs.

▶ Direct Objects

All direct objects are usually nouns or pronouns.

A **direct object** is a noun or pronoun that answers the question *What?* or *Whom?* after an action verb.

To find a direct object, first find the subject and the action verb in a sentence. Then ask yourself *What?* or *Whom?* after the verb. The answer to either question will be a direct object. In the example sentences on the next page, subjects are underlined once and verbs are underlined twice. Notice that the direct object comes after the verb.

DIRECT OBJECTS	Sharks have many **teeth.**
	(Sharks have what? *Teeth* is the direct object.)
	Predators know **them** very well.
	(Predators know whom? *Them* is the direct object.)

To find the direct object in a question, change the question into a statement.

QUESTION	Did you see the eagles?
STATEMENT	You did see the **eagles.**

Two or more direct objects together are called a **compound direct object.**

COMPOUND DIRECT OBJECTS	Adam bought a **camera** and **binoculars.**
	(Adam bought what? The compound direct object is *camera* and *binoculars*.)

Verbs that are followed by a direct object are called transitive verbs. You can learn more about action verbs and transitive verbs on pages L75–L79.

PRACTICE YOUR SKILLS

● Check Your Understanding
Finding Direct Objects

 General Interest **Write each direct object.**

1. Ducks will lay eggs only in the morning.

2. You can make eleven omelets with an ostrich egg.

3. Chimpanzees use twigs and rocks as tools.

4. A robin has almost three thousand feathers.

5. Did you see eagles on your trip to the lake?

6. Some earthworms have ten hearts.

7. Lemon sharks grow new teeth every two weeks.

8. One type of spider can spin a web in twenty minutes.

9. Bats squeal and use their ears for navigation.

10. Will a wolf abandon its pups?

● Check Your Understanding
Finding Direct Objects

Science Topic **Write each direct object.**

11. Have you seen the bats under the bridge?

12. Every spring the bats use the bridge as a nursery.

13. A mother bat raises one baby at a time.

14. At night the bats eat insects.

15. They prefer moths and other pests.

16. A small area of the bridge can contain five hundred bats.

17. People watch the bats at dusk.

18. Bats have hands with fingers and feet with toes.

19. By summer the baby bats can eat adult food.

20. The bats leave the bridge in the fall and fly to Mexico.

● Connect to the Writing Process: Drafting
Writing Sentences with Direct Objects

Write a sentence that answers each question. Then underline each direct object in your sentences.

21. What do you see directly in front of you?

22. Whom did you visit recently?

23. What did you eat for dinner last night?

24. How many pencils and pens do you have?

25. What kinds of books do you like best?

Communicate Your Ideas

APPLY TO WRITING
Field Notes: *Direct Objects*

Your science club has assigned you to observe the
bats that live under the local bridge. You observe the
scene shown in the picture. Write a short paragraph
for your science club that describes the behavior of
the bats. Use direct objects in your sentences. When
you finish, underline the direct objects you used.

► Indirect Objects

If a sentence has a direct object, it can also have an indirect object.

An **indirect object** is a noun or pronoun that answers the question *To or for whom?* or *To or for what?* after an action verb.

To find an indirect object, first find the direct object. Then ask yourself, *To whom? For whom? To what?* or *For what?* about the direct object. The answer to any of these questions will be an indirect object. Remember that in order to have an indirect object, a sentence must have a direct object.

INDIRECT OBJECT   Ken bought **Nathan** three hamburgers.

(*Hamburgers* is the direct object. Ken bought the hamburgers for whom? *Nathan* is the indirect object.)

INDIRECT OBJECT   The yellow paint gave the **playscape** a bright appearance.

(*Appearance* is the direct object. The paint gave a bright appearance to what? *Playscape* is the indirect object.)

Notice that an indirect object always comes before a direct object in a sentence.

To find the indirect object in a question, change the question into a statement.

QUESTION   Will you show everyone that watermelon?

STATEMENT   You will show **everyone** that watermelon.
       ⌐— i.o. —⌐   ⌐— d.o. —⌐

Two or more indirect objects together are called a **compound indirect object.**

COMPOUND
INDIRECT
OBJECT

⌐i.o.⌐　⌐i.o.⌐　　　⌐d.o.⌐
Dad gave **Gene** and **Lani** his old football.

(Dad gave the football to whom?
The compound indirect object is *Gene*
and *Lani*.)

Sometimes using an indirect object is awkward. A
prepositional phrase can often make the sentence
read more clearly.

INDIRECT OBJECT | Ted brought the **children** ice cream sandwiches.

PREPOSITIONAL PHRASE | Ted brought ice cream sandwiches **for the children.**

PRACTICE YOUR SKILLS

● Check Your Understanding
Finding Indirect Objects

Contemporary Life **Write each indirect object.**

1. We fed the ducks bread crumbs.

2. Dad cooked us hamburgers on the grill.

3. Sara showed us the delicious dessert.

4. Will you pass me the ketchup?

5. My mom found everyone at the picnic a shady spot for lunch.

6. Did Steve make Mary that fried chicken?

7. You must give Rosemarie and him some lemonade.

8. Have you given Sandra the recipe?

9. Please take your sister this cookie.

10. Susan will reserve us the shelter for our next picnic.

● Check Your Understanding
Finding Indirect Objects

Math Topic **Write each indirect object.**

11. Our teacher read the class several biographies of famous mathematicians.

12. Ms. Gomez taught our class the Pythagorean theorem.

13. Then she showed several students a picture of Archimedes.

14. The picture gave me a more vivid impression of him.

15. Archimedes gave Syracuse and Sicily the invention of the catapult.

16. Archimedes gave geometry many original contributions.

17. He brought the Egyptians the invention of the screw pump.

18. His theories taught me much math and science.

19. Ms. Gomez saved the class an interesting article about early Greek mathematicians.

20. Next week our science instructor will teach us Einstein's theories.

Revising Sentences with Indirect Objects

21.–25. Choose any five of the sentences above and rewrite them without indirect objects. In some cases you may have to write two sentences to convey the same meaning, or you may have to use a prepositional phrase.

APPLY TO WRITING

E-mail Message: *Indirect Objects*

Your mother is away on business this week and wants to know what you have been learning and doing in school. Write your mother an E-mail message that tells her what you have learned this week. Be sure to use indirect objects in your message.

✓ QuickCheck Mixed Practice

Contemporary Life **Write each complement in the following sentences. Then label each one *direct object* or *indirect object.***

1. Have you ever eaten an artichoke or an avocado?

2. I tasted both at the food fair.

3. Anton cooked everyone a Mexican meal.

4. Grandmother made Martina and me sweet potato candy.

5. For decoration, people sometimes put flowers on cakes.

6. Please pass us the eggrolls and the chopsticks from the Asian display.

7. Did you show him the stuffed pitas?

8. Two new students were nibbling scones and biscuits at the fair.

9. Anna showed Peter and Maria her cooking project.

10. Mrs. Pallone kept the same booth as last year.

11. The judges awarded Chet first prize for most unusual recipe.

12. Rona saved me a seat at a table in the German tent.

13. Make your little brother and sister some baklava.

14. We bought Flora some fortune cookies.

15. I brought Will and Betsy a fresh-baked piece of shortbread.

▶ Predicate Nominatives

Direct objects and indirect objects follow action verbs. Two other kinds of complements follow linking verbs. They are called **subject complements** because they identify, rename, or describe the subject. One kind of subject complement is called a predicate nominative.

A **predicate nominative** is a noun or a pronoun that follows a linking verb and identifies, renames, or explains the subject.

To find subject complements, you must be able to recognize linking verbs.

You can learn more about linking verbs on pages L83–L87.

COMMON LINKING VERBS	
Be VERBS	is, are, am, was, were, be, being, been, shall be, will be, can be, should be, would be, may be, might be, has been
OTHERS	appear, become, feel, grow, look, remain, seem, smell, sound, stay, taste, turn

To find a predicate nominative, first find the subject and the verb. Check to see if the verb is a linking verb. Then find the noun or the pronoun that identifies, renames, or explains the subject. This word will always be a predicate nominative. In the following examples, the arrows point to the subjects and the predicate nominatives.

PREDICATE NOMINATIVES

That park is a **preserve.**

(The predicate nominative *preserve* renames the subject *park*.)

The U.S.A. has become a powerful country.

(The predicate nominative *country* renames the subject *U.S.A.*)

Two or more predicate nominatives together are called a **compound predicate nominative.**

COMPOUND PREDICATE NOMINATIVES

The states of most interest were **Texas** and **New York.**

(Both predicate nominatives, *Texas* and *New York*, rename the subject *states*.)

Notice that a predicate nominative can never be part of a prepositional phrase.

Iceland is **one** of the islands near the Arctic Circle.

(The predicate nominative *one* identifies the subject *Iceland. Islands* is not the predicate nominative because it is part of the prepositional phrase *of the islands.*)

PRACTICE YOUR SKILLS

 Check Your Understanding
Finding Predicate Nominatives

Geography Topic **Write each predicate nominative.**

1. Diamonds are extremely hard and rare stones.

2. The prairie sunsets were spectacular sights.

3. Those huge trees are maples.

4. The main resources of South Asia are soil, water, and climate.

5. The longest rivers in the world are the Amazon and the Nile.

6. The land in Pennsylvania may be a good source of coal.

7. Saudi Arabia remains a major producer of oil.

8. Rhode Island is the smallest state.

9. My favorite countries are the United States and Mexico.

10. California has become one of the candidates for a major earthquake.

Supplying Predicate Nominatives

<table>
<tr><td>Contemporary
Life</td><td>**Write a predicate nominative that completes each sentence. Beside the predicate nominative, write the word it renames. If you use a pronoun as a predicate nominative, use only *I, you, he, she, it, we,* or *they*.**</td></tr>
</table>

11. My favorite musician is ▪.

12. Two of my favorite musical instruments are the ▪ and the ▪.

13. My brother Roy will become a ▪.

14. The instruments featured are ▪ and ▪.

15. Their soloist is a ▪.

16. Eric will remain ▪ of the band.

17. Mrs. Davis is my ▪.

18. The soloist in Sunday's concert will be ▪.

19. My favorite song is ▪.

20. The drummers in the band are ▪ and ▪.

● Connect to the Writing Process: Revising
Revising Sentences with Predicate Nominatives

Rewrite the following sentences so that they contain a different predicate nominative.

21. When I grow up, I want to be a musician.

22. My favorite instrument is the piano.

23. My favorite types of music are classical and jazz.

24. One of the best schools for the study of music is Juilliard.

25. I will be a concert pianist.

APPLY TO WRITING

Introduction: *Predicate Nominatives*

The guidance counselor has asked you to introduce a new student to your classmates and show the newcomer around the school tomorrow. You decide to write a few notes that will help you remember what to tell the new student. Write introductions about some of the people in your class. Include predicate nominatives that will tell something interesting about each person.

 Predicate Adjectives

The second kind of a subject complement is the predicate adjective.

> A **predicate adjective** is an adjective that follows a linking verb and modifies the subject.

To find a predicate adjective, first find the subject and the verb. Check to see if the verb is a linking verb. Then find an adjective that follows the verb and describes the subject. This word will be the predicate adjective.

PREDICATE
ADJECTIVES
The bear's den was very **warm.**

(The predicate adjective *warm* describes the subject *den—warm den.*)

Recently the weather has become **warmer.**

(The predicate adjective *warmer* describes the subject *weather—warmer weather.*)

Two or more predicate adjectives together are called a **compound predicate adjective.**

COMPOUND PREDICATE ADJECTIVES	These bears are **big** and **powerful.**
	(The predicate adjectives *big* and *powerful* both describe the subject *bears.*)
	The dens of the bears look **dark** and **warm.**
	(The predicate adjectives *dark* and *warm* both describe *dens.*)

You can learn more about adjectives on pages L99–L109.

PRACTICE YOUR SKILLS

● Check Your Understanding
Finding Predicate Adjectives

Science Topic **Write each predicate adjective.** (Some sentences may have a compound predicate adjective.)

1. That polar bear is hungry again.
2. Its claws are long and sharp.
3. Polar bears seem cuddly.
4. The Arctic winter is dark and cold.
5. The mother polar bear appears thin after the long winter season.
6. The den seems warm in the spring.
7. The bears appear curious about the scientists.
8. That huge bear is dangerous.
9. The ice is bright and slippery.
10. The bear's head looks long and pointy.

Supplying Predicate Adjectives

Contemporary Life	**Write a predicate adjective that completes each sentence. Avoid overused adjectives such as *good, nice,* and *wonderful.***

11. All of the original poems that Terry wrote are ■.

12. Dawn looked ■ and ■ during her oral presentation.

13. The poet was ■.

14. After waiting thirty minutes for the presentation to start, the class became ■.

15. After finishing her writing projects, Natalie always seemed so ■.

16. Alana appeared ■ after her recitation even though she made a mistake.

17. That new poem sounds ■.

18. Kyle's volume is too ■.

19. Both Ray and Alice were ■ during Tanya's presentation.

20. Many of the original poems from this year's class sound ■ and ■.

● Connect to the Writing Process: Drafting
Writing Sentences with Predicate Nominatives and Predicate Adjectives

21.–24. **Write four sentences about a poem you like. Include a predicate nominative in two of the sentences and a predicate adjective in the other two sentences. Label each complement *predicate nominative* or *predicate adjective.***

APPLY TO WRITING

Writer's Craft: *Analyzing the Use of Complements*

Writers often use adjectives to help convey a mood or feeling. In this passage, Tolkien writes about Bilbo's final journey home after all his adventures. Read the following paragraph and answer the questions.

He had many hardships and adventures before he got back. The Wild was still the Wild, and there were many other things in it in those days beside goblins; but he was well guided and well guarded— the wizard was with him, and Beorn for much of the way—and he was never in great danger again. Anyway by mid-winter Gandalf and Bilbo had come all the way back, along both edges of the Forest, to the doors of Beorn's house; and there for a while they both stayed. Yule-tide was warm and merry there; and men came from far and wide to feast at Beorn's bidding. The goblins of the Misty Mountains were now few and terrified, and hidden in the deepest holes they could find; and the Wargs had vanished from the woods, so that men went abroad without fear. Beorn indeed became a great chief afterwards in those regions and ruled a wide land between the mountains and the wood. . . .

—*J.R.R. Tolkien,* The Hobbit

- Write each underlined word from the passage and label it *direct object, predicate nominative,* or *predicate adjective.*
- Write the verb that each direct object follows. What do you notice about each verb?

- Write the verb that each predicate nominative or predicate adjective follows. What do you notice about each of these verbs?

- Write the word that each predicate nominative or predicate adjective renames. Why might a writer use predicate nominatives and predicate adjectives instead of using all direct objects?

QuickCheck Mixed Practice

History Topic **Write each complement in the following sentences. Label each complement *predicate nominative* or *predicate adjective*.**

1. Television became very popular in the 1950s.

2. *Howdy Doody* was a favorite children's program of the time.

3. The characters Howdy Doody and Clarabelle the Clown were comical.

4. For more than twenty million teenagers, the most popular show in the late 1950s was *American Bandstand*.

5. Davy Crockett was one of the most admired TV characters of the decade.

6. Davy Crockett was a frontiersman.

7. Popular clothes for boys during those years were chino pants and motorcycle jackets.

8. Pedal pushers, bobby socks, and poodle skirts were fashionable for girls.

9. Hula hoops became a fad in 1958.

10. TV dinners in little aluminum foil dishes first became popular in 1954.

Sentence Patterns

Nearly every sentence you write follows one of five different patterns. Each pattern may be expanded by adding modifiers and prepositional phrases.

PATTERN 1: S-V (subject–verb)

    S   V
Clocks chime.

          S   V
Certain clocks in the store chime on the hour.

PATTERN 2: S-V-O (subject–verb–direct object)

    S   V   O
Roots prevent erosion.

       S   V   O
The roots of trees often prevent erosion of the soil.

PATTERN 3: S-V-I-O (subject–verb–indirect object–direct object)

     S   V   I   O
Aunt May sends me postcards.

    S   V   I   O
My Aunt May frequently sends me postcards from Idaho.

PATTERN 4: S-V-N (subject–verb–predicate nominative)

    S   V   N
Dogs are friends.

    S   V   N
Dogs of all sizes usually are excellent friends.

PATTERN 5: S-V-A (subject–verb–predicate adjective)

    S   V   A
Books are expensive.

    S   V   A
Books about art are often quite expensive.

To find the pattern of a certain sentence, drop all the modifiers and prepositional phrases.

          S   V   O
~~My~~ grandparents own a ~~small~~ farm ~~in Nebraska~~.

Determining Sentence Patterns

Write the sentence pattern that each sentence follows.

1. The branches of the old tree swayed in the wind.
2. Everyone in the audience grew very restless.
3. A hen often turns its eggs.
4. One of my neighbors is a farmer.
5. The small kitten raced around the room.
6. Some Chinese typewriters have 5,700 keys.
7. The blacksmith gave the black horse a new shoe.
8. The evening air suddenly felt very cold.
9. The secretary in the office gave me an application.
10. That song is this week's top single.

Expanding Sentence Patterns

Expand each sentence by adding modifiers or prepositional phrases or both.

1. (S-V) Eagles fly.
2. (S-V-O) Judges presented medals.
3. (S-V-I-O) Friends gave us presents.
4. (S-V-N) Neighbors are students.
5. (S-V-A) Photographs are old.
6. (S-V) Jake studies.
7. (S-V-O) Ms. Ubach reads stories.
8. (S-V-I-O) Mom sent Dad flowers.
9. (S-V-N) We have been friends.
10. (S-V-A) Hikers were weary.

Diagraming Complements

A subject, a verb, and sometimes a complement make up the **sentence base**. Complements are diagramed on the baseline or are attached to it.

Direct Objects   A direct object is placed on the baseline after the verb. The direct object and the verb are separated by a short vertical line. Notice in the second example that the parts of a compound direct object are placed on parallel horizontal lines. The conjunction is placed on a broken line.

That camera takes clear pictures.

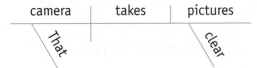

The team manager thoroughly cleaned the uniforms and the equipment.

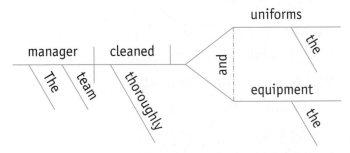

Indirect Objects   An indirect object is diagramed on a horizontal line that is connected to the verb by a slanted line. Notice in the second example that the parts of a compound indirect object are diagramed on parallel horizontal lines. The conjunction is placed on a broken line.

The school counselor gave Beth some good advice.

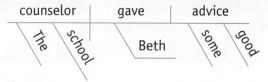

Give Carla and Rick our concert tickets.

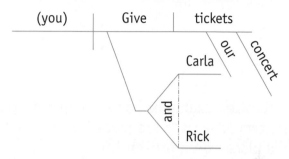

Subject Complements   The predicate nominative and the predicate adjective are diagramed alike. They are placed on the baseline after the verb. These subject complements are separated from the verb by a slanted line that points back toward the subject. The first example below shows how to diagram a predicate nominative. The second example shows how to diagram a predicate adjective.

The trophies were small bronze statues.

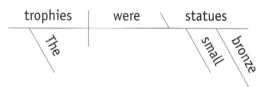

Our house is very old.

Notice in the next example that the parts of a compound subject complement are placed on parallel lines. The conjunction is placed on a broken line.

His favorite foods are corn dogs and hamburgers.

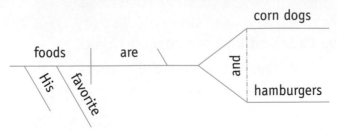

Each of the following examples has a compound predicate adjective. The two adjectives are placed on parallel lines. The conjunction is placed on a broken line.

The leather belt feels soft and smooth.

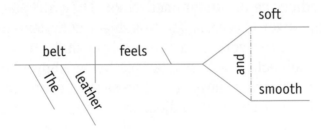

The soup was cold and watery.

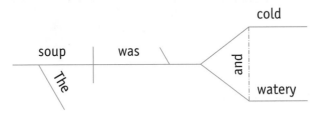

PRACTICE YOUR SKILLS

Diagraming Complements

Diagram the following sentences or copy them. If you copy them, draw one line under each subject and two lines under each verb. Then label each complement with the following abbreviations:

direct object = *d.o.*   predicate nominative = *p.n.*
indirect object = *i.o.*   predicate adjective = *p.a.*

1. Animals set boundaries.
2. These boundaries are exact.
3. Usually a territory is a safe place.
4. They give animals courage.
5. A small dog will chase a larger dog.
6. A territory usually includes space and food.
7. The spring day was clear and crisp.
8. The bird songs were signals and markers.
9. Have you heard these beautiful melodies?
10. Our teacher promised the other students and me more information about boundaries.

Finding Direct and Indirect Objects

Write each complement. Then label each one *direct object* or *indirect object*. (Some sentences have compound complements.)

1. Christopher Columbus brought cattle to America on his second voyage.
2. The director gave the actors their scripts for the play.
3. The United States once issued a five-cent bill.
4. I have the key to the apartment.
5. Mr. David gave Marita and me a project.

Finding Subject Complements

Write each complement. Then label each one *predicate nominative* or *predicate adjective*. (Some sentences have compound complements.)

1. Many animals are record holders.
2. The giraffe's neck, for example, is the longest.
3. The outstanding feature of the albatross is its wings.
4. Its twelve-foot wingspan is quite impressive.
5. The puma appears normal on the ground.
6. Then this cat becomes a bird or Olympic jumper.
7. The remarkable puma is the champion of the twenty-three-foot-high jump from a standing position.
8. The tiger is also athletic and energetic.
9. The tiger, however, remains a distant second to the puma.
10. The tiger's higest jump is only thirteen feet.

Identifying Complements

Write each complement. Then label each one *direct object,* ***indirect object, predicate nominative,* or *predicate adjective.***

1. Samuel Wilson was only a boy in 1775.

2. Nevertheless, he played an important role in the American Revolution.

3. Immediately after Paul Revere's ride through town, Sam told the people in each house the bad news.

4. His father and brother were Minutemen.

5. Years later the government gave Sam the job of meat inspector.

6. Uncle Sam became his nickname.

7. Someone drew a picture of Sam.

8. This picture eventually became a symbol of the United States.

9. "Uncle Sam" was famous overnight.

10. The workers in the meat plant were proud of their old friend with the white pointed beard.

Using Complements

Write five sentences that follow the directions below. (The sentences may come in any order.) Write about one of the following topics or a topic of your own choice: a recent movie you have seen or book you have read.

Write a sentence that . . .

1. includes a direct object.

2. includes an indirect object and a direct object.

3. includes a predicate nominative.

4. includes a predicate adjective.

5. includes a compound predicate adjective.

Then underline and label each complement.

Language and *Self-Expression*

Frida Kahlo (1907–1954) was a Mexican artist. After she was severely injured in a traffic accident at age nineteen, she taught herself to paint. Many of her paintings were self-portraits painted from the mirrors she hung around her bed during her recovery.

Frida Kahlo felt that the watermelons she painted in some way represented a life force. Think of an object or living creature that you feel embodies a life force in the same way. It can be a plant, an animal, a building, or another object. Write a short composition describing the object you have chosen and explaining how you feel it represents life. Use direct and indirect objects, predicate nominatives, and predicate adjectives in your writing.

Prewriting Make a word web to describe the object you have chosen. Write your object in the center. Around it should be words that describe it and reasons it represents life to you.

Drafting Use your word web to create a first draft of your composition. In it, be sure you explain what your object is and why you feel it embodies a life force.

Revising Read your composition aloud to a classmate. Ask your classmate to comment on any ideas in your writing that are unclear or confusing. Make any changes necessary to clarify your writing.

Editing Go over your composition for errors in spelling, capitalization, and punctuation. Be sure you have used complements correctly.

Publishing With your classmates, read your composition aloud into a tape recorder. Title the tape of all your compositions "Long Live Life."

Another Look

A **complement** is a word or group of words that completes the meaning of subjects and verbs.

Kinds of Complements

A **direct object** is a noun or pronoun that answers the question *What?* or *Whom?* after an action verb. *(pages L157–L158)*

An **indirect object** is a noun or pronoun that answers the question *To or for whom?* or *To or for what?* after an action verb. *(pages L161–L162)*

A **predicate nominative** is a noun or pronoun that follows a linking verb and identifies, renames, or explains the subject. *(pages L165–L167)*

A **predicate adjective** is an adjective that follows a linking verb and modifies the subject. *(pages L169–L170)*

COMMON LINKING VERBS	
Be **Verbs**	is, are, am, was, were, be, being, been, shall be, will be, can be, should be, would be, may be, might be, has been
Others	appear, become, feel, grow, look, remain, seem, smell, sound, stay, taste, turn

Other Information About Complements

Predicate nominatives and predicate adjectives, called **subject complements,** follow linking verbs. *(pages L165–L167, L169)*

Recognizing all the compound constructions *(pages L158, L162, L166, and L170)*

Posttest

Directions

Write the letter of the term that correctly identifies the underlined word in each sentence.

EXAMPLE   **1.** Marianne ran her first <u>marathon</u> in October.

      1 A direct object
         B indirect object
         C predicate nominative
         D predicate adjective

ANSWER   **1 A**

1. Marianne was the youngest <u>racer</u> in her group.

2. The other runners in the competition seemed much <u>older</u>.

3. Marianne stretched her <u>muscles</u> first.

4. She gave <u>herself</u> fifteen minutes to warm up.

5. The official blew his <u>whistle</u>.

6. Marianne's pace was <u>slow</u> at first.

7. The course was very <u>hilly</u>.

8. Several hills on the path were a real <u>challenge</u> for Marianne.

9. People on the sidelines passed <u>Marianne</u> glasses of water.

10. The runners were not <u>energetic</u> now.

L184 Complements

1 A direct object
   B indirect object
   C predicate nominative
   D predicate adjective

2 A direct object
   B indirect object
   C predicate nominative
   D predicate adjective

3 A direct object
   B indirect object
   C predicate nominative
   D predicate adjective

4 A direct object
   B indirect object
   C predicate nominative
   D predicate adjective

5 A direct object
   B indirect object
   C predicate nominative
   D predicate adjective

6 A direct object
   B indirect object
   C predicate nominative
   D predicate adjective

7 A direct object
   B indirect object
   C predicate nominative
   D predicate adjective

8 A direct object
   B indirect object
   C predicate nominative
   D predicate adjective

9 A direct object
   B indirect object
   C predicate nominative
   D predicate adjective

10 A direct object
   B indirect object
   C predicate nominative
   D predicate adjective

Phrases

Directions
Write the letter of the term that correctly identifies the underlined word or group of words in each sentence.

EXAMPLE
1. One of the first medical schools was established <u>in ancient Egypt</u>.
   1 **A** preposition
     B adjective phrase
     C adverb phrase
     D appositive

ANSWER
1 **C**

1. Galen, <u>a Greek physician</u>, made many important observations in Egypt.
2. <u>Because of</u> Galen's studies, medicine became a part of European science.
3. Arabs <u>of the Middle East</u> also studied medicine.
4. Persian doctors practiced <u>in Baghdad</u> in the 700s.
5. They traveled <u>from town to town</u> with their medical offices.
6. These Persians, <u>skillful doctors</u>, rode camels.
7. The Muslims moved <u>into</u> Spain in 711 with their medical knowledge.
8. There, students <u>of medicine</u> learned the Persian techniques.
9. Italian professors, <u>teachers of the Roman methods</u>, added Muslim medical knowledge to their curriculum.
10. Arab scholars were also known <u>for mathematics</u>.

1	A	preposition	6	A	preposition
	B	adjective phrase		B	adjective phrase
	C	adverb phrase		C	adverb phrase
	D	appositive phrase		D	appositive phrase
2	A	preposition	7	A	preposition
	B	adjective phrase		B	adjective phrase
	C	adverb phrase		C	adverb phrase
	D	appositive phrase		D	appositive phrase
3	A	preposition	8	A	preposition
	B	adjective phrase		B	adjective phrase
	C	adverb phrase		C	adverb phrase
	D	appositive phrase		D	appositive phrase
4	A	preposition	9	A	preposition
	B	adjective phrase		B	adjective phrase
	C	adverb phrase		C	adverb phrase
	D	appositive phrase		D	appositive phrase
5	A	preposition	10	A	preposition
	B	adjective phrase		B	adjective phrase
	C	adverb phrase		C	adverb phrase
	D	appositive phrase		D	appositive phrase

Mary Cassatt. *At the Theatre (Woman in a Loge)*, ca. 1879.
Pastel on paper, 21¹³/₁₆ by 18⅛ inches. The Nelson-Atkins Museum of Art.

Describe Describe the source of light in this painting. How does the artist use texture in the painting?

Analyze How do you think the woman feels about what she is experiencing?

Interpret What sort of person do you think the woman is? Why do you think so?

Judge Is it easier to learn about a person through a painting or through a written description? Explain.

At the end of this chapter, you will use the artwork to stimulate ideas for writing.

Prepositional Phrases

Unlike a sentence, a phrase does not have a subject or verb. However, a **phrase** is a group of related words that acts as a single part of speech. You already know about one kind of phrase—a prepositional phrase.

A **prepositional phrase** is a group of words that begins with a preposition, ends with a noun or a pronoun, and is used as an adjective or adverb.

Since all prepositional phrases begin with a preposition, you should be familiar with the following list of common prepositions. Notice that some prepositions have more than one word. These prepositions are called **compound prepositions.**

COMMON PREPOSITIONS

about	below	inside	to
above	beneath	into	toward
according to	beside	like	under
across	between	near	underneath
after	beyond	of	until
against	by	off	up
along	down	on	upon
among	during	out of	up to
around	except	over	with
at	for	past	within
because of	from	since	without
before	in	through	
behind	in front of	throughout	

PREPOSITIONAL PHRASES	The story **of Cesar Chavez** is interesting.
	He worked **throughout his lifetime.**

PRACTICE YOUR SKILLS

● Check Your Understanding
Finding Prepositional Phrases

 History Topic **Write each prepositional phrase.**

1. Cesar Chavez was born in 1927 in the Southwest near Yuma, Arizona.
2. He would later become an important leader of farm workers.
3. After the stock market crash in 1929, the Chavez family became migrant farm workers.
4. Chavez enlisted in the Navy during World War II.
5. In 1952, he was recruited by Fred Ross as a worker for the Community Service Organization.
6. With the CSO, Cesar Chavez worked for the aid of the poor.
7. By 1958, Cesar Chavez had become the national director of the CSO.
8. He resigned from the CSO in 1962 and started a farm workers' union.
9. Cesar Chavez changed the system through nonviolent means.
10. With his dedication, he helped many migrant farm workers.

▶ Adjective Phrases

An adjective phrase is a prepositional phrase that is used like a single adjective.

SINGLE ADJECTIVE	A **quiet** sidewalk lines the Seine riverbank.
ADJECTIVE PHRASE	A sidewalk **with cafes** lines the Seine riverbank.

Notice that both the adjective *quiet* and the prepositional phrase *with cafes* tell something about the *sidewalk*.

> An **adjective phrase** is a prepositional phrase that modifies a noun or pronoun.

An adjective phrase also answers the same question that a single adjective answers: *Which one?* or *What kind?* In the following sentences, an arrow goes from each adjective phrase to the word it describes.

WHICH ONE?	The postcard **of Paris** is mine.
	I prefer the picture **of the** *Mona Lisa.*
WHAT KIND?	James likes stories **about medieval Paris.**
	We need a hotel room **with four beds.**

Notice that in all of these examples, an adjective phrase comes directly after the noun it modifies. Of course, a sentence can have more than one adjective phrase. Sometimes an adjective phrase modifies a pronoun, as in the following examples.

One **of my friends** wrote a report **about Paris.**

The Louvre **in Paris** is a museum **of exceptional quality.**

PRACTICE YOUR SKILLS

● Check Your Understanding
Finding Adjective Phrases

Geography
Topic

Write each adjective phrase.

1. The most famous city in France is Paris.
2. Paris is the capital of France.
3. It is one of the largest French cities.
4. Paris is also one of the major European cities.
5. Each of the twenty districts within Paris has its own mayor.
6. The most famous painting at the Louvre is the *Mona Lisa*.
7. The street in front of the Louvre is called the Triumphal Way.
8. A famous architect completed a renovation of the Louvre.
9. The view from the Eiffel Tower is breathtaking.
10. The sidewalk beneath the tower is a popular tourist area.

● Check Your Understanding
Finding Adjective Phrases

Contemporary
Life

Write each adjective phrase. Then write the word that the phrase modifies.

11. The lake beyond those hills has an excellent sailing course.
12. One of my friends owns a sailboat.
13. The dock across the lake is vacant.
14. Six friends on the committee organized a pancake breakfast for the sailors.

15. The sailboat with the torn sail left the race.

16. The day after tomorrow should be a good time for us.

17. The sails on our boat have double rows of stitches.

18. The three smallest boats at the race were the fastest boats.

19. The best sailor on the water is Toby.

20. The McFarlins own the boat beside ours.

● Connect to the Writing Process: Drafting
Drafting Sentences with Adjective Phrases

Write a sentence that uses each of the following prepositional phrases as an adjective phrase. Remember to place each phrase after the noun or the pronoun it modifies.

21. of students

22. with the green stripes

23. near the ocean

24. on the lake

25. from my aunt

Communicate Your Ideas

APPLY TO WRITING

News Article: *Adjective Phrases*

Your sports club has asked you to write an article about your team for the local newspaper. As you write your article, describe different team members and their positions. Be sure to use adjective phrases in your description. Underline the phrases you used.

Misplaced Adjective Phrases

In the preceding exercises, all the adjective phrases came directly after the noun or pronoun they described. Sometimes, however, an adjective phrase will get too far from the word it describes. When it does, it is called a **misplaced modifier.** Sometimes a misplaced modifier confuses the meaning of a sentence, and sometimes it just makes the sentence sound silly.

<table>
<tr><td>MISPLACED
MODIFIERS</td><td>The teacher gave the popcorn to the children without butter and salt.</td></tr>
<tr><td></td><td>(Because the phrase is misplaced, the sentence seems to be saying that only children without butter and salt got the popcorn.)</td></tr>
<tr><td></td><td>On the moon Tad gave a talk about the huge craters.</td></tr>
<tr><td></td><td>(Because of this misplaced modifier, a reader would think that Tad was on the moon.)</td></tr>
</table>

To correct a misplaced modifier, place the adjective phrase next to the word it describes.

<table>
<tr><td>CORRECT
MODIFIERS</td><td>The teacher gave the popcorn without butter and salt to the children.</td></tr>
<tr><td></td><td>(Now the popcorn is missing the butter and salt, not the children.)</td></tr>
<tr><td></td><td>Tad gave a talk about the huge craters on the moon.</td></tr>
<tr><td></td><td>(Now the craters, not Tad, are on the moon.)</td></tr>
</table>

PRACTICE YOUR SKILLS

● Check Your Understanding
Finding Misplaced Adjective Phrases

Contemporary Life **Write each misplaced adjective phrase.**

1. Our teacher in the cafeteria talked about good manners.

2. The librarian gave books without library cards to the children.

3. Our school has many activities for students with no sports emphasis.

4. The school has an excellent academic record beyond that street.

5. That unusually large classroom is vacant across the hall.

6. The best teacher is Mrs. Emerson in the English department.

7. The shady area is called the Peace Garden in front of our school.

8. That student was lost from another school.

9. The principal handed passes to the students for a local amusement park.

10. The boy was shouting with the backpack on one shoulder.

● Connect to the Writing Process: Editing
Correcting Sentences with Misplaced Adjective Phrases

11.–20. Rewrite the sentences from the preceding exercise so that the adjective phrases are in the proper place.

▶ Adverb Phrases

Like a single adverb, a prepositional phrase can describe a verb. This kind of phrase is called an adverb phrase.

SINGLE ADVERB	The snail crawled **slowly.**
ADVERB PHRASE	The snail crawled **at a slow pace.**

Both the adverb *slowly* and the prepositional phrase *at a slow pace* tell how the snail crawled.

An **adverb phrase** is a prepositional phrase that is used mainly to modify a verb.

Because an adverb phrase does the same job as a single adverb, it also answers the same questions: *Where? When?* or *How?* Occasionally an adverb phrase will also answer the question *Why?* In the following sentences, an arrow goes from each adverb phrase to the verb it describes.

WHERE?	Everyone went **to the garden.**
	The snail crept **toward the house.**
WHEN?	They waited **for a few minutes.**
	Within the hour the snail arrived.
HOW?	**With a smile** Maria watched the snail.
	Without any directions the snail found the garden.
WHY?	He waited **because of the terrible storm.**
	Snails eat plants **for survival.**

As these examples show, an adverb phrase can come anywhere in a sentence. In the following example, notice that the adverb phrase modifies the whole verb phrase.

During science class I must finish this snail project.

Also, just like adjective phrases, more than one adverb phrase can be in a sentence, and both adverb phrases can modify the same verb.

For three hours snails have been eating **in the garden.**

PUNCTUATION WITH ADVERB PHRASES

If a short adverb phrase comes at the beginning of a sentence, usually no comma is needed. However, a comma should be placed after an introductory adverb phrase of four or more words or one that ends in a date.

No Comma	**From the deck** you can see the garden.
Comma	**From the front deck,** you can see the garden.
	In 1998, only a few snails lived in the garden.

PRACTICE YOUR SKILLS

● Check Your Understanding
Finding Adverb Phrases

Science Topic **Write each adverb phrase.**

1. A snail lives inside a tough spiral shell.

2. On its slow travels, a snail drags its shell on its back.

3. A snail creeps on a large footlike structure.

4. Many snails have a slimy fluid under this foot.

5. With this fluid snails can crawl up vertical surfaces.

6. A snail can climb safely over a razor blade.

7. In a dangerous situation, a snail pulls its head inside its shell.

8. Within its tough shell, the snail hides from most enemies.

9. Land snails usually live in shady, damp places.

10. With a long, toothed "tongue," a snail scrapes its food off surfaces.

● Check Your Understanding
Finding Adverb Phrases

Sports Topic **Write each adverb phrase. Then write the word or words each adverb phrase modifies.**

11. The baseball whizzed by the batter.

12. A hush descended over the crowd.

13. Within a few hours, David Cone pitched a perfect baseball game.

14. David Cone looked around the baseball field carefully.

15. The catcher sent the signals across the field.

16. Toward the eighth inning, the fans became quiet.

17. Anxious faces appeared in the dugout.

18. David Cone pitched the entire game without a base runner.

19. After the game he celebrated and thanked the fans.

20. This perfect baseball game will live forever in sports history.

Punctuating Adverb Phrases

Edit the following sentences for proper use of commas with adverb phrases. If a sentence is correct, write C.

21. In Cooperstown, you will find the Baseball Hall of Fame.

22. Until last week, I had no idea where it was.

23. On several occasions, Joe has visited there.

24. In the spring my family toured it.

25. In the famous hall we learned about the players.

Communicate Your Ideas

APPLY TO WRITING
Friendly Letter: *Adverb Phrases*

Your family watches a baseball game in this large stadium as part of your vacation. Write a letter to your cousin that tells about the stadium and the game you saw there. Use adverb phrases correctly.

Sports Topic **Write each prepositional phrase. Then label each one *adjective* or *adverb*.**

1. Basketball was invented in 1891.

2. At the time no major sport was played in winter.

3. A man at a Massachusetts YMCA school had a wonderful idea.

4. This person was James A. Naismith, the father of basketball.

5. Basketball provided a sport between the football season and the baseball season.

6. The origin of its name is an interesting story.

7. Naismith had no money for fancy equipment.

8. In a hall he nailed peach baskets on opposite walls.

9. The game's name came from the peach baskets.

10. Another necessary piece of equipment for the new game was a tall ladder.

11. The bottoms of the peach baskets were not removed.

12. At the start everyone used an old soccer ball.

13. The players divided into two teams.

14. Each of the teams defended a basket.

15. For a score a player would throw the ball into the opposite basket.

16. Sometimes a side had fifty players on a team.

17. With that many players, there wasn't much space for team play or skill.

18. Eventually the number on a basketball team decreased to five.

Appositives and Appositive Phrases

In order to explain or identify a noun or pronoun in your writing, occasionally you will have to add another noun or pronoun called an appositive.

Next is Gino's favorite class, **physical education.**

(*Physical education* is the appositive. It explains what Gino's favorite class is.)

Leroy and Guy, **the captains**, meet with the coach.

(*Captains* identifies who Leroy and Guy are. *Captains* is the appositive.)

An **appositive** is a noun or pronoun that identifies or explains another noun or pronoun in the sentence.

When an appositive has a modifier, it is called an **appositive phrase.**

That shoe, **the one with the black sole**, belongs to my brother.

(*The one with the black sole* is the appositive phrase. It explains which shoe.)

Ask Mr. Berry, **the director of the band**, for tickets to the game.

(*The director of the band* is the appositive phrase. It explains who Mr. Berry is.)

The preceding examples also show that a prepositional phrase can be part of an appositive phrase.

You may have noticed that the appositives and appositive phrases in the examples on the preceding page were separated from the rest of the sentence by commas. Appositives and appositive phrase are often, but not always, enclosed in commas. The following guidelines can help you decide when to use commas.

PUNCTUATION WITH APPOSITIVES AND APPOSITIVE PHRASES

If the information in an appositive is essential to the meaning of a sentence, no commas are needed. The information is essential if it identifies a person, place, or thing. However, a comma is needed before and after an appositive or appositive phrase if the information is not essential to the meaning of the sentence.

You can usually tell whether the information is essential or nonessential by reading the sentence without the appositive. If it makes sense without the appositive, the appositive is nonessential.

ESSENTIAL	The movie **Brian's Song** is about football. (*Brian's Song* is the appositive. If *Brian's Song* were dropped, the sentence would not have enough information. There are many movies about football. Therefore, the appositive is essential and no commas are needed.)
NONESSENTIAL	*Brian's Song*, **a movie about football**, is a very sad movie. (*A movie about football* is the appositive phrase. If the appositive phrase were dropped, the sentence would still make sense. Therefore, the appositive phrase is not essential and needs a comma before and after it.)

You can learn more about using commas with appositives on pages L550–L551.

PRACTICE YOUR SKILLS

● Check Your Understanding
Finding Appositives and Appositive Phrases

Contemporary Life **Write each appositive or appositive phrase.**

1. Mr. Rich, our football coach, is looking forward to a great season this year.

2. Todd, the team captain, has been working hard all summer.

3. Tomorrow is the game against our rival school Central.

4. The referee, the one with the black hat, gave our team a penalty.

5. The song "Fire Away" will be our fight song this year.

6. The coach called for a new play, Blue 42.

7. Our receiver, the one with the school record, caught the pass in the end zone.

8. Billy, our kicker, scored the winning point.

9. Mrs. Johnson, the journalism teacher, said we should interview Billy.

10. Arthur Donovan, the opposing coach, congratulated our school.

● Connect to the Writing Process: Editing
Punctuating Sentences with Appositives or Appositive Phrases

Write each sentence, using commas correctly with appositives or appositive phrases. If a sentence is correct, write C.

11. My brother, Bob, likes to read.

12. The book, *Tom Sawyer*, is one of his favorites.

13. *Huckleberry Finn* a book by Mark Twain is also a favorite.

14. Tom my younger brother enjoys building models with his friends.

15. His favorite model, the *Titanic,* is on display in his room.

Communicate Your Ideas

APPLY TO WRITING

E-mail Message: *Appositives and Appositive Phrases*

Your older cousin has volunteered to chaperone your next scout camping trip. Before he arrives, he wants to know something about the others in your troop. Write him an E-mail message that will help introduce him to your friends in the scout troop. To better describe your friends, use appositives and appositive phrases. Be sure to punctuate them correctly.

 QuickCheck Mixed Practice

Literature Topic **Write each appositive or appositive phrase. Beside it, write the word it identifies or explains.**

1. William Sydney Porter, a writer, lived in Austin, Texas.

2. He is known to most people by his pseudonym, O. Henry.

3. O. Henry, a gifted storyteller, impressed many types of people.

4. In 1894, he started a comic magazine, *The Rolling Stone*.

5. The magazine, a humorous weekly, failed after a few issues.

6. After he moved to Houston, Porter took a job as a journalist on the local paper, *The Post*.

7. O. Henry, a talented writer, published many different types of short stories.

8. His most famous collection, *The Four Million*, appeared in 1906.

9. This collection includes one of his best stories, "The Gift of the Magi."

10. The story, a tale of sacrifice and irony, takes place at Christmas.

11. Another short story, "The Ransom of Red Chief," takes place in the Old South.

12. Two characters, Bill Driscoll and the storyteller, decide to kidnap the only child of a prominent citizen.

13. The child, Red Chief, is so wild that the kidnappers pay his father to take him back!

14. The collection *Heart of the West* contains stories set mostly in Texas.

15. Little is known about the personal life of O. Henry, a very private man.

Diagraming Phrases

Phrases are diagramed close to the word they modify.

Prepositional Phrases An **adjective phrase** is connected to the noun or pronoun it modifies. An **adverb phrase** is connected to the verb it modifies.

The boy on the red bike waved.

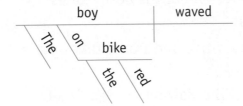

For an hour the wind blew steadily.

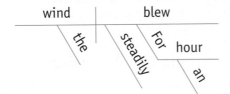

Appositives and Appositive Phrases An appositive is diagramed in parentheses next to the word it identifies or explains.

We like Ben Rosen, a baseball player for a local team.

That watch, the gold one, is a present from my grandmother:

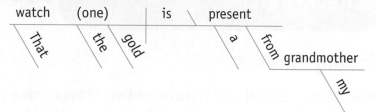

PRACTICE YOUR SKILLS

Diagraming Phrases

Diagram the following sentences or copy them. If you copy them, draw one line under each subject and two lines under each verb. Put parentheses around each phrase. Then label each one *adjective, adverb,* or *appositive.*

1. The Great Ice Age, a time of much change, occurred over two million years ago.

2. During this time huge ice sheets formed.

3. They covered large portions of the earth.

4. One glacier in New York was mammoth.

5. It covered the tops of the Catskill Mountains.

6. These mountains, an eastern range, are quite high.

7. The glaciers acted like rivers of ice.

8. They ground everything in their paths.

9. Minnesota and Wisconsin, two Midwestern states, have many lakes because of glacial melt.

10. States with great glacial erosion include New York and Ohio.

CheckPoint

Finding Phrases

**Write each prepositional phrase and each appositive phrase.
Then label each one *adjective, adverb,* or *appositive*.**

1. *Voyager 2* discovered huge ice cliffs on Miranda, Uranus's moon.

2. Pluto, the smallest planet, was not discovered until 1930.

3. Because of the *Apollo* space missions, the moon has been mapped quite accurately.

4. Without a telescope you can see approximately fifteen hundred stars in a clear night sky.

5. The first record of an eclipse of the sun was in China on October 22, 2136 B.C.

6. In 1865 Jules Verne, a French writer, wrote a story about space travel to the moon.

7. According to his book, the launch site for this journey was Florida.

8. After one hundred years, his story actually happened.

9. The future of space travel is being planned now by scientists.

10. During the next fifty years, people might be traveling between the earth and another planet.

11. Would you travel to another planet?

12. Mars, the red planet, would be an interesting choice.

13. Saturn with its rings is further away.

14. Venus can often be seen in the night sky.

15. The planet closest to the sun is Mercury.

Identifying Phrases

Write each phrase. Then write the word the phrase modifies, describes, or renames.

1. New York was named after an English royal family.
2. Monaco, a Mediterranean principality, has a total population of only 29,000 people.
3. The horse went to the creek and took a drink.
4. Jamie owns a cat without a tail.
5. Swifts, the world's fastest flyers, may spend weeks in the air.
6. Little League Baseball began in 1939.
7. A grove of cherry trees grew along the riverbank.
8. The classic book *Gulliver's Travels* was written by Jonathan Swift, an Irish clergyman.
9. The big oak door near us swung slowly open.
10. Comets travel around the sun in egg-shaped paths.

Using Phrases

Write five sentences that follow the directions below. (The sentences may come in any order.) Write about one of the following topics or a topic of your own choice: recommendations for making homeroom, study hall, or the cafeteria better.

Write a sentence that . . .

1. includes an adjective phrase.
2. includes an adverb phrase.
3. includes an introductory adverb phrase.
4. includes an appositive.
5. includes an appositive phrase.

Then underline and label each phrase.

Language and *Self-Expression*

Mary Cassatt (1844–1926) studied art at the Pennsylvania Academy of Fine Arts and then went to Europe to paint. Edgar Degas, a French Impressionist painter, was so impressed by her work that he invited her to join the Impressionists.

In this painting, the woman is obviously intrigued by what she is viewing or hearing. Imagine what is onstage below her. Write a review of the performance she is experiencing. In your review, use prepositional and appositive phrases to add interest to your writing.

Prewriting Jot down reporter's notes as if you are at the performance. Answer the reporter's questions *Who? What? When?* and *Where?* Then jot down your opinion and reasons for your answers.

Drafting Use your notes to write a first draft of your review. Include factual information about the performance as well as your opinion and the reasons supporting it.

Revising Reread your review. Be sure you have included all the necessary facts and have supported your opinion adequately. Correct any misplaced modifiers.

Editing Go over your review for errors in spelling and punctuation. Be sure any nonessential appositives are set off with commas, and check to see that introductory prepositional phrases of four words or more are followed by commas.

Publishing Read your review aloud and compare it with classmates' interpretations of the performance the woman in the painting is watching.

 **Another Look**

A **prepositional phrase** is a group of words that begins with a preposition, ends with a noun or pronoun, and is used as an adjective or adverb.

An **adjective phrase** is a prepositional phrase that is used to modify a noun or a pronoun.

Misplaced Adjective Phrases

To correct a misplaced adjective phrase, place the phrase next to the word it describes. *(page L194)*

An **adverb phrase** is a prepositional phrase that is used mainly to modify a verb.

PUNCTUATION WITH ADVERB PHRASES
If a short adverb phrase comes at the beginning of a sentence, usually no comma is needed. However, a comma should be placed after an introductory adverb phrase of four or more words or one that ends in a date.

NO COMMA	**From the deck** you can see the garden.
COMMA	**From the front deck,** you can see the garden.
	In 1998, only a few snails lived in the garden.

An **appositive** is a noun or a pronoun that identifies or explains another noun or pronoun in the sentence.

An appositive used with modifiers forms an **appositive phrase**.

Posttest

Directions

Write the letter of the term that correctly identifies the underlined word or group of words in each sentence.

EXAMPLE
1. A movie was filmed <u>in our town</u>.
   - 1 **A** preposition
     - **B** adjective phrase
     - **C** adverb phrase
     - **D** appositive phrase

ANSWER
1 **C**

1. The movie, <u>a science-fiction thriller</u>, had some famous actors in it.

2. For days the crew set up scenes <u>around town</u>.

3. <u>Because of</u> their work, there were traffic jams everywhere.

4. A scene <u>about an alien</u> was shot at our school.

5. It was shot <u>on a weekend</u>, but the students came and acted as extras.

6. Early Saturday morning the crew pulled lights and props <u>out of boxes</u>.

7. The star, <u>a handsome man</u>, wouldn't look at any of us.

8. He sat alone <u>in a corner</u> and rehearsed his lines for the day's scene.

9. In our part of the movie, the alien was moving <u>toward</u> us.

10. We couldn't really see the alien, <u>a horrible, slimy beast</u>, because it would be added later with a computer.

1
 A   preposition
 B   adjective phrase
 C   adverb phrase
 D   appositive phrase

2
 A   preposition
 B   adjective phrase
 C   adverb phrase
 D   appositive phrase

3
 A   preposition
 B   adjective phrase
 C   adverb phrase
 D   appositive phrase

4
 A   preposition
 B   adjective phrase
 C   adverb phrase
 D   appositive phrase

5
 A   preposition
 B   adjective phrase
 C   adverb phrase
 D   appositive phrase

6
 A   preposition
 B   adjective phrase
 C   adverb phrase
 D   appositive phrase

7
 A   preposition
 B   adjective phrase
 C   adverb phrase
 D   appositive phrase

8
 A   preposition
 B   adjective phrase
 C   adverb phrase
 D   appositive phrase

9
 A   preposition
 B   adjective phrase
 C   adverb phrase
 D   appositive phrase

10
 A   preposition
 B   adjective phrase
 C   adverb phrase
 D   appositive phrase

CHAPTER 8

Verbals and Verbal Phrases

 **Pretest**

Directions
Write the letter of the term that correctly identifies the underlined word or group of words in each sentence.

EXAMPLE
1. Our school worked hard <u>to put on a carnival</u>.
   - **1 A** participial phrase
   - **B** infinitive
   - **C** infinitive phrase
   - **D** prepositional phrase

ANSWER
   1 C

1. The carnival was <u>to raise money for a new gym</u>.
2. Each class was responsible <u>for an activity</u>.
3. The class had <u>to plan a booth</u> and set it up.
4. <u>Acting wisely</u>, our class decided on a dart game.
5. <u>To win</u>, you have to hit a balloon with a dart.
6. We had great <u>stuffed</u> animals to give to the winners.
7. Fortunately, the sun decided <u>to shine</u> on the day of the carnival.
8. The <u>excited</u> crowd milled around the booths.
9. A boy <u>sitting on a board</u> could be dunked into a vat of water at one popular booth.
10. Players had to toss a ball <u>at a lever</u>.

1 **A** participle
   B participial phrase
   C infinitive phrase
   D prepositional phrase

2 **A** participle
   B participial phrase
   C infinitive phrase
   D prepositional phrase

3 **A** participle
   B participial phrase
   C infinitive phrase
   D prepositional phrase

4 **A** participle
   B participial phrase
   C infinitive phrase
   D prepositional phrase

5 **A** participle
   B participial phrase
   C infinitive
   D infinitive phrase

6 **A** participle
   B participial phrase
   C infinitive phrase
   D prepositional phrase

7 **A** participle
   B infinitive
   C infinitive phrase
   D prepositional phrase

8 **A** participle
   B participial phrase
   C infinitive
   D prepositional phrase

9 **A** participle
   B participial phrase
   C infinitive phrase
   D prepositional phrase

10 **A** participle
   B participial phrase
   C infinitive
   D prepositional phrase

Rogier van der Weyden.
*Lady Wearing a Gauze
Headdress*, ca. 1435.
Oil on wood, 18⁵⁄₁₆ by 12½ inches.
Gemaeldegalerie, Berlin.

Describe What does the painting show? When do you think the subject lived?

Analyze How does the artist use light for emphasis? What other aspects of the painting emphasize the subject's face?

Interpret What do you think the woman in the painting is thinking? Why do you think so?

Judge How do you feel about this painting? Why?

At the end of this chapter, you will use the artwork to stimulate ideas for writing.

Some words are not what they appear to be. For example, the words *yelping* and *wounded* in the following sentences are a form of the verbs *yelp* and *wound*. However, they are not verbs in the following sentences. Instead, they are acting like adjectives. *Yelping* is describing the coyote, telling which coyote. *Wounded* is describing the coyote, telling what kind of coyote.

In the following sentences, each subject is underlined once, and each verb is underlined twice.

> The **yelping** coyote attracted the scientists' attention.
>
> Lee found a **wounded** coyote.

Yelping and *wounded* are examples of a **verbal**, a form of a verb that is used as another part of speech—such as an adjective or noun.

In this chapter you will learn about two kinds of verbals: **participles** and **infinitives.** Often these verbals are linked with related words to form **verbal phrases.** Because verbals are verb forms, they will make your writing livelier and more interesting to read.

▶ Participles

Participles are probably the most often used verbals. In fact, the words *yelping* and *wounded* in the previous examples are both participles.

A participle is a verb form that is used as an adjective.

There are two forms of a participle: **present participles** and **past participles.** Present participles are easy to recognize because they always end in *-ing.* Past participles usually end in *-ed* or *-d.* Some, however, have irregular endings, such as *-n, -t,* or *-en.*

PARTICIPLES		
VERB	**PRESENT PARTICIPLE**	**PAST PARTICIPLE**
move	moving	moved
shout	shouting	shouted
blow	blowing	blown
lose	losing	lost
freeze	freezing	frozen

Since a participle is used as an adjective, it describes a noun or pronoun. It also answers the adjective question *Which one?* or *What kind?*

We were too near that **snarling** coyote.

(Which coyote?)

The **shouting** man disrupted the wildlife meeting.

(Which man?)

The **blowing** wind howled all night at the game preserve.

(What kind of wind?)

The **lost** pup was found very quickly.

(Which pup?)

The scientists ate **frozen** dinners.

(What kind of dinners?)

You can learn more about forming past participles on pages L307–L325.

PRACTICE YOUR SKILLS

● Check Your Understanding
Finding Participles

Science Topic **Write each participle.**

1. The scientists could hear the howling coyotes.

2. The coyote's expanding range presents a challenge for scientists.

3. A coyote can live anywhere from the frozen mountains to the hot deserts.

4. A starving coyote will scavenge in trash cans.

5. A coyote will change its breeding habits for adaptation.

6. Controlled hunts wiped out the coyote population in central Texas and much of North Dakota.

7. Lost pets often become prey for coyotes.

8. A hunting coyote will stalk its prey patiently.

9. Exhausted animals are no match for the coyote's stamina.

10. The coyote is a protected species in only twelve states.

● Check Your Understanding
Finding the Words Participles Describe

General Interest **Write each participle. Then write the word each participle modifies.**

11. A determined schoolteacher made an unusual bicycle trip.

12. Byron Vouga has no functioning kidneys.

13. Two failed transplants resulted in dialysis three times a week.

14. The courageous Vouga planned an exhausting cross-country bicycle trip.

15. Vouga endured blistering heat and many other trials as a fund-raiser for the fight against kidney disease.

16. Scheduled stops at clinics for Vouga's dialysis were part of the trip.

17. Vouga met many unrecognized heroes who live with kidney disease every day.

18. One person has been on dialysis for twenty years and still works at a towing service.

19. Byron Vouga is truly an amazing man and an inspiration to others.

20. His challenging task brings hope to many people with kidney disease.

Participle or Verb?

It is very easy to confuse a participle with the verb of a sentence because a participle is a form of a verb and looks very much like a verb. However, to be a verb, a participle must always have one or more helping verbs.

PARTICIPLE	The **glowing** lights up ahead were bright.
VERB	The tiny candles **were glowing** in the dark room.
PARTICIPLE	Clean up the **splattered** paint before the show.
VERB	The paint **was splattered** across the stage floor.

PRACTICE YOUR SKILLS

● Check Your Understanding
Distinguishing Between Participles and Verbs

Contemporary Life **Label each underlined word *P* for participle or *V* for verb.**

1. The <u>dancing</u> children delighted the audience.
2. Marcie had <u>spoken</u> to the audience about the show.
3. Clap your hands with the <u>syncopated</u> rhythm.
4. The singers were <u>standing</u> under the bright lights.
5. By the end of the show, everyone was <u>singing</u>!
6. We gave the actors a <u>standing</u> ovation.
7. Everyone was <u>dancing</u> in the aisles.
8. Beth's <u>spoken</u> monologue went well.
9. Mrs. Owen <u>syncopated</u> the soprano part.
10. The <u>singing</u> dog was a great addition to the show.

② Participial Phrases

More often than not, participles are joined with related words to form a **participial phrase.** Those related words often include a complement, an adverb, or an adverb phrase.

PARTICIPLE WITH A COMPLEMENT	The explorer, **strumming his guitar,** sang softly.
PARTICIPLE WITH AN ADVERB	**Sitting up,** Sacajawea noticed several Shoshones.
PARTICIPLE WITH A PREPOSITIONAL PHRASE	She found her people **living near the Rockies.**

PUNCTUATION WITH PARTICIPIAL PHRASES

A participial phrase that comes at the beginning of a sentence is always followed by a comma.

Listening carefully, Sacajawea translated for the men.

Participial phrases that come in the middle or at the end of a sentence may or may not need commas. If the information in the phrase is essential, no commas are needed. Information is essential if it identifies a person, place, or thing in the sentence.

If the information in a participial phrase is not essential, commas are needed to separate it from the rest of the sentence. A participial phrase is nonessential if it can be removed without changing the meaning of the sentence.

ESSENTIAL	The boat **tied to the pier** was damaged.
	(Commas are not needed because the participial phrase is needed to identify which boat was damaged. *The boat was damaged* is not clear by itself.)
NONESSENTIAL	Sacajawea, **dancing joyfully,** recognized her people.
	(Commas are needed because the participial phrase could be removed from the sentence without changing the meaning: *Sacajawea recognized her people.*)

The best way to decide whether commas are needed or not needed is to read the sentence without the participial phrase. If it makes sense alone, add commas. If the sentence does not make sense alone, do not add commas.

You can learn more about essential and nonessential phrases on page L202.

● Check Your Understanding
Finding Participial Phrases

History Topic **Write each participial phrase.**

1. Pushing deep into the land to the northwest, Lewis and Clark hoped for a route to the Pacific.

2. The Corps of Discovery, chosen carefully by Lewis and Clark, explored the Louisiana Territory.

3. Born around 1787, Sacajawea did not join the Lewis and Clark expedition until 1805.

4. Sacajawea, known also as Bird Woman, served as an interpreter and guide for the expedition.

5. Taken captive as a child, she had grown up in a Hidatsa village far from her Shoshone people.

6. Knowing that Sacajawea was a Shoshone, the explorers wanted her help.

7. The Rocky Mountains, looming ahead, provided a natural rest stop.

8. Needing horses, Lewis and Clark stopped at a nearby Shoshone village.

9. Immediately Sacajawea recognized several Shoshone mounted on horses.

10. Weeping with joy, Sacajawea was reunited with her people.

11. Sacajawea, serving as an interpreter, helped Lewis and Clark buy several horses.

12. Riding Shoshone horses over the mountains, the explorers pushed onward.

13. Lewis and Clark, traveling further west, drew closer to the Pacific Ocean.

Check Your Understanding
Recognizing Participial Phrases as Modifiers

Science Topic **Write each participial phrase. Then write the word each phrase modifies.**

14. Viewed through a telescope, Saturn is one of the most unusual objects in the sky.

15. Saturn, named for an ancient Roman god, is yellow and gray.

16. Known as the ringed planet, Saturn is easily recognized.

17. Saturn is one of the giant outer planets characterized by large size and low density.

18. Composed mostly of hydrogen and helium, Saturn's atmosphere is not fit for human life.

19. Saturn's rings, first seen by Galileo in 1610, make it a unique planet.

20. Looking through a telescope, you can see six of Saturn's twenty satellites.

21. The largest satellite rotating around Saturn is called Titan.

22. Titan's diameter is about 3,200 miles, measuring larger than the planets of Mercury and Pluto.

23. Discovered in 1655, Titan has a substantial atmosphere.

24. Hidden by its thick atmosphere, the surface of the satellite is not easily seen.

25. The atmosphere of Titan, consisting chiefly of nitrogen, cannot support the life forms of the earth.

26. The smallest satellite rotating around Saturn is called Pan.

Writing Sentences with Participial Phrases

Write ten original sentences, using at least one of the following participial phrases in each sentence.

27. gazing at the night sky

28. known for its brightness

29. revolving around the planet

30. seen from Earth

31. sighted in the eastern sky

32. shining under the stars

33. hidden in the darkness

34. made up of gases

35. looking up at the clouds

36. found in the atmosphere

● Connect to the Writing Process: Editing
Punctuating Participial Phrases

Rewrite each sentence, adding or deleting commas with participial phrases. If a sentence is correct, write C.

37. Wandering through the planetarium, we learned many amazing facts about the beautiful night sky.

38. Tom reading from one of the displays learned about stars and sailors.

39. Ancient sailors navigating without fancy instruments used the stars for guidance across the ocean.

40. The full moon shining above also helped ancient navigators.

41. Shaking his head in amazement Mr. Guerrero said that ancient people must have been brave.

APPLY TO WRITING

Descriptive Paragraph: *Participles and Participial Phrases*

After a trip to the local planetarium, your class has decided to help plan a planetarium for the local elementary school. Your group has been asked to write descriptions of planets and stars for the display. Write a descriptive paragraph about a planet, star, or constellation for elementary school children. Use some participles and participial phrases in your description.

Misplaced Participial Phrases

In the last chapter, you learned that an adjective phrase that gets too far away from the word it describes is called a **misplaced modifier.** Because a participial phrase acts like an adjective it also must be close to the word it describes.

A participial phrase—like the one that follows—also becomes a misplaced modifier if it gets too far away from the word it describes.

MISPLACED MODIFIER	We saw a beautiful swan **riding along in our car.**
	(This sentence says that the swan was riding in our car.)
MISPLACED MODIFIER	**Drinking a soda,** the gorilla watched Tim.
	(This sentence says that the gorilla was drinking a soda.)

To correct a misplaced modifier, find the word that the phrase describes. Then place the phrase right next to that word.

CORRECT MODIFIER	**Riding along in our car,** we saw a beautiful swan.
	(Because the participial phrase is close to the word it is describing, the sentence now makes sense. It is we who are riding, not the swan.)
CORRECT MODIFIER	The gorilla watched Tim **drinking a soda.**
	(Now it is Tim, not the gorilla, who is drinking the soda.)

PRACTICE YOUR SKILLS

● Check Your Understanding
Finding Participial Phrases

Contemporary Life **Write C for each participial phrase that is placed correctly and I for each participial phrase that is placed incorrectly.**

1. Maria and Keisha watched a camel waiting for their popcorn.

2. Tanya, tired from the long walk on the trail, noticed a bobcat.

3. Singing clearly and loudly, Rico heard the rare bird.

4. Shawna took a picture of a lion panting in the hot sun.

5. Walking through the city zoo, Chen saw a ferocious tiger.

6. Tony enjoyed the seal swimming in its pool.

7. Morgan watched a raccoon talking quietly with her friends.

8. Swinging from the trees, the children laughed at the chimpanzee.

9. The elephants eyed the children spraying water from their trunks.

10. A giraffe, chewing on some leaves, cautiously watched Nita.

● Connect to the Writing Process: Revising
Correcting Misplaced Participial Phrases

11.–15. **Rewrite the incorrect sentences from the preceding exercise. Move the phrases so that the sentences make sense.**

⊚ Infinitives

An infinitive is another type of verbal. Because an infinitive usually begins with the word *to,* it looks quite different from a participle.

> An **infinitive** is a verb form that usually begins with *to.* It is used as a noun, an adjective, or an adverb.

An infinitive has several uses. It is used in almost all the ways a noun is used. An infinitive can also be used as an adjective or an adverb.

NOUN	**To relax** isn't easy during a big shopping trip.
	(*To relax* is the subject. It tells what the sentence is about.)
	My brother likes **to shop.**
	(My brother likes what? *To shop* is the direct object.)
ADJECTIVE	The best movie **to see** is at Cinema City.
	(*To see* describes the movie. It tells which movie.)
	Which is the best CD **to buy?**
	(*To buy* describes the CD. It tells which CD.)
ADVERB	They went to the mall **to plan.**
	(*To plan* tells why they went to the mall.)
	Gary will stay here **to eat.**
	(*To eat* tells why he will stay.)

PRACTICE YOUR SKILLS

● Check Your Understanding
Recognizing Infinitives

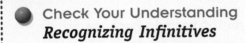

Contemporary Life **Write each infinitive.**

1. Kathy really likes to shop.
2. The best mall to visit is the Northgate Mall.
3. I visited the mall only to look.
4. To shop isn't the only reason for visiting the mall.
5. Danny likes to eat.
6. Which is the best restaurant to try?
7. My Mom will go with us to supervise.
8. Do you know which way to go?
9. Is Jill's mother going to drive?
10. My Mom likes to browse.

Infinitive or Prepositional Phrase?

Because an infinitive begins with the word *to*, it can be easily confused with a prepositional phrase that also begins with the word *to*. Just remember that an infinitive is the word *to* plus a verb form. A prepositional phrase is the word *to* plus a noun or pronoun.

INFINITIVE   It is important **to succeed.**

(The phrase ends with a verb form, *succeed.*)

PREPOSITIONAL PHRASE   They have already gone **to school.**

(The phrase ends with a noun, *school.*)

● Check Your Understanding

Distinguishing Between Infinitives and Prepositional Phrases

Language Arts
Topic

Label each underlined phrase *I* for infinitive or *PP* for prepositional phrase.

1. There are many different factors that contribute <u>to research</u>.

2. It is important <u>to plan</u> your research paper very carefully.

3. Once you have completely developed your plan, get <u>to work</u>.

4. <u>To research</u> for any topic will require some supplies.

5. Organize all of your research information according <u>to type</u>.

6. You should plan <u>to school</u> yourself thoroughly in your topic.

7. If you follow a schedule, your research should proceed according <u>to plan</u>.

8. Several people went <u>to school</u> and wrote their papers in the computer lab.

9. It is difficult <u>to work</u> when it is noisy in the room.

10. If your final draft is long, you will need lots of patience <u>to type it</u>.

▶ Infinitive Phrases

Like a participle, an infinitive can be combined with modifiers or a complement to form an infinitive phrase.

An **infinitive phrase** is an infinitive with its modifiers and complements—all working together as a noun, adjective, or an adverb.

An infinitive phrase can be made up of several different combinations of words.

INFINITIVE WITH AN ADVERB	At the rink we want **to skate quickly.**
INFINITIVE WITH A PREPOSITIONAL PHRASE	Nelson hopes **to qualify for the Olympics.**
INFINITIVE WITH A COMPLEMENT	During practice we tried **to set a record.**

CONNECT TO WRITER'S CRAFT

Many times a writer will use infinitive phrases to do the work of nouns, adjectives, or adverbs. This adds variety to writing. In some cases, it makes the writing sound more natural. Notice how the writer uses the underlined infinitives and infinitive phrases in the following passage. Consider how the passage would sound if she had used other parts of speech.

Once he follows me across the bridge, though, and on past the gristmill, I start to worry. Looks like he's fixing to follow me all the way to our house. I'm in trouble enough coming home with my clothes wet. My ma's mama died of pneumonia, and we don't ever get the chance to forget it. And now I got a dog with me, and we were never allowed to have pets.

—*Phyllis Reynolds Naylor,* Shiloh

PRACTICE YOUR SKILLS

● Check Your Understanding
Finding Infinitive Phrases

Sports Topic **Write each infinitive phrase.**

1. Two-year-old Bonnie Blair learned to skate from her siblings.
2. They did not want Bonnie to use double runners on her skates.
3. Double runners make it easier for a child to stand up on skates.
4. Bonnie quickly learned to take a few steps on the skates.
5. She always wanted to skate in the Olympics.
6. Bonnie, a good student, was allowed to graduate from high school early.
7. A group of police officers decided to help Bonnie.
8. They raised $7,000 to pay for her Olympic training costs.
9. Bonnie knows what it is like to win at the Olympics.
10. She has many gold medals to prove her ability.

● Check Your Understanding
Finding Infinitive Phrases

Literature Topic **Write each infinitive phrase.**

11. Samuel Clemens was apprenticed to work as a printer.
12. Instead he became a journalist and began to write for a living.
13. He decided to use the pen name Mark Twain.

14. Rivermen used the call "mark twain" to mark the depth of the river.

15. In 1871, he quit journalism to devote his full attention to literature.

16. By 1875, he was able to produce several short stories as well as the novel *Tom Sawyer*.

17. A European trip enabled him to gather materials for several stories, including *The Prince and the Pauper*.

18. By 1884, he was able to publish *Huckleberry Finn*.

19. Because of financial gambles, Twain had to declare bankruptcy in 1894.

20. However, he continued to write a number of popular novels and short stories.

Connect to the Writing Process: Drafting
Writing Sentences with Infinitive Phrases

Write five sentences, using the following infinitive phrases.

21. to read a good book

22. to study hard

23. to copy in my notebook

24. to photograph the scene

25. to research the topic well

Communicate Your Ideas

APPLY TO WRITING

Persuasive Letter: *Infinitives and Infinitive Phrases*

Your school's soccer team has earned a spot in the state competition. However, the school does not have enough money to pay for travel expenses. Write a letter to the school board to persuade them to help finance the trip. Be sure to use infinitives and infinitive phrases in your letter. Check that you can identify them.

 Write each verbal or verbal phrase. Then label each one *participle, participial phrase, infinitive,* or *infinitive phrase.*

1. Searching the ocean floor carefully, treasure hunters look for remains of old ships.

2. Stolen treasure is rumored to be near the town of Wellfleet, Massachusetts.

3. Barry Clifford hopes to find the remains of the pirate ship *Whydah*.

4. The *Whydah*, laden with heavy treasure, sank in a storm on April 26, 1717.

5. The storm caused the ship to break apart.

6. To aid Clifford in his search, several experts have signed on his workboat *Vast Explorer II*.

7. The best artifact to find is the hull with the treasures of the ship.

8. A smiling diver emerges with black disks in his hands.

9. The diver floating in the water has found some coins.

10. He boards the research vessel to show them to an eager crew.

Diagraming Verbals and Verbal Phases

Before diagraming a sentence with a verbal in it, you will have to determine how the verbal is used.

Participial Phrases   Because a participial phrase is always used as an adjective, it is diagramed under the word it describes—the same way an adjective would be diagramed. The participle, however, is written in a curve. Notice that the second participial phrase, *making a nest*, has a direct object. It is diagramed like a regular direct object with a line between it and the verb form *making*.

A single participle is diagramed exactly the same way the participle *looking* or *making* is diagramed below—except it would have no complement or modifiers.

Looking out the window, we watched a bird making a nest.

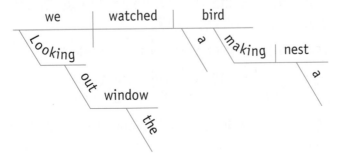

Infinitive Phrases   Because an infinitive phrase can be used as an adjective, an adverb, or a noun, it is diagramed in several ways. The first example shows how to diagram an infinitive phrase that is used as a noun, the subject of a sentence. Notice that *to make* has the direct object *impression* that is diagramed like a regular direct object with a line between it and the verb form *to make*. The second example shows how to diagram an infinitive phrase that is used as an adjective.

To make a good impression is very important.

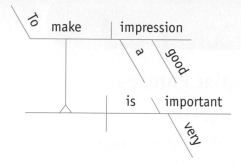

These are the best directions to get to my house.

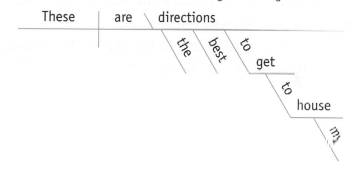

PRACTICE YOUR SKILLS

Diagraming Verbal Phrases

Diagram the following sentences or copy them. If you copy them, draw one line under each subject and two lines under each verb. Then put parentheses around each verbal phrase and label each one *participial* or *infinitive*.

1. My father planted the lemon tree growing in our yard.
2. He wanted to plant it.
3. He likes to eat the lemons.
4. Looking at the tree, my father remembered his old home.
5. To keep the tree alive is very important.
6. I plan to water it.
7. The lemons, picked in the summer, are helpful.
8. We use them to make lemonade.
9. Sipping that delicious drink, I am cool immediately.
10. The tree, surviving for years, might last forever.

Finding Participial Phrases

Write each participial phase.

1. The Sahara Desert, covering approximately 3.5 million square miles, is the largest desert in the world.

2. Extinct volcanoes, crossing the Sahara from west to east, form a chain of mountains.

3. Scattered along the base of the Atlas Mountains, narrow strips of good soil break up the enormous stretch of desert.

4. These fertile areas, called oases, are rest areas for travelers.

5. Linked to the world by small air fields, some oases have grown into towns or villages.

Finding Infinitive Phrases

Write each infinitive phrase.

1. In a famous experiment at Yale University, chimpanzees learned to operate a "Chimp-O-Mate."

2. To earn chips to buy food from the machine, the chimpanzees performed certain kinds of work.

3. Some chimpanzees were willing to put off their purchases until the next day.

4. Others would grow impatient and try to shake the machine for oranges or bananas.

5. To the delight of the scientists, however, the chimpanzees quickly learned to use the right method.

Finding Verbal Phrases

Write each verbal phrase. Then label each one *participial* or *infinitive*. If a sentence does not have a verbal phrase, write *none*.

1. Have you ever traveled to Connecticut?
2. To see all the sights, my family visited the state last summer.
3. Harriet Beecher Stowe, known for her book *Uncle Tom's Cabin*, once lived in Hartford, the capital of Connecticut.
4. Living next door to her, Mark Twain also wrote many of his books in Hartford.
5. Also in Hartford, the first cookbook written by an American was published in 1796.
6. We went to see the home of Noah Webster.
7. His first book, published in 1783, was *Blue-Backed Speller*.
8. Later, of course, Webster published his famous dictionary, used now throughout the world.
9. His name is still remembered today.
10. Known for its charm, Connecticut is a great place.

Using Verbal Phrases

Write five sentences that follow the directions below.

1. Include the participial phrase *singing at the top of his lungs* at the beginning of a sentence.
2. Include the participial phrase *won by the girl's basketball team* in a sentence.
3. Include the participial phrase *falling asleep at night* at the beginning of a sentence.
4. Include the infinitive phrase *to prevent the flu* at the beginning of a sentence.
5. Include the infinitive phrase *to see a rodeo* in a sentence.

When you have finished, underline and label each phrase.

Language and *Self-Expression*

Rogier van der Weyden was made the official painter for the Flemish city of Bruges in 1435. Many of his paintings have religious themes, and he often focused on the interplay of light and shadow in his work.

Imagine what the woman in the picture might have been thinking. Write a diary entry for her on the day the painting was completed, explaining what was happening in her life that made her look as she does.

Prewriting Try to place yourself in the mind of this fifteenth-century woman from Bruges, in what is now Belgium. Was she thinking of chores she had to finish, people she knew and loved, a meeting she would have later? Freewrite what you believe her thoughts might have been at the time.

Drafting Use your freewriting to create a first draft of the woman's diary entry for a day in 1435. Keep in mind the issues that might have concerned her at the time. Use participial phrases and infinitive phrases in your writing.

Revising Have a classmate read your diary entry. Ask your partner for feedback on how well you have captured the woman's thoughts. Add any details you may have omitted.

Editing Go over your diary entry for errors in spelling. Be sure you have set off any introductory and nonessential participial phrases with commas.

Publishing Make a final copy of your entry. Gather it together with classmates' entries to create a diary for the lady in the gauze headdress.

 **Another Look**

A **verbal** is a form of a verb that is used as another part of speech.

A **participle** is a verb form that is used as an adjective.

A participle joined with related words forms a **participial phrase**.

Punctuation with Participial Phrases

A participial phrase that comes at the beginning of a sentence is followed by a comma. *(page L222)*

Essential participial phrases do not require commas. *(page L222)*

Nonessential participial phrases are separated from the rest of the sentence with commas. *(page L222)*

Misplaced Participial Phrases

A participial phrase becomes a misplaced modifier if it gets too far away from the word it describes. *(page L227)*

To correct a misplaced participial phrase, find the word that the phrase describes. Place the phrase next to that word. *(page L227)*

An **infinitive** is a verb form that usually begins with *to*. It is used as a noun, an adjective, or an adverb.

An **infinitive phrase** is an infinitive with its modifiers and complements—all working together as a noun, adjective, or adverb.

Other Information About Verbals and Verbal Phrases

Recognizing present participles *(page L218)*

Recognizing past participles *(page L218)*

Distinguishing between participles and verbs *(page L220)*

Distinguishing between infinitives and prepositional phrases *(page L230)*

Posttest

Directions

Write the letter of the term that correctly identifies the underlined word or group of words in each sentence.

EXAMPLE

1. In the 1800s, <u>spinning</u> machines and other inventions changed industry.

 1 A participle
  B participial phrase
  C infinitive
  D preposition

ANSWER   **1 A**

1. The growth of railroads brought new growth <u>to Europe and America</u>.

2. The steel industry also began <u>to grow</u>.

3. People such as farmers and tradesmen found their jobs <u>disappearing quickly</u>.

4. Factory work began <u>to replace other work</u>.

5. <u>Working</u> conditions were often harsh and difficult.

6. <u>Repeated</u> activity led to many injuries.

7. Children <u>in the factories</u> could not go to school.

8. These children often had no fresh food or milk <u>to eat and drink each day</u>.

9. Factory workers, <u>working fourteen-hour days</u>, often didn't make enough money to live.

10. They were forced <u>to live in the same dwelling with many other people</u>.

1 A participle
   B participial phrase
   C infinitive phrase
   D prepositional phrase

2 A participle
   B participial phrase
   C infinitive
   D infinitive phrase

3 A participle
   B participial phrase
   C infinitive phrase
   D prepositional phrase

4 A participle
   B participial phrase
   C infinitive phrase
   D prepositional phrase

5 A participle
   B participial phrase
   C infinitive phrase
   D prepositional phrase

6 A participle
   B participial phrase
   C infinitive phrase
   D prepositional phrase

7 A participle
   B participial phrase
   C infinitive phrase
   D prepositional phrase

8 A participle
   B participial phrase
   C infinitive phrase
   D prepositional phrase

9 A participle
   B participial phrase
   C infinitive phrase
   D prepositional phrase

10 A participle
    B participial phrase
    C infinitive phrase
    D prepositional phrase

CHAPTER 9

Clauses

Pretest

Directions

Write the letter of the term that correctly identifies the underlined group of words in each sentence.

EXAMPLE
1. <u>When we finished breakfast,</u> we visited the Raptor Center.
   1 **A** adjective clause
     B adverb clause
     C independent clause
     D simple sentence

ANSWER
1 **B**

1. The Raptor Center is a place <u>that the county funds</u>.
2. <u>When people find hurt birds</u>, they bring them there.
3. <u>Vets help cure the birds</u>, and they are released.
4. <u>Some birds are too badly hurt to return to nature.</u>
5. These birds, <u>which can still fly short distances</u>, are trained to perform.
6. <u>The trainers show us some birds, and the birds perform for us.</u>
7. <u>When we last visited</u>, there was an injured owl.
8. The owl ignored us, but <u>it knew we were watching</u>.
9. An amazing thing <u>that the owl does</u> is to swivel its head nearly 360 degrees.
10. <u>We stood behind it until it turned its head completely around to look at us.</u>

1 A adjective clause
   B adverb clause
   C independent clause
   D simple sentence

2 A adjective clause
   B adverb clause
   C independent clause
   D simple sentence

3 A adjective clause
   B adverb clause
   C independent clause
   D simple sentence

4 A compound sentence
   B complex sentence
   C independent clause
   D simple sentence

5 A adjective clause
   B adverb clause
   C independent clause
   D simple sentence

6 A compound sentence
   B complex sentence
   C independent clause
   D simple sentence

7 A adjective clause
   B adverb clause
   C independent clause
   D simple sentence

8 A adjective clause
   B adverb clause
   C independent clause
   D simple sentence

9 A adjective clause
   B adverb clause
   C independent clause
   D simple sentence

10 A compound sentence
    B complex sentence
    C independent clause
    D simple sentence

Charles Burchfield.
November Sun Emerging,
1956–1959.
Watercolor on paper, 37 ½ by
31 ¾ inches. Courtesy of SBC
Communications, Inc.

Describe   What does this landscape show? How can you tell what time of year it is?

Analyze   Why do you think the artist chose to emphasize the sun in this painting?

Interpret   Think about your own environment at this time of year. What memories does it bring about? What emotions do you think the artist wanted to invoke in the viewer?

Judge   How does this painting make you feel? How might you express these thoughts and feelings in writing?

At the end of this chapter, you will use the artwork to stimulate ideas for writing.

Independent and Subordinate Clauses

In this chapter you will learn about three kinds of sentences: simple, compound, and complex. However, before you can fully understand them, you must know about a group of words called a clause.

> A **clause** is a group of words that has a subject and a verb.

Since the clause has a subject and a verb, it is easy to see the difference between a phrase and a clause. In the following examples, subjects are underlined once, and verbs are underlined twice.

PHRASE	We will eat **after lessons.**
CLAUSE	We will eat **after we finish our lessons.**

There are two kinds of clauses. One kind is called an independent, or main clause.

> An **independent, or main, clause** can stand alone as a sentence because it expresses a complete idea.

When an independent clause stands by itself, it is called a sentence. It only becomes an independent clause when it appears in a sentence with another clause.

> independent clause   independent clause
> Sara looked for shells, but the tide came in.

Since these two clauses are independent clauses, they both could stand alone as single sentences.

> Sara looked for shells. The tide came in.

The second kind of clause is called a subordinate clause, or dependent clause. Because it is dependent, it needs another clause to give it meaning. In other words, a dependent clause cannot stand alone as a sentence.

> A **subordinate, or dependent, clause** cannot stand alone as a sentence because it does not express a complete thought.

Notice that the subordinate clauses in the following examples do not express a complete thought—even though they have both a subject and a verb.

subordinate clause   independent clause
After we swam, we ate a huge lunch.

    independent clause   subordinate clause
I just had the salad that my mother prepared.

PRACTICE YOUR SKILLS

● Check Your Understanding
Distinguishing Between Independent and Subordinate Clauses

Contemporary Life **Label each underlined clause *I* for independent or *S* for subordinate.**

1. If the sky is dark and cloudy, you should bring an umbrella.

2. Unless you call first, I will leave for the beach at noon.

3. I like this beach because it is almost never crowded.

4. Since the tide is in, the water is high.

5. We will eat <u>when Terry and Yolanda finally get here</u>.

6. <u>Before the rain started</u>, we played a game of volleyball.

7. <u>Although it was raining almost the entire afternoon</u>, we stayed at the beach.

8. <u>Sometimes we surf</u> while we are at the beach with our friends.

9. I watched television <u>after I got home from the beach</u>.

10. Someone <u>knocked on the door</u> as soon as I got home.

Communicate Your Ideas

APPLY TO WRITING

Letter: *Independent and Dependent Clauses*

Your teacher has asked you to write a letter to a newspaper reporter, telling the reporter what you think the students in your class would learn about journalism if he or she visited your class. Before you begin your letter, make a list of some of the things you would like to learn from your guest. Then write your letter using both main (independent) clauses and subordinate (dependent) clauses in some of your sentences. When you have finished writing the letter, underline the main clauses once and the subordinate clauses twice.

Like phrases, subordinate clauses can be used in more than one way. They can be used as adverbs and adjectives.

▶ Adverb Clauses

A subordinate clause can be used in the same way a single adverb or an adverb phrase is used. Such a clause is called an adverb clause.

SINGLE ADVERB	The eagles arrived **late.**
ADVERB PHRASE	The eagles arrived **after the first storm.**
ADVERB CLAUSE	The eagles arrived **after the snow had begun.**

An **adverb clause** is a subordinate clause that is used mainly to modify a verb.

An adverb clause answers the adverb question *How? When? Where? How much?* or *To what extent?* In addition, an adverb clause answers the question *Under what circumstances?* or *Why?* Notice in the following examples that an adverb clause modifies the whole verb phrase.

HOW?	The eagle flew **as if it were suspended in the sky.**
WHEN?	**When the guide arrives,** the eagle watch will begin.

WHERE?	Eagles roost **where they can find good hunting.**
TO WHAT EXTENT?	Eagles search for prey **until they are successful.**
WHY?	You should bring your binoculars **so that you can see the eagles.**

verb phrase

Subordinating Conjunctions

Adverb clauses begin with a subordinating conjunction. A few of the subordinating conjunctions in the following box—such as *after, before, since,* and *until*—can also be used as prepositions. Just remember that those words are subordinating conjunctions if they are followed by a group of words with a subject and a verb.

SUBORDINATING CONJUNCTIONS

after	as though	since	unless
although	because	so	until
as	before	so that	when
as far as	even though	than	whenever
as if	however	therefore	where
as long as	if	though	wherever
as soon as	in order that	thus	while

When **the eagles return to the nest,** they will feed their babies.

The eagle has keen eyesight *so that* **it can easily spot prey.**

Always place a comma after an adverb clause that comes at the beginning of a sentence.

Because we were early, we saw many eagles.

PRACTICE YOUR SKILLS

Check Your Understanding

Supplying Subordinating Conjunctions

Science Topic **Write a subordinating conjunction in each blank to create a subordinate clause.**

1. ▓ the bald eagle is our national bird, it is protected from hunters.

2. ▓ the bald eagle has been our national symbol since 1782, many people want to protect it.

3. ▓ pesticides were used, many eagles died in the 1970s.

4. ▓ the bald eagle became an endangered species, scientists studied it carefully.

5. It proved to be a relatively easy task ▓ eagles reuse the same nest sites.

6. Eagles are convenient to study ▓ several pairs of eagles nest in a small area.

7. ▓ the first chick feeds for several days, it will outgrow its younger siblings.

8. The female bald eagle needs to be large and strong ▓ she can provide for her young.

9. ▓ eagles mainly hunt young sea otters, they also prey on other small mammals.

10. Most eagles are good hunters ▓ they prey on fish.

Finding Adverb Clauses

General Interest	**Write the adverb clause in each sentence. Then write the word or words that the adverb clause modifies.**

11. Although Detroit is called "the Motor City," its football team is named after an animal.

12. Because George Richards owned a radio station, the team's owner held a contest to name the new football team.

13. The team became the Detroit Lions after the contest had ended.

14. When the team won many games the first season, fans cheered.

15. After the Lions won the Western Division title in 1935, they advanced to the championship.

16. New York fans were disappointed when the Lions beat the Giants.

17. As soon as the game was over, Detroit celebrated.

18. Though they had won the championship in 1935, Detroit was 7–3 in 1936.

19. It would be several seasons before the Lions had another championship.

20. Until the team acquired some new players, winning seasons would be scarce.

● Connect to the Writing Process: Drafting
Writing Sentences with Adverb Clauses

Write five original sentences, using the following adverb clauses. Be sure you use commas correctly.

21. because football is so popular

22. as soon as the game starts

23. after we scored the winning touchdown

24. since we will go to the state championship this year

25. before we go to the playoffs

● Connect to the Writing Process: Editing
Punctuating Sentences with Adverb Clauses

Rewrite the following sentences, adding or removing commas where needed. If a sentence is correct, write C.

26. Whenever I watch football I like to cheer for my team.

27. While the game is on, you shouldn't talk to my dad.

28. As soon as it's halftime we will get a pretzel at the snack bar.

29. Our team should spend some time on fundamentals, unless they want to repeat last year's performance.

30. We should get our tickets before the game is sold out.

Communicate Your Ideas

APPLY TO WRITING

News Story: *Adverb Clauses*

Your school's football team has won the district championship. Write a news story for the school newspaper that describes highlights of the game. Provide information about important plays and key players. Be sure to use adverb clauses in your description.

▶ Adjective Clauses

A subordinate clause can also be used like a single adjective or an adjective phrase. Such a clause is called an adjective clause.

SINGLE ADJECTIVE	It is a **great** story.
ADJECTIVE PHRASE	It was a story **beyond our expectations.**
ADJECTIVE CLAUSE	It was a story **that we will never forget.**

An **adjective clause** is a subordinate clause that is used to modify a noun or a pronoun.

An adjective clause answers the adjective question *Which one?* or *What kind?* Usually an adjective clause will modify the noun or pronoun directly in front of it.

WHICH ONE?	The story **that tells how Arthur found Excalibur** is my favorite.
WHAT KIND?	It is a legend **that is often repeated.**

Relative Pronouns

Most adjective clauses begin with a relative pronoun. A **relative pronoun** relates an adjective clause to the noun or the pronoun that the clause describes.

RELATIVE PRONOUNS				
who	whom	whose	which	that

Sometimes a relative pronoun just begins an adjective clause, but sometimes it is the subject of the adjective clause.

> I haven't read another story **that I like.**
>
> I haven't read another story **that is like Arthur's story.**

PUNCTUATION WITH ADJECTIVE CLAUSES

No punctuation is used with an adjective clause that contains information that is essential to identify a person, place, or thing in the sentence.

ESSENTIAL   A story **that was written about King Arthur** won the writing contest.

Arthur was a great leader **who united the British people.**

A comma or commas, however, should set off an adjective clause that is nonessential. A clause is nonessential if it can be removed from the sentence without changing the basic meaning of the sentence. A clause is usually nonessential if it modifies a proper noun.

NONESSENTIAL   Thomas Malory, **who wrote many King Arthur stories,** lived hundreds of years after King Arthur.

Arthur, **whose adventures were many,** may have actually lived during the Dark Ages.

The relative pronoun *that* is used in an essential clause and *which* is usually used in a nonessential clause.

> The play **that is about King Arthur** is *Camelot*.
>
> *Camelot*, **which is about King Arthur,** is my favorite play.

PRACTICE YOUR SKILLS

● Check Your Understanding

Finding Adjective Clauses

History Topic **Write each adjective clause.**

1. King Arthur, who is the subject of many legends, may have been a real person.

2. There are few stories that are like Arthur's.

3. The Dark Ages, which were perhaps the times in which Arthur lived, were very chaotic.

4. Arthur, whose leadership skills were great, united the British people against the Saxon raiders.

5. Arthur's rule was one that would not soon be forgotten.

6. Sir Thomas Malory, who lived during the Middle Ages, wrote about King Arthur.

7. His book, which details the adventures of Arthur's knights, exaggerates some of the stories.

8. Lancelot, who was portrayed as Arthur's best knight, may not have been from France.

9. Merlin, who was believed to be a wizard, was probably just Arthur's adviser.

10. In any case it is a story that intrigues many readers.

● Check Your Understanding

Identifying the Words that Adjective Clauses Describe

Contemporary Life **Write each adjective clause. Then write the word or words that each adjective clause describes.**

11. Joan, who is reading a book about Robin Hood, enjoys legends.

12. It was her love of old legends that interested me in the King Arthur stories.

13. Marco, whose report about the Dark Ages was excellent, wants to write his own book about King Arthur.

14. Missy's report, which was about castles, contained many details.

15. The report that Mrs. Johns liked the best was about ancient legends.

16. Mrs. Johns, who reads widely about historical people and events, learned something new about the Dark Ages from Sue's report.

17. Rahul, who wants to be an archaeologist, wrote about the search for Camelot.

18. The ancient castle, which has never been found, might be fictitious.

19. Jonathan, whose paper was written on the bus, did not hope for a good grade.

20. The paper, which had not been well researched, needed more work, additional information, and a great deal more thought.

● Connect to the Writing Process: Drafting
Writing Sentences with Adjective Clauses

Write five original sentences, using the following adjective clauses. Be sure to use commas correctly.

21. that I like

22. who is sitting beside me

23. whom I know to be an expert

24. which is her nickname

25. whose computer is broken

Punctuating Sentences with Adjective Clauses

Rewrite the following sentences, adding or removing commas where needed. If a sentence is correct, write C.

26. Our school library which is huge is a good place for research.

27. Mrs. Engel, who is our librarian, is a wonderful resource person.

28. The place in the library that I like best is the technology room.

29. Jim whose knowledge of computers is amazing is a good friend to take to the library.

30. Mrs. Engel whom I respect highly always finds the right book for me.

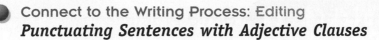

Communicate Your Ideas

APPLY TO WRITING
Friendly Letter: *Adjective Clauses*

Your pen pal is coming for a visit and will be spending time with you at your school. Write a letter to your pen pal describing some of your classmates. Also describe your school and the classes that you are taking. Use adjective clauses in your sentences so that your pen pal can better picture what you are writing about. When you have finished writing your letter, underline each adjective clause. Check that you have punctuated all clauses correctly.

Sports Topic **Label each underlined clause *adverb* or *adjective*.**

1. Although he had been diagnosed with cancer in 1996, Lance Armstrong overcame the disease.

2. Lance Armstrong, who looks to his mother for inspiration, trained hard for the 1999 Tour de France.

3. Armstrong was not discouraged though doctors had given him only a 50–50 chance for recovery.

4. When Armstrong crossed the finish line at the end of the race, he had accomplished the impossible.

5. The Tour de France, which is a cycling event, takes place every year in July.

6. Even though Armstrong was in good physical condition, doctors credit his recovery to his positive attitude.

7. Armstrong says, "If you ever get a second chance in life, you've got to go all the way."

8. Lance Armstrong, who held a commanding lead after three stages of the event, rode hard every day.

9. As soon as he crossed the finish line, a great cheer went up.

10. Many Americans, who interrupted their vacations, congratulated Lance Armstrong, the winner.

Misplaced Adjective Clauses

To make your meaning clear, always put an adjective clause next to the word it describes. An adjective clause that

gets too far away from the word it describes is called a
misplaced modifier.

MISPLACED	Miriam saw a duck **who had a pair of binoculars.**
	(This sentence says that the duck had the binoculars.)
CORRECT	 Miriam, **who had a pair of binoculars,** saw a duck.
	(Now Miriam has the binoculars.)
MISPLACED	The duck wanted the food **that was swimming in the water.**
	(This sentence says that the food was swimming.)
CORRECT	The duck **that was swimming in the water** wanted the food.
	(Now the duck is swimming.)

PRACTICE YOUR SKILLS

● Check Your Understanding
Recognizing Misplaced Adjective Clauses

Contemporary Life **Write *C* if an adjective clause is placed correctly and *I* if an adjective clause is placed incorrectly.**

1. Bethany, who had a bag of bread crumbs, watched a pigeon.

2. A goose that had a bump on its head lunged for the bag.

3. David threw some crumbs to a duck who enjoys feeding the birds.

4. A grackle that was flying overhead wanted some food.

5. A dog that had no collar chased some of the ducks.

6. My sister that had been abandoned observed a nest.

7. Koreen threw some crumbs to the swans who had an extra bag.

8. A turtle that was eager to investigate climbed to the shore.

9. Marta explored the pool whose love of wildlife is well known.

10. Deb saw a duck who never really wanted to come along.

11. The duck, which was following its mother, lagged behind.

12. People waited in line who wanted to ride the paddleboats.

13. The line, which curved around several times, was very long.

14. Stephen, who was holding his brother's hand, became impatient.

15. He picked up some tiny pebbles and threw them into the water that were on the ground.

● Connect to the Writing Process: Revising
Correcting Sentences with Misplaced Adjective Clauses

16.–22. Rewrite the incorrect sentences from the preceding exercise, placing the adjective clauses properly. Be sure to use commas where needed.

If you understand the different kinds of sentences, you will be able to add variety to your writing by using them. In this section, you will learn about three kinds of sentences: simple, compound, and complex.

Simple and Compound Sentences

A simple sentence is the foundation on which the other kinds of sentences are built.

> A **simple sentence** is a sentence that has one subject and one verb.

In the following examples, the subjects are underlined once and the verbs are underlined twice.

> ONE SUBJECT, ONE VERB   <u>Softball</u> <u>is</u> my favorite sport.

In a simple sentence, either the subject or the verb, or both, can be compound.

> COMPOUND SUBJECT   <u>Amelia</u> and her <u>team</u> <u>flew</u> to the softball championships in New York City.

> COMPOUND VERB   <u>Mia-Lu</u> <u>threw</u> the first pitch and <u>struck</u> the first batter out.

There are other kinds of sentences besides simple sentences. For example, two or more related simple sentences can be placed together to make a compound sentence.

A **compound sentence** is made up of two or more simple sentences, usually joined by a comma and a coordinating conjunction: *and, but, or*, or *yet.*

If the comma and the conjunction are dropped from a compound sentence, two simple sentences will remain.

COMPOUND SENTENCE	The game will begin at four o'clock, **but** the buses will leave at two o'clock.
SIMPLE SENTENCES	The game will begin at four o'clock. The buses will leave at two o'clock.

PRACTICE YOUR SKILLS

● Check Your Understanding
Recognizing Simple and Compound Sentences

Sports Topic **Label each sentence *simple* or *compound.***

1. Softball began in Chicago in 1887.

2. Softball fields require less space than baseball fields.

3. A game of softball is similar to a game of baseball, but the bases on a softball field are closer together.

4. Softball bases are sixty feet apart, but baseball requires ninety feet between bases.

5. A softball pitcher stands 40 to 46 feet from home plate, but the distance in baseball is 60.5 feet.

6. The circumference of a softball usually measures twelve inches and is larger than a baseball's circumference.

7. A baseball is about nine inches in circumference.

8. Baseball players usually leave the base before a pitch, but softball players always wait for a pitch.

9. Baseball allows a choice of pitches, but softball pitchers always throw underhand.

10. A softball team has nine or ten players and plays only seven innings.

Compound Sentence or Compound Verb?

Sometimes you can mistake a sentence with a compound verb for a compound sentence. Just remember that a compound sentence must have two sets of subjects and verbs. In the following examples, subjects are underlined once and verbs are underlined twice.

COMPOUND SENTENCE	The children cheered, and Mom gave them some pie.
COMPOUND VERB	The children cheered and pointed at the chocolate pie.

PUNCTUATION WITH COMPOUND SENTENCES

There are several ways to connect the independent clauses in a compound sentence. One way is to join them with a comma and a conjunction.

Chocolate is the most popular flavor, **but** vanilla runs a close second.

You can also join independent clauses with a semicolon and no conjunction.

Chocolate is the most popular flavor; vanilla runs a close second.

You can learn more about punctuating compound sentences on pages L536–L537 and L611.

PRACTICE YOUR SKILLS

● Check Your Understanding
Distinguishing Between Simple and Compound Sentences

Health Topic **Label each sentence *simple* or *compound*.**

1. Yogurt is a good source of calcium, and cheese contains calcium, too.

2. On advice from the Indians, the Pilgrims planted corn and found many uses for it.

3. Potato leaves are definitely poisonous, but the potato itself is not.

4. Spinach is a good source of iron and other minerals and can be eaten raw.

5. Three types of roots are onions, turnips, and parsnips.

6. Tomatoes are categorized as fruits, but many people think of tomatoes as vegetables.

7. Trout is a very nutritious fish; it contains many nutrients.

8. Raw carrots are crunchy, tasty, and good for you, too.

9. Ice cream contains vitamin D but has a great deal of fat.

10. Chocolate may be junk food, but it tastes good to most people.

● Connect to the Writing Process: Drafting
Writing Simple and Compound Sentences

Use the independent clauses at the top of the next page to form five simple or compound sentence. You may use a clause more than once.

11. the hamburgers smell delicious

12. they are still pink

13. the picnic starts at one o'clock

14. I don't have a ride

15. Tom made a pie

● Connect to the Writing Process: Editing
Punctuating Compound Sentences

Rewrite the following compound sentences. Be sure that commas, conjunctions, and semicolons are used properly. If a sentence is punctuated correctly, write C.

16. Jennifer wanted to have watermelons at the picnic; but they weren't in season.

17. Ashley made a chocolate cake but she left it at home.

18. Brian cooked the hot dogs he burned only a few.

19. Bob wanted to bring cantaloupe yet he couldn't find any.

20. Michael made brownies; they were delicious.

Communicate Your Ideas

APPLY TO WRITING

Proposal: *Simple and Compound Sentences*

Your class wants to hold a picnic for an end-of-the-year activity. Before you can announce the picnic to the student body, you must submit a proposal to the student council that outlines your plans. Where will the picnic be held? Who will supply the food? What kinds of activities will take place? Make sure that your proposal contains both simple and compound sentences.

Complex Sentences

You can recognize complex sentences if you understand independent and subordinate clauses.

A **complex sentence** consists of one independent clause and one or more subordinate clauses.

┌─── subordinate clause ───┐ ┌─── independent clause ───┐
Before the rain started, I closed the car windows.

┌─── independent clause ───┐ ┌─── subordinate clause ───┐
We stayed in the cabin that we had rented the year

┐
before.

┌─────── independent clause ───────┐ ┌── subordinate clause ──
Dan and I hiked to the general store, which was about a

──────┐
mile away.

CONNECT TO WRITER'S CRAFT

Writers often use many different kinds of sentences in their writing. This technique keeps the reader from getting bored because it creates variety. Notice how the writer uses simple, compound, and complex sentences in the following passage.

At the end of the fourth period, the score was 47–32. Coach made the boys do three laps around the gym before he let them shower. On the last lap, Coach joined them and tried to be jolly, but the teams just looked at the floor, breathing hard. The cheerleaders were gone. The shafts of sunlight that had blazed on the gym floor were gone. The heater was off, and the janitor was pulling the windows shut.

—*Gary Soto*, Taking Sides

PRACTICE YOUR SKILLS

● Check Your Understanding

Distinguishing Between Simple, Compound and Complex Sentences

History Topic **Label each sentence *simple, compound,* or *complex.***

1. Many people associate Benjamin Franklin only with the discovery of electricity, but he had many other notable accomplishments as well.

2. Although he had only two years of formal schooling, Franklin was an avid reader.

3. Franklin found a job as a printer, and he began to publish *Poor Richard's Almanac.*

4. His business expanded further when he did government printing.

5. He also operated a bookshop, and he became a clerk of the Pennsylvania Assembly.

6. Franklin, who served as postmaster of Philadelphia, retired at the age of forty-two.

7. Franklin began yet another career in 1740 when he invented the Franklin stove.

8. He also read papers about electricity and began a series of experiments.

9. Franklin became famous when the Royal Society in London published his discoveries.

10. Benjamin Franklin was a man of many talents, yet few people recognize the breadth of his achievements.

11. There have been postage stamps in Franklin's honor, and some money bears his face.

12. The Franklin Institute in Philadelphia is named for him.

Punctuating Complex Sentences

Rewrite the following sentences, adding commas where needed. If a sentence is correct, write C.

13. As Franklin traveled throughout the colonies he reorganized the American postal system.

14. In October 1776, Franklin sailed for France, where he gained French aid.

15. Though he was nearly eighty years old Benjamin Franklin became the first United States government minister to France.

16. Franklin outfitted John Paul Jones who owned the ship the *Bonhomme Richard.*

17. When Franklin returned home in 1785 he accepted his election as president of Pennsylvania.

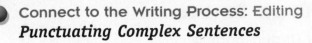

Communicate Your Ideas

APPLY TO WRITING

Summary: *Compound and Complex Sentences*

Your social studies class is creating a display for the local history museum. Because space is limited, only a few important people from history can be included. Persuade your teacher to include a display about a historical figure you admire by writing a short summary about that person. Be sure to include compound and complex sentences in your summary.

Literature Topic **Label each sentence *simple, compound,* or *complex.***

1. Hans Christian Andersen was born in 1805 and died almost seventy years later.

2. He wrote 156 fairy tales, but his most famous tale was "The Ugly Duckling."

3. Andersen grew up in Denmark and lived in a one-room house.

4. Although his father was a shoemaker, he could not afford leather shoes for his own children.

5. Andersen was tall and lanky, and his hands and feet were large.

6. His eyes were small and very close together, and his nose was too big for his face.

7. People made jokes about him or ignored him.

8. As he played by himself, he carved a tiny theater.

9. He made up short plays and acted out all the parts.

10. After he saw a real play at the age of seven, he longed for the stage.

11. Later he went to Copenhagen, but no theater there would hire him.

12. When he wasn't successful, Andersen went back to school and earned good grades.

13. When he wrote his first fairy tale at the age of thirty, he never expected success.

14. People all over the world loved his stories, and they still read them today.

Diagraming Sentences

Each clause must have its own baseline in a diagram. As a result, only a simple sentence will have one baseline.

Compound Sentences   A compound sentence is diagramed like two simple sentences, but the diagrams are connected by a broken line. The broken line joins the two verbs. The conjunction that joins the two sentences is written on this line.

You prepare the salad, and I will cook the stew.

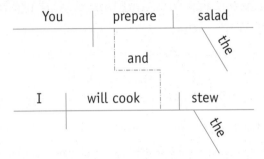

Complex Sentences   An adverb clause is diagramed beneath the independent clause—regardless of the order in a sentence. The subordinating conjunction belongs on a broken line that connects the verb in the adverb clause to the word the clause modifies in the independent clause.

If you finish your homework, you can go to the movies.

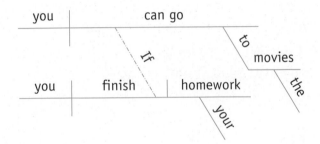

An adjective clause is also diagramed beneath the independent clause. The relative pronoun is connected by a broken line to the noun or the pronoun the clause modifies. Keep in mind that a relative pronoun can also be the subject of an adjective clause.

We liked the movie that is playing at the new theater.

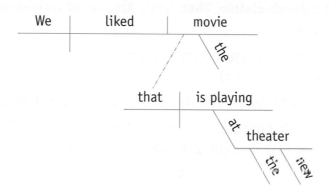

PRACTICE YOUR SKILLS

Diagraming Sentences

Diagram the following sentences or copy them. If you copy them, draw one line under each subject and two lines under each verb. Put any subordinate clauses in parentheses and draw arrows to the words they modify.

1. Virginia became the tenth state when it joined the Union in 1788.

2. Virginia is rich in history, and it is the birthplace of eight U.S. presidents.

3. It has many historical sites that have been preserved.

4. Williamsburg, which is a Colonial village, is an unusual place.

5. In the workshops blacksmiths make iron products, and weavers and glassblowers give demonstrations.

Finding Adverb Clauses

Write each adverb clause. Then write the word or words the clause describes.

1. Although there are no trees on the Aleutian Islands, other plants grow there.

2. As it sped through the air, the arrow hissed like a snake.

3. When the automobile was new and strange in 1896, it was shown in Barnum and Bailey's Circus.

4. Wrap the glasses carefully so that they don't break.

5. Mexican jumping beans jump because bugs live inside them.

Finding Adjective Clauses

Write each adjective clause. Then write the word or words the clause describes.

1. According to research there is no nation that does not enjoy music.

2. Clay pipes and wooden drums are often found in the graves of people who died thousands of years ago.

3. Musicians who lived in the Middle Ages often played a flute and beat a drum at the same time.

4. The bagpipe, which is generally considered a Scottish instrument, is also found in Africa and Asia.

5. Many folksongs that have been sung for centuries have only lately been written down.

Identifying Subordinate Clauses

Write each subordinate clause. Then label each one *adv.* for *adverb* or *adj.* for *adjective*.

1. Those who dwell among the beauties and mysteries of the earth are never alone or weary of life.—Rachel Carson

2. Big Red could do anything because a dog with his brains could be taught anything.—James Kjelgaard

3. Slang is language that rolls up its sleeves, spits on its hands, and goes to work.—Carl Sandburg

4. Home is all the words that call you in for dinner, over to help, into a hug, and out of a dream.—Michael J. Rosen

5. When I was a babe, I was warmed by the sun, rocked by the winds, and sheltered by the trees.—Geronimo

Using Sentence Structure

Write five sentences that follow the directions below. (The sentences may come in any order.) Write about one of the following topics or a topic of your choice: a job or occupation that sounds interesting to you and why you might choose that profession for yourself one day.

1. Write a simple sentence.

2. Write a complex sentence with an introductory adverb clause.

3. Write a complex sentence with an adjective clause.

4. Write a compound sentence joined by a comma and a conjunction.

5. Write a compound sentence joined by a semicolon.

When you have finished, label each sentence. Then check the punctuation of each one.

Language and *Self-Expression*

Charles Burchfield (1893–1967) grew up in Ohio, and many of his paintings reflect his childhood memories. He focuses on landscapes of the Midwest and often tries to capture natural phenomena, like the wind, in his work.

Burchfield's painting shows the beauty that can be found in a November landscape. What is your favorite time of year and why? Write a brief composition explaining why you have chosen this time of year. Tell what it means to you and why you prefer it. Use simple, compound, and complex sentences.

Prewriting Create a main-idea and details chart for your essay. For the main idea, write which time of year is your favorite. In the details section, write down any reasons you have that support your main idea. You can include both facts and opinions.

Drafting Use your main idea and details chart as the basis for your first draft. Try to explain clearly what time of year you favor and why.

Revising Ask a classmate to read your composition. Have your partner tell you if you have explained your preference clearly and convincingly. If your writing sounds choppy, try combining some simple sentences to make compound or complex sentences.

Editing Check your writing for errors in spelling or punctuation. Be sure you have placed commas after introductory adverb clauses, between clauses in compound sentences, and to set off nonessential adjective clauses.

Publishing Collect your composition along with classmates' in a book of seasons.

Another Look

A **clause** is a group of words that has a subject and a verb.

Kinds of Clauses
An **independent (or main) clause** can stand alone as a sentence because it expresses a complete idea. *(page L247)*

A **subordinate (or dependent) clause** cannot stand alone as a sentence because it does not express a complete thought. *(page L248)*

An **adverb clause** is a subordinate clause that is used mainly to modify a verb. Adverb clauses begin with a subordinating conjunction.

Punctuation with Adverb Clauses
Always place a comma after an adverb clause that comes at the beginning of a sentence. *(page L252)*

An **adjective clause** is a subordinate clause that is used to modify a noun or a pronoun. Most adjective clauses begin with a relative pronoun.

Punctuation with Adjective Clauses
No punctuation is used with an essential adjective clause. *(page L256)*

A comma or commas should set off a nonessential adjective clause. *(page L256)*

Kinds of Sentences
A **simple sentence** is a sentence that has one subject and one verb. *(page L263)*

A **compound sentence** is made up of two or more simple sentences, usually joined by a comma and the coordinating conjunction *and, but, or,* or *yet. (page L264)*

A **complex sentence** consists of one independent clause and one or more subordinate clauses. *(page L268)*

 **Posttest**

Directions
Write the letter of the term that correctly identifies the underlined group of words in each sentence.

EXAMPLE

1. An ancient civilization, <u>which existed around 2500 B.C.,</u> was based in the Indus Valley.
   1 A adjective clause
      B adverb clause
      C independent clause
      D simple sentence

ANSWER

1 A

1. <u>Archaeologists found the remains of two cities there.</u>
2. <u>Although the cities were built thousands of years ago,</u> they were laid out in a very modern way.
3. <u>Streets intersected at right angles, and they were broad and long.</u>
4. <u>Each home had a sewer system,</u> so sewage disposal wasn't a problem.
5. The cities, <u>which were twin capitals of the area,</u> were called Harappa and Mohenjo-Daro.
6. <u>Because the cities were not rivals,</u> archeologists think a strong central government must have existed.
7. The cities were built of bricks <u>that were dried in ovens.</u>
8. <u>The city of Harappa contained a huge granary,</u> which held grain to feed the entire population.
9. <u>The people of the area made cloth and pottery, and they also farmed.</u>
10. Gold and silver jewelry <u>that was excavated from the area</u> shows that fine quality was standard.

1 A compound sentence
   B complex sentence
   C independent clause
   D simple sentence

2 A adjective clause
   B adverb clause
   C independent clause
   D simple sentence

3 A compound sentence
   B complex sentence
   C independent clause
   D simple sentence

4 A adjective clause
   B adverb clause
   C independent clause
   D simple sentence

5 A adjective clause
   B adverb clause
   C independent clause
   D simple sentence

6 A adjective clause
   B adverb clause
   C independent clause
   D simple sentence

7 A compound sentence
   B complex sentence
   C independent clause
   D simple sentence

8 A adjective clause
   B adverb clause
   C independent clause
   D simple sentence

9 A compound sentence
   B complex sentence
   C independent clause
   D simple sentence

10 A adjective clause
   B adverb clause
   C independent clause
   D simple sentence

CHAPTER 10

Sentence Fragments and Run-ons

 **Pretest**

Directions
Read the passage. Write the letter of the best way to write each group of underlined words. If the underlined words contain no error, write *D*.

EXAMPLE   We tasted red-hot chili <u>peppers</u>.
                                          (1)
                <u>During our visit</u>.
                1 A peppers, during our visit
                   B peppers during our visit
                   C peppers, and during our visit
                   D No error

ANSWER   **1 B**

Native to Central America, peppers are used <u>in</u>

<u>cooking. Throughout the world</u>. <u>Some peppers are sweet</u>
            (1)   **(2)**
<u>some have sharp, spicy flavors.</u> Although they are high

<u>in vitamins A and C, peppers are low</u> in calories.
            (3)
Different kinds of <u>peppers varying from</u> mild to
                        (4)
extremely hot. Peppers are named after their place of

origin. For example, El Paso chilies <u>come from the city</u>
                                            (5)
<u>of El Paso in Texas.</u>

1 **A** in cooking, throughout the world
   B in cooking throughout the world
   C In cooking throughout the world
   D No error

2 **A** Some peppers are sweet, some have sharp, spicy
           flavors.
   B Some peppers are sweet or some have sharp, spicy
           flavors.
   C Some peppers are sweet. Some have sharp, spicy
           flavors.
   D No error.

3 **A** in vitamins A and C, and peppers are low
   B in vitamins A and C. Peppers are low
   C in vitamins A and C but peppers are low
   D No error

4 **A** peppers. Varying from
   B peppers vary from
   C peppers that vary from
   D No error

5 **A** come from the city of El Paso. In Texas.
   B coming from the city of El Paso in Texas.
   C come from the city of El Paso, it is in Texas.
   D No error

Romare Bearden. *Sunset and Moonrise with Maudell Sleet,* 1978. Collage on board, 41 by 29 inches. Estate of Romare Bearden. © Romare Bearden Foundation/Licensed by VAGA, New York, NY.

Describe Who is the focus of this painting? What is the setting?

Analyze How do size and color emphasize the figure in the foreground? What message does the painting convey about the woman and her environment?

Interpret How could a writer represent the same relationships?

Judge Do you think this collage or the written word would better express the relationship between this woman and the world around her? Explain your answer.

At the end of this chapter, you will use the artwork to stimulate ideas for writing.

Sentence Fragments

You have learned that a sentence must have a subject and a verb to express a complete thought. A group of words that does not have either a subject or a verb is called a sentence fragment.

A **sentence fragment** is a group of words that does not express a complete thought.

In each of the following examples, the subject is underlined once and the verb is underlined twice. To be complete, a sentence must have both a subject and a verb, and must express a complete thought.

No Subject	**Spoke** to the band after the show.
	(*Who spoke to the band?*)
Complete Sentence	Brenda spoke to the band after the show.
	(Now the sentence has a subject.)
No Verb	Joe's **cousin** from Detroit.
	(What does he *do?*)
Complete Sentence	Joe's **cousin** from Detroit **plays** in a band.
	(Now the sentence has a verb.)

When you edit your writing, always carefully check for any missing subjects or missing verbs.

CONNECT TO WRITER'S CRAFT

Writers often use fragments in creative writing for dialogue or for incomplete thoughts. Fragments, however, are not usually appropriate in formal writing, such as school assignments and business letters.

PRACTICE YOUR SKILLS

● Check Your Understanding
Identifying Sentence Fragments

Music Topic **Label each group of words *sentence* or *sentence fragment*.**

1. No one thought the Beatles had much talent in the early 1960s.
2. Said they were a musical disaster.
3. The band began its career in England.
4. Their unusual style.
5. The Beatles' arrival in America.
6. Their appearance on the Ed Sullivan show was one of the highest-rated programs of its day.
7. Their music was a hit.
8. Thousands of fans.
9. Sold 2.5 million albums and singles in four weeks' time.
10. The fans went crazy.
11. Dozens of girls fainted at the Beatles' appearances across America.
12. The Beatles were the first rock and roll band to play at Carnegie Hall.
13. Had an amazing tour across most of the United States.
14. Apparently, the critics were wrong.
15. Changed rock and roll music forever.

● Connect to the Writing Process: Revising
Correcting Sentence Fragments

16.–20. Rewrite the sentence fragments from the preceding exercise to make complete sentences.

APPLY TO WRITING

Concert Review: *Sentence Fragments*

You have just attended a concert given by your favorite band. Write a review for your school paper. Describe the band and what they played. Be sure to avoid using sentence fragments in your review.

✓ QuickCheck Mixed Practice

Contemporary Life

Write S if the fragment is missing a subject or V if the fragment is missing a verb.

1. The reed for the clarinet.
2. Dropped the case on the ground.
3. Had sprung open.
4. My new clarinet.
5. Picked it up and tried the mouthpiece.
6. A crack on the mouthpiece.
7. Told my band teacher.
8. My mom and dad.
9. The price for the repairs.
10. My allowance for the next ten weeks.
11. Once dropped.
12. Plays the trumpet.
13. Practices every day.
14. My brother.
15. Would rather play the drums.

Phrase Fragments

A sentence must have a subject and a verb to be complete. Since a phrase does not have either a subject or a verb, it can never stand alone as a sentence. When phrases are written alone, they result in **phrase fragments.** The words in **bold** type are examples of different kinds of phrase fragments. Notice that they are capitalized and punctuated as if they were sentences.

PREPOSITIONAL PHRASE	We waited for them for an hour. **On the edge of the garden.**
APPOSITIVE PHRASE	Have you ever met Mrs. Cho? **The famous gardener.**
PARTICIPIAL PHRASE	The children watched the rabbits. **Nibbling on some lettuce.**
INFINITIVE PHRASE	**To keep your plants healthy.** You must care for your garden daily.

PRACTICE YOUR SKILLS

● Check Your Understanding
Identifying Phrase Fragments

 Contemporary Life **Label each group of words *S* for sentence or *PF* for phrase fragment.**

1. In the garden on a hot day.

2. The cucumber plants are very green this year.

3. Watering the garden with a hose.

4. I saw the birds eating the tomatoes again.

5. To stop them from eating all my plants.

6. I work hard to guard against bugs.

7. For the best gardener in my family.

8. My dad knows how to make plants grow.

9. At the end of a long day.

10. We enjoy fresh vegetables from our garden.

Ways to Correct Phrase Fragments

When you edit your writing, always look for phrase fragments. If you find any, you can correct them in one of two ways: either add a subject and a verb to make the phrase a separate sentence, or attach a phrase to a related group of words that has a subject and a verb.

The following examples show how to correct the phrase fragments on the preceding page.

CORRECTED PREPOSITIONAL PHRASE FRAGMENT	We waited for them for an hour. **We stood on the edge of the garden.** (subject and verb added)
	We waited for them an hour **at the edge of the garden.** (attached to a sentence)

CORRECTED APPOSITIVE PHRASE FRAGMENT	Have you ever met Mrs. Cho? **She is the famous gardener.** (subject and verb added)
	Have you ever met Mrs. Cho, **the famous gardener?** (attached to a sentence)

CORRECTED PARTICIPIAL PHRASE FRAGMENTS	The children watched the rabbits. **They were nibbling on some lettuce.**
	(subject and verb added)
	The children watched the rabbits **nibbling on some lettuce.**
	(attached to a sentence)

| CORRECTED INFINITIVE PHRASE FRAGMENT | **To keep your plants healthy,** you must care for your garden daily. |
| | (attached to a sentence) |

PRACTICE YOUR SKILLS

 Check Your Understanding

Identifying Phrase Fragments

History Topic **Label each group of words S for sentence or *PF* for phrase fragment.**

1. George Washington Carver was a professor of agriculture.

2. At the Tuskegee Institute.

3. George Washington Carver was an ecologist.

4. To teach people about using the soil productively.

5. Carver spent much of his childhood tending the family vegetable garden.

6. Collecting new flowers.

7. As a quiet child.

8. Soon young Carver was known as the "plant doctor."

9. To help people take care of the land.

10. Carver's work resulted in many new uses for the peanut plant.

● Connect to the Writing Process: Revising
Correcting Phrase Fragments

11.–15. Rewrite the phrase fragments from the preceding exercise to make complete sentences.

Communicate Your Ideas

APPLY TO WRITING
Instructions: *Phrase Fragments*

You are going away on vacation and a friend is going to take care of your garden. Write your friend a short paragraph that gives instructions for taking care of your garden. Be sure to avoid using phrase fragments.

Clause Fragments

Because a subordinate clause has a subject and a verb, it can look very much like a complete sentence. However, when a subordinate clause stands alone, it becomes a **clause fragment** because it does not express a complete thought. The words in **bold** type below are examples of clause fragments. Notice that they are punctuated and capitalized as if they were complete sentences.

ADVERB CLAUSE FRAGMENTS	**Before the hunt began.** The dogs played with the pups.
	We stayed behind. **So that we could observe the pups more carefully.**
ADJECTIVE CLAUSE FRAGMENTS	Tim is the best person. **Who can explain the dogs' behavior.**
	Is this the dog? **That we should tag for the scientist?**

PRACTICE YOUR SKILLS

● Check Your Understanding
Recognizing Clause Fragments

 General Interest · **Label each group of words S for sentence or CF for clause fragment.**

1. Since it is called a wild dog.

2. Wild dogs are not house pets gone bad.

3. Tim McNutt spent many years researching African wild dogs.

4. Who is a wildlife biologist.

5. Wild dogs are most like wolves.

6. Which are nearly as endangered as the black rhino.

7. People mistakenly believe that wild dogs are bad animals.

8. Although they live in a pack.

9. Wild dogs sometimes make kills by themselves.

10. Because they have a tightly structured social system.

Ways to Correct Clause Fragments

When you edit your written work, you can correct clause fragments in one of two ways: either change the subordinate clause to an independent clause, or attach a clause fragment to a related sentence next to it.

The following examples show how to correct the clause fragments on the preceding page.

CORRECTED ADVERB CLAUSE FRAGMENTS	**Before the hunt began,** the dogs played with the pups.
	(attached to a sentence)
	We stayed behind. **We could observe the pups more carefully.**
	(made into an independent clause)
CORRECTED ADJECTIVE CLAUSE FRAGMENTS	Tim is the best person. **He can explain the dogs' behavior.**
	(made into an independent clause)
	Is this the dog **that we should tag for the scientist?**
	(attached to a sentence)

When writers use dialogue, they occasionally use fragments. People often speak in fragments. Writers imitate normal conversation so that their writing sounds natural. Notice the combination of sentences and fragments in the following excerpt.

"Yeah, something like that."

"And how old is this kid?"

"About twelve, maybe a little older."

"And for this you swore me to secrecy?"

"Sheri said the treasure could be in the millions," I said. "You want everybody in the neighborhood out looking for it?"

—*Walter Dean Myers,* The Mouse Rap

PRACTICE YOUR SKILLS

● Check Your Understanding
Recognizing Clause Fragments

Literature Topic **Label each group of words S for sentence or CF for clause fragment.**

1. Jean Craighead George wrote *Julie of the Wolves.*

2. Since the author studied wolf behavior.

3. Many people have learned much about wolves.

4. After they have read *Julie and the Wolves.*

5. Julie, who is the main character.

6. She runs away from home.

7. The setting of the story is not a friendly one.

8. Which is located in the frozen North.

9. The wolves find her and save her life.

10. Before she freezes to death.

● Connect to the Writing Process: Revising
Revising Sentence Fragments

11.–15. Rewrite the clause fragments from the preceding exercise to make complete sentences.

Communicate Your Ideas

APPLY TO WRITING
E-mail Message: *Clause Fragments*

Your family has just visited a nature preserve, and you think it would be a good place for your science class to visit. Write an E-mail message to your science teacher describing your trip. Explain that you would like to have your class visit the nature preserve. Give enough details to convince your teacher, and be sure to avoid using clause fragments.

Run-on Sentences

When people write too fast, they sometimes combine several thoughts together as one sentence. The result is a run-on sentence.

A **run-on sentence** is two or more sentences that are written together and are separated by a comma or no mark of punctuation at all.

In each of the following examples, the subject of the sentence is underlined once and the verb is underlined twice.

WITH A COMMA   The crocodile is hunting, it will search for frogs.

The bear is tired, it will sleep now.

WITH NO COMMA   The orca missed its prey another orca got the seal.

White tigers are rare they have blue eyes.

PRACTICE YOUR SKILLS

● Check Your Understanding
Identifying Run-on Sentences

Science Topic **Label each group of words *S* for sentence or *RO* for run-on.**

1. Bears climb trees like cats, they sink their claws into the bark.

2. Birds use their bills for many purposes.

3. Locusts can travel three hundred miles nonstop their average air speed can reach eight miles per hour.

4. Some centipedes have 28 legs others have as many as 354 legs.

5. A trout can live in a lake for as long as four years.

6. A cheetah can reach speeds of over sixty miles per hour.

7. Humans are very seldom bitten or attacked by vampire bats these flying mammals do not like human blood.

8. Lionesses do most of the hunting lions defend the territory.

9. Cobras prey on other poisonous snakes they subdue them with very strong venom.

10. Great white sharks are the only sharks that regularly attack mammals.

Ways to Correct Run-on Sentences

Basically there are two ways to correct a run-on sentence. You can either turn the run-on sentence into separate sentences or create a compound sentence.

RUN-ON SENTENCE	We rushed into the village the elephant had already left.
SEPARATE SENTENCES	We rushed into the village. **The** elephant had already left.
COMPOUND SENTENCE	We rushed into the village, **but** the elephant had already left.

PRACTICE YOUR SKILLS

● Check Your Understanding
Identifying Run-on Sentences

General Interest **Label each group of words S for sentence or RO for run-on.**

1. In India, people and elephants compete for resources.

2. Elephants are enormous animals, they need a large amount of space.

3. India has a very large population and needs land for farming.

4. Elephants destroy vegetable crops the farmers become angry.

5. Game wardens have no choice but to capture such animals.

6. A captured elephant is transported to a wildlife refuge it gets a second chance.

7. Conservationists are looking for a better solution to the problem.

8. Some experts believe that people can learn to live with wild animals.

9. An elephant often returns to the same grazing area, when people move into these areas elephants become upset.

10. An angry elephant can cause a lot of damage it is a very big animal.

● Connect to the Writing Process: Revising
Correcting Run-on Sentences

11.–15. Rewrite the run-on sentences from the preceding exercise to make complete sentences.

General
Interest
Correct each fragment or run-on sentence. Add capital letters, commas, conjunctions, and end marks where needed. If a sentence is correct, write C.

1. The first subway in the world opened in London. On January 10, 1863.

2. A large trench was dug a pavement was laid over it.

3. The trains were powered by steam engines, the smoke from the engines filled the tunnels with terrible fumes.

4. Ten feet of water once filled the tunnels the subway shut down briefly.

5. About thirty years later, London's first "tube tunnel" was built.

6. And instantly became a success.

7. In a tube line, a tunnel is actually bored through the ground.

8. Under the foundations of buildings.

9. The first tube line used electric power.

10. And it still runs today.

11. In 1897, Boston completed the first subway system.

12. That ran in the United States.

13. It ran only 1½ miles.

14. And used trolley cars on the subway tracks.

15. New York's subway finally opened in 1904, more than two billion people now ride it every year.

CheckPoint

Identifying Sentences, Fragments, and Run-ons

Label each group of words *S* for sentence, *F* for fragment, or *R* for run-on.

1. Robert Louis Stevenson wrote many books, one of them was *Treasure Island*.
2. The warmth of a wool poncho on a cold day.
3. Benjamin Franklin wanted the wild turkey as our national bird.
4. Through the front door of the Mason's apartment.
5. Mavis and her sister earned their lifesaving certificates last year.
6. Corey bowed, the audience stood and cheered.
7. The horseshoe crab has two pairs of eyes.
8. Enjoyed a salad of bananas, oranges, and papayas.
9. Ostriches cannot fly they have small, weak wings.
10. The display of Indian art at the Boswell Museum.
11. To play in the championship game.
12. Cathy reading her favorite book.
13. The bell rang the students went into class.
14. The weather has turned warmer.
15. In front of the door of the yellow house.
16. Bob Holley, the artist who painted that picture.
17. Since tomorrow is Monday.
18. The baseball player who hit the most home runs.
19. Behind the wall was a garden.
20. The dog barked, the cat ran.

Correcting Sentence Fragments

Write a complete sentence using each sentence fragment.

1. In the pocket of an old coat.
2. Can't find today's newspaper.
3. The parade with bands and floats.
4. Pulled over to the side of the road.
5. And ran onto the field.
6. A large school of fish beneath the boat.
7. Rock squirrels with black stripes on their backs.
8. The limb of the spruce tree.
9. Owned a red car with white stripes.
10. On the trees at the farm.

Correcting Sentence Errors

Rewrite the following paragraph correcting the sentence fragments and run-on sentences.

In 1844, young Elizabeth Blackwell wanted to become a doctor, medical schools did not accept women students at that time. Blackwell was very determined, however. For a while she studied. With private teachers. Then in 1846, a medical school in New York. Finally admitted her as a student. After she finished her studies, she could not find a job at any established hospital. Therefore, she founded her own hospital. For women and children. Today the Blackwell Medal is awarded to women physicians it recognizes their achievements as doctors.

Language and *Self-Expression*

Romare Bearden used collage to express what he felt about the people and the society in which he lived. In *Sunset and Moonrise with Maudell Sleet,* for example, Bearden portrays a woman he recalled from his childhood in Charlotte, North Carolina. In his own words, "She was a strong woman with a green thumb." How did he show this in this collage?

Think of individuals who have made a vivid impression on you. Is there one individual who possesses a special ability or quality you admire? What words best describe the person?

Write a story about your subject in a few clear, organized paragraphs. Use phrases and clauses to add details about your subject and to vary your writing.

Prewriting Use a story map to identify ideas and examples to include in the beginning, middle, and ending of the story.

Drafting Use your story map to focus only on examples that demonstrate your point. Present a vivid image of your character that sets the tone in your first sentence. Close with a summary sentence that states the main idea of the story.

Revising Read your story aloud. Then ask yourself questions to help you react to your own writing. Are my ideas clearly presented? Do I need more details? Will others enjoy reading this story? Be sure you have written in complete sentences.

Editing Fix sentence fragments and run-on sentences, correcting punctuation as needed.

Publishing Prepare a final copy of your story. If possible, attach a photograph of the subject. Share your story with family and friends.

Another Look

A **sentence fragment** is a group of words that does not express a complete thought.

A phrase has no subject or verb. Because a phrase does not express a complete thought, it can never stand alone as a sentence. When phrases are written alone, they result in **phrase fragments.** *(pages L286–L288)*

A subordinate clause has a subject and a verb, but it does not express a complete thought. When a subordinate clause stands alone, it becomes a **clause fragment.** *(pages L290–L291)*

A **run-on sentence** is two or more sentences that are written together and are separated by a comma or no mark of punctuation at all

A **sentence** is a group of words that expresses a complete thought. It has a subject and verb.

Other Information About Fragments and Run-ons

When you edit your writing, always carefully check for any missing subjects or missing verbs, phrase fragments, clause fragments, and run-on sentences.

Correcting sentence fragments *(page L283)*
Correcting phrase fragments *(pages L287–L288)*
Correcting clause fragments *(page L291)*
Correcting run-on sentences *(page L295)*

Directions
Read the passage. Write the letter of the best way to write each group of underlined words. If the underlined words contain no error, write D.

EXAMPLE   The mandarin <u>orange is one. Of my favorite</u>
                                          (1)
               <u>fruits</u>.
        1 **A** orange being one of my favorite fruits.
           B orange is one of my favorite fruits.
           C orange. Is one of my favorite fruits.
           D No error

ANSWER   1 **B**

The word *mandarin* has <u>several meanings all of them</u> are
                                          (1)
interesting. There is the <u>mandarin orange. That originated in</u>
                                          (2)
<u>China</u>. It is sweet and juicy, and it's easy to peel. <u>In the</u>

<u>Chinese Empire. A mandarin is</u> an official of rank. Also, the
                (3)
official spoken language in China is Mandarin. <u>It is based on a</u>

<u>dialect spoken in and around Beijing.</u> When it refers to a style
                (4)
of <u>Chinese dress, and the word *mandarin* describes a short,</u>
                                          (5)
<u>stand-up collar.</u>

1   **A**   several meanings, all of them
    B   several meanings. All of them
    C   several meanings. That all of them
    D   No error

2   **A**   mandarin orange, that originated in China.
    B   mandarin orange and originated in China.
    C   mandarin orange that originated in China.
    D   No error

3   **A**   In the Chinese Empire, a mandarin is
    B   In the Chinese Empire a mandarin. Is
    C   In the Chinese Empire, a mandarin being
    D   No error

4   **A**   It is based on a dialect. Spoken in and around Beijing.
    B   It is based on a dialect spoken. In and around Beijing.
    C   It is based. On a dialect spoken in and around Beijing.
    D   No error

5   **A**   Chinese dress, the word *mandarin* describes a short,
            stand-up collar.
    B   Chinese dress. The word *mandarin* describes a short,
            stand-up collar.
    C   Chinese dress, the word *mandarin* to describe a short,
            stand-up collar.
    D   No error

CHAPTER 11

Using Verbs

· · · · · · ·

Directions
Read the passage and write the letter of the word or group of words that belongs in each underlined space.

EXAMPLE   Turtles __(1)__ resilient to survive.
     1 A is
       B are
       C have to be
       D has to be

ANSWER   **1 C**

Baby sea turtles face many dangers. Just hatching __(1)__ a bit iffy. __(2)__ this. Some crabs __(3)__ sea turtle eggs, and adult turtles sometimes crush the nesting eggs of other turtles. Only one hatchling in one thousand __(4)__ to adulthood. Even as hatchlings scramble to the sea, predators __(5)__ to gobble them up.

Other hazards are threatening the survival of adult turtles. Pollution and poaching __(6)__ two. Actually, humans are sea turtles' greatest threat. Poachers __(7)__ turtles to meet the demand for turtle parts. Toxins __(8)__ turtles on land and in the sea. Unchecked, such problems __(9)__ sea turtles to extinction. Who __(10)__ the sea turtles' survival in the twenty-first century?

1 **A** is
   B being
   C was
   D has been

2 **A** Considers
   B Considered
   C Consider
   D Considering

3 **A** ate
   B eating
   C eats
   D eat

4 **A** has survived
   B survived
   C survives
   D is surviving

5 **A** tried
   B try
   C tries
   D have tried

6 **A** had been
   B was
   C are
   D will

7 **A** hunting
   B hunted
   C hunts
   D hunt

8 **A** harm
   B harmed
   C have harmed
   D will harm

9 **A** brings
   B could bring
   C takes
   D could take

10 **A** has assured
   B will assure
   C assures
   D assure

David Strickland. *Case Alien,* 1991.
Metal machinery parts and glass. 104 by 46 by 63 inches. Private Collection.

Describe   Describe the sculpture. Identify objects
the artist used to assemble this sculpture.

Analyze   What mood does *Case Alien* express? How
does Strickland use exaggeration,
contrast, and knowledge of the human
body to express the mood?

Interpret   How might a writer create the same
mood?

Judge   Do you think this sculpture or a written
description would more effectively create
this mood? Give reasons for your answer.

At the end of this chapter, you will use the artwork to
stimulate ideas for writing.

The Principal Parts of Verbs

You know that a verb shows action or makes a statement about the subject of a sentence. A verb also tells when the action happens.

PRESENT ACTION	Each day I **call** Suzanne.
PAST ACTION	Yesterday I **called** her.
FUTURE ACTION	Tomorrow I **will call** Tasha.

Notice that a verb changes its form to show the time of the action. The different forms of a verb are made from the basic parts of a verb, called principal parts.

The **principal parts** of a verb are the present, the present participle, the past, and the past participle.

Following are the principal parts of the verb *call*. Notice that the present participle and the past participle must have a helping verb when they are used as verbs.

PRESENT	I often **call** my friend after dinner.
PRESENT PARTICIPLE	I *am* **calling** her tonight.
PAST	I **called** her last week.
PAST PARTICIPLE	I *have* **called** her six times so far this month.

You can learn more about helping verbs on page L80.

▶ Regular Verbs

Most verbs form their past and past participle just like the verb *call*—by adding *-ed* or *-d* to the present. These verbs are called regular verbs.

A **regular verb** forms its past and past participle by adding *–ed* or *–d* to the present.

The principal parts of the verbs *talk, bake, stop,* and *carry* are listed below. Notice that the present participle is formed by adding *–ing* to the present form. Also, as the rule says, the past is formed by adding *–ed* or *–d* to the present.

REGULAR VERBS			
PRESENT	**PRESENT PARTICIPLE**	**PAST**	**PAST PARTICIPLE**
talk	(is) talking	talked	(have) talked
bake	(is) baking	baked	(have) baked
stop	(is) stopping	stopped	(have) stopped
carry	(is) carrying	carried	(have) carried

Sometimes when you add a word ending such as *–ing* or *–ed* to verbs such as *bake, stop,* and *carry,* the spelling changes. If you are unsure of the spelling of a verb form, look it up in the dictionary.

You can learn more about spelling on pages L640–L669.

PRACTICE YOUR SKILLS

● Check Your Understanding
Writing the Principal Parts of Regular Verbs

Make four columns on your paper. Label them *present, present participle, past,* and *past participle*. Then write the four principal parts of each of the following regular verbs on the following page. Use *is* when you write the present participle and *have* when you write the past participle. If you are unsure of the spelling of a verb form, look it up in the dictionary.

1. climb	**6.** stop
2. drag	**7.** use
3. suppose	**8.** earn
4. paint	**9.** skip
5. wish	**10.** move

● Connect to the Writing Process: Drafting
Writing Sentences with Regular Verbs

Write five sentences, using the instructions below.
Remember to use a helping verb with the present
participle and past participle.

11. Write a sentence using the present form of *laugh*.

12. Write a sentence using the past form of *cry*.

13. Write a sentence using the present participle form
of *play*.

14. Write a sentence using the past participle form of
hope.

15. Write a sentence using the present participle form
of *dream*.

▶ Irregular Verbs

Although most verbs form their past and past participle by
adding –*ed* or –*d*, a few verbs do not. These verbs are called
irregular verbs.

An **irregular verb** does not form its past and past
participle by adding –*ed* or –*d* to the present.

Irregular verbs can be divided into groups according to the
way they form their past and past participles. You should
remember that the word *is* is not part of the present
participle and *have* is not part of the past participle. Still,

they have been added to the following lists of irregular verbs. They are there to remind you that all present and past participles must have a form of these helping verbs when they are used in a sentence.

Group 1 These irregular verbs have the same form for the present, the past, and the past participle.

PRESENT	PRESENT PARTICIPLE	PAST	PAST PARTICIPLE
burst	(is) bursting	burst	(have) burst
cut	(is) cutting	cut	(have) cut
let	(is) letting	let	(have) let
put	(is) putting	put	(have) put
set	(is) setting	set	(have) set

Group 2 These irregular verbs have the same form for the past and the past participle.

PRESENT	PRESENT PARTICIPLE	PAST	PAST PARTICIPLE
bring	(is) bringing	brought	(have) brought
buy	(is) buying	bought	(have) bought
catch	(is) catching	caught	(have) caught
leave	(is) leaving	left	(have) left
make	(is) making	made	(have) made
say	(is) saying	said	(have) said
teach	(is) teaching	taught	(have) taught

PRACTICE YOUR SKILLS

● Check Your Understanding
Using the Correct Verb Form

Sports Topic **Label each underlined verb form *past* or *past participle*.**

1. Yesterday no one in the stadium <u>left</u> before the end of the game.

2. Jimmy's old football uniform has finally <u>burst</u> its seams.

3. Who <u>made</u> the winning touchdown last night?

4. Has everyone <u>brought</u> his playbooks to today's practice?

5. Coach has <u>said</u> that many times before.

6. You should have <u>put</u> your uniform in your locker at the end of practice.

7. Coach <u>taught</u> us a new play.

8. I <u>let</u> Joe block for me.

9. Danny <u>brought</u> us each a basket of candy from the cheerleaders.

10. I have <u>made</u> the starting lineup.

● Connect to the Writing Process: Editing
Correcting Sentences with Irregular Verbs

Rewrite the following sentences, replacing the underlined verb with the correct verb form.

11. John <u>bursted</u> through the other team's weak defense.

12. The referee <u>putted</u> the ball on the thirty-five-yard line.

13. The coach should have <u>letted</u> me play.

14. On his last run, Gary <u>brung</u> our team to within scoring distance.

15. Benjamin had <u>catched</u> the football very close to the goal line.

16. When we beat Central in the last game, we <u>maked</u> the playoffs.

● Connect to Speaking: Reading a Summary
Correcting the Use of Irregular Verbs

> Oral
> Expression
> **Read the following game summary aloud, correcting any irregular verbs that have been used incorrectly.**

Last night when our team leaved the field, Coach was very proud. He sayed that he had never before seen such a great effort by the whole team. The local newspaper sayed that our team is sure to win the playoffs now. The sensational overtime win putted us in first place and brung us to the championship level.

Group 3 These irregular verbs form the past participle by adding –*n* to the past.

PRESENT	PRESENT PARTICIPLE	PAST	PAST PARTICIPLE
break	(is) breaking	broke	(have) broken
choose	(is) choosing	chose	(have) chosen
freeze	(is) freezing	froze	(have) frozen
speak	(is) speaking	spoke	(have) spoken
steal	(is) stealing	stole	(have) stolen

Group 4 These irregular verbs form the past participle by adding −n to the present.

PRESENT	PRESENT PARTICIPLE	PAST	PAST PARTICIPLE
blow	(is) blowing	blew	(have) blown
drive	(is) driving	drove	(have) driven
give	(is) giving	gave	(have) given
grow	(is) growing	grew	(have) grown
know	(is) knowing	knew	(have) known
see	(is) seeing	saw	(have) seen
take	(is) taking	took	(have) taken
throw	(is) throwing	threw	(have) thrown

PRACTICE YOUR SKILLS

 Check Your Understanding
Determining the Correct Verb Form

Sports Topic **Write the correct verb form for each sentence.** Remember that *have, has,* or *had* is used with the past participle.

1. Has anyone (saw, seen) the film clip of Mark McGwire's seventieth season home run?

2. McGwire had (broke, broken) the record for most home runs in a season.

3. By the end of the 1998 baseball season, he had (drove, driven) seventy home runs out of the ballpark.

4. His last home run was a moment that has been (froze, frozen) in time.

5. No one has (stole, stolen) McGwire's special memories of that season.

6. During the following season, McGwire (blew, blowed) his five hundredth career home run ball out of the park in August.

7. McGwire has (took, taken) his record-breaking feats in stride.

8. McGwire (threw, throwed) himself into playing great baseball.

9. He has (spoke, spoken) to the press about his records.

10. He says that as a child, he never (knew, knowed) that he would have such a great baseball career.

● **Check Your Understanding**
Using the Correct Verb Form

General Interest **Write the past or the past participle of each verb in parentheses. Remember that *have, has,* or *had* is used with the past participle.**

11. Over the past few years, bears have (drive) people to take extra precautions in national parks.

12. A grizzly bear (break) the spine of a salmon with a snap of its jaws.

13. In the past grizzly bears have (choose) to be active at night when humans were near.

14. Bears in campgrounds (give) many groups of campers a fright.

15. Some campers have (see) bears climbing into tents in search of food.

16. The grizzly population has (grow) in mountainous areas.

17. One bear even (take) some fruit from a basket.

18. Those bears should have (know) to stay away from the ranger station.

● **Connect to the Writing Process: Editing**
Correcting Sentences with Irregular Verbs

Write the following sentences, replacing any incorrect verb with the correct verb form. If a sentence is correct, write C.

19. A bear had broke into Grandma's smokehouse.

20. Fortunately, the bear choose only the smallest piece of meat.

21. Grandma has spoke with the local game warden.

22. Last year a bear steal three of Grandma's hams.

23. She should have known that bears would want the food.

Group 5   These irregular verbs form the past and past participle by changing a vowel. The *i* in the present changes to an *a* in the past and a *u* in the past participle.

PRESENT	PRESENT PARTICIPLE	PAST	PAST PARTICIPLE
begin	(is) beginning	began	(have) begun
drink	(is) drinking	drank	(have) drunk
ring	(is) ringing	rang	(have) rung
sing	(is) singing	sang	(have) sung
swim	(is) swimming	swam	(have) swum

Group 6 These irregular verbs form the past and past participle in other ways.

PRESENT	PRESENT PARTICIPLE	PAST	PAST PARTICIPLE
come	(is) coming	came	(have) come
do	(is) doing	did	(have) done
eat	(is) eating	ate	(have) eaten
go	(is) going	went	(have) gone
ride	(is) riding	rode	(have) ridden
run	(is) running	ran	(have) run
wear	(is) wearing	wore	(have) worn
write	(is) writing	wrote	(have) written

PRACTICE YOUR SKILLS

● Check Your Understanding
Determining the Correct Verb Form

Contemporary Life   **Write the correct verb form for each sentence.** Remember that *have, has,* or *had* is used with the past participle.

1. Has Patrick ever (did, done) this kind of rodeo work before?

2. The steer (ran, run) crazily into the center of the ring.

3. Have you ever (went, gone) to a rodeo?

4. I (began, begun) barrel racing when I was seven years old.

5. The starting bell (rang, rung) three minutes ago.

6. Has Nick ever (wore, worn) that blue plaid cowboy shirt?

7. Jessica (drank, drunk) three glasses of water after her barrel race.

8. Do you know who (sang, sung) the national anthem?

9. Have you (wrote, written) a thank-you note to the judging committee?

10. My head (swam, swum) after I tripped and fell in front of the stands.

● Check Your Understanding
Using the Correct Verb Form

Music Topic **Write the past or the past participle of each verb in parentheses. Remember that *have, has,* or *had* is used with the past participle.**

11. The three tenors (do) a second encore at the end of their performance.

12. Had those four sopranos ever (sing) together before?

13. The critics should have (eat) their words about the concert.

14. The conductor must have (ride) to rehearsal with the drummer, because they were both late.

15. The singers should have (come) an hour before the show.

16. Rehearsal had (begin) without the dancers on the stage.

17. All the musicians (wear) special jackets for the evening's first performance with the tenors.

18. Who (write) that aria?

19. After holding the bass drum all evening, my arms felt as if I had (swim) across the river and back.

20. The bells have (ring) for the start of the third movement.

● Check Your Understanding
Finding the Principal Parts in a Dictionary

Make four columns on your paper. Label them *present, present participle, past* and *past participle*. Use a dictionary to find the principal parts of the following verbs and write them in the correct columns.

21. think

22. raise

23. win

24. lead

25. tear

26. fly

27. bite

28. shake

29. catch

30. spring

● Connect to the Writing Process: Editing
Correcting Sentences with Irregular Verbs

Rewrite each of the following sentences, replacing any incorrect verb forms with the correct verb form. If a sentence is correct, write C.

31. Shannon sung her first solo at the concert last night.

32. The concert almost begun without her and Samantha.

33. Shannon had wrote the song especially for her performance.

34. Marti did a dance after Shannon's solo.

35. Christina's parents come to the concert at intermission.

● **Connect to Speaking:** Making an Announcement
Correcting Improperly Used Verbs

> Oral
> Expression

Read the following intercom announcement aloud to a classmate or your teacher. As you read, correct any verb errors you see.

We are holding auditions for the talent show on Thursday. If you have ever sang a song, please come. If you have ever did any karate performances, you are welcome too. Make sure you have wrote your name on the list. We will call and tell you the time for auditions.

Communicate Your Ideas

APPLY TO WRITING

Biography: *Principal Parts of Verbs*

Your school band has applied to perform in a very important competition. Before you can submit an audition tape, you must send in a "biography" of the band and its accomplishments. Your band director has asked you to write this biography for the judges of the competition. Be sure to use the principal parts of verbs correctly so that you impress the judges.

 QuickCheck Mixed Practice

> History
> Topic

Write the past or the past participle of each verb in parentheses.

1. People (write) and (say) why their city should be the nation's capital.

2. Congress finally (decide) to create a new city.

3. Congress (pass) a bill in 1790 giving permission to the president to choose a site.

4. George Washington (go) to several places and finally (choose) the place where the city now stands.

5. He (know) it was a good location because the Potomac River (run) deep enough for ships.

6. Maryland and Virginia (give) the land to the federal government.

7. President Washington then (bring) in a French architect to design the new city.

8. The architect (begin) to draw plans with broad avenues.

9. He (divide) the city into four sections with the Capitol building in the center.

10. He then (make) designs of beautiful government buildings and monuments.

11. The name of this ten-mile-square area, the District of Columbia, (come) from the name Christopher Columbus.

12. The architect and a planning commission (name) the city Washington in honor of the country's first president.

13. By 1800, builders had nearly (complete) the President's house.

14. President John Adams and his wife (ride) to their new home.

15. Soon other members of the government also (move) to Washington, D.C.

▶ Six Problem Verbs

The following sets of verbs are called problem verbs because their meanings are often confused—causing problems.

bring and *take*

Bring indicates motion toward the speaker. *Take* indicates motion away from the speaker.

PRESENT	PRESENT PARTICIPLE	PAST	PAST PARTICIPLE
bring	(is) bringing	brought	(have) brought
take	(is) taking	took	(have) taken

BRING   David **brings** us doughnuts every morning.

David is **bringing** us doughnuts today.

David **brought** us doughnuts yesterday.

David **has brought** us doughnuts every day this week.

TAKE   Please **take** this chocolate cake now to Mrs. Jones.

Tom **is taking** the chocolate cake to Mrs. Jones today.

Sara **took** a library book to Mrs. Jones yesterday.

I **have taken** magazines to Mrs. Jones every Saturday.

PRACTICE YOUR SKILLS

● Check Your Understanding
Using the Correct Verb Form

> **Oral Expression** **Read these sentences aloud to practice using the correct verb form.**

1. What are you <u>taking</u> to Bill's party tomorrow?
2. Sue <u>brought</u> me a pie for dessert.
3. <u>Bring</u> your CD player to my house before the party.
4. Joe <u>took</u> a ladder to Bill's house to help with the decorations.
5. Denise is <u>bringing</u> her volleyball net here.

● Check Your Understanding
Using* Bring *and* Take *Correctly

> **Science Topic** **Write the correct form of *bring* or *take*.**

6. A wolf (brings, takes) food to its pups.
7. The pups (bring, take) food from the adult wolf.
8. The pups (bring, take) the food to a corner and examine it.
9. An adult wolf (brings, takes) its pups along on hunts when the pups are about six months old.
10. Wolves were (brought, taken) to Yellowstone Park away from their natural habitat.

learn and *teach*

Learn means "to gain knowledge." *Teach* means "to instruct" or "to show how."

PRESENT	PRESENT PARTICIPLE	PAST	PAST PARTICIPLE
learn	(is) learning	learned	(have) learned
teach	(is) teaching	taught	(have) taught

LEARN

Sheila **learns** music very quickly.

Sheila is **learning** to play the piano.

Sheila **learned** two songs yesterday.

Sheila **has learned** some Mozart pieces already.

TEACH

Teach me this overture.

Mr. Davidson **is teaching** me a new aria.

Mr. Davidson **taught** me a trumpet solo last week.

Mr. Davidson **has taught** me a concerto already.

PRACTICE YOUR SKILLS

● Check Your Understanding
Using the Correct Verb Form

Oral Expression | **Read these sentences aloud to practice using the correct verb form.**

1. I promise I will <u>learn</u> this movement by Friday.

2. Mrs. Arnold has <u>taught</u> piano for many years.

3. Sarah is <u>learning</u> a new solo for the concert.

4. We <u>learned</u> about Mozart in class today.

5. Mr. Johns <u>taught</u> us many facts about Mozart's music.

● Check Your Understanding
Using **Learn** *and* **Teach** *Correctly*

> Music Topic **Write the correct form of *learn* or *teach*.**

6. Mozart (learned, taught) a great deal about music from his father, Leopold.

7. Before he was six years old, young Wolfgang had (learned, taught) to compose symphonies.

8. Many children have (learned, taught) one of his earliest compositions, "Twinkle, Twinkle, Little Star."

9. Mozart's father had (learned, taught) Wolfgang to play a number of instruments.

10. His music (learns, teaches) people many things about patterns of music.

leave and *let*

Leave means "to depart" or "go away." *Let* means "to allow" or "permit."

PRESENT	PRESENT PARTICIPLE	PAST	PAST PARTICIPLE
leave	(is) leaving	left	(have) left
let	(is) letting	let	(have) let

LEAVE   When do you **leave** for Boston?

Brenda **is leaving** for Chicago.

Sue **left** a few minutes ago on the plane to Baltimore.

Marty **has left** for San Francisco.

LET   I **let** the cat sleep on my bed.

I **am letting** the cat sleep there tonight.

I **let** the cat sleep on my bed all last week.

I **have let** the cat sleep on my bed many times before.

You can learn more about other problem verbs in A Writer's Glossary of Usage on pages L460–L476.

PRACTICE YOUR SKILLS

 Check Your Understanding
Using the Correct Verb Form

Oral Expression   **Read these sentences aloud to practice using the correct verb form.**

1. <u>Let</u> me take your suitcase.

2. I will put it in our car by the curb and <u>leave</u> it there.

3. Mark is <u>letting</u> me take care of his dog while he is away.

4. Denise placed her tickets on the counter and <u>left</u> them there.

5. I have <u>let</u> Kathy use my suitcase for her vacation three times now.

Using Leave and Let Correctly

Contemporary Life **Write the correct form of *leave* or *let*.**

6. Please (leave, let) me drive you to the airport.

7. Has Judy's plane (left, let) yet?

8. Margie had (left, let) yesterday for Denver.

9. I am (leaving, letting) Jane borrow my camera for her trip to Greece.

10. What time does your plane (leave, let) the gate?

Connect to the Writing Process: Editing
Using Problem Verbs

Rewrite each sentence, replacing the incorrect verb with the correct verb form.

11. Please learn me to read the train schedule.

12. Let your suitcase with the ticket agent.

13. You should bring a jacket on your trip to Denver.

14. I taught to read an airport departure board when I was very young.

15. Kelly left me take her hair dryer on the trip since mine was broken.

Communicate Your Ideas

APPLY TO WRITING

Friendly Letter: *Problem Verbs*

Your best friend will be joining you on your vacation after a few days. Write your friend a letter that tells what to expect about your destination. Be sure to use problem verbs correctly.

General Interest **Write the correct form of each verb in parentheses.**

1. The Chicago Field Museum (learned, taught) us about a dinosaur fossil.

2. The work (brought, took) many scientists to the museum.

3. Scientists have (learned, taught) much about dinosaurs from this fossil.

4. The fossil, named Sue, was (brought, taken) to Chicago because of the work of a paleontologist named Sue Hendricksen.

5. Once a fossil has been discovered, scientists seldom (leave, let) the site.

6. They hope to (learn, teach) about how the dinosaurs lived.

7. The Chicago Museum hopes to (leave, let) the public view the bones soon.

8. They hope that Sue will (bring, take) many visitors to the museum.

9. The scientists will (leave, let) the excavation site as they found it.

10. Paleontologists have (learned, taught) that dinosaurs suffered from gum disease.

Verb Tense

Every verb has six tenses: the present, past, future, present perfect, past perfect, and future perfect.

The time expressed by a verb is called the **tense** of the verb.

PRESENT	I **paint** pictures.
PAST	I **painted** a picture in art class yesterday.
FUTURE	I **will paint** another picture tomorrow.
PRESENT PERFECT	I **have painted** pictures for almost a year.
PAST PERFECT	I **had painted** pictures before I attended kindergarten.
FUTURE PERFECT	I **will have painted** fifteen pictures by June.

▶ Uses of the Tenses

The preceding examples of the verb *paint* show that verbs in the English language have six basic tenses. All of these tenses can be formed from the principal parts of a verb, along with the helping verbs *have, has, had, will,* and *shall.*

Present tense is used to express an action that is going on now. To form the present tense, use the present form (the first principal part of the verb) or add *–s* or *–es* to the present form.

| PRESENT TENSE | I **sculpt** clay. |
| | Pam **begins** her art lessons with a sketch. |

Past tense expresses an action that already took place or was completed in the past. To form the past tense of a regular verb, add –*ed* or –*d* to the present form. To form the past tense of an irregular verb, check a dictionary, or look for it on pages L309–L325.

| PAST TENSE | I **sculpted** some clay in art class yesterday. |
| | Pam **began** her creative art lessons last week. |

Future tense is used to express an action that will take place in the future. To form the future tense, use the helping verb *shall* or *will* with the present form.

| FUTURE TENSE | I **shall sculpt** more clay figures tomorrow. |
| | Pam **will begin** an art lesson tomorrow. |

You can learn more about the correct use of shall *and* will *on page L471.*

Present perfect tense expresses an action that was completed at some indefinite time in the past. It also expresses an action that started in the past and is still going on. To form the present perfect tense, add *has* or *have* to the past participle.

| PRESENT PERFECT TENSE | I **have sculpted** clay for two years. |
| | Pam **has begun** art lessons this morning. |

Past perfect tense expresses an action that took place before some other action. To form the past perfect tense, add *had* to the past participle.

> PAST PERFECT TENSE
>
> I **had sculpted** clay before I took lessons.
>
> Pam **had begun** art lessons before she turned ten years old.

Future perfect tense expresses an action that will take place before another future action or time. To form the future perfect tense, add *shall have* or *will have* to the past participle.

> FUTURE PERFECT TENSE
>
> I **will have sculpted** more than three new pieces by the end of the month.
>
> By Saturday, Pam **will have begun** her art lessons.

▶ Conjugation of a Verb

A **conjugation** is a list of all the singular and plural forms of a verb in all six tenses. The following is a conjugation of the irregular verb *fall*, whose four principal parts are *fall, falling, fell,* and *fallen*.

CONJUGATION OF THE VERB *FALL*	
Present	
SINGULAR	PLURAL
I fall	we fall
you fall	you fall
he, she, it falls	they fall

Past

SINGULAR	PLURAL
I fell	we fell
you fell	you fell
he, she, it fell	they fell

Future

SINGULAR	PLURAL
I shall/will fall	we shall/will fall
you will fall	you will fall
he, she, it will fall	they will fall

Present Perfect Tense

SINGULAR	PLURAL
I have fallen	we have fallen
you have fallen	you have fallen
he, she, it has fallen	they have fallen

Past Perfect Tense

SINGULAR	PLURAL
I had fallen	we had fallen
you had fallen	you had fallen
he, she, it had fallen	they had fallen

Future Perfect Tense

SINGULAR	PLURAL
I will/shall have fallen	we will/shall have fallen
you will have fallen	you will have fallen
he, she, it will have fallen	they will have fallen

The present participle is used to conjugate the progressive forms of a verb. You can learn more about the progressive forms of verbs on pages L336–L337.

PRACTICE YOUR SKILLS

● Check Your Understanding
Identifying Verb Tenses

Science Topic **Label the tense of each underlined verb as *present, past, future, present perfect, past perfect,* or *future perfect.***

1. A cheetah <u>becomes</u> an adult when it is only two years old.

2. A mother cheetah <u>has brought</u> her cubs part of a gazelle.

3. In a single day, a mother cheetah <u>has hunted</u> a number of times.

4. A female cheetah <u>will catch</u> live prey for her cubs to practice hunting.

5. The cheetah <u>broke</u> sixty miles per hour during the hunt.

6. After the cheetah <u>had stalked</u> its prey, it burst into a run.

7. Cheetahs <u>live</u> in dry grassland areas of Africa.

8. A cheetah <u>will accelerate</u> to top speed in three seconds.

9. The cheetah <u>has hunted</u> in the plains of Africa for thousands of years.

10. The cheetah <u>makes</u> facial expressions with the bold black lines around its muzzle.

● Check Your Understanding
Writing Different Tenses

Write the verbs, following the instructions below.

11. Write the present tense of *call.*

12. Write the past tense of *burst.*

13. Write the present perfect tense of *say*.

14. Write the future tense of *teach*.

15. Write the past perfect tense of *stop*.

16. Write the future perfect tense of *talk*.

● Connect to the Writing Process: Revising
Changing Tenses of Verbs

Rewrite the following sentences so that each underlined verb is in the past perfect tense.

17. The cheetah <u>survives</u> well in the wild.

18. Cheetahs <u>have climbed</u> trees to get a good view of their territory.

19. Cheetah cubs <u>have led</u> sheltered lives.

20. By the end of the day, cheetah cubs <u>will have played</u> for many hours.

21. The cheetah <u>will continue</u> to thrive.

Communicate Your Ideas

APPLY TO WRITING

Descriptive Paragraph: *Tenses of Verbs*

Your science class is setting up a petting zoo for the children of a local day-care center. You plan to teach the students a little about each of the animals. Write a descriptive paragraph about an animal that will be in the petting zoo so that young children can learn about the animal. After you have finished, reread your description. Check that you used the correct form of verbs.

▶ Shifts in Tense

When you write a story, you can tell your readers when
the story takes place by the tense of the verbs you use. As
you write, however, be sure to keep your tenses consistent.
For example, if you are telling a story that took place in the
past, use the past tense of verbs. If you suddenly shift to the
present, you will probably confuse your readers.

**Avoid unnecessary shifts in tense within a sentence or
within related sentences.**

A shift in tense can occur within a sentence itself or within
related sentences.

INCONSISTENT	*past* After I **rode** my bike a few miles, the *present* tire **goes** flat.
INCONSISTENT	*present* After I **ride** my bike a few miles, the *past* tire **went** flat.
CONSISTENT	*present* After I **ride** my bike a few miles, the tire *present* **goes** flat.
CONSISTENT	*past* After I **rode** my bike a few miles, the *past* tire **went** flat.
INCONSISTENT	*past* By the time I **fixed** the flat, the clouds *present* **pour** rain.
INCONSISTENT	*present* By the time I **fix** the flat, the clouds *past* **poured** rain.
CONSISTENT	*present* By the time I **fix** the flat, the clouds *present* **pour** rain.
CONSISTENT	*past* By the time I **fixed** the flat, the clouds *past* **poured** rain.

Professional writers often use the same verb tense to create a particular mood. Notice how this writer uses the same tense consistently in the following passage so that you feel as if you are there.

> The lovely Miss Gomez pales. After a moment of painful hesitation, she rips the telegram open. *Zzzzzt!* She gasps. *Aurggg!* Her face goes chalky white.
>
> —*Avi*, Who Was That Masked Man Anyway?

PRACTICE YOUR SKILLS

● Check Your Understanding

Identifying Shifts in Verb Tense

Contemporary Life **Write *S* If a sentence contains a shift in verb tense. If a sentence is correct, write *C*.**

1. Before you leave for the race, check your equipment and gear.

2. When I checked my bike before the race, I find a flat rear tire.

3. Because I didn't have a patch kit, I will not ride in the race.

4. Joe says that he has a patch kit.

5. I told him that I will need a patch for my flat tire.

6. Joe gave me the kit, and I fixed the flat tire very quickly.

7. After I fix the flat tire, I left for the big bicycle race.

8. The new tire will help my performance and gave me more traction on the wet roads.

9. When I told the other riders about my flat, they shared their biking stories with me.

10. After I finished the race, I thanked Joe for his extra help.

● Connect to the Writing Process: Revising
Correcting Shifts in Verb Tense

11.–15. Rewrite the sentences in the preceding exercise that contain shifts in verb tense.

Communicate Your Ideas

APPLY TO WRITING

Introduction: *Shifts in Verb Tense*

A famous athlete is coming to your school to share tips on competing. Your coach has asked you to write a brief introduction that highlights some of the athlete's accomplishments for the students who may not be familiar with this person. Jot down notes about what the athlete has done. Then write the introduction. Be sure to avoid shifting verb tenses improperly in your introduction.

▶ Progressive Verb Forms

Each of the six tenses has a **progressive form.** These forms are used to express continuing or ongoing action. The progressive forms add a special meaning to verbs that the regular tenses do not. Notice the differences in meaning in the following examples.

PRESENT	The groom **brushes** the horse.
	(*Brushes* shows that the groom can or does brush the horse.)
PRESENT PROGRESSIVE	The groom **is brushing** the horse.
	(*Is brushing* shows that the groom is brushing the horse right now.)

To form the progressive, add a form of the verb *be* to the present participle. Notice in the following examples that all of the progressive verb forms end in *–ing*.

PRESENT PROGRESSIVE	I am falling.
PAST PROGRESSIVE	I was falling.
FUTURE PROGRESSIVE	I will (shall) be falling.
PRESENT PERFECT PROGRESSIVE	I have been falling
PAST PERFECT PROGRESSIVE	I had been falling.
FUTURE PERFECT PROGRESSIVE	I will (shall) have been falling.

PRACTICE YOUR SKILLS

● Check Your Understanding
Identifying Progressive Verb Forms

Contemporary Life **Write each verb phrase.**

1. By today's end, we will have been announcing the Kentucky Derby for twenty-five years.

2. We will be watching the entrance of the horses.

3. The horses have been prancing in anticipation of the race.

4. The favorite has been racing well all season.

5. Last year he had been placing second or third on a regular basis.

6. Today his trainer is hoping for a win.

7. The horses will be entering the post parade in a moment.

8. The gray horse is pawing the ground impatiently.

9. The jockeys are planning their strategy.

10. Earlier the crowd was acting restless.

● **Connect to the Writing Process: Revising**
Changing Verb Tenses

Rewrite each of the following sentences so that it contains a progressive verb.

11. The greatest names in thoroughbred racing have gathered in Louisville.

12. The horses have practiced for weeks.

13. The crowd roars.

14. The horses enter the starting gate.

15. The gates fly open.

Communicate Your Ideas

APPLY TO WRITING

News Story: *Progressive Forms of Verbs*

The editor of the school paper wants you to write your story on last Friday's big game in a way that makes the readers feel they are watching the game all over again. Write a description of the action of the game, using progressive tenses of verbs.

Science
Topic
Write each underlined verb in the tense that is indicated in parentheses.

1. Nile crocodiles live (present perfect progressive) in Africa for many years.

2. By the time it reach (present) maturity, a crocodile weigh (present) up to 2,220 pounds.

3. Crocodiles grow (present perfect) to twenty feet.

4. Some ancient people believe (past) that the crocodile was sly.

5. Crocodiles continue (future) to thrive because people preserve (future) their habitat.

6. The crocodile survive (past perfect) due to its toughness.

7. During the last wet season the crocodiles live (past) in rain puddles.

8. By midday a crocodile wait (future progressive) patiently for its prey.

9. A crocodile strike (future) at its prey in seconds.

10. Yesterday a crocodile lunge (past perfect) for a zebra.

11. A crocodile drown (present) its prey.

12. At the end of three months, a female crocodile sit (future perfect) on her nest almost constantly.

13. The crocodiles' diet depend (future) on the type of prey that wander (future) near the water.

14. Some crocodiles survive (present perfect) a year without eating.

15. The crocodile's tail propel (past) it through the water.

Using the Correct Verb Form

Rewrite the following sentences, replacing incorrect verbs with correct verb forms. If a sentence needs no change, write C.

1. Julio has accidentally broke the light bulb.
2. My cousin has often sang solos with the choir.
3. I have drunk the last glass of milk.
4. They have chose Connie as the captain of the team.
5. We swum at the town beach yesterday morning.
6. Matthew done everything on the list.
7. The lake had nearly frozen by morning.
8. Who throwed the ball into our court?
9. The wind has blown the leaves around the yard.
10. The grass has already growed another inch.

Using the Correct Verb Form

Write each underlined verb in the tense that is indicated in parentheses.

1. I <u>break</u> (*past*) the silence with a cackling laugh.
2. Linda <u>live</u> (*past perfect*) in Ohio before she moved here.
3. Most bats <u>sleep</u> (*present*) upside down.
4. I <u>write</u> (*present perfect*) for a free catalog.
5. Tomorrow the sun <u>rise</u> (*future*) over those mountains.
6. Brian said that he <u>mail</u> (*past perfect*) two invitations.
7. Nancy <u>save</u> (*present perfect*) enough money for a new bicycle.
8. Who <u>carry</u> (*future*) the flag in tomorrow's parade?

Using Problem Verbs

Write the correct verb form for each sentence.

1. Margaret Hey's family (brought, took) a unique approach to clutter cleanup.
2. Here's an idea I (learned, taught) from *Family Fun,* October 1999.
3. (Leave, Let) the junk and save the collectibles.
4. The Hey's home museum (learns, teaches) visitors about family collectibles.
5. Books are available that (learn, teach) new collectors what to look for.
6. Some collectors (bring, take) their "junk" to antique road shows.
7. My friend (brought, took) his 1940s comics to have them evaluated.
8. Items (brought, taken) out of their protective wrapping lose some of their value.
9. Artists (leave, let) creative possibilities develop where they will.
10. "Heaps of junk" (left, let) in some artists' hands can become works of beauty or humor.

Using Verbs Correctly

Write five sentences that follow the directions below.

Write a sentence that . . .

1. includes the future tense of *begin.*
2. includes the past tense of *choose.*
3. includes the future perfect tense of *eat.*
4. includes the present progressive form of *race.*
5. includes the past progressive form of *throw.*

Language and *Self-Expression*

David Strickland's *Case Alien* illustrates how an imaginative eye can create a fanciful alien from what others consider a pile of junk.

Strickland used exaggeration and contrast to create a humorous alien—head, chest, arms, legs from tractor parts and bits of glass for bulging eyes. Think of someone in your life who makes you see funny or unexpected possibilities. Describe your subject in a few paragraphs. Use verb forms correctly and avoid tense changes. Write sentences that express the vivid images and the mood your subject creates.

Prewriting Draw a cluster diagram with objects or actions that show your subject's humor. Then order the objects from most to least humorous.

Drafting Begin with a sentence that sets the tone of your writing. Review your list of objects and select the most humorous ones. Remember to use exaggeration and contrast for effect.

Revising Read aloud your description to a classmate. Then ask him or her if your description of the subject creates a funny image. If your partner does not think the subject is funny, ask what you can do to add humor.

Editing Change any overused words. Check that you have used correct verb forms. Be sure that you have not changed tense in the same sentence.

Publishing Prepare a final copy. Read your work to the class, and ask them to sketch your subject.

Another Look

The **principal parts** of a verb are the present, the present participle, the past, and the past participle.

A **regular verb** forms its past and past participle by adding -ed or -d to the present. *(pages L307–L308)*

An **irregular verb** does not form its past and past participle by adding -ed or -d to the present. *(pages L309–L325)*

The **tense** of a verb is the time expressed by the verb.

To form the **present tense**, use the present form (the first principal part of the verb) or add -s or -es to the present form. *(pages L328–L329)*

To form the **past tense** of a regular verb, add -ed or -d to the present form. To form the past tense of an irregular verb, check the dictionary, or look for it on pages L309–L325. *(page L329)*

To form the **future tense,** use the helping verb *shall* or *will* with the present form. *(page L329)*

Present perfect tense expresses an action that was completed at some indefinite time in the past. It also expresses an action that started in the past and is still going on. To form the present perfect tense, add *has* or *have* to the past participle. *(page L329)*

Past perfect tense expresses an action that took place before some other action. To form the past perfect tense, add *had* to the past participle. *(page L330)*

Future perfect tense expresses an action that will take place before another future action or time. To form the future perfect tense, add *shall have* or *will have* to the past participle. *(page L330)*

A **conjugation** is a list of all the singular and plural forms of a verb in all six tenses.

Other Information About Verbs

Using the correct forms of problem verbs *(pages L321–L325)*
Avoiding shifts in tense *(page L334)*
Using progressive verb forms *(pages L336–L337)*

Posttest

Directions
Read the passage and write the letter of the word or group of words that belongs in each underlined space.

    EXAMPLE
    1. In what year __(1)__ you born?

        1 A was
           B were
           C have
           D are

    ANSWER
    1 B

People are living longer today! In the past, many people __(1)__ their lives in one century. My mother __(2)__ from 1907 to 1987—eighty years. My life __(3)__ two centuries. For example, I __(4)__ my birth in 1940. Most likely, I __(5)__ before 2040 or soon after. By then, I __(6)__ in the twentieth and the twenty-first centuries.

Imagine your life spanning three centuries. __(7)__ about it. It __(8)__ to others. Why not you? You __(9)__ to be 115 years old or even older. If you live to the year 2100, you __(10)__ in the twentieth, twenty-first, and twenty-second centuries.

1 **A** lives
   B live
   C lived
   D has lived

2 **A** lives
   B is living
   C have lived
   D lived

3 **A** spans
   B will span
   C is spanning
   D will span

4 **A** celebrated
   B is celebrating
   C was celebrating
   D had celebrated

5 **A** died
   B dies
   C had died
   D will die

6 **A** will have lived
   B will live
   C lives
   D had lived

7 **A** Thinks
   B Think
   C Thinking
   D Thinked

8 **A** happening
   B happens
   C has happened
   D will happen

9 **A** has lived
   B could live
   C had lived
   D will have lived

10 **A** will have lived
   B live
   C lives
   D has lived

CHAPTER 12

Using Pronouns

Directions
Read the passage and write the letter of the word or group of words that belongs in each underlined space.

EXAMPLE   Mark and _(1)_ visited ancient ruins in Egypt.

      1 A her
         B him
         C I
         D me

ANSWER   **1 C**

Archaeology is the study of past civilizations. _(1)_ involves uncovering, or excavating, clues about people and _(2)_ cultures. An archaeologist studies artifacts, or handmade objects, found at excavations called "digs." _(3)_ are interested in _(4)_ digs and artifacts. Each artifact reveals information to historians and _(5)_.

In 1922, Howard Carter and _(6)_ archaeological team uncovered the entrance to King Tutankhamen's tomb. One of the greatest archaeological finds of all time was Carter's and _(7)_. For over three thousand years, this tomb and _(8)_ treasures had remained undisturbed. King Tut, as he is often called today, had been buried as king of Egypt with great treasures to honor _(9)_. _(10)_ could have foreseen such an amazing contribution to Egyptian culture?

1	**A**	He	**6**	**A**	my
	B	She		**B**	his
	C	It		**C**	your
	D	They		**D**	her
2	**A**	their	**7**	**A**	his
	B	my		**B**	ours
	C	his		**C**	it's
	D	our		**D**	theirs
3	**A**	No one	**8**	**A**	it's
	B	Someone		**B**	its
	C	Everybody		**C**	them
	D	Many		**D**	theirs
4	**A**	these	**9**	**A**	her
	B	her		**B**	him
	C	this		**C**	us
	D	we		**D**	them
5	**A**	it	**10**	**A**	Whom
	B	we		**B**	Who
	C	his		**C**	He
	D	us		**D**	Whose

Artist unknown, Egyptian.
*Tutankhamen, mask from
mummy case,* ca. 1343 B.C.
Gold, lapis lazuli, and cornelian,
height 21¼ inches. Egyptian
Museum, Cairo.

Describe Look at the mask. What objects did the
artist use to make Tutankhamen's mask?

Analyze How does the artist's use of repeated
patterns focus your attention?

Interpret What do you think was the artist's
purpose or goal when making
Tutankhamen's mask? How did the artist
accomplish his goal?

Judge Which of the facial features is the most
striking? Would you prefer to read a
character description about Tutankhamen
or to see his mask? Explain your answer.

At the end of this chapter, you will use the artwork to
stimulate ideas for writing.

The Cases of Personal Pronouns

The personal pronouns *he, him,* and *his* can all refer to the same person because pronouns have cases.

> Bob said **he** would take **his** brother with **him** to the stables.

Case is the form of a noun or pronoun that indicates its use in a sentence.

In English there are three cases: the nominative case, the objective case, and the possessive case.

NOMINATIVE CASE (used for subjects and predicate nominatives)		
	SINGULAR	PLURAL
FIRST PERSON	I	we
SECOND PERSON	you	you
THIRD PERSON	he, she, it	they

OBJECTIVE CASE (used for direct objects, indirect objects, and objects of prepositions)		
	SINGULAR	PLURAL
FIRST PERSON	me	us
SECOND PERSON	you	you
THIRD PERSON	him, her, it	them

POSSESSIVE CASE		
(used to show ownership or possession)		
	SINGULAR	PLURAL
FIRST PERSON	my, mine	our, ours
SECOND PERSON	your, yours	your, yours
THIRD PERSON	his, her, hers, its	their, theirs

PRACTICE YOUR SKILLS

● Check Your Understanding
Identifying the Cases of Personal Pronouns

Contemporary Life **Write the pronouns in each sentence. Label each pronoun *nominative*, *objective*, or *possessive*.**

1. They are going to the stables.
2. That is he on the tall chestnut horse.
3. I left my saddle in the barn.
4. We like riding through the countryside.
5. That saddle belongs to me.
6. Our riding instructor taught us to groom the horses.
7. My horse kept tossing its head.
8. Justin had trouble with his horse, too.
9. We tried to control our horses, but they wouldn't behave.
10. Please tell me how to keep my horse from stopping suddenly.

 The Nominative Case

The following list shows all the personal pronouns in the nominative case.

NOMINATIVE CASE		
	SINGULAR	PLURAL
FIRST PERSON	I	we
SECOND PERSON	you	you
THIRD PERSON	he, she, it	they

Pronouns in the nominative case are used two ways in sentences: as subjects and as predicate nominatives.

> The **nominative case** is used both for subjects and for predicate nominatives.

SUBJECT   **They** went to the library.

PREDICATE NOMINATIVE   The lady with the red book is **she.**

You can learn more about personal pronouns on pages L57–L58.

Pronouns Used as Subjects

A subject names the person, place, or thing the sentence is about. A pronoun used as a subject is in the nominative case.

SUBJECTS   **He** wrote his report.
              Did **they** drive to the library?

              (Turn a question into a statement: *They did drive to the library.* Then it is easy to find the subject.)

Sometimes a sentence has more than one subject.

> COMPOUND SUBJECT   Anna and (I, me) study daily.

To find the correct pronoun, say the sentence as if the pronoun stood alone.

> CORRECT   **I** study daily.
> INCORRECT   **Me** study daily.

When you separate the choices, it becomes easy to see and hear which pronoun is correct. In this sentence, the nominative case *I* is the correct form to use.

> CORRECT   Anna and **I** study daily.

You can learn more about finding subjects on pages L5–L9.

PRACTICE YOUR SKILLS

● Check Your Understanding
Using Pronouns as Subjects

 Read each sentence aloud, trying each pronoun separately. Then read the sentence again, choosing the correct pronoun.

1. Last night Fred and (I, me) studied social studies at the library.

2. The Riveras and (we, us) are going to the library after school today.

3. Are Marya and (he, him) doing a science experiment together?

4. Chuck and (she, her) are working together on their history project.

5. The Roys and (they, them) are taping our presentations.

6. Brendan and (I, me) made a model of the White House.

7. After school Tony and (he, him) went to Mr. Bennett's tutorial.

8. Have Min and (she, her) finished their math project?

9. Ali and (I, me) wrote a speech for our presentation together.

10. My parents and (they, them) will meet us at the local library.

● Check Your Understanding
Using Pronouns as Subjects

Science Topic **Write the correct personal pronoun for each sentence.**

11. (I, me) enjoyed reading *Born Free* by Joy Adamson.

12. (She, Her) adopted a lion cub.

13. (It, Their) was named Elsa.

14. George was Joy's husband, and (he, him) studied lions.

15. Together (they, them) learned much about these animals.

16. (We, Us) all have benefited from the Adamsons' experience.

17. Although Joy loved Elsa, (she, her) knew that the lion deserved to be free.

18. George and Joy did not want to give Elsa up, but (they, them) did.

19. George and (she, her) taught Elsa to be a wild lion.

20. Joy and (he, him) were very sad when Elsa finally set out on her own.

Pronouns Used as Predicate Nominatives

A **predicate nominative** is a word that follows a linking verb and identifies or renames the subject. A pronoun used as a predicate nominative is in the nominative case.

PREDICATE NOMINATIVE	My government teacher is **she.**
	Is the man from the Senate **he?**
	(Turn a question into a statement. *The man from the Senate is he.* It is easy to see that *he* renames *man.*)

In a compound predicate nominative, there is an easy way to choose the correct pronoun. Turn the sentence around. Use each pronoun as a subject. Then say the sentence as if the pronoun stood alone.

PREDICATE NOMINATIVE	The boys on stage are Bill and (he, him). Bill and (he, him) are the boys on stage.
CORRECT	**He** is on stage.
INCORRECT	**Him** is on stage.
CORRECT	The boys on stage are Bill and **he.**

Some of the sentences with pronouns used as predicate nominatives in this section may *sound* wrong, even though they are correct. When you write, you can avoid these awkward-sounding sentences. Simply reverse the sentences. Turn the predicate nominatives into subjects.

AWKWARD	My government teacher is **she.**
BETTER	**She** is my government teacher.
AWKWARD	The boys on stage are **Bill and he.**
BETTER	**Bill and he** are the boys on stage.

Expressions like *It's me* or *That's him* are becoming acceptable for informal use, especially in speech. When you write, however, the correct expressions to use are *It is I* and *That is he.*

You can learn more about linking verbs on pages L83–L87.

You can learn more about predicate nominatives on pages L165–L167.

PRACTICE YOUR SKILLS

● Check Your Understanding
Using Pronouns as Predicate Nominatives

Oral Expression

Turn each sentence around to make the predicate nominative the subject. Say each pronoun aloud to find out which one is correct. Read each sentence aloud again, choosing the correct pronoun.

1. The best candidate is (she, her).

2. The two people next to Senator Jensen are Mr. Ricker and (she, her).

3. The election monitors will be the teachers or (we, us).

4. The two candidates were Carlos and (I, me).

5. The winners of the election are Tara and (he, him).

● Check Your Understanding
Using Pronouns as Predicate Nominatives

Contemporary Life

Write the correct personal pronoun for each sentence.

6. The best actor to play Romeo was (he, him).

7. That's (he, him) in the movie with Clare Danes.

8. My two favorite actors are Leonardo DiCaprio and (she, her).

9. That's (I, me) in the picture with the movie star.

10. The winner of the award for best actress will be Whoopi Goldberg or (she, her).

11. The extras in the movie will be the boys from Detroit or (we, us).

12. Was that (she, her) in the hot pink costume at the movie premiere last night?

13. My favorite directors are Steven Spielberg and (he, him).

14. The two stunt doubles were Sidney and (I, me).

15. That was (they, them) in the opening scene.

● Check Your Understanding
Supplying Pronouns in the Nominative Case

Contemporary Life **Complete each sentence by writing an appropriate pronoun. Do not use *you* or *it*.**

16. Sandra and ▨ are riding the bus to school this year.

17. It's ▨ in the front seat.

18. On the night before school starts, ▨ can never get any sleep.

19. Laura and ▨ just got new clothes for school.

20. When did Wade and ▨ leave for school?

21. Our car pool drivers will be the Samlers and ▨.

22. Two new people in my class this year are Judy and ▨.

23. Were the teachers and ▨ at the conference?

24. Was the first person on the bus Sarah or ▨?

25. Did the Parkses and ▨ meet in front of the school?

● Connect to the Writing Process: Editing
Correcting Nominative Case Errors

If an underlined pronoun is in the wrong case, write it correctly. If it is in the correct case, write C.

26. The library aides for our class this year are Grace and <u>her</u>.

27. Is that <u>he</u> by the cafeteria?

28. The twins and <u>me</u> are making plans for a special treat at lunch.

29. Bob and <u>me</u> often like to work on science projects together.

30. Rico and <u>her</u> will have the same homeroom teacher this year.

31. The teachers and <u>them</u> are looking at the new mural.

32. The driver of the first car in the pickup line is <u>she</u>.

33. Mr. Santos and <u>us</u> are going to the science museum.

34. The cafeteria workers on the cleanup crew are <u>they</u>.

35. Should Cindy and <u>me</u> wait for you?

● Connect to the Writing Process: Drafting
Writing Sentences with Nominative Case Pronouns

Write five sentences, following the instructions below.

36. Use *she* as a subject.

37. Use *Patty and I* as a compound subject.

38. Use *neighbors and I* as a compound subject.

39. Use *they* as a predicate nominative.

40. Use *Ken and he* as a compound predicate nominative.

APPLY TO WRITING

Friendly Letter: *Nominative Case Pronouns*

You have started school and your grandmother wants to know all about the first couple of weeks. Write her a friendly letter that describes your first two weeks of school. Be sure to use pronouns in the nominative case both as subjects and as predicate nominatives. When you are finished, underline the nominative case pronouns you used.

QuickCheck Mixed Practice

Literature Topic **Write the correct personal pronoun for each sentence.**

1. (We, Us) are reading *Where the Red Fern Grows.*
2. (It, they) was written by Wilson Rawls.
3. I think my favorite writer is (he, him).
4. The main character works hard so that (he, him) can afford to buy some hunting dogs.
5. When the dogs arrive, (they, them) are little pups.
6. The boy and the dogs become friends, and (they, them) have many adventures together.
7. Ann is small, but (she, her) can think for herself.
8. I think my favorite dog is (she, her).
9. Old Dan is bigger, but (he, him) gets into trouble.
10. Little Ann and (he, him) have all sorts of adventures hunting together.

 The Objective Case

The following list shows all the personal pronouns in the
objective case.

	OBJECTIVE CASE	
	SINGULAR	PLURAL
FIRST PERSON	me	us
SECOND PERSON	you	you
THIRD PERSON	him, her, it	them

Pronouns in the objective case are used in three ways in
sentences.

The **objective case** is used for direct objects, indirect
objects, and objects of prepositions.

DIRECT OBJECT	Barry will call **her** tonight after his flight.
INDIRECT OBJECT	Mom gave **us** new suitcases.
OBJECT OF A PREPOSITION	Is Corey going with **them** to the airport?

Pronouns Used as Direct and Indirect Objects

A pronoun used as a direct object or an indirect object is
in the objective case. A **direct object** follows an action verb
and answers the questions *Whom?* and *What?*

DIRECT OBJECT	Tom took **us** to the station.
	(Tom took whom? *Us* is the direct object.)

Did your dad take **you** to the station?

(Turn a question into a statement. *Your dad did take you to the station.* Your dad did take whom? *You* is the direct object.)

You can learn more about direct objects on pages L157–L158.

An **indirect object** comes before a direct object and answers the question *To or for whom?* or *To or for what?*

INDIRECT OBJECT Ron gave **her** a ticket.

(Ron gave what? *Ticket* is the direct object. Ron gave a ticket to whom? *Her* is the indirect object.)

Give **them** some film.

(Give what? *Film* is the direct object. Give film to whom? *Them* is the indirect object.)

Mom wrote **her** the instructions.

(Wrote what? *Instructions* is the direct object. Wrote for whom? *Her* is the indirect object.)

You can learn more about indirect objects on pages L161–L162.

To choose the correct pronoun for a compound object, just say the sentence as if the pronoun stood alone.

DIRECT OBJECT Mom called Marty and (I, me).

INCORRECT Mom called **I.**

CORRECT Mom called **me.**

CORRECT Mom called Marty and **me.**

INDIRECT OBJECT	Gail gave Emma and (she, her) a camera.
INCORRECT	Gail gave **she** a camera.
CORRECT	Gail gave **her** a camera.
CORRECT	Gail gave Emma and **her** a camera.

PRACTICE YOUR SKILLS

● Check Your Understanding
Using Pronouns as Direct and Indirect Objects

 Read each sentence aloud, trying each pronoun separately. Then read the sentence aloud again, choosing the correct pronoun.

1. Give Mom or (we, us) your suitcase.

2. Grandpa told Pepe and (I, me) stories about his last vacation.

3. Did you see the Wilsons or (they, them) this morning?

4. You should have called (we, us) from the airport.

5. Will you drive Aretha and (I, me) to the train station?

6. Mr. Sims promised Pedro and (I, me) a reduced rate on our tickets.

7. Show Earl and (he, him) the pictures from your trip.

8. Did you find Aaron and (she, her) at the wax museum?

9. The onlookers applauded Betty-Sue and (he, him) at the subway station.

10. Evelyn sent Alma and (they, them) a postcard.

Using Pronouns as Direct and Indirect Objects

Write the correct personal pronoun for each sentence.

11. Joe told (we, us) the new plays for Saturday's game.

12. Give the equipment manager or (they, them) your uniform.

13. The cheerleaders sent Tom and (he, him) some goody bags before the game.

14. Did you see my neighbors or (they, them) in the stands at the game?

15. The crowd cheered Robert and (he, him) for their great team effort.

16. You should have asked (we, us) for help with the new plays.

17. Did you find Alex and (she, her) after the football game yesterday?

18. Will you throw David and (I, me) a few practice passes now?

19. Show Eddie and (he, him) the videotape from the game.

20. Coach Burns promised Sam and (I, me) jobs as mascots last season.

Pronouns Used as Objects of Prepositions

A prepositional phrase begins with a preposition, such as *to, for, near,* or *by.* A prepositional phrase ends with the object of the preposition. A pronoun that is used as the object of a preposition is in the objective case.

OBJECTS OF PREPOSITIONS	Is the party for **me?**
	(*For me* is the prepositional phrase.)
	The video was about **him.**
	(*About him* is the prepositional phrase.)

An easy way to choose the correct pronoun in a compound object of a preposition is to say the sentence as if the pronoun stood alone.

OBJECT OF A PREPOSITION	The birthday party was planned by Ian and (she, her).
INCORRECT	The birthday party was planned by **she.**
CORRECT	The birthday party was planned by **her.**
CORRECT	The birthday party was planned by Ian and **her.**

CONNECT TO SPEAKING AND WRITING

A common mistake occurs with the preposition *between*. When people try to sound formal or correct, they will often use nominative case pronouns after *between*. However, all pronouns used as objects of a preposition should be in the objective case. In this case, the more common-sounding expression is correct.

INCORRECT	The cheesecake was divided between **she** and **I.**
CORRECT	The cheesecake was divided between **her** and **me.**

You can learn more about prepositions and prepositional phrases on pages L189–L197.

PRACTICE YOUR SKILLS

● Check Your Understanding
Using Pronouns as Objects of Prepositions

Oral
Expression
Read each sentence aloud, trying each pronoun separately. Then read the sentence aloud again, choosing the correct pronoun.

1. The party is for Tony and (he, him).

2. Jody will give a party for Glen and (I, me) next month.

3. This present is from Keith and (she, her).

4. The bill for the cake will be paid by the Morrisons and (we, us).

5. Is that orange soda for Barney or (he, him)?

6. Hard workers like (they, them) should be invited.

7. I will share my good party pictures with you and (she, her).

8. Send those clear photographs to the Smiths and (they, them).

9. Who will dance with Sara and (they, them)?

10. This is a photograph of Tony and (we, us).

● Check Your Understanding
Using Pronouns as Objects of Prepositions

Contemporary
Life
Write the correct personal pronoun for each sentence.

11. The duet was written for Barry and (she, her).

12. The play will be financed by the Smiths and (we, us).

13. Good singers like (they, them) should audition.

14. I will share my script with you and (she, her).

15. Will someone run lines with Ben and (I, me)?

16. Arthur's musical ability was a surprise for (we, us).

17. The play was directed by Thomas and (he, him).

18. Give these costumes to Billy and (they, them).

19. Is that prop for Will or (he, him)?

20. The play was about (she, her).

Check Your Understanding
Supplying Pronouns in the Objective Case

Contemporary Life **Complete each sentence by writing an appropriate pronoun. Do not use *you* or *it*.**

21. Mr. Porter gave Maureen and ▇ usher uniforms.

22. Has Justin given the scripts to Doyle and ▇?

23. Will you give Janine and ▇ some makeup?

24. Leila ran across the stage after Rona and ▇.

25. The Langs invited Cora and ▇ to opening night.

26. My sister always beats Carlos and ▇ to the theater after school.

27. Jeff won't go on without Ronnie and ▇.

28. Mom offered Joyce and ▇ a ride home from rehearsal.

29. Rico just received his costume from Rob and ▇.

30. Dad bought Liz and ▇ a CD of the musical.

Connect to the Writing Process: Editing
Correcting Objective Case Errors

If an underlined pronoun is in the wrong case, write it correctly. If it is in the correct case, write *C*.

31. Mr. Daniels drove Doris and I to play practice.

32. These are the scripts for the new actors and he.

33. Has Jamie given Douglas and she any lines yet?

34. Please give Amanda and <u>he</u> some advice on learning their lines.

35. One line is enough for Sharon and <u>me</u>.

Connect to the Writing Process: Drafting
Writing Sentences with Objective Case Pronouns

Write five sentences, following the instructions below.

36. Use *him* as a direct object.

37. Use *James or her* as a compound direct object.

38. Use *us* as an indirect object.

39. Use *Carrie and me* as a compound indirect object.

40. Use *me* as the object of the preposition *about*.

Communicate Your Ideas

APPLY TO WRITING

Announcement: *Pronouns in the Objective Case*

Your drama coach has asked you to write an announcement reminding the cast of the play to attend a special rehearsal today after school. Before you begin writing, jot down answers to the following questions:

- What is the rehearsal for?
- At what time is the rehearsal?
- Where is the rehearsal?
- What should students bring with them?

Be sure to use pronouns in the objective case correctly. When you have finished, underline the objective pronouns you used.

Contemporary
Life **Write the correct personal pronoun for each sentence.**

1. Give Mrs. Nesbitt or (we, us) your topic for your research paper.

2. The teacher gave Sheila and (I, me) a special classroom job.

3. I will share all of my history notes with you and (she, her).

4. Give Melinda and (he, him) some of those large index cards.

5. Dad showed Joan and (he, him) a good Website for research.

6. Who wants to go to the library with Sam and (I, me)?

7. Mrs. Nesbitt told Myrna and (he, him) the good news about the special books.

8. Those science books are reserved for Sandy and (I, me).

9. Show Carl and (he, him) the Internet connection.

10. You should have asked (we, us) for some help with your topic.

11. The teacher promised Dave and (she, her) an extra day for research.

12. Please teach (I, me) the correct form for an outline.

13. Give these encyclopedias to (she, her).

14. Ask Mr. Venegas about (they, them).

15. Mrs. Nesbitt dropped (he, him) a hint about an article for his paper.

The Possessive Case

The following list shows all the personal pronouns in the possessive case.

POSSESSIVE CASE		
	SINGULAR	PLURAL
FIRST PERSON	my, mine	our, ours
SECOND PERSON	your, yours	your, yours
THIRD PERSON	his, her, hers, its	their, theirs

The **possessive case** is used to show ownership or possession.

Possessive pronouns are divided into two groups: (1) those used like adjectives to modify nouns, and (2) those used alone.

USES OF POSSESSIVE PRONOUNS	
USED LIKE ADJECTIVES	my, your, his, her, its, our, your, their
USED ALONE	mine, yours, his, hers, its, ours, yours, theirs

My dog is brown, but **hers** is gray.

Her dog is young, but **mine** is old.

Pronouns used as adjectives are sometimes called possessive *adjectives.*

Although apostrophes are used with possessive nouns, they are not used with possessive forms of personal pronouns.

POSSESSIVE NOUN	Is this **Jill's** dog?
POSSESSIVE PRONOUN	Is this dog **hers?** (not *her's*)

PRACTICE YOUR SKILLS

● Check Your Understanding
Using Possessive Pronouns

Oral Expression **Read each sentence aloud, trying each pronoun separately. Then read the sentence aloud again, choosing the correct pronoun.**

1. Where is (your, yours) dog?

2. (My, Mine) is walking in front of the judges' stand.

3. That dog looks a lot like (her, hers).

4. (Their, Theirs) golden retriever won the dog show last year.

5. The dog with the red collar is (our, ours).

6. Which one is (your, yours)?

7. (Her, Hers) poodle is very well behaved.

8. It looks as if the ribbon will be (their, theirs).

9. I had hoped that (my, mine) dog would get a ribbon this year.

10. (Our, Ours) dog did win the obedience portion of the contest.

● Check Your Understanding
Using Pronouns in the Possessive Case

Sports Topic **Write the correct personal pronoun for each sentence.**

11. Which pair of skates is (your, yours)?

12. I got (my, mine) new skates last week.

13. (Our, Ours) skating instructor is teaching us to spin.

14. Are those skates (her, hers)?

15. (Their, Theirs) class is going to a competition next week.

Correcting Possessive Pronouns

If an underlined pronoun is incorrect, write it correctly. If it is correct, write C.

16. I like <u>mine</u> new skating instructor.

17. <u>Her</u> suggestions are easy to follow.

18. The first class on the ice was <u>our</u>.

19. <u>Yours</u> skates were in the locker room.

20. The team with the most first-place ribbons is <u>theirs</u>.

Possessive Pronoun or Contraction?

Because some contractions sound like personal pronouns, people sometimes confuse them in their writing.

POSSESSIVE PRONOUNS AND CONTRACTIONS	
POSSESSIVE PRONOUNS	its, your, their, theirs
CONTRACTIONS	it's (it is), you're (you are), they're (they are), there's (there is)

The best way to separate these words in your mind is to say the two words that a contraction stands for.

POSSESSIVE PRONOUN OR CONTRACTION	(You're, Your) grill is here.
INCORRECT	**You are** grill is here.
CORRECT	**Your** grill is here.

You can learn more about contractions on pages L605–L606.

PRACTICE YOUR SKILLS

● Check Your Understanding

Oral Expression	**Read each sentence aloud, trying each word separately. Remember to say the two words that make up a contraction. Then read each sentence again, choosing the correct pronoun.**

1. Where is (your, you're) apartment?

2. (Its, It's) going to rain tomorrow, so the picnic will have to be at your place.

3. (Hers, Her's) is the best place for a cookout.

4. (Their, They're) car just drove up to your apartment building.

5. (Your, You're) the perfect person to host this picnic.

6. (Theirs, There's) a surprise waiting for you after the picnic.

7. The watermelon is (ours, our's).

8. We should join them at (their, they're) house.

9. My soda lost (its, it's) fizz by the end of the picnic.

10. (Theirs, There's) is the only sugar-free dessert.

● Connect to the Writing Process: Drafting
Writing Sentences with Possessive Pronouns and Contractions

Write sentences, using one of the following words in each.

11. mine   **16.** it's

12. hers   **17.** they're

13. its   **18.** you're

14. your   **19.** there's

15. his   **20.** ours

APPLY TO WRITING

Writer's Craft: *Analyzing the Use of Pronouns*

Read these lines from the poem "Oranges" by Gary Soto. Then answer the following questions about the use of pronouns.

> Outside,
> A few cars hissing past,
> Fog hanging like old
> Coats between the trees.
> I took my girl's hand
> In mine for two blocks,
> Then released it to let
> Her unwrap the chocolate.
> I peeled my orange
> That was so bright against
> The gray of December
> That, from some distance,
> Someone might have thought
> I was making a fire in my hands.
>
> —*Gary Soto,* "Oranges"

- List the personal pronouns in this poem.
- Label how each pronoun was used: subject, predicate nominative, direct object, indirect object, object of the infinitive, object of the preposition, possessive pronoun.
- Was there any type of pronoun that the writer did not use? If so, what is it?
- How would the poem be different if the poet had not used pronouns?

Science Topic **Write the correct personal pronoun for each sentence.**

1. Last week (I, me) learned about sharks in science.

2. Sharks make (their, they're) homes in the temperate oceans around the world.

3. Long teeth help the shark capture (it, its) prey.

4. The best-known shark scientists are Dr. Eugenie Clark and (he, him).

5. The shark was swimming toward (they, them).

6. When one diver was bothered by a shark, she gave (it, its) a sharp blow to the head.

7. The surprised shark left (she, her) alone.

8. Most great white sharks are quite large, and (they, them) can weigh as much as seven thousand pounds.

9. Dr. Eugenie Clark and (she, her) will be lecturing at our school next week.

10. We hope she will tell (we, us) some new information about sharks.

11. Carl and (she, her) did not know that sharks have boneless skeletons.

12. (Their, Theirs) bodies are sleek.

13. Have Karen and (he, him) seen the shark exhibit at the aquarium?

14. Laurie pointed out the model of the shark to Frank and (I, me).

15. (They're, Their) babies are called pups.

Pronoun Problem: *Who* or *Whom?*

In an earlier chapter you learned that some pronouns are called **interrogative pronouns** because they are used to ask questions. The interrogative pronouns *who* and *whom* have case just as personal pronouns do.

Because *who* is in the nominative case, it is used as a subject.

> SUBJECT **Who** wrote that book?

Because *whom* is in the objective case, it is used as a direct object or an object of the preposition.

> DIRECT OBJECT **Whom** did you suspect?
> (Turn a question into a statement:
> *You did suspect whom?*
> *Whom* is the direct object.)
>
> OBJECT OF THE PREPOSITION From **whom** did you get that information?
> (*From whom* is a prepositional phrase.)

Whose can also be used an interrogative pronoun. It always shows possession.

> **Whose** books are these? (whose as an adjective)
> Looking at both stacks of books, we didn't know **whose** were **whose!** (whose as a pronoun)

Be careful not to confuse the pronoun *whose* with the contraction *who's*. *Who's* stands for *who is*.

You can learn more about interrogative pronouns on pages L62–L63.

PRACTICE YOUR SKILLS

● Check Your Understanding
Using Who and Whom Correctly

Contemporary Life **Write the correct word in parentheses for each sentence.**

1. (Whose, Who's) is this mystery book?
2. (Who, Whom) is your favorite character in the book?
3. About (who, whom) was the novel written?
4. (Who, Whom) is the author?
5. (Who, Whom) did you believe was really telling the truth?
6. (Whose, Who's) was the best alibi?
7. From (who, whom) did you pick up most of your clues?
8. (Who, Whom) did the detective question about the crime?
9. (Who, Whom) committed the crime?
10. (Whose, Who's) giving the book report on the next mystery story?

● Connect to the Writing Process: Drafting
Writing Sentences with Interrogative Pronouns

Write five sentences, following the instructions below.

11. Use *who* as a subject.
12. Use *whose* as a possessive pronoun.
13. Use *whom* as the object of a preposition.
14. Use *whom* as a direct object.
15. Use *who's* as a subject and verb.

Pronouns and Their Antecedents

The word that a pronoun refers to, or replaces, is called the pronoun's **antecedent.**

PRONOUNS AND ANTECEDENTS	**Ruth** left **her** ticket at the house.
	The **McGanns** are selling **their** cottage.

In the preceding sentences, *Ruth* is the antecedent of *her,* and *McGanns* is the antecedent of *their.* A pronoun and its antecedent should agree because they refer to the same person, place, or thing.

A pronoun must agree in number and gender with its antecedent.

Number is the term that indicates whether a noun or a pronoun is singular (one) or plural (more than one). A pronoun must be singular if its antecedent is singular. It must be plural if its antecedent is plural.

SINGULAR	**James** can't find **his** camera.
PLURAL	The **girls** can't find **their** cameras.

A pronoun must also agree with its antecedent in gender. **Gender** tells whether a noun or a pronoun is masculine, feminine, or neuter. *He, him,* and *his* are masculine. *She, her,* and *hers* are feminine. *It* and *its* are neuter.

MASCULINE	**Andrew** said that **he** wasn't feeling well.
FEMININE	**Judy** finished **her** vacation early.
NEUTER	The **car** blew **its** tire.

Plural pronouns such as *them* and *their* can refer to masculine, feminine, or neuter antecedents.

PRACTICE YOUR SKILLS

● Check Your Understanding
Making Pronouns and Their Antecedents Agree

Contemporary Life
Complete each sentence by writing an appropriate pronoun.

1. Janice is going on vacation with ▮ best friend.
2. Mom and Dad packed ▮ bags for the trip.
3. Thomas packed ▮ suitcase yesterday.
4. Susan forgot to pack ▮ bathing suit.
5. My brothers brought ▮ sleeping bags to the car this morning.
6. Did the girls bring ▮ hair dryers?
7. A raccoon ate ▮ breakfast on our hotel doorstep.
8. Ellen signed ▮ name on the postcard for Mr. Lee.
9. Peter took ▮ binoculars to the Grand Canyon.
10. Will the children remember ▮ toothbrushes?

● Connect to the Writing Process: Editing
Correcting Errors with Pronouns and Their Antecedents

Rewrite the following sentences, making sure each pronoun agrees with its antecedent. If a sentence is correct, write C.

11. Michelle found her camera on the sofa.
12. Jane finished his hamburger.
13. A pigeon flapped her wings and begged for food.
14. The boys took his video games on the trip to Alaska.
15. The Smiths are sending their children to camp for the summer.

Pronouns and Their Antecedents L377

⏵ Indefinite Pronouns as Antecedents

Sometimes an indefinite pronoun can be the antecedent of a personal pronoun. Some indefinite pronouns are singular and some are plural.

COMMON INDEFINITE PRONOUNS	
SINGULAR	anybody, anyone, another, anything, each, either, everybody, everyone, everything, neither, nobody, nothing, no one, one, somebody, someone, something
PLURAL	both, few, many, several

A personal pronoun must be singular if its antecedent is one of the singular indefinite pronouns.

SINGULAR   **One** of the girls can't find **her** shoes.

Somebody in the boys' gym lost **his** sneakers.

When the gender of a singular indefinite pronoun is not known, use *his or her* to refer to the indefinite pronoun.

SINGULAR   Everyone must practice **his or her** sprints.

Although the previous sentence is correct, it might still sound awkward. You can often eliminate an awkward sentence by rewriting it in the plural form.

PLURAL   All track team **members** must practice **their** sprints.

A personal pronoun must be plural if its antecedent is one of the plural indefinite pronouns.

PLURAL   **Several** of the girls can't find **their** coats in the locker room.

Many of the boys forgot **their** towels.

PRACTICE YOUR SKILLS

● Check Your Understanding
Making Pronouns and Their Antecedents Agree

Sports Topic   **Complete each sentence by writing an appropriate personal pronoun.**

1. Each of the girls on the track team wore ▮ school sweater to the game.

2. Only one of the other school teams wore ▮ sweaters to the game.

3. Both of my sisters like ▮ track coach very much.

4. Neither of my brothers remembered ▮ equipment for the meet today.

5. Several of the shoes in the locker room do not have ▮ laces.

6. Everyone on the boys' team wore ▮ jacket in honor of the victory.

7. Someone in the girls' locker room left ▮ locker open.

8. Many of the boys on the team take ▮ equipment home with them.

9. Either of my brothers will give you ▮ discus.

10. Few of the boys on the team have had ▮ physical examinations yet.

Correcting Errors with Pronouns and Their Antecedents

Rewrite the following sentences, making sure each pronoun agrees with its antecedent. If a sentence is correct, write C.

11. Everybody on the girls' teams tried his best.

12. Many of the spectators brought its cameras.

13. The city has improved his track fields.

14. Did anyone on the boys' team lose his key?

15. Each of the team members has their own locker.

Communicate Your Ideas

APPLY TO WRITING

Profile: *Pronouns and Their Antecedents*

The adviser to the school paper has asked you to profile the members of your track team. Write a short description of some of the people on your team. Be sure to use pronouns and their antecedents correctly.

Unclear or Missing Antecedents

If the pronouns you use do not have clear antecedents, the meaning of your writing or speaking can become confusing.

Every personal pronoun should clearly refer to a specific antecedent.

UNCLEAR	I don't like the ski lift because **you** might get stuck.
	(*You* is incorrectly used because it does not refer to the person being spoken to. Instead, it refers to the speaker.)
CLEAR	I don't like the ski lift because **I** might get stuck.
MISSING	After a long day of skating, **it** felt good.
	(What does *it* refer to in this sentence? The antecedent is missing.)
CLEAR	After a long day of skating, the **fire** felt good.

PRACTICE YOUR SKILLS

● Check Your Understanding
Recognizing Unclear or Missing Antecedents

Contemporary Life   **Write *I* for each antecedent that is unclear or missing and *C* for each antecedent that is used correctly.**

1. Jimmy likes the winter because he can go skiing.
2. At the end of a long day of skiing, it tastes delicious.

3. I knew Sally was a good skier, but I had never seen any of her skiing until yesterday.

4. I like skiing because you get to be outside.

5. Sue's ankle was swollen, but now it has disappeared.

6. Mom got a new ski pole so that she can ski better.

7. I enjoy watching other skiers because you can learn different techniques.

8. Ken emptied his pockets and let them fall to the floor.

9. I have never tried a ski jump, but I still enjoy skiing.

10. I usually go skiing early in the morning because then I have the whole day to ski.

● Connect to the Writing Process: Revising
Correcting Sentences with Unclear or Missing Antecedents

11.–16. **Rewrite the incorrect sentences from the preceding exercise, making the antecedents clear.**

Communicate Your Ideas

APPLY TO WRITING

Persuasive Paragraphs: *Unclear or Missing Antecedents*

Your friend wants to take up a new sport or hobby but is not sure which one to try. You want your friend to try something that you like to do so that the two of you can spend more time together. In a paragraph or two, persuade your friend to try your favorite sport or hobby by explaining all the good things about your favorite activity. Be sure to avoid missing or unclear antecedents.

Contemporary Life

Correct each underlined pronoun that is used incorrectly. If the pronoun is correct, write C.

1. <u>Whom</u> is cooking the dinner tomorrow night?

2. Everyone says John is a good cook, but I have never tasted any of <u>it</u>.

3. Each of the people in my group will bring <u>our</u> favorite dessert to the dinner.

4. From <u>whom</u> did you get this recipe?

5. Most of the recipe books in my house do not have <u>its</u> covers.

6. Few of the boys want to admit that <u>their</u> cooking skills are good.

7. My dad likes to get up early Saturday mornings because <u>you</u> have more time to make breakfast.

8. <u>Who's</u> is that cake?

9. Carrie emptied the pitcher and let <u>it</u> pour into the sink.

10. Mom got a new mixer so that <u>she</u> can make cakes more easily.

11. Clarence made a chocolate cake for <u>his</u> girlfriend.

12. The Browns are making <u>its</u> favorite casserole dish.

13. <u>Who</u> will you invite to the dinner?

14. My parents and <u>us</u> are looking forward to this holiday dinner.

15. Neither of my sisters remembered <u>her</u> table manners.

Using Pronouns in the Correct Case

Write the correct personal pronoun for each sentence.

1. The coach put James and (I, me) in the game in the last quarter.
2. Michael went to the basketball game with Rebecca and (she, her).
3. Did Eli or (he, him) make this bread?
4. Joan snapped a picture of Lana and (I, me).
5. Ron didn't know for (who, whom) the invitation to the party was intended.
6. Uncle George told Dad and (we, us) some good jokes.
7. That climb won't be hard for Sam and (she, her).
8. It must be (they, them) on the dock.
9. Did (he, him) and Rudy study their Spanish notes at the library today?
10. (Who, Whom) went to the store for potatoes earlier today?

Correcting Pronoun Errors

Write each sentence using the correct pronoun form. If a sentence needs no change, write C.

1. Mr. Daniels drove Doris and I to the stadium.
2. The cooks tonight are Grace and her.
3. For whom was the money intended?
4. Mom gave Megan and he the good news.
5. The Wongs and us are having a barbecue on the Fourth of July weekend.

6. Whom could that be in the plaid shirt?
7. Joyce went canoeing with Ginnie and we.
8. May Allie and me go for a swim after lunch?
9. The invitation is for Martha and me.
10. Rico and him live on the same street.

Making Pronouns Agree with Antecedents

Write a personal pronoun that correctly completes each sentence.

1. Neither of the boys could finish ▨ dinner.
2. Julie hasn't found ▨ glasses yet.
3. Many of the members have paid ▨ club dues.
4. Somebody has left the lights on in ▨ car.
5. A few of the fathers played soccer with ▨ daughters.
6. Should Carlos bring ▨ sunscreen to the beach?
7. Each of my sisters is looking for a job during ▨ summer vacation.
8. A turtle must carry ▨ home all the time.
9. One of the girls left ▨ sweater on the bus.
10. All of the students must turn in ▨ homework.

Using Pronouns Correctly

Write ten sentences that follow the directions below.

Write a sentence that . . .

1. includes *Bill and I* as the subject.
2. includes *him and her* as the indirect object.
3. includes the words *your* and *you're*.
4. includes the word *who*.
5. includes *everyone* as the subject.

Language and *Self-Expression*

An unknown artist made the mummy case for Tutankhamen in Egypt about 1340 B.C. The gold, precious stones, and craftsmanship show how members of the royal family were honored after death. The headdress with its serpent symbols represents a pharaoh of Egypt. King Tut was a youthful and well-loved pharaoh. How does the artist capture these attributes?

Choose a positive role model and write a character sketch about him or her. Use pronouns correctly and avoid unclear or incorrect antecedents. Include symbols and images that represent characteristics of your subject's personality and community status.

Prewriting Draw a cluster diagram showing symbols that depicts your subject's contributions or personality. Rank the symbols from most to least important.

Drafting Begin with a sentence that identifies your subject and sets the tone of his or her personality. Choose two or three symbols that best signify the person's contributions, and draw comparisons.

Revising Ask a partner to read your sketch for clarity. If your partner finds a symbol confusing, discuss its importance, and make changes as needed. Check pronoun usage.

Editing Reword sentences in which pronoun antecedents are unclear. Check for correct possessive forms of pronouns.

Publishing Prepare a final copy of your character sketch. Draw a mask and ask classmates to identify your subject before sharing your sketch with them.

Another Look

Case is the form of a noun or pronoun that indicates its use in a sentence.

The Cases of Personal Pronouns
The **nominative case** is used for subjects and predicate nominatives. *(pages L349–L354)*

The **objective case** is used for direct objects, indirect objects, and objects of prepositions. *(pages L349 and L359)*

The **possessive case** is used to show ownership or possession. *(pages L350 and L368)*

A **direct object** follows an action verb and answers the question *Whom?* or *What? (pages L359–L360)*

An **indirect object** comes before a direct object and answers the questions *To or for whom?* or *To or for what? (page L360)*

Possessive pronouns can be used as pronoun adjectives or alone. *(page L368)*

Some pronouns are called **interrogative pronouns** because they are used to ask questions. The interrogative pronouns *who* and *whom* have case just like personal pronouns. *(page L374)*

Pronouns and Their Antecedents
A pronoun must agree in number and gender with its antecedent. *(page L376)*

Number is the term that indicates whether a noun or a pronoun is singular (one) or plural (more than one). *(page L376)*

Gender is the term that indicates whether a noun or a pronoun is masculine, feminine, or neuter. *(page L376)*

Every personal pronoun should clearly refer to a specific antecedent. *(page L381)*

Other Information About Pronouns
Using pronouns as subjects *(pages L351–L352)*
Using pronouns as predicate nominatives *(pages L354–L355)*
Using pronouns as direct and indirect objects *(pages L359–L361)*
Using pronouns as objects of prepositions *(pages L362–L363)*
Using possessive pronouns and contractions correctly *(page L370)*
Using indefinite pronouns as antecedents *(pages L378–L379)*

Posttest

Directions

Read the passage and write the letter of the word or group of words that belongs in each underlined space.

EXAMPLE   I shared __(1)__ lunch with somebody on the tour bus in Egypt.

        1 A mine
           B me
           C its
           D my

ANSWER   **1 D**

__(1)__ on __(2)__ tour bus is fascinated with the history of ancient Egypt. __(3)__ are learning much about Egyptian culture on this tour. The tour guide explained that ancient Egyptians cared very much about __(4)__ appearance. An Egyptian woman, for example, would paint __(5)__ nails red with henna and wear large, round earrings. An Egyptian man would shave __(6)__ beard and head with a razor.

__(7)__ have learned other interesting facts about Egypt on this tour as well. As early as 5000 B.C., writing in the form of hieroglyphs appeared. __(8)__ could have taken our first chariot ride in Egypt in 1600 B.C! __(9)__ also learned that between 1567 B.C. and 1070 B.C., Egypt had __(10)__ first female pharoah, Queen Hatshepsut, and later a boy king, Tutankhamen.

1 **A** Many
   B All
   C Everyone
   D Few

2 **A** its
   B mine
   C our
   D them

3 **A** Us
   B It
   C I
   D We

4 **A** their
   B his or her
   C his or hers
   D theirs

5 **A** your
   B my
   C his
   D her

6 **A** my
   B his
   C her
   D their

7 **A** Me
   B Us
   C You
   D We

8 **A** You and me
   B You and I
   C You and my
   D You and him

9 **A** She
   B We
   C They
   D Them

10 **A** their
   B its
   C his
   D my

CHAPTER 13

Subject and Verb Agreement

• •

Directions
Read the passage and write the letter of the word or group of words that belongs in each underlined space.

> EXAMPLE
>
> I _(1)_ the birds and squirrels in my backyard.
>
> **1 A** enjoys
> **B** enjoy
> **C** enjoying
> **D** will enjoys
>
> ANSWER   **1 B**

Natural resources and wildlife often _(1)_ easy to identify. Regional environmental education centers are great resources. They _(2)_ hands-on experience. _(3)_ you have a center near you? The center near me _(4)_ programs year round. One program about the history and methods of making maple syrup _(5)_ for this month. Another, Animal Tracking Techniques, draws some amateur detectives every time it is offered.

In northeastern Pennsylvania, white-tailed deer and red foxes _(6)_ familiar backyard visitors. A gaggle of geese _(7)_ temporarily on small ponds. Groundhogs, on the other hand, _(8)_ housekeeping. They _(9)_ underground homes and make huge holes in the yard. Either woodpeckers or sapsuckers _(10)_ the biggest nuisance award because they drill holes in houses.

1 A has been
   B am
   C is
   D are

2 A provides
   B provide
   C was providing
   D providing

3 A Doing
   B Doesn't
   C Do
   D Does

4 A have offered
   B offer
   C offers
   D offering

5 A is scheduled
   B are scheduled
   C were scheduled
   D have been
      scheduled

6 A are
   B is
   C am
   D was

7 A lands
   B have landed
   C were landed
   D do land

8 A does set up
   B has set up
   C sets up
   D set up

9 A has built
   B build
   C is building
   D builds

10 A win
   B wins
   C winning
   D has win

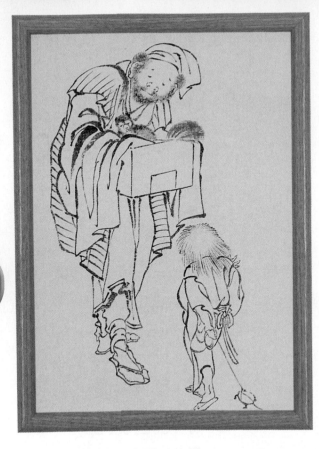

Katsushika Hokusai.
Man and Boy, Edo period
(1658–1868).
Ink on paper, 12 $^{11}/_{16}$ by 8$^{11}/_{16}$
inches. Freer Gallery of Art,
Washington, D.C.

Describe What figures are in this drawing? What
kinds of lines do you see? Where are lines
repeated or dark?

Analyze What elements does the artist use to
create unity between the two figures?

Interpret What message do you think the artist is
trying to express about the man and the
boy?

Judge Do you think this drawing or a story
about these characters would more
effectively express the same ideas? Why
do you think as you do?

At the end of this chapter, you will use the artwork as a
visual aid for writing.

Agreement of Subjects and Verbs

Something is wrong with these sentences.

> He don't like spaghetti.
> Is you taking Spanish this year?

Read the following sentences. This time the form of the verbs has been changed.

> He **does**n't like spaghetti.
> **Are** you taking Spanish this year?

Now the sentences are correct because there is agreement between each verb and its subject. One basic agreement rule applies to all subjects and verbs.

A verb must agree with its subject in number.

 Number

Number is the term used to indicate whether a word is singular or plural. In this chapter you will see that nouns, pronouns, and verbs all have number and that the number of a subject and a verb must agree.

The Number of Nouns and Pronouns

The plural of most nouns is formed by adding –s or –es to the singular form.

	REGULAR NOUNS	
SINGULAR	truck	potato
PLURAL	trucks	potatoes

A few nouns, however, form their plurals in other ways. A dictionary always lists an irregular plural.

IRREGULAR NOUNS		
SINGULAR	mouse	child
PLURAL	**mice**	**children**

Pronouns can also be singular or plural. *I, he, she,* and *it* are singular, and *we* and *they* are plural. *You* can be singular or plural.

You can learn about spelling plural nouns on pages L647–L651.

PRACTICE YOUR SKILLS

● Check Your Understanding
Determining the Number of Nouns and Pronouns

Label each word *singular* or *plural*.

1. Ohio **5.** they **9.** glove **13.** flower

2. test **6.** lamps **10.** she **14.** it

3. boxes **7.** shoe **11.** we **15.** flags

4. vases **8.** men **12.** horse **16.** car

The Number of Verbs

In the present tense, most verbs add *–s* or *–es* to form the singular. Plural forms in the present tense do not end in *–s* or *–es.*

SINGULAR   PLURAL

The boy { sings.   The boys { sing.
         laughs.   laugh.
         catches.   catch.

Be, have, and *do,* however, have special singular and plural forms in the present tense. *Be* also has special forms in the past tense.

	FORMS OF *BE, HAVE,* AND *DO*	
	SINGULAR	PLURAL
be	am, is (present) was (past)	are (present) were (past)
have	has	have
do	does	do

In the following examples, each subject is underlined once, and each verb is underlined twice.

SINGULAR   She is my best friend.
Patty was my best friend.
Lance has a new friend.

PLURAL   They are my friends also.
Tim and my cousin were good friends.
The Morrisons have some nice friends.

PRACTICE YOUR SKILLS

● Check Your Understanding
Determining the Number of Verbs

Write each verb and label it *singular* or *plural*.

1. Alvin enjoys
2. twins have
3. students play
4. he was
5. truck has

6. we do
7. it is
8. they drive
9. pictures are
10. Pauline does

▶ Singular and Plural Subjects

The number of a verb must agree with the number of its noun or pronoun subject.

A singular subject takes a singular verb.

A plural subject takes a plural verb.

To make a verb agree with its subject, ask yourself two questions: *What is the subject?* and *Is the subject singular or plural?* Then choose the correct verb form. In the following sentences, each subject is underlined once, and each verb is underlined twice.

SINGULAR	Kristen dances gracefully.
PLURAL	They dance gracefully.
SINGULAR	Matt was in a hurry.
PLURAL	They were in a hurry.

PRACTICE YOUR SKILLS

● Check Your Understanding
Making Subjects and Verbs Agree

 Read the following sentences aloud, trying out both forms of the verb in parentheses. Ask yourself whether the subject is singular or plural. Read each sentence aloud again, choosing the correct verb form.

1. Susan (practices, practice) her new dance routine every day.

2. They (studies, study) ballet on Tuesday nights.

3. Geraldine (stretches, stretch) her legs before she starts to dance.

4. Madame (instructs, instruct) her pupils in the most difficult ballet movements.

5. The girls (performs, perform) for their parents.

6. The dancers (is, are) beautiful in their costumes.

7. The dance school (has, have) almost one hundred pupils.

8. Jenny (do, does) enjoy her dance classes.

9. The students (were, was) at class on time.

10. They (surprises, surprise) their teacher constantly.

Check Your Understanding
Making Subjects and Verbs Agree

Science
Topic
Write each subject and label it *singular* or *plural*. Then write the form of the verb in parentheses that agrees with the subject.

11. Brown pelicans (dives, dive) into the ocean for fish.

12. A white pelican (scoops, scoop) fish out of the water just below the surface.

13. Mockingbirds (eats, eat) insects.

14. Owls (flies, fly) almost noiselessly.

15. The short-eared owl (helps, help) control rodents.

16. All birds (has, have) special colors and songs.

17. Male blue jays (is, are) a different color than female blue jays.

18. An average condor (have, has) a wingspan of more than nine feet.

19. A duck's webbed feet (acts, act) as paddles.

20. The trumpeter swan (is, are) the largest of all water birds.

Correcting for Subject and Verb Agreement

Write correctly each sentence in which the subject and verb do not agree. If a sentence is correct, write C.

21. Ravens are very clever birds.

22. The bald eagle are the symbol of the United States and its national bird.

23. The mockingbird imitate the calls of many different kinds of birds.

24. Cardinals likes evergreen trees for their nests.

25. A robin likes earthworms.

26. Urban pigeons lives in towns and cities.

27. The mourning dove are named for its sad, cooing call.

28. Ostriches mainly eats plants.

29. Penguins spend most of their time in the ocean.

30. Hawks look for prey on the ground below them.

Communicate Your Ideas

APPLY TO WRITING

Descriptive Paragraph: *Subject-Verb Agreement*

A local biologist is preparing a presentation about birds in your area. He will be making a presentation to the city council so that they can make decisions about future development. The biologist has asked the students at your school to write a descriptive paragraph about their favorite types of birds and their habits. Be sure that the subjects and verbs agree in your description.

Science
Topic
Write each subject and label it *singular* or *plural*. Then write the form of the verb in parentheses that agrees with the subject.

1. Big cats (is, are) predators.
2. The lion (is, are) the king of beasts.
3. Lions (lives, live) in the African grassland.
4. They (eats, eat) gazelles, antelopes, and zebras.
5. A male lion (weighs, weigh) almost 550 pounds.
6. Lionesses (do, does) most of the hunting for the pride.
7. All the lions (cares, care) for the lion cubs.
8. A pride (contains, contain) as many as forty lions.
9. Lions (sleeps, sleep) most of the day.
10. The lion (creeps, creep) up on its unsuspecting prey.
11. India (is, are) home to a small population of lions.
12. Cubs (has, have) a thick spotted coat.
13. They (is, are) very social animals.
14. The leopard (is, are) a relative of the lion.
15. It (hunts, hunt) smaller prey than the lion.
16. The lion's most familiar relative (is, are) the house cat.
17. Many people (enjoys, enjoy) the company of a cat.
18. Like the lion, cats (is, are) good hunters.
19. Birds (chirps, chirp) loudly from the trees at the sight of a cat.
20. A cat (lies, lie) quietly and patiently.

Common Agreement Problems

Making certain subjects and verbs agree creates problems. Some of the more common problems are explained in the following section.

▶ Verb Phrases

You may recall that the main verb plus one or more helping verbs is called a **verb phrase.** If a sentence has a verb phrase, the first helping verb must agree in number with the subject. In all of the following examples, the subject is underlined once, the verb is underlined twice, and the first helping verb is in bold type.

SINGULAR   Chris **is** looking for Coach.

(*Chris* and the helping verb *is* agree because they are both singular.)

PLURAL   They **have** been waiting for the coach.

(*They* and the first helping verb *have* agree because they are both plural.)

The first helping verb must agree in number with the subject.

The following list shows the singular and plural forms of common helping verbs.

COMMON HELPING VERBS	
SINGULAR	am, is, was, has, does
PLURAL	are, were, have, do

SINGULAR	The <u>player</u> <u>**is** <u>throwing</u></u> the ball now.
	Your <u>team</u> <u>**does** <u>practice</u></u> hard once or twice a day.
PLURAL	Many <u>teams</u> <u>**are** <u>being honored</u></u> every year.
	Your <u>teammates</u> <u>**are** <u>going</u></u>, too.

PRACTICE YOUR SKILLS

● Check Your Understanding
Making Subject and Verb Phrases Agree

Sports Topic **Write each subject and label it *singular* or *plural*. Then write the helping verb in parentheses that agrees with the subject.**

1. The first football game (was, were) played between Rutgers and Princeton.
2. Downhill skiers (has, have) raced at over 120 miles per hour.
3. Helmets (was, were) first introduced to the major baseball leagues in 1941.
4. Soccer (does, do) require a lot of skill.
5. Basketball (was, were) invented by James Naismith.
6. Ice hockey (is, are) played mostly in the northern states.
7. Cyclists (has, have) raced through France for many years.
8. Runners (do, does) practice for many hours.
9. The first marathon (was, were) held in Greece.
10. Tennis (was, were) played in the Middle Ages.

Writing Sentences Using Subject and Verb Agreement

Write five sentences that follow the instructions below.

11. Write a sentence using *football* and a present-tense helping verb.

12. Write a sentence using *soccer* and a past-tense helping verb.

13. Write a sentence using *skaters* and a past-tense helping verb.

14. Write a sentence using *skis* and a present-tense helping verb.

15. Write a sentence using *coaches* and a past-tense helping verb.

● Connect to the Writing Process: Editing
Correcting Subject and Verb Agreement

Rewrite each sentence in which the subject and verb do not agree. If a sentence is correct, write C.

16. Table tennis are becoming a popular indoor sport.

17. Jerry is playing today.

18. Floyd do like tennis.

19. Anna was introduced to cricket in England.

20. Bill were practicing hard yesterday.

▶ *Doesn't* or *Don't?*

When contractions are used, agreement with a subject can be confusing. When you check for agreement, always say the individual words of a contraction.

The verb part of a contraction must agree in number with the subject.

INCORRECT	That <u>ant</u> **don**'t <u>look</u> good on the kitchen counter.
CORRECT	That <u>ant</u> **does** not <u>look</u> good on the kitchen counter.
	That <u>ant</u> **does**n't <u>look</u> good on the kitchen counter.
INCORRECT	<u>Tim</u> and his <u>father</u> **does**n't <u>like</u> ants in the kitchen.
CORRECT	<u>Tim</u> and his <u>father</u> **do** not <u>like</u> ants in the kitchen.
	<u>Tim</u> and his <u>father</u> **don**'t <u>like</u> ants in the kitchen.

The preceding rule applies to all other contractions as well. Keep in mind which contractions are singular and which are plural.

CONTRACTIONS	
SINGULAR	**does**n't, **has**n't, **is**n't, **was**n't
PLURAL	**don**'t, **have**n't, **are**n't, **were**n't

PRACTICE YOUR SKILLS

🔵 Check Your Understanding
Making Subject and Verb Phrases Agree

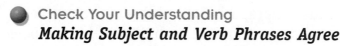

Science Topic **Write each subject. Then write the contraction in parentheses that agrees with the subject.**

1. Scientists (doesn't, don't) ignore the importance of ants.

2. Ants (wasn't, weren't) crawling on that plant.

3. Weaver ants (doesn't, don't) live on the ground.

4. Those ants (wasn't, weren't) unusual.

5. Some ants (doesn't, don't) live underground.

6. Some of the ants (isn't, aren't) leaving the nest.

7. I (hasn't, haven't) ever seen a herdsman ant.

8. The queen and the workers (hasn't, haven't) arrived yet.

9. That ant (isn't, aren't) crawling very fast along the garden path.

10. Aphids and mealybugs (doesn't, don't) like any kind of ants.

● Connect to the Writing Process: Editing
Correcting for Subject and Verb Agreement

Rewrite each sentence in which the subject and verb do not agree. If a sentence is correct, write C.

11. Herdsman ants doesn't like to stay in one place.

12. Plants aren't always homes for ants.

13. Some ants hasn't been studied yet.

14. Ants and plants doesn't always support each other.

15. Those ants weren't very large.

▶ Interrupting Words

Sometimes words—a prepositional phrase, for example—can come between a subject and its verb. When this happens, people sometimes make a mistake in agreement. They make the verb agree with the word it is closer to, rather than with the subject.

The agreement of a verb with its subject is not changed by any interrupting words.

In the following examples, each subject and verb agree in number—in spite of the words that come between them. The best way to find the correct agreement in these sentences is to mentally take out all of the prepositional phrases. Then it is easy to see just the remaining subject and verb.

SINGULAR   A list of new drivers is available.
             (*Is* agrees with the subject *list,* not with the object of the preposition *drivers*—even though *drivers* is closer to the verb.)

PLURAL   The drivers in that room are winners.
             (*Are* agrees with the subject *drivers,* not with the object of the preposition *room*—even though *room* is closer to the verb.)

Compound prepositions—such as *in addition to, as well as,* and *along with*—often begin interrupting phrases. Make sure the verb always agrees with the subject, not the object of the preposition.

My sister as well as many other race fans was visiting the NASCAR Museum.
(*Was* agrees with the subject *sister*—not with *fans,* the object of the preposition *as well as.*)

PRACTICE YOUR SKILLS

● Check Your Understanding
Making Interrupted Subjects and Verbs Agree

Sports Topic **Write each subject and label it *singular* or *plural.* Then write the form of the verb in parentheses that agrees with the subject.**

1. The car with the rainbow on its door (sits, sit) on the pit road.

2. The drivers at the track (seems, seem) friendly.

3. Throughout the years the friendship among the drivers (has, have) remained strong.

4. The TV announcers, along with the fans, (enjoys, enjoy) a good race.

5. The driver with the most wins this year (is, are) Dale Jarrett.

6. The driver in the shiny black car (was, were) very nervous.

7. People like Jeff Gordon (appears, appear) self-confident.

8. The three drivers from South Carolina (is, are) leading the field.

9. The paint on the new car at the track (was, were) beautiful and bright.

10. A rainbow of colors (decorates, decorate) the hood of the car.

● Connect to the Writing Process: Editing
Correcting Subject and Verb Agreement

Rewrite the sentences in which the subject and verb do not agree. If a sentence is correct, write C.

11. The announcers from the TV station at the track is preparing for the race.

12. The fans, in addition to the announcers, are waiting for the green flag.

13. The drivers in the red and white cars is on the same winning team.

14. The driver with the fewest wrecks on his record is Mark Martin.

15. The track with the most dangerous turns are in New York.

▶ Inverted Order

In most sentences the subject comes before the verb. This is a sentence's **natural order**. In some sentences, however, the verb or part of a verb phrase comes before the subject. Such a sentence has **inverted order**. A verb always agrees with its subject, whether the sentence is in its natural order or in inverted order.

> The subject and verb of an inverted sentence must agree in number.

There are several types of inverted sentences. When you are looking for the subject in an inverted-order sentence, turn the sentence around to its natural order.

INVERTED ORDER	In the supply closet is some gum.
NATURAL ORDER	Some gum is in the supply closet.
QUESTION	Has Coach answered your request?
NATURAL ORDER	Coach has answered your request.
SENTENCE BEGINNING WITH *HERE*	Here is my favorite catcher's mitt.
NATURAL ORDER	My favorite catcher's mitt is here.
SENTENCE BEGINNING WITH *THERE*	There were six members present at the meeting.
NATURAL ORDER	Six members were present at the meeting.
	(Sometimes *here* or *there* must be dropped for the sentence to make sense.)

The words *here* and *there* are never the subject of a sentence.

● Check Your Understanding
Making Subjects and Verbs in Inverted Order Agree

Contemporary Life **Write each subject and label it *singular* or *plural*. Then write the form of the verb in parentheses that agrees with the subject.**

1. There (is, are) only one baseball game after school this week.

2. When (does, do) your sister Maria pitch?

3. (Has, Have) your practices for games been challenging this year?

4. Here (is, are) my glove for the catcher.

5. In the dugout there (was, were) two heavy bags full of bats.

6. Where (was, were) the catcher at four o'clock yesterday afternoon?

7. On top of the pitcher's mound (stands, stand) a strong pitcher.

8. (Does, Do) Tito and his brother stay after practice?

9. Here (is, are) some socks from my bag.

10. (Was, Were) there any foul balls in the game last night?

● Connect to the Writing Process: Drafting
Writing Sentences Using Subject and Verb Agreement

Write four sentences, following the instructions below.

11. Write a sentence that begins with the word *here*.

12. Write a question.

13. Write a sentence that begins with the word *there*.

14. Write a sentence that begins with a prepositional phrase and is in inverted order.

Correcting Subject and Verb Agreement

Write correctly each sentence in which the subject and verb do not agree. If a sentence is correct, write C.

15. When does the players arrive?

16. On the bus were two of my favorite gloves.

17. Here are the umpire.

18. There was two mascots for our team last year.

19. By the pitcher's mound was a small glove.

20. Do that glove belong to one of the infielders?

Communicate Your Ideas

APPLY TO WRITING

E-mail Message: *Subject-Verb Agreement*

You missed baseball practice yesterday and need to know if everything is in order before the big game. Write an E-mail message to a friend who is on the team. Ask your friend to tell you what you missed. Be sure that the subjects and verbs in inverted order in your message agree in number.

✔ QuickCheck Mixed Practice

General Interest **Write each subject. Then write the form of the verb in parentheses that agrees with the subject.**

1. The largest cat in the Americas (is, are) the jaguar.

2. Elephants in Africa (has, have) large ears and flat heads.

3. In the jungle (roam, roams) many wild animals.
4. A queen ant in a colony (lives, live) about ten to twenty years.
5. There (was, were) two alligators in the mud at the edge of the lake.
6. A jellyfish (has, have) little or no color.
7. Bees (doesn't, don't) want to be disturbed.
8. When (do, does) the birds migrate?
9. (Wasn't, Weren't) those birds unusual?
10. The ostrich (is, are) known for its speed.
11. Cheetahs (has, have) run at over sixty miles per hour.
12. There (isn't, aren't) many gray wolves left.
13. The dry deserts of Saudi Arabia (contains, contain) many types of beetles.
14. In the mountains (is, are) many types of sheep.
15. Sharks (do, does) swim constantly.
16. A catfish (has, have) two to four pairs of whiskers.
17. One stage in the life of a butterfly (is, are) the caterpillar stage.
18. The chimpanzees of Africa (is, are) known for their intelligence and playfulness.
19. (Does, Do) lobsters live in freshwater or salt water?
20. Here in the field (is, are) the hives for the bees.

When you edit your writing, pay attention to the following agreement problems as well.

▶ Compound Subjects

A **compound subject** is two or more subjects that have the same verb. A compound subject is usually joined by a single conjunction, such as *and,* or *or,* or by a pair of conjunctions, such as *either/or* or *neither/nor.*

> **When subjects are joined by *and,* the verb is usually plural.**

When a subject is more than one, it is plural. The verb, therefore, must also be plural to agree with the subject. In all of the following examples, the subject is underlined once and the verb is underlined twice.

PLURAL VERBS   Cathy **and** Beth take the early bus to work.

This trunk **and** those suitcases have traveled many miles.

Breakfast **and** lunch are served in the dining car.

Agreement between the subject and the verb follows a different rule, however, when a compound subject is joined by *or, either/or,* or *neither/nor.*

> **When subjects are joined by *or, either/or,* or *neither/nor,* the verb agrees with the closer subject.**

SINGULAR VERB	**Either** <u>Mercury</u> **or** <u>Venus</u> <u>is</u> very small. (The verb is singular because *Venus*, the subject closer to it, is singular.)
PLURAL VERB	**Neither** the <u>moon</u> **nor** the <u>planets</u> **have** <u>risen</u> yet. (The verb is plural because *planets*, the subject closer to it, is plural.)
SINGULAR VERB	**Either** those high <u>buildings</u> **or** that <u>tree</u> <u>is</u> <u>blocking</u> the telescope. (The verb is singular because *tree*, the subject closer to it, is singular.)
PLURAL VERB	**Either** that <u>tree</u> **or** those <u>buildings</u> **are** <u>blocking</u> the telescope. (The verb is plural because *buildings*, the subject closer to it, is plural.)

PRACTICE YOUR SKILLS

 Check Your Understanding
Making Verbs Agree with Compound Subjects

General Interest **Write the correct form of the verb in parentheses.**

1. The sun and the moon (seems, seem) almost the same size in the sky.
2. Saturn and Jupiter (has, have) moons.
3. Comets and meteors (travels, travel) through space.
4. Either that moon or that planet (is, are) rising in the east.
5. Neither Mercury nor Venus (is, are) cold.

6. Pluto and Neptune (has, have) no life.

7. Neither wind nor rain (occurs, occur) on the surface of the moon.

8. Either Venus or Mars (has, have) clouds.

9. Some asteroids and comets (passes, pass) close to Earth.

10. The sun and the moon (sets, set) in the west.

● Check Your Understanding
Making Verbs Agree with Compound Subjects

General Interest **Write the correct form of the verb in parentheses.**

11. Sopranos and tenors (sings, sing) the high parts.

12. Either the altos or the basses (has, have) the harmony.

13. Neither the sopranos nor the altos (remembers, remember) their cues.

14. The piano and the flutes (plays, play) the introduction.

15. The drums and the oboe (starts, start) the second section.

16. The piano and the drums (is, are) considered percussion instruments.

17. Neither the trumpets nor the trombones (has, have) the melody.

18. Either the soloist or the conductor (bows, bow) after the music is over.

19. The clarinets and the oboes (sounds, sound) similar.

20. Neither the saxophones nor the piccolo (has, have) a part in this song.

● Connect to the Writing Process: Drafting
Writing Sentences with Compound Subjects

Write the correct form of the verb in parentheses. Then complete each sentence.

21. Juan and his brothers (was, were) ■.

22. The basses or the tenors (has, have) ■.

23. The chimes and the triangle often (ring, rings) ■.

24. That old, broken piano and those new flutes (was, were) ■.

25. Sopranos and altos (is, are) ■.

● Connect to the Writing Process: Editing
Correcting Subject and Verb Agreement

Rewrite the sentences in which the subject and verb do not agree. If a sentence is correct, write C.

26. My flute and the twins' clarinets is out of tune again.

27. The woodwinds and the brass horns have the best parts in the concert.

28. The soloist and the altos likes to sing harmony together.

29. Neither Katharine's reed nor Michael's keys was broken in practice.

30. Either the bassoons or the tuba were flat during the recital.

▶ Collective Nouns

A **collective noun** names a group of people or things. The words in the box at the top of the next page are examples of collective nouns.

COMMON COLLECTIVE NOUNS			
band	committee	flock	orchestra
bunch	congregation	gang	school
class	crew	group	swarm
cluster	crowd	herd	team
colony	family	league	tribe

The way you use a collective noun determines what verb to use.

Use a singular verb with a collective noun subject that is thought of as a unit. Use a plural verb with a collective noun that is thought of as individuals.

The crew **is** sailing in the Memorial Day race next weekend.

(The crew as a whole, as one unit, is sailing in the Memorial Day race next weekend. Therefore, the verb is singular.)

The crew **are** not agreeing on the color of the new uniforms.

(The individuals on the crew are acting separately because they are not agreeing with one another. If they were acting as a unit, all members would be in agreement. Therefore, the verb is plural.)

To make the second sentence even clearer, you could add the word *members* after *crew*. Then the agreement between *members* and *are* would be very clear.

The crew members **are** not agreeing on the color of the new uniforms.

PRACTICE YOUR SKILLS

● Check Your Understanding
Making Verbs Agree with Collective Nouns

Contemporary Life **Write the correct form of the verb in parentheses.**

1. A large and curious crowd (has, have) gathered at the dock.

2. The ship's crew (is, are) arguing over the type of sails to use.

3. A flock of seagulls (flies, fly) low in the sky overhead.

4. The band (tunes, tune) their instruments before they play for the sailors.

5. The judging committee (makes, make) a final inspection of the ship.

6. The captain's family (wishes, wish) him good luck.

7. The sailors' league (checks, check) the boat carefully.

8. The team (disagrees, disagree) over the official start time for the race.

9. This class of boats (is, are) very fast.

10. A pod of dolphins (swims, swim) with the boat during the first part of the race.

● Connect to the Writing Process: Editing
Correcting Subject and Verb Agreement

Rewrite each sentence in which the subject and verb do not agree. If a sentence is correct, write C.

11. The orchestra plays every night on the cruise ship.

12. A flock of gulls land on the deck of the big ship every afternoon.

13. My family like sailing.

14. The enthusiastic crowd cheers loudly for their favorite boat.

15. The crew prepare for a long race.

APPLY TO WRITING

Postcard: *Subject-Verb Agreement with Collective Nouns*

Your family has been away on vacation. Write a postcard to a relative or friend and describe an activity you and every other member of your family enjoyed. Why did each of you like this activity? Be sure to include collective nouns used as subjects and make the verbs agree with them.

General Interest **Write the form of the verb in parentheses that agrees with the subject.**

1. An ant colony (is, are) very complex.

2. Termites and ants (does, do) a lot of damage to homes and lawns.

3. In Texas, bees and ants (is, are) considered pests by many people.

4. A swarm (flies, fly) to find its new home.

5. People and animals (has, have) been disturbed by ants.

6. Either ants or bees (stings, sting) people.

7. The cattle herd (avoids, avoid) ant mounds.

8. Neither fleas nor ticks (are, is) very pleasant to encounter.

9. Either termites or ants (damages, damage) homes.

10. A termite colony (does, do) need to be watched carefully.

11. Fire ants (has, have) particularly painful stings.

12. Burning sensations like fire (is, are) the painful reminder of the sting of these ants.

13. There (has, have) always been many kinds of termites in wooded areas.

14. (Doesn't, Don't) hungry termites silently eat away at all the wood in homes?

15. Warm areas of the country (has, have) more problems with ants and termites than cooler areas.

Agreement Problems with Pronouns

When certain pronouns are used as subjects, they can present some subject-verb agreement problems.

▶ *You* and *I* as Subjects

The singular pronouns *you* and *I* are exceptions to the two rules for agreement between subjects and verbs. *You* is always used with a plural verb even when *you* refers to one person. In the following examples, the subject is underlined once and the verb is underlined twice.

> PLURAL VERBS   Anne, you are always very organized.
>
>   Boys, you work very hard.

I usually takes a plural verb.

> PLURAL VERBS   I study models of ships.
>
>   I have a new math teacher.

The only exceptions are the verbs *am* and *was*.

> SINGULAR VERBS   I am ready to study.
>
>   I was sick yesterday.

CONNECT TO WRITER'S CRAFT

Sometimes a writer will ignore the rules for subject-verb agreement in order to tell the reader something about the characters' backgrounds. Notice the underlined verbs in the passage at the top of the next page. What should the correct verb forms be?

"What are you getting up so soon for, Sam?" asked Bill.

"Me?" says I. "Oh, I got a kind of pain in my shoulder. I thought sitting up would rest it."

"You're a liar!" says Bill. "You're afraid. You was to be burned at sun-rise, and you was afraid he'd do it. And he would, too, if he could find a match."

—*O. Henry*, "The Ransom of Red Chief"

PRACTICE YOUR SKILLS

Check Your Understanding
Making Verbs Agree with **You** *and* **I**

Contemporary
Life

Write the correct form of the verb in parentheses.

1. I (likes, like) history class.

2. You (is, are) the best student in our mathematics class.

3. I (has, have) some homework.

4. You (has, have) a report to prepare for geography class tomorrow.

5. We (was, were) in English class.

6. You (needs, need) Internet access to finish your report.

7. You (was, were) very amusing in this year's school play.

8. This year you (studies, study) hard.

9. I always (wears, wear) this old shirt to gym class.

10. You (has, have) a lot of homework to do this weekend.

● Connect to the Writing Process: Editing
Correcting Subject and Verb Agreement

Rewrite each sentence in which the subject and verb do not agree. If a sentence is correct, write C.

11. I likes my math class this year.

12. You reads a lot of nonfiction books.

13. I enjoy science.

14. You finish your math homework quickly.

15. I types faster than you.

▶ Indefinite Pronouns

An indefinite pronoun—such as *someone, many,* and *all*—can be the subject of a sentence. Indefinite pronouns have number. Some are singular and some are plural.

A verb must agree in number with an indefinite pronoun used as a subject.

The following list shows the number of common indefinite pronouns.

COMMON INDEFINITE PRONOUNS	
SINGULAR	anybody, anyone, each, either, everybody, everyone, neither, nobody, no one, one, somebody, someone
PLURAL	both, few, many, several

Singular indefinite pronouns used as subjects always take a singular verb. Plural indefinite pronouns used as subjects always take a plural verb. Interrupting words do not affect this agreement.

SINGULAR	<u>Everyone</u> <u><u>is</u></u> ready.
	(*Is* agrees with the singular indefinite pronoun *everyone.*)
	<u>One</u> of my sisters <u><u>was</u></u> there.
	(*Was* agrees with the singular indefinite pronoun *one,* not with the object of the preposition *sisters.*)
PLURAL	<u>Many</u> <u>play</u> at this field each day.
	(*Play* agrees with the plural indefinite pronoun *many.*)
	<u>Several</u> in the group <u><u>go</u></u> to soccer camp each summer.
	(*Go* agrees with the plural indefinite pronoun *several,* not the object of the preposition *group.*)

You can learn more about indefinite pronouns on pages L60–L61.

PRACTICE YOUR SKILLS

● Check Your Understanding
Making Verbs Agree with Indefinite Pronouns

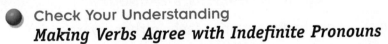

Contemporary Life | **Write each subject and label it *singular* or *plural*. Then write the form of the verb in parentheses that agrees with the subject.**

1. Many of the stadium lights (has, have) burned out.

2. Each of our soccer players (is, are) wearing green shorts.

3. A few of the uniforms (was, were) the wrong size.

4. One of those players (is, are) hurt.

5. Somebody on the team (plays, play) very aggressively.

6. Either of the two game plans (is, are) workable.

7. Several on the team (has, have) worked very hard.

8. Everybody on the team (does, do) practice almost every day.

9. Many on the team (has, have) their own soccer balls.

10. No one at the game (was, were) from middle school.

● Check Your Understanding
Making Verbs Agree with Indefinite Pronouns

Contemporary Life **Write each subject and label it *singular* or *plural*. Then write the form of the verb in parentheses that agrees with the subject.**

11. One of the suitcases (has, have) a hole in it.

12. Each of the tourists (has, have) eaten some dinner in the small café.

13. Several of my friends (takes, take) pictures.

14. (Has, Have) everyone slept well?

15. Neither of the twins (has, have) ever gone to the beach.

16. Both of the tickets (has, have) been ordered.

17. Nobody (was, were) waiting at the train station.

18. Many of the students on our bus (listens, listen) to their headphones.

19. Everybody on the plane (cheers, cheer) loudly when we arrive.

20. Somebody in our hotel (is, are) a singer.

● Connect to the Writing Process: Drafting
Writing Sentences with Indefinite Pronouns

Write five sentences, using the following indefinite pronouns as subjects.

21. many

22. few

23. both

24. nobody

25. someone

● Connect to the Writing Process: Editing
Correcting Subject and Verb Agreement

Rewrite each sentence in which the subject and verb do not agree. If a sentence is correct, write C.

26. A few of the suitcases is missing.

27. Several of the tourists are tired.

28. No one like our hotel.

29. Many of the sightseers does enjoy travel.

30. Few want to return home.

Communicate Your Ideas

APPLY TO WRITING

Brochure: *Subject-Verb Agreement*

The sponsor of your school's travel club has asked you to create a brochure. This brochure will help new students understand what the travel club is all about. Create a brochure that details some of the trips your club has taken. Be sure that indefinite pronouns agree with the verbs in your sentences.

General
Interest **Write the correct form of the verb in parentheses.**

1. Coins (has, have) been around for more than 2,500 years.

2. Once only kings and rich people (was, were) coin collectors.

3. Now more than five million people throughout the world (takes, take) part in this hobby.

4. Many of the collectors (does, do) it as an investment.

5. This hobby (is, are) often begun with just a handful of pennies.

6. There (is, are) a few pennies with a value of $115!

7. A Jefferson nickel or a Roosevelt dime (is, are) also a good addition to a collection.

8. The condition of rare coins (is, are) very important to buyers.

9. Collectors (doesn't, don't) hold any of the coins in their hands.

10. The moisture from hands (has, have) stained many valuable coins.

11. Coin dealers across the country (rates, rate) coins.

12. One of the best ratings (is, are) "extremely fine."

13. The surfaces of these coins (shows, show) little or no wear.

14. Pennies in "extremely fine" condition (is, are) worth twenty-five cents.

15. (Has, Have) you ever wanted to start a coin collection?

Selecting Subjects and Verbs That Agree

Write the form of the verb in parentheses that agrees with each subject.

1. The canals on Mars (is, are) probably dry riverbeds.
2. Many of my friends (was, were) at the mall today.
3. Here (is, are) five quarters from my allowance.
4. (Does, Do) a normal caterpillar have sixteen legs?
5. A trumpeter and a drummer (is, are) needed tonight.
6. In the small pond (was, were) several goldfish.
7. One of those oranges (is, are) enough for me.
8. (Has, Have) you noticed the school's new flag?
9. A boxer or a collie (is, are) a good pet.
10. The orchestra (does, do) not have a violin section.

Making Subjects and Verbs Agree

Find and write the verbs that do not agree with their subjects. Then write each sentence correctly. If a sentence needs no change, write C.

1. The herd is easily quieted on warm nights.
2. One of the books have a funny title.
3. Haven't Lou or Max mowed the lawn yet?
4. There is many tiny creatures in a drop of water.
5. Behind the garage is three grapevines.
6. Was you afraid of that Doberman?
7. Stacy and I have been friends since fifth grade.
8. Each of those flowers have its own special scent.

Editing for Subject and Verb Agreement

Write the following paragraphs, correcting each verb that does not agree with its subject.

One of the world's greatest masterpieces are the Great Sphinx at Giza, Egypt. A sphinx is a mythical animal with the head of a human and the body of a lion. Many sphinxes was built in Egypt, but the Great Sphinx are the oldest of its kind. The features of the sphinx resembles King Khafre, the king at that time.

The body and the head is carved from a natural cliff in the center of a large stone quarry. However, the outstretched paws of the sphinx was added. The figure were originally covered with painted plaster, and there is still some traces of the plaster. The Great Sphinx is 66 feet high and 240 feet long. Its nose alone measure 5 feet 7 inches. The crew at the dig were astounded by its size.

Using Subject and Verb Agreement

Write a sentence that . . .

1. includes *doesn't* at the beginning.
2. includes *there* at the beginning.
3. includes *my dog and cat* as the subject.
4. includes *either Tim or his brothers* as the subject.
5. includes *anyone* as the subject.

Language and *Self-Expression*

Katsushika Hokusai's *Man and Boy* uses a single color and varied line strokes to create interesting characters. Hokusai's curved lines express harmony and diagonal lines suggest movement. Where do you see hints of harmony or illusions of movement in this artwork?

Hokusai used line strokes in the way a writer might use words to express ideas. Write a short story about Hokusai's characters or others you know—real or imaginary. Be sure that the subjects and verbs agree in number. Then record your story and share it with your classmates.

Prewriting Complete a story map by naming each character and listing interesting details about him or her. Identify the setting and the mood of the situation. Determine the problem between the characters. Then figure out a solution.

Drafting Begin with a sentence that introduces the characters. Point out friction between characters that might lead to the problem. Describe the setting in which the characters will meet, and then develop the problem and solution.

Revising Have a classmate read your story. Then ask him or her to visualize the characters. Discuss whether the problem and solution are realistic. To add variety use inverted sentences, compound subjects, and collective nouns.

Editing Check agreement between subjects and verbs. Make sure that collective nouns have been used correctly.

Publishing Prepare a final copy and make an audio recording to share with classmates.

Another Look

Number is the term used to indicate whether a word is singular or plural.

Agreement of Subjects and Verbs
A singular subject takes a singular verb. *(page L396)*
A plural subject takes a plural verb. *(page L396)*

Common Agreement Problems
The main verb plus one or more helping verbs is called a **verb phrase.** The first helping verb must agree in number with the subject. *(page L400)*
The verb part of a contraction must agree in number with the subject. *(pages L402–L403)*
The agreement of a verb with its subject is not changed by the interruption of prepositional phrases. *(pages L404–L405)*

Inverted Order
A sentence is in **natural order** when the subject comes before the verb. When the verb comes before the subject, for example in a question, the sentence is in **inverted order.** *(page L407)*
The subject and verb of an inverted sentence must agree in number. *(page L407)*

Compound Subjects
A **compound subject** is two or more subjects that have the same verb. *(pages L411–L412)*
When subjects are joined by *and,* the verb is usually plural. *(page L411)*
When subjects are joined by *or, either/or,* or *neither/nor,* the verb agrees with the closer subject. *(pages L411–L412)*

Collective Nouns
A **collective noun** names a group of people or things. *(pages L414–L415)*

Other Information About Subject-Verb Agreement
Using the singular pronouns *you* and *I (pages L419–L420)*
Using indefinite pronouns as subjects *(pages L421–L422)*

Posttest

Directions
Read the passage and write the letter of the word or group of words that belongs in each underlined space.

EXAMPLE   My friends and I __(1)__ recycling bins in every classroom.

    1 A places
       B have placed
       C has placed
       D is placing

ANSWER   **1 B**

Opportunities for students to learn about their environment __(1)__ many. Topics __(2)__ seasonal changes, animals, and endangered species, to name just a few. Projects and field trips __(3)__ hands-on experience. A class visiting local recycling centers, wetlands, farms, or fisheries __(4)__ first hand about local resources. __(5)__ you want to sample freshly made maple syrup at the end of a program on methods of collecting maple syrup?

Vacations are a super way to learn about the environment. People __(6)__ more interesting vacations! Whale-watch weekends __(7)__ more popular in recent years. Recently friends and I __(8)__ a humpback whale as she reeled in schools of sun eels. First, she __(9)__ bubbles under the water to get the sun eels into one spot. Then she opened her mouth and __(10)__ hundreds of them.

1   **A**   are
     B   is
     C   was
     D   be

2   **A**   does include
     B   including
     C   includes
     D   include

3   **A**   offers
     B   offer
     C   offering
     D   is offering

4   **A**   learns
     B   were learning
     C   are learning
     D   learn

5   **A**   Doing
     B   Do
     C   Done
     D   Does

6   **A**   looks for and finds
     B   has look for and has find
     C   are looking for and are finding
     D   is looking for and finding

7   **A**   has becoming
     B   have become
     C   becomes
     D   has become

8   **A**   were watching
     B   was watching
     C   have watch
     D   has watch

9   **A**   blow
     B   have blown
     C   blew
     D   is blown

10   **A**   am scooping
     B   has scooped up
     C   scoop up
     D   scooped up

CHAPTER 14

Using Adjectives and Adverbs

 **Pretest**

Directions
Read the passage and write the letter of the modifier that belongs in each underlined space.

EXAMPLE   Hiking is __(1)__ inexpensive.
        1 A   more fairly
            B   most fair
            C   fairly
            D   fairest

ANSWER   **1 C**

Hiking is growing __(1)__ each day. In 1999, about 50 million Americans went hiking. That's 100 percent __(2)__ than the number of hikers during the 1980s. It is one of the __(3)__ expensive of all recreational activities. In addition, trails are __(4)__. If you're interested, check the state parks in your area. If there are several parks in your state, one of them may be __(5)__ to you than the others.

    Trails in state parks are __(6)__ well marked. Also, trail maps provide __(7)__ information about landmarks along the trail itself. Hikers are __(8)__ cautioned to stay on marked trails. The __(9)__ trails in the park may become crowded. However, experienced hikers don't stray from the trails as __(10)__ as inexperienced ones.

1	A	popularer	6	A	usually
	B	most popular		B	usual
	C	more popular		C	most usual
	D	popularly		D	more usual

2	A	most	7	A	more useful
	B	more		B	useful
	C	much		C	usefuler
	D	much more		D	usefulest

3	A	little	8	A	regular
	B	less		B	regularly
	C	littler		C	more regular
	D	least		D	most regularly

4	A	availabler	9	A	most popular
	B	available		B	popularest
	C	availablely		C	popularer
	D	more available		D	more popular

5	A	closer	10	A	most often
	B	more closer		B	more often
	C	closest		C	oftener
	D	close		D	often

Paul Cézanne. *Mont Sainte-Victoire Seen from the Bibemus Quarry,* ca. 1897.
Oil on canvas, 25⅓ by 31¼. The Baltimore Museum of Art.

Describe   Describe what you see. To what do your
eyes keep returning? What shapes and
colors emphasize the mountain?

Analyze   What ideas do you think Paul Cézanne is
trying to express about this landmark? He
uses shape, color, and lighting to give a
three-dimensional effect. Where do you
see this?

Interpret   How might a writer express similar ideas
in writing?

Judge   Do you think Cézanne's painting or a
story with vivid sensory images would
more effectively express the same ideas?
Explain.

At the end of this chapter, you will use the artwork to
stimulate ideas for writing.

Comparison of Adjectives and Adverbs

Adjectives and adverbs usually change form when they are used to compare two or more people or things. Most adjectives and adverbs have three forms to show differences in the degree of comparison.

Most adjectives and adverbs have three degrees of comparison: the positive, the comparative, and the superlative.

The **positive degree** is used when no comparison is being made.

ADJECTIVE	This bear is **big.**
ADVERB	The bee works **quickly.**

The **comparative degree** is used when two people, things, or actions are being compared.

ADJECTIVE	This black bear is **bigger** than the other black bear.
ADVERB	The bees work **more quickly** than the snails.

The **superlative degree** is used when more than two people, things, or actions are being compared.

ADJECTIVE	This black bear is the **biggest** bear in the entire forest.
ADVERB	Of all the insects, I think bees work **most quickly.**

You can learn more about adjectives and adverbs on pages L99–L125.

PRACTICE YOUR SKILLS

● Check Your Understanding

Identifying the Degree of Comparison

Science Topic **Label each underlined adjective or adverb P for positive, C for comparative, or S for superlative.**

1. Of the mammals on both land and sea, the blue whale is the largest.

2. Scientists have recently discovered the smallest mammal.

3. The tiny rodent is less than an inch long.

4. A cheetah can run faster than a lion.

5. A baby orca rapidly puts on weight.

6. A pack of wolves will hunt larger prey than a single wolf will hunt.

7. A peacock has the most impressive display of feathers.

8. Does the snail crawl more slowly than the turtle?

9. Of all the fish in the river, that salmon jumps highest.

10. A cobra's venom is poisonous.

▶ Regular Comparison

Almost all adjectives and adverbs form the comparative and superlative degrees in the same manner. These forms depend on the number of syllables in the modifier.

Add *–er* to form the comparative degree and *–est* to form the superlative degree of one-syllable modifiers.

ONE-SYLLABLE MODIFIERS			
	POSITIVE	**COMPARATIVE**	**SUPERLATIVE**
ADJECTIVE	smart	smart**er**	smart**est**
	hot	hot**ter**	hot**test**
ADVERB	near	near**er**	near**est**
	fast	fast**er**	fast**est**

Sometimes a spelling change occurs when *–er* or *–est* is added to certain modifiers, such as *hot*. Look in a dictionary to check the spelling of such words.

Many two-syllable modifiers are formed exactly like one-syllable modifiers. There are some two-syllable modifiers, however, that would be difficult to say with *–er* or *–est*. Words like *usefuller* and *usefullest* would sound awkward. For such two-syllable modifiers, *more* and *most* should be used to form the comparative and superlative degrees. *More* and *most* are generally used with adverbs that end in *–ly*.

Use *–er* or the word *more* to form the comparative degree and *–est* or the word *most* to form the superlative degree of two-syllable modifiers.

TWO-SYLLABLE MODIFIERS			
	POSITIVE	**COMPARATIVE**	**SUPERLATIVE**
ADJECTIVE	narrow	narrow**er**	narrow**est**
	happy	happi**er**	happi**est**
	helpless	**more** helpless	**most** helpless
ADVERB	soon	soon**er**	soon**est**
	slowly	**more** slowly	**most** slowly

Notice that a spelling change occurs in many modifiers that end in *y*, such as *happy*. The *y* changes to *i* before *-er* or *-est* is added.

All modifiers with three or more syllables form their comparative and superlative degrees by using *more* and *most*.

Use *more* to form the comparative degree and *most* to form the superlative degree of modifiers with three or more syllables.

THREE-SYLLABLE MODIFIERS		
	POSITIVE	COMPARATIVE	SUPERLATIVE
ADJECTIVE	horrible	**more** horrible	**most** horrible
ADVERB	eagerly	**more** eagerly	**most** eagerly

PRACTICE YOUR SKILLS

 Check Your Understanding

Forming Regular Comparisons of Modifiers

Oral Expression
Read the following sentences aloud, trying out each word or group of words in parentheses. Then read the sentence aloud again, choosing the correct word or group of words.

1. Paul is the (tallest, most tall) member of the basketball team.

2. Bob runs (quicklier, more quickly) than Larry does.

3. Coach is one of the (helpfulest, most helpful) people I know.

4. The crowd stared (curiouslier, more curiously) at the other team than they did at us.

5. Gene plays his position (powerfullest, most powerfully) of all the team members.

6. That was the (longest, most long) game this year.

7. Danny made the (beautifullest, most beautiful) shot in the whole game.

8. The game was over (sooner, more soon) than I expected.

9. Our coach was (happier, more happy) than the other coach.

10. We won by the (narrowest, most narrow) margin all season.

● Check Your Understanding
Forming the Comparison of Modifiers

Copy each modifier. Then write its comparative and superlative forms.

11. quick	**16.** merrily	**21.** cold	**26.** curious
12. quiet	**17.** dangerous	**22.** neatly	**27.** early
13. slowly	**18.** rapidly	**23.** careful	**28.** weakly
14. great	**19.** dry	**24.** big	**29.** pretty
15. witty	**20.** steadily	**25.** thin	**30.** long

● Check Your Understanding
Using the Correct Form of Modifiers

Contemporary Life   **Write the correct modifier in each sentence.**

31. Marty wasn't sure which was (easier, easiest), rowing or paddling.

32. Does the canoe or the rowboat glide (faster, fastest)?

33. Juan faced the situation (more bravely, most bravely) than I did.

34. Of the two boats, which do you think is (bigger, biggest)?

35. Of the five rowers, Barry rows the (more skillfully, most skillfully).

36. Which of the two rowing teams is (more powerful, most powerful)?

37. Of the ten races I've seen this year, this was (more enjoyable, most enjoyable).

38. Joe is the (stronger, strongest) member of the rowing team.

39. A canoe can move (more quickly, most quickly) than a barge.

40. Which race was the (shorter, shortest), the first or the last?

▶ Irregular Comparison

A few adjectives and adverbs are compared in an irregular manner.

IRREGULAR MODIFIERS		
POSITIVE	**COMPARATIVE**	**SUPERLATIVE**
bad/badly	worse	worst
good/well	better	best
little	less	least
much/many	more	most

POSITIVE	The salad was **good.**
COMPARATIVE	It was **better** than yesterday's salad.
SUPERLATIVE	It was the **best** salad we have ever had.

PRACTICE YOUR SKILLS

● Check Your Understanding
Forming Comparisons of Modifiers

Oral
Expression

Read the following sentences aloud, trying out each word in parentheses. Then read each sentence aloud again, choosing the correct word.

1. This is the (goodest, best) place for a picnic.

2. Did you do (weller, better) in the potato sack races than Sita?

3. Sue ate the (less, least) amount of anyone at the picnic.

4. Margaret had (mucher, more) chicken than Sharlene had.

5. That was the (baddest, worst) potato salad I have ever eaten.

● Check Your Understanding
Supplying the Correct Form of Modifiers

Contemporary
Life

Read the first sentence in each group. Then write the comparative and superlative forms of the underlined modifier in the two sentences below it.

6. I have little interest in science fiction.
I have ▇ interest in fables.
I have the ▇ interest in biographies.

7. You read quite well.
You read ▇ than my sister.
You read the ▇ of all the students in my class.

8. The book this week is good.
I think it is ▇ than last week's book.
In fact, it is the ▇ book I have read so far this month.

9. <u>Many</u> people in my class buy books.
■ people use the library.
However, ■ people prefer to borrow books from each other.

10. I feel <u>bad</u> about the ending of this book.
I felt ■ about the ending of last week's book.
Two weeks ago, I felt ■ of all.

● Connect to the Writing Process: Editing
Using the Correct Form of Modifiers

Write C if the modifiers in each sentence are used correctly. If a modifier is used incorrectly, rewrite the sentence.

11. Which do you like goodest, animal stories or science fiction?

12. That book is definitely the worst one I have read all year.

13. Leslie couldn't decide which book she liked most, the mystery or the fairy tale.

14. Who reads fastest, Lee or Shirley?

15. That science encyclopedia is the bigger book in the whole library.

Communicate Your Ideas

APPLY TO WRITING

Writer's Craft: *Analyzing the Use of Modifiers*

Writers often use modifiers to create a specific effect on their audience. At the top of the next page is a passage from *Where the Red Fern Grows*. Read it and answer the questions that follow.

As I skipped along, it was hard for me to realize all the wonderful things that had happened to me in such a few short years. I had two of the finest little hounds that ever bawled on the trail of a ringtail coon. I had a wonderful mother and father and three little sisters. I had the best grandpa a boy ever had, and to top it all, I was going on a championship coon hunt. It was no wonder that my heart was bursting with happiness. Wasn't I the luckiest boy in the world?

—*Wilson Rawls*, Where the Red Fern Grows

- Make a list of adjectives and adverbs in this paragraph and identify which degree of comparison is being used. Some modifiers have only a positive degree.

- Are there any irregular comparisons? If so, what are they?

- Why do you think the writer used several superlative forms? What effect do these forms have on you?

QuickCheck Mixed Practice

Contemporary Life

Find and write each incorrect modifier. Then write it correctly.

1. Which type of music do you like best, classical or jazz?

2. Of the three composers, Mozart is the more challenging.

3. Is jazz, classical, or pop the harder to play on the guitar?

4. Who wrote the best music, Ludwig van Beethoven or Johann Sebastian Bach?

5. That composition was the more difficult piece I have ever played.

6. That song was without a doubt the worse song I've heard all year!

7. Which instrument plays most loudly, the tuba or the piccolo?

8. Of all the instruments my brother can play, I like the baritone the less.

9. Of all my music, I have played the Mozart piece more recently.

10. Which composition came earliest in the program, "Für Elise" or the *Moonlight Sonata?*

11. I am least eager to hear the symphony than Cynthia is.

12. He couldn't decide which he liked most, the trumpet or the flute.

13. Which music do you think is prettiest, rock or classical?

14. Of all the symphony's concerts, I think the first one was better.

15. Jazz is my more favorite type of music.

Problems with Modifiers

In addition to knowing the comparative and superlative forms of modifiers, you also need to be aware of a few other possible problems when you use adjectives and adverbs.

Other and *Else*

When you compare one thing to another in a group, do not make the mistake of comparing the first thing with itself. Instead add the word *other* or *else* to your comparison.

Add *other* or *else* when comparing a member of a group to the rest of the group.

INCORRECT	David sings louder than any boy in the chorus. (David is being compared to all boys in the chorus, which means that he is also being compared to himself because he is in the chorus.)
CORRECT	David sings louder than any **other** boy in the chorus. (Now he is being compared only to the other boys, not to himself.)
INCORRECT	Kay dances better than anyone in the play. (Because Kay is in the play, she is also being compared to herself.)
CORRECT	Kay dances better than anyone **else** in the play. (Now she is being compared only to other students, not to herself.)

When you speak and write, be sure that your comparisons are logical. Notice the difference between these two sentences.

Seventh graders' math assignments are more difficult than sixth graders.

Seventh graders' math assignments are more difficult than sixth graders' assignments.

Although the first sentence may sound logical when you speak, it becomes illogical when you write. The first sentence incorrectly compares math assignments to sixth grade students. The second correctly compares math assignments to math assignments.

PRACTICE YOUR SKILLS

● Check Your Understanding
Identifying Problems with Other *or* Else

Contemporary Life | **Read the following sentences, looking for problems with *other* or *else*. Write C if the sentence is correct and *I* if the sentence is incorrect.**

1. Harry learned his lines more quickly than anyone in the play.

2. Our play was better than any other play performed by seventh graders.

3. Sally sings better than any singer in the play.

4. Mrs. Constanza dedicated more of her time to the production than anyone else at our school.

5. My mom took more pictures of the dress rehearsal than anyone did.

6. Sharon had stage fright worse than anyone in the cast.

7. No one was as calm as Juan.

8. Jori got the part because she is taller than any other student who auditioned.

9. Mrs. Constanza was more nervous than the other teachers.

10. Sam sang louder than any other performer in the cast.

11. Barry recited more lines of dialogue than any other cast member.

12. Chen practiced his lines harder than anyone for this play.

● Connect to the Writing Process: Editing
Correcting Errors with Other *or* Else

13.–18. Rewrite the incorrect sentences from the preceding exercise, using *other* or *else* correctly.

▶ Double Comparisons

You should use only one method of forming the comparative or the superlative form of a modifier. Using both methods—for example, –er and *more* together—results in a **double comparison.**

Do not use both –er and *more* to form the comparative degree or both –est and *most* to form the superlative degree.

DOUBLE COMPARISON	Our winter weather comes **more earlier** than yours.
CORRECT	Our winter weather comes **earlier** than yours.

DOUBLE COMPARISON	We drove through the **most foggiest** area in the valley.
CORRECT	We drove through the **foggiest area** in the valley.

PRACTICE YOUR SKILLS

● Check Your Understanding
Identifying Double Comparisons

Geography Topic **Read the following sentences, looking for problems with double comparisons. Write C if the sentence is correct and I if the sentence is incorrect.**

1. The weather in Texas is more drier than the weather in Pennsylvania.

2. Some people think the hills of Austin are prettier than the hills of Pittsburgh.

3. The terrain west of Austin becomes more steeper than the terrain east of Austin.

4. Spanish explorers arrived in Texas earlier than the French arrived in Pennsylvania.

5. People in Texas can swim outside for a more longer time than people in Pennsylvania.

6. Many agree that sunrises on the Gulf Coast are the prettiest they have ever seen.

7. Most Texans believe that their chili is more tastier than Northern chili.

8. Texas is the most biggest state in the continental United States.

Using Adjectives and Adverbs

9. Some of the most interesting architecture in the state can be seen in Austin.

10. Winter in Texas is warmer than in Pennsylvania.

● Connect to the Writing Process: Editing
Correcting Errors with Double Comparisons

11.–15. Rewrite the incorrect sentences from the preceding exercise so that there are no double comparisons.

▶ Double Negatives

The following is a list of common negative words. Notice that all of these words begin with *n*.

COMMON NEGATIVES	
never	none
no	not (and its contraction *n't*)
no one	nothing

Two of these words should not be used together to express the same idea. When they are, the result is a **double negative.**

Avoid using double negatives.

DOUBLE NEGATIVE	Ken does**n't** know **nothing** about animals.
CORRECT	Ken does**n't** know anything about animals.
CORRECT	Ken knows **nothing** about animals.

● Check Your Understanding
Identifying Double Negatives

Science Topic **Read each of the following sentences, looking for double negatives. Write *C* if the sentence is correct and *I* if the sentence is incorrect.**

1. Porpoises don't have no gills.

2. Some salamanders don't have no lungs, so they breathe through their skin.

3. Most people didn't know anything about dodo birds until they became extinct.

4. Some squirrels can't never find the acorns they bury.

5. An eagle won't let anything harm its chicks.

6. That mongoose has not done nothing about the cobra in the garden.

7. The scientists have never seen that species before.

8. There is no way to protect endangered species without education.

9. That caterpillar hasn't never stopped eating parsley.

10. A newly hatched hornbill cannot leave the nest until its feathers grow.

● Connect to the Writing Process: Editing
Correcting Errors with Double Negatives

11.–15. **Rewrite the incorrect sentences from the preceding exercise, eliminating the double negatives.**

▶ *Good or Well?*

Good is always an adjective. *Well* is usually an adverb. However, when *well* means "in good health," it is used as an adjective.

ADJECTIVE	The music sounded **good.**
	(*Good* is a predicate adjective that describes *music.*)
ADVERB	He always plays **well.**
	(*Well* is an adverb that tells how he plays.)
ADJECTIVE	The conductor doesn't feel **well** today.
	(*Well* means "in good health.")

You can learn more about predicate adjectives and linking verbs on pages L69–L70.

PRACTICE YOUR SKILLS

● Check Your Understanding
Using Good *or* Well

General Interest **Write *good* or *well* to correctly complete each sentence.**

1. Vacuum the rug ▓.
2. Janice dances ▓.
3. I feel quite ▓.
4. The steak looks ▓.
5. It's running ▓.

6. The lunch tasted ▓.
7. The Lions played ▓.
8. That rain feels ▓.
9. Sandra dives ▓.
10. Tim's voice is ▓.

● Connect to the Writing Process: Editing
Correcting Errors with Good *or* Well

Rewrite the following sentences if they contain errors with *good* or *well*. If a sentence is correct, write *C.*

11. The new band sounds good.
12. They played good at their first concert.
13. The conductor was not feeling well.
14. The flute section did well with the solo.

APPLY TO WRITING

Persuasive Letter: *Comparison with Modifiers*

Susan Merritt. *Picnic Scene,* ca. 1853.
Watercolor and collage on paper, 26 by 36½ inches. The Art Institute of Chicago.

Pablo Picasso. *Guernica*, 1937.
Oil on canvas, 136¾ by 305 inches. Centro de Arte Reina Sofia, Madrid, Spain.

Your mother wants to hang one of these two paintings
in your room. Persuade your mother to choose one
of them by writing her a letter in which you compare
the two paintings. Tell her which you prefer. Be sure to
use comparisons correctly in your letter.

Science Topic **Rewrite the following paragraphs, correcting the use of modifiers.**

Which is most famous, a rabbit or a hare? There's no question about it. Rabbits win every time. After all, who hasn't never read about Bugs Bunny, Peter Rabbit, or Brer Rabbit?

A rabbit is different from a hare. Of the two animals, the rabbit is smallest. A rabbit has more shorter ears and legs than a hare. Rabbits build their nests in burrows. Their young are born blind. A newly born hare, on the other hand, has fully opened eyes. In addition, a rabbit doesn't have no hair when it is born, but a newborn hare has a full coat of hair. Newborn hares are able to hop more earlier than baby rabbits. Young hares are born in an open field. As a result they can take better care of themselves sooner than young rabbits.

All rabbits and hares run and jump good. They jump faster than any animal in the forest. A running jackrabbit takes a more higher leap every sixth stride. By doing this, it is able to look around for any possible danger. The strong hind legs of rabbits make them fast runners.

Both kinds of animals are more activer at night than in the day. Rabbits and hares eat plants, but they don't eat no meat.

Using the Correct Forms of Modifiers

Write the correct modifier in parentheses for each sentence.

1. This is the (heavier, heaviest) crate I have ever lifted.
2. Of my two uncles, I think Uncle Pete is (older, oldest).
3. Our young chickens are coming along (good, well).
4. Of all the people at the tryouts for the play, Ned was the (more, most) talented.
5. Sandy types (more, most) accurately than Eric.
6. Both pieces of meat look good, but this piece tastes (better, best).
7. There aren't (no, any) erasers for the chalkboard in homeroom.
8. Because Rico didn't sing (good, well) at rehearsal, he is nervous about the concert.
9. Your skates are (newer, more newer) than mine.
10. Mr. Lyons looks (good, well) in a three-piece suit.

Correcting Errors with Modifiers

Write the following sentences, correcting each error. If the sentence needs no change, write C.

1. This bread is more fresher than those rolls.
2. Doesn't no one have a flashlight?
3. I think a panther looks more fiercer than a tiger.
4. He learned his lesson good.
5. I play basketball more better than soccer.
6. Which do you like better, swimming in the ocean or swimming in a lake?

7. We didn't have no practice for three days.
8. Tim's was the most biggest trout caught today.
9. You can't ever depend on the weather in New England.
10. The lost notebook doesn't have no name on it.

Forming the Comparison of Modifiers

Write the correct form of each modifier indicated below. Then use each word in a sentence.

1. the comparative of *quickly*
2. the superlative of *long*
3. the comparative of *little*
4. the superlative of *fast*
5. the comparative of *bad*
6. the comparative of *energetic*
7. the superlative of *helpful*
8. the superlative of *good*
9. the comparative of *clear*
10. the comparative of *bravely*

Using Adjectives and Adverbs

Write five sentences that follow the directions below. Write a sentence that . . .

1. uses a form of *little* to compare three pets.
2. uses the word *other* in a comparison.
3. uses the word *else* in a comparison.
4. includes the word *good*.
5. includes the word *bad*.

Language and *Self-Expression*

Paul Cézanne used shape, color, and lighting to present three-dimensional scenes to help others visualize places and landmarks as he did. For example, in this painting Cézanne draws viewers into the quarry to look up at the mountain and see its majesty. He actually painted many views of Mont Sainte-Victoire to help people experience it from many angles.

What landmark or favorite place do you know well? Choose one and express your ideas about it in a few paragraphs. Use adjectives and adverbs to give vivid details and to make comparisons. Avoid double negatives.

Prewriting Make a chart with three columns. Label them *background, foreground, center.* Then under each column write sensory details—what you see, hear, feel, smell, and taste—as you remember your special place.

Drafting Use your chart as you write. Introduce your subject and then verbally "walk" your reader through in this special place. Close with a statement that summarizes your special place.

Revising Put your writing aside for a while. When you return to it, check that the order in which you have described your subject makes sense. If necessary, reorder ideas to make your description logical.

Editing Check that you used adjectives and adverbs correctly to make comparisons. Be sure that you have not used any double negatives.

Publishing Prepare a final copy and place it in a folder. If you have a photo of the place, use it on the cover.

Another Look

Most adjectives and adverbs have three **degrees of comparison:** the positive, the comparative, and the superlative.

Comparison of Adjectives and Adverbs

The **positive degree** is used when no comparison is being made. *(page L435)*

The **comparative degree** is used when two people, things, or actions are being compared. *(page L435)*

The **superlative degree** is used when more than two people, things, or actions are being compared. *(page L435)*

Regular Comparison

Add *-er* to form the comparative degree and *-est* to form the superlative degree of one-syllable modifiers. *(pages L436–L437)*

Use *-er* or *more* to form the comparative degree and *-est* or *most* to form the superlative degree of two-syllable modifiers. *(pages L437–L438)*

Use *more* to form the comparative degree and *most* to form the superlative degree of modifiers with three or more syllables. *(page L438)*

Irregular Comparison

The modifiers *bad, badly, good, well, little, much,* and *many* have special forms of comparison. *(page L440)*

Problems with Modifiers

Add *other* or *else* when comparing a member of a group to the rest of the group. *(page L445)*

Do not use both *-er* and *more* to form the comparative degree or *-est* and *most* to form the superlative degree. *(pages L447–L448)*

Two negative words should not be used together to express a negative idea. *(page L449)*

Good is always an adjective. *Well* can be used as an adverb. When *well* means in good health, it is used as an adjective. *(pages L450–L451)*

Posttest

Directions
Read the passage and write the letter of the modifier that belongs in each underlined space.

EXAMPLE   Hikers __(1)__ carry backpacks.

    1 **A** more usually

        B usually

        C usual

        D most usual

ANSWER   **1 B**

Backpacks include items that are nice to have as well as items that are __(1)__ . For example, a brush is nice to have, but you might need snacks __(2)__ . Forgetting a swimsuit may be bad, but having no dry clothes may be __(3)__ . In some areas, the possibility of __(4)__ temperature changes makes lightweight layered clothing preferable. Your __(5)__ supply, however, is good, clean water.

Experienced hikers are __(6)__ kind to their feet. They choose footwear that is __(7)__ for their feet. Many people find low-cut lightweight boots the __(8)__ . These day-hiking boots offer less protection than the __(9)__ boots worn by weekend hikers. There is not __(10)__ worse than sore feet at the end of a long day.

1   **A**   importantly
     B   more importantly
     C   most importantly
     D   more important

6   **A**   especial
     B   most especial
     C   more especially
     D   especially

2   **A**   many
     B   much
     C   more
     D   most

7   **A**   appropriate
     B   appropriately
     C   more appropriately
     D   appropriatest

3   **A**   badder
     B   worse
     C   worst
     D   more bad

8   **A**   goodest
     B   better
     C   best
     D   wellest

4   **A**   suddener
     B   sudden
     C   suddenly
     D   suddenest

9   **A**   heaviest
     B   more heavy
     C   heavier
     D   more heavily

5   **A**   most necessary
     B   more necessary
     C   necessariest
     D   most necessariest

10   **A**   nothing
     B   anything
     C   no
     D   none

A Writer's Glossary of Usage

The basic elements of usage appeared in the last four chapters. In this section, you will find specific areas that often cause difficulty for students of English. To make it easier for you to use this guide as a reference, entries are arranged alphabetically.

When you examine "A Writer's Glossary of Usage," notice the variety in language levels, two of which are standard English and nonstandard English. **Standard English,** used by the majority of English-speaking people around the world, has a set pattern of rules and conventions. On the other hand, **nonstandard English** is used by people of varying regions and dialects. It has many differences and includes slang words. Using nonstandard English with friends is not necessarily incorrect; however, it is not acceptable in certain situations. When you write or speak in formal situations, such as in school assignments, you should use standard English.

Examples of both formal and informal English are shown in the glossary. **Formal English** conforms to the accepted rules for grammar, usage, and mechanics in writing. Some typical examples of formal English include business letters, technical reports, and well-written essays. Although **informal English** follows most of the conventional rules of standard English, it contains words and phrases that may not sound appropriate in formal writing. Informal English is frequently used in magazines, newspapers, fiction, and personal writing aimed at general audiences.

a, an Use *a* before words beginning with consonant sounds and *an* before words beginning with vowel sounds.

> It was **an** evening filled with excitement.
> After the movies, we went to **a** restaurant.

accept, except *Accept* is a verb that means "to receive with consent." *Except* is usually a preposition that means "but" or "other than."

> **Except** for an emergency, the teacher will not **accept** any late papers.

affect, effect *Affect* is a verb that means "to influence" or "to act upon." *Effect* is usually a noun that means "a result" or "an influence." As a verb, *effect* means "to accomplish" or "to produce."

> The lively debate **affected** the audience in different ways.
>
> On most, the **effect** was a positive one.
>
> At least it **effected** a needed change in policy.

ain't This contraction is nonstandard English. Avoid it in your writing.

> NONSTANDARD   The newspaper **ain't** going to be delivered today.
>
> STANDARD   The newspaper **isn't** going to be delivered today.

all ready, already *All ready* means "completely ready." *Already* means "previously."

> Are you surprised that my suitcase is **all ready** to be taken to the car?
>
> Because you wanted to leave early, I had **already** packed it.

To avoid confusion between *all ready* and *already*, remember that the word *all* can mean "everything" or "everyone." For example, if you say or write that something is *all ready* or that a group is *all ready*, you are actually saying that everything is ready or that everyone is ready.

a lot People very often write these two words incorrectly as one. There is no such word as "alot." *A lot*, even as two words, should be avoided in formal writing.

INFORMAL	**A lot** of people gathered to honor the graduates.
FORMAL	**A large number** of people gathered to honor the graduates.

among, between These words are both prepositions. *Among* is used when referring to three or more people or things. *Between* is used when referring to two people or things.

> You should be able to find one pair of shoes **among** the many that are on display.
>
> I cannot choose **between** the sandals and the sneakers.

amount, number *Amount* refers to a singular word. *Number* refers to a plural word.

> The large **amount** of help probably accounts for the **number** of happy people.

anywhere, everywhere, nowhere, somewhere Do not add *s* to any of these words.

> You will find the book you lost **somewhere**.

at Do not use *at* after *where*.

> NONSTANDARD   Do you know **where** the new stadium is **at?**
>
> STANDARD   Do you know **where** the new stadium is?

PRACTICE YOUR SKILLS

● Check Your Understanding
Finding the Correct Word

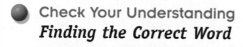 **Write the word in parentheses that correctly completes each sentence.**

1. (Among, Between) the many skills to master, none is more important than reading.

2. You have (all ready, already) learned some reading strategies.

3. The ability to read well (affects, effects) your life.

4. It has a direct (affect, effect) on whether you enjoy reading.

5. It also can (affect, effect) your comprehension.

6. Reading fiction, for example, (ain't, isn't) always easy because a plot has many twists and turns.

7. A varied (amount, number) of strategies are available to help you.

8. When you begin reading, you need to create (a, an) interaction (among, between) yourself and the text.

9. (A, An) reading log allows you to record (many, a lot) of your thoughts.

10. With an open mind and a reading log, you are (all ready, already) to start an exciting journey.

Write the underlined words from the following paragraph. If a word is used correctly, write C beside it. If a word is used incorrectly, write the correct form of the word.

Most teachers will <u>except</u> any reading log response to the text <u>except</u> a plot summary. Any place in the text where you find a problem <u>at</u>, you should list possible questions. If a certain character <u>effects</u> you, you can describe your feelings. <u>Anywheres</u> you find a line or passage you especially like, explain the <u>effect</u> it has on you. If a situation reminds you of a book you have <u>all ready</u> read, compare the similarities <u>between</u> the two. With these strategies, you can gain a large <u>amount</u> of practice. You should then be <u>all ready</u> for an intelligent class discussion.

bad, badly *Bad* is an adjective and often follows a linking verb. *Badly* is used as an adverb. In the first two examples, *sounds* is a linking verb.

NONSTANDARD   Do you think the speech sounds **badly?**

STANDARD   Do you think the speech sounds **bad?**

STANDARD   I very **badly** wanted to be the last to speak.

You can learn more about using adjectives and adverbs on pages L435–L459.

bring, take *Bring* indicates motion toward the speaker. *Take* indicates motion away from the speaker.

> If you **bring** me an application, I'll **take** it to the office.

You can learn more about using problem verbs on pages L321–L325.

can, may *Can* expresses ability. *May* expresses possibility or permission.

> None of my students **can** write as well as Eddie.
> **May** I see some of his writing?

doesn't, don't *Doesn't* is singular and must agree with a singular subject. *Don't* is plural and must agree with a plural subject or with the singular pronouns *I* and *you*.

> A cat **doesn't** usually like dogs.
> Cats **don't** usually like dogs.

double negative Words such as *but* (when it means "only"), *hardly, never, no, none, no one, nobody, not* (and its contraction *n't*), *nothing, nowhere, only, barely,* and *scarcely* are all negatives. Do not use two negatives to express one negative meaning.

> NONSTANDARD **Hardly no one** failed the test.
> STANDARD   **Hardly anyone** failed the test.
> STANDARD   **No one** failed the test.

You can learn more about the use of negatives on page L449.

fewer, less *Fewer* is plural and refers to things that can be counted. *Less* is singular and refers to quantities and qualities that cannot be counted.

> The **fewer** exercises you do, the **less** chance you have of passing your final exam.

good, well *Good* is an adjective and often follows a linking verb. *Well* is an adverb and often follows an action verb. However, when *well* means "in good health" or "satisfactory," it is used as an adjective.

> The team looked **good** in practice.
>
> (adjective)
>
> Our new quarterback threw **well** in practice.
>
> (adverb)
>
> Let's hope he feels **well** for the first game.
>
> (adjective meaning "in good health")

You can learn more about using adjectives and adverbs on pages L435–L459.

have, of Never substitute *of* for the verb *have*. When speaking, many people make a contraction of *have*. For example, they might say, "We should've gone." Because *'ve* sounds like *of, of* is often mistakenly substituted for *have* in writing.

> NONSTANDARD   I know that I should **of** gone.
> STANDARD   I know that I should **have** gone.

in, into Use *in* when you are referring to a place. Use *into* when you want to express motion from one place to another.

> Is your towel **in** the locker?
>
> Don't forget to put it **into** your backpack when you leave.

its, it's *Its* is a possessive pronoun and means "belonging to it." *It's* is a contraction for *it is*.

> When we find **its** entrance, let's explore the cave.
>
> I think **it's** too dangerous until we know more about **its** tunnels.

PRACTICE YOUR SKILLS

● Check Your Understanding
Finding the Correct Word

General Interest **Write the word in parentheses that correctly completes each sentence.**

1. (Fewer, Less) people now depend solely on automobiles for transportation than ever before.

2. (Its, It's) not uncommon for people to travel by helicopter, dogsled, canoe, kayak, or ferry boat.

3. You (can, may) wish to travel on a cruise ship.

4. Going through the Inside Passage, the ship (brings, takes) you close enough to view beautiful scenery.

5. You never could (have, of) seen as much by car.

6. Travel by water is also a (good, well) way to visit interesting cities and sights.

7. Be sure to (bring, take) a journal with you!

8. If you watch (good, well), a pod of whales might surface near the ship.

9. Possibly you'll spy an eagle atop (its, it's) nest.

10. When the ship sails (in, into) each port, you might ride ashore in a boat called a *tender.*

● Connect to the Writing Process: Editing
Recognizing Correct Usage

Write the underlined words from the following paragraph. If a word is used correctly, write C beside it. If a word is used incorrectly, write the correct form of the word.

Kayaks <u>can</u> be navigated through the canals in the city of Ketchikan. <u>Its</u> also known as "the Salmon

Capital of the World." You might feel badly about missing a feast if you don't go to a salmon bake. One spectacular sight is the rain forest with its collection of totem poles. In Juneau, you can find it difficult to walk on the steep streets. If you badly want to walk on ice, take a helicopter ride to Mendenhall Glacier. After most cruise ships leave Juneau, they travel into Glacier Bay. The glaciers, which gleam like diamonds, don't hardly seem real. Although Sitka has less people than Ketchikan and Juneau, it is a historic place. You doesn't want to miss seeing the icons in St. Michael's Cathedral.

Communicate Your Ideas

APPLY TO WRITING
Description: *Word Usage*

Jack London, a well-known American author, rose to fame when he published *The Call of the Wild,* a novel about Buck. Buck is a dog who fights for survival in the rugged but beautiful territory of Alaska. In the following excerpt from his novel, London paints a vivid picture of spring emerging in the wilderness. Read the description on the next page carefully, then follow the instructions.

Each day the sun rose earlier and set later. It was dawn by three in the morning, and twilight lingered till nine at night. The whole long day was a blaze of sunshine. The ghostly winter silence had given way to the great spring murmur of awakening life. . . . The sap was rising in the pines. The willows and aspens were bursting out in young buds. Shrubs and vines were putting on fresh garbs of green.

—*Jack London*, The Call of the Wild

Imagine that the school newspaper editor has asked you to write a description of this nature scene to include in its next edition. Use any five of the glossary words from *a/an* through *its/it's*, and write a description of the scene in the picture. Be sure to use the correct form of the words.

learn, teach *Learn* means "to gain knowledge." *Teach* means "to instruct or "to show how."

After the students **learn** about ratios, you can **teach** them about proportions.

You can learn more about using problem verbs on pages L321–L325.

leave, let *Leave* means "to depart" or "to go away from." *Let* means "to allow" or "to permit."

NONSTANDARD	I wish you would **leave** me do my job.
STANDARD	I wish you would **let** me do my job.
STANDARD	If you feel that way about it, I'll **leave** now.

lie, lay *Lie* means "to rest or recline." *Lie* is never followed by a direct object. Its principal parts are *lie, lying, lay,* and *lain. Lay* means "to put or set (something) down." *Lay* is usually followed by a direct object. Its principal parts are *lay, laying, laid,* and *laid.*

> LIE   If I **lie** down now, I'll feel like going with you later.
>
>   I was **lying** on the sofa when the phone rang.
>
>   I **lay** there yesterday.
>
>   In fact, I have **lain** there many times before.
>
> LAY   **Lay** the directions on the table before you leave.
>
>   (*Directions* is the direct object.)
>
>   Are you **laying** the directions on the seat of my car?
>
>   Isn't that where you **laid** the grocery list yesterday?
>
>   When I have **laid** reminders on the table, you never could find them.

You can learn more about using problem verbs on pages L321–L325.

passed, past *Passed* is the past tense of the verb *pass.* As a noun *past* means "a time gone by." As an adjective *past* means "just gone" or "elapsed." As a preposition *past* means "beyond."

> The way he **passed** the football reminded me of a play in the **past.**
>
> (*past* as a noun)
>
> Our quarterback has thrown the football **past** his receiver twice in the **past** two games.
>
> (*past* as a preposition and then as an adjective)

rise, raise *Rise* means "to move upward" or "to get up." *Rise* is never followed by a direct object. Its principal parts are *rise, rising, rose,* and *risen. Raise* means "to lift (something) up," "to increase," or "to grow something." *Raise* is usually followed by a direct object. Its principal parts are *raise, raising, raised,* and *raised.*

> If you want to **rise** early, be sure to set your alarm.
>
> Then I won't have to **raise** my voice to make sure you're up on time.
> (*Voice* is the direct object.)

shall, will Formal English uses *shall* with first-person pronouns and *will* with second- and third-person pronouns. Today *shall* and *will* are used interchangeably with *I* and *we,* except that *shall* is used with *I* and *we* for questions.

> **Shall** I ask permission to leave?
> No, they **will** dismiss us soon.

sit, set *Sit* means "to rest in an upright position." *Sit* is never followed by a direct object. Its principal parts are *sit, sitting, sat,* and *sat. Set* means "to put or place (something)." Set is usually followed by a direct object. Its principal parts are *set, setting, set,* and *set.*

> Please **set** your book down before we **sit** down for dinner.
> (*Book* is the direct object.)

than, then *Than* is a subordinating conjunction and is used for comparisons. *Then* is an adverb and means "at that time" or "next."

NONSTANDARD	I can't believe you're older **then** her.
STANDARD	When the others found out that I was older **than** she, they **then** let me go with them.

that, which, who As relative pronouns, *that* refers to people, animals, or things; *which* refers to animals or things; and *who* refers to people.

> Our class enjoyed the art exhibit **that** we attended.
>
> Several of the paintings, **which** were located upstairs, were portraits of famous people.
>
> The guide **who** directed the tour provided us with useful information.

PRACTICE YOUR SKILLS

● Check Your Understanding
Finding the Correct Word

Contemporary Life **Write the word in parentheses that correctly completes each sentence.**

1. Expectations receive more attention now (than, then) in the (passed, past).

2. When teachers (raise, rise) their expectations, students usually respond.

3. This concept results in (learning, teaching) students to (set, sit) higher goals.

4. When students (raise, rise) to a new level, (than, then) they are often rewarded.

5. As a result, students (learn, teach) the connection that (lays, lies) between success and recognition.

6. The recognition (that, which, who) students receive comes in a variety of forms.

7. Some teachers (shall, will) display superior assignments on the bulletin board.

8. This reward (leaves, lets) students enjoy peer recognition also.

9. Students (that, who) have reached or (passed, past) certain goals sometimes receive certificates.

10. Complimentary postcards, (which, who) praise a student's efforts, may be sent to parents.

Connect to the Writing Process: Editing
Using Correct Forms of Verbs

Write the underlined verbs. If the verb is used correctly, write *C* beside it. If the verb is used incorrectly, write the correct form of the verb.

The teacher informed the students that if they lay down on the job, this failure might lay in a lack of effort. The students set attentively through the class. They are sitting their goals for success. The teacher further explained that they should be setting their minds on their goals. A goal helps sit the tone for achievement. As a result, the teacher who raised the issue saw a sharp raise in students' attitudes. At the end of the year, students had raised their grades. Their self-esteem had raised also.

their, there, they're *Their* is a possessive pronoun. *There* is usually an adverb, but sometimes it begins an inverted sentence. *They're* is a contraction for *they are.*

The students will have **their** class pictures taken tomorrow.

There is a mirror **there** in case it's needed.

They're going to have retakes in a few weeks.

theirs, there's *Theirs* is a possessive pronoun. *There's* is a contraction for *there is.*

> If **theirs** isn't ready, ask if they want a bite of ours.
> **There's** enough to share with them.

them, those Never use *them* as a subject or a modifier.

NONSTANDARD	**Them** are the skates I bought.
	(subject)
STANDARD	**Those** are the skates I bought.
NONSTANDARD	**Them** skates are like mine.
	(adjective)
STANDARD	**Those** skates are like mine.

this here, that there Avoid using *here* or *there* in addition to *this* or *that.*

NONSTANDARD	Have you and Jason been to **that there** new restaurant?
STANDARD	Have you and Jason been to **that** new restaurant?

CONNECT TO SPEAKING AND WRITING

The word *this* indicates that a person or thing is nearby, or here. *That* indicates that a person or thing is far away, or there. When you say *this here* or *that there*, what you are really saying is "this here here" or "that there there."

to, too, two *To* is a preposition. *To* also begins an infinitive. *Too* is an adverb that modifies a verb, an adjective, or another adverb. *Two* is a number.

A Writer's Glossary of Usage

Are they going **to** the beach **to** play volleyball?

If it's not **too** hot, the **two** of them will play there.

Can I go **too** if I want **to** watch?

use to, used to Be sure to add the *d* to *use*.

NONSTANDARD	She **use to** have a miniature doll collection.
STANDARD	She **used to** have a miniature doll collection.

way, ways Do not substitute *ways* for *way* when referring to a distance.

NONSTANDARD	The rocket went a **long ways** over the ocean.
STANDARD	The rocket went a **long way** over the ocean.

where Do not substitute *where* for *that*.

NONSTANDARD	I noticed **where** the days are getting longer.
STANDARD	I noticed **that** the days are getting longer.

who, whom *Who,* a pronoun in the nominative case, is used as either a subject or a predicate nominative. *Whom,* a pronoun in the objective case, is used as a direct object, an indirect object, or an object of a preposition.

Who will take your place in the play? (subject)

Whom did the director suggest? (direct object)

whose, who's *Whose* is a possessive pronoun or an adjective. *Who's* is a contraction for *who is*.

> **Whose** presentation was the best?

> **Who's** the winner?

your, you're *Your* is a possessive pronoun. *You're* is a contraction for *you are*.

> After the dance, we're all going to **your** house.

> **You're** sure we'll have enough time?

PRACTICE YOUR SKILLS

● Check Your Understanding
Finding the Correct Word

> Geography Topic **Write the word in parentheses that correctly completes each sentence.**

1. (Their, There, They're) will likely be a variety of assignments for special credit in (your, you're) geography class.

2. Map drawing allows students (to, too, two) visualize the shape of (that, that there) particular country.

3. Filling in names of important cities helps with learning (to, too, two).

4. (Them, Those) maps are both informative and creative.

5. Frequently guest speakers who (use to, used to) live in another country give interesting and valuable talks.

6. (Those, Them) interested in a particular country might do more research.

7. Students (who, whom) enjoy cooperative learning might prefer to work in groups of (to, too, two) or more.

8. Students have great fun when they plan a trip to the country of (their, there, they're) choice.

9. (Their, There, They're) required to calculate the mileage of the trip (their, there, they're).

10. When (your, you're) deciding what clothes to pack for (this, this here) trip, think about the climate of the country you are visiting.

Connect to the Writing Process: Editing
Recognizing Correct Usage

Write the underlined words. If a word is used correctly, write C beside it. If a word is used incorrectly, write the correct form of the word.

Learning about other people's culture is exciting because theirs is different from your own. A cultural-awareness day serves too purposes. Them are the enjoyment and involvement of everyone in class. Advance planning is necessary to decide whose responsible for different projects. One group, whose focus is language, might learn key phrases to teach too the class. Another might concentrate on the food of that there country. Students who like to cook could prepare native dishes. Others whom are artistic might design costumes worn in <u>that</u> country. <u>Them</u> games that are popular <u>they're</u> could be played too. At the end of the project, <u>your</u> certain to have come a long <u>ways</u> in understanding another culture.

APPLY TO WRITING

Sentences: *Pronouns*

The words *who, whom, whose,* and *who's* can be very confusing to use. Suppose your teacher asked you to help another student who is having difficulty using these pronouns. To help the student, write an original sentence for each word. Briefly explain the reason for each word choice.

QuickCheck   Mixed Practice

Geography Topic   **Write the word in parentheses that correctly completes each sentence.**

1. (Shall, Will) we take a glimpse (in, into) the center of Europe?

2. One fascinating country (whose, who's) neutrality is known (everywhere, everywheres) is Switzerland.

3. Switzerland is (good, well) known for its mountains.

4. The Swiss Alps, (that, which, who) are one of three geographical regions in the country, are also (among, between) the world's most famous mountain ranges.

5. (Their, There, They're) also part of the literary (passed, past) in Johanna Spyri's story of *Heidi*.

6. If you travel to Mount Titlis, you (can, may) eat in a mountaintop restaurant.

7. (Theirs, There's) (not any, not no) better dining experience (than, then) fondue.

8. (Fewer, Less) sights are more interesting than watching the cows descend from the mountains.

9. The cows have large cowbells around (their, there, they're) necks and are often decorated with ribbons and flowers.

10. In no place (accept, except) Bern, the capital of Switzerland, (shall, will) you find a bear pit in the middle of the city!

11. Another unusual attraction is the Clock Tower, which has moving characters (who, whom) tell time.

12. At Lake Lucerne, you (can, may) want to ride a cogwheel train up the mountain.

13. Beautiful resort hotels (set, sit) high atop the mountains.

14. You will be favorably (affected, effected) by the many Swiss chalets (that, who) create a pretty (affect, effect).

15. (Your, You're) trip won't be complete if you (doesn't, don't) buy Swiss chocolate.

CHAPTER 15

Capital Letters

 **Pretest**

Directions
Read the passage and decide which underlined word or words should be capitalized. Write the letter of the correct answer. If the underlined word or words contain no error, write **D**.

EXAMPLE

In 1903, American author Jack London published *the call of the wild*.
(1)

1 **A** *The Call of the Wild*
  B *The Call Of The Wild*
  C *The Call of The Wild*
  D No error

ANSWER

1 **A**

The early 1900s was a period of exciting "firsts." In 1901, <u>baseball's American league</u> was formed to compete
(1)
with the National League. American <u>explorer robert e.</u>
(2)
<u>peary</u> reached the North Pole in 1909. The year 1916 brought Jeannette Rankin to the <u>U.S. house of</u>
(3)
<u>representatives</u> as its first female member. By 1921, mystery writer Agatha Christie had published her <u>first</u>
<u>hercule poirot story</u>. In 1928, *Steamboat Willie,* the first
(4)
sound cartoon, featured <u>walt disney's Mickey Mouse</u>.
(5)

1 **A** baseball's American League

  B Baseball's American league

  C Baseball's American League

  D No error

2 **A** explorer Robert e. peary

  B explorer Robert E. Peary

  C Explorer Robert E. Peary

  D No error

3 **A** u.s. house of representatives

  B U.S. House of representatives

  C U.S. House of Representatives

  D No error

4 **A** first Hercule Poirot story

  B First Hercule Poirot story

  C First Hercule Poirot Story

  D No error

5 **A** walt Disney's mickey mouse

  B Walt Disney's mickey mouse

  C Walt Disney's Mickey Mouse

  D No error

Sonia Terk Delaunay.
(Detail) *Study for Portugal,*
ca. 1937.
Gouache on paper, 14¼ by 37
inches. The National Museum of
Women in the Arts.

Describe   Describe the setting and what is
happening.

Analyze   What colors and shapes do you see? How
does the artist imply lines within the
painting?

Interpret   What ideas do you think the artist is
trying to show by using few outlines and
strong lines? How could a writer express
similar ideas?

Judge   Do you think this painting or a written
work would more satisfyingly express the
same ideas? Explain your answer.

At the end of this chapter, you will use the artwork to
stimulate ideas for writing.

Rules of Capital Letters

Capital letters and punctuation marks were not used when writing first began. They were developed over the years to make written communication easier for the reader to read and understand.

First Words

Without capital letters and end marks, one sentence would run into another. Among other things, a capital letter is a clear signal that a new sentence is beginning. A capital letter also begins a line of poetry, certain parts of a letter, and some parts of an outline.

Sentences

A capital letter always begins a new sentence.

Capitalize the first word in a sentence.

STATEMENT	**L**ast night's frost threatened the delicate flowers.
QUESTION	**W**ere your roses damaged in last night's frost?

Lines of Poetry

A capital letter also signals the beginning of a new line of poetry in most poems.

Capitalize the first word in a line of poetry.

Out walking in the frozen swamp one
　　gray day,
I paused and said, "I will turn back
　　from here.
No, I will go on farther—and we
　　shall see."

　　　　　　　　　　　　—*Robert Frost*, "The Wood Pile"

CONNECT TO WRITER'S CRAFT

　　A few modern poets purposely misuse capital letters or do not use any capital letters at all in their poetry. If you are quoting such a poem, copy it exactly as the poet wrote it. Notice the lack of capital letters in the following poem.

who knows if the moon's
a balloon, coming out of a keen city
in the sky—filled with pretty people?
　　　　　　—*E. E. Cummings*, "Who Knows If the Moon's"

Parts of Letters

Capital letters bring attention to certain parts of a letter.

Capitalize the first word in the greeting of a letter and the first word in the closing of a letter.

GREETINGS AND CLOSINGS		
GREETING	**D**ear Terri,	**G**entlemen:
CLOSING	**S**incerely,	**V**ery truly yours,

Outlines

The main points of an outline begin with a capital letter. The capital letters help draw attention to the important points in the outline.

Capitalize the first word of each item in an outline and the letters that begin major subsections of the outline.

 I. **Severe weather storms**
  A. **Tornadoes**
  B. **Hurricanes**
  C. **Thunderstorms**
  D. **Cyclones**

 II. **Mild weather storms**
  A. **Snow**
  B. **Rain**
  C. **Sleet**
  D. **Wind**

 ## The Pronoun *I*

The pronoun *I* is always capitalized, whether it stands alone or is part of a contraction.

Capitalize the pronoun *I*, both alone and in contractions.

ALONE	Did you see the enormous snowball that **I** made?
CONTRACTIONS	Next winter **I'm** going to visit San Antonio, Texas.
	Everyone says **I'll** like the sights in San Antonio.

You can learn about capital letters with direct quotations on page L576.

Practice Your Skills

Capitalizing First Words and I

Mathematics Topic	**Write correctly each word that should be capitalized.**

1. before snowy Canada converted to the metric system, my family took a trip to Montreal.

2. montreal is a beautiful city.

3. it has incredible museums.

4. consumer goods in Montreal were measured by the Canadian system.

5. for example, gasoline was sold by the imperial gallon.

6. an imperial gallon is equal to approximately five U.S. quarts.

7. the imperial gallon sold for about $1.50, but the U.S. gallon cost about $1.15.

8. my father asked me to calculate the relative cost of gasoline in Canada and the United States.

9. furthermore, i had to figure which price was the better bargain.

10. i'll never forget how long it took me to calculate the costs.

11. the vacation was delayed until i could figure out the relative costs.

12. thank goodness Canada has converted to the metric system.

13. to this day i get nervous thinking about imperial gallons in wintry Canada.

14. our vacation went splendidly.

Rewrite the following letter, adding capital letters where needed.

dear Mr. Grieb,

    now that the English class is over, i wish to thank you for talking to our class about poetry. your information was appreciated by the whole class. i found this quotation that i think you'll enjoy. Algernon Charles Swinburne wrote:

sleep; and if life were bitter to thee, pardon,
if sweet, give thanks; thou hast no more to live;
and to give thanks is good, and to forgive.

    i hope that you are able to visit our English class again soon.

            sincerely,

            Monica

Communicate Your Ideas

APPLY TO WRITING

Thank-You Note: *Capital Letters*

Write a personal thank-you note to someone at your school who has helped you in some way. Be sure to tell that person what service he or she provided and why you appreciated it. Use capital letters as needed.

▶ Proper Nouns

A **noun** is the name of a person, a place, a thing, or an idea. A **proper noun** is the name of a particular person, place, thing, or idea.

COMMON AND PROPER NOUNS	
COMMON NOUNS	PROPER NOUNS
girl	Serena
city	Seattle
road	Evergreen Road
school	Teague Middle School
law	the United States Constitution
team	Texas Rangers
mountain	Pike's Peak
language	English

Capitalize proper nouns and their abbreviations.

Study the following groups of rules for capitalizing proper nouns. Refer to them when you edit your writing.

You can learn more about nouns on pages L47–L52.

Names of persons and animals should be capitalized. Also capitalize the initials that stand for people's names.

NAMES OF PERSONS AND ANIMALS	
PERSONS	Marianne, M. W. Raymond, Jon Davies, Jr.
ANIMALS	Arnold, Bambi, Maggie, Rover, Spot, Willie

You can learn more about the capitalization of people's titles on pages L506–L507.

PRACTICE YOUR SKILLS

● Check Your Understanding
Capitalizing Proper Nouns

History Topic **Write correctly each word that should be capitalized.**

1. Rita likes American colonial history more than her friend fred does.

2. Planter james madison called for a Constitutional Convention.

3. Back in 1786, madison wanted to revise the Articles of Confederation.

4. At first george washington was not enthusiastic.

5. Finally washington agreed with james madison and alexander hamilton that changes were needed.

6. Fifty-five delegates went to ben franklin's hometown.

7. They were to work with madison, hamilton, and franklin on the United States constitution.

8. The delegates chose washington as presiding officer.

9. james madison's plan called for a two-house Congress.

10. On the other hand, william patterson favored a one-house plan.

11. The British leader william e. gladstone greatly admired the united states constitution.

12. Twenty-six-year-old jonathan dayton was the youngest signer.

13. Eighty-one-year-old benjamin franklin was the oldest.

14. Another signer was gunning bedford, jr.

Geographical names that name particular places and bodies of water are capitalized.

GEOGRAPHICAL NAMES	
STREETS, HIGHWAYS	Preston Road (Rd.), New Jersey Turnpike, Thirty-third Street (St.) (The second part of a hyphenated numbered street is *not* capitalized.)
CITIES, STATES	Austin, Texas (**TX**), Orlando, Florida (**FL**)
COUNTIES, PARISHES, TOWNSHIPS	Orange County, Louisiana Parish, Washington Township
COUNTRIES	France, Mexico, Greece, India, United States of America (**U.S.A.**)
CONTINENTS	Australia, South America, Europe
WORLD REGIONS	Northern Hemisphere, South Pole
ISLANDS	Virgin Islands, Galveston Island
MOUNTAINS	Rocky Mountains, Mount (Mt.) Ida
FORESTS AND PARKS	Ocala National Forest, Little Brown Park, Yellowstone National Park
BODIES OF WATER	Lake Michigan, the Pacific Ocean, the Po River, Hudson Bay
SECTIONS OF THE COUNTRY	the South, the West, New England, the Midwest (Simple compass directions are not capitalized. *Go south on Center Street.*)

Words such as *city, street, lake, ocean,* and *mountain* are capitalized only when they are part of a proper noun.

> We live near some lakes, but they are small compared to the Great Lakes.

PRACTICE YOUR SKILLS

● Check Your Understanding
Capitalizing Geographical Names

History Topic **Write correctly each word that should be capitalized.**

1. In 1840, the united states had three thousand miles of railroad track.

2. By 1850, workers were constructing railroads in all of the states east of the mississippi river.

3. One of these railroads linked new york city and buffalo, ny.

4. Others linked such cities as baltimore, md, and wheeling, wv.

5. Railway builders linked these eastern lines with lines in ohio, indiana, and illinois.

6. Railway lines went around both lake erie and lake michigan.

7. Before the railroads many depended on the mississippi river to transport goods.

8. The goods were put on ships in new orleans, louisiana.

9. The ships sailed around florida to cities in the east.

10. From the east to past the rocky mountains, north america was opened up by the railroad.

Names of historical importance should be capitalized. Capitalize the names of historical events, periods, and documents. (Prepositions, such as the *of* in Bill of Rights, are not capitalized.)

HISTORIC NAMES	
EVENTS	World War II (**WWII**), the Boston Tea Party, the Treaty of Versailles
PERIODS OF TIME	the Middle Ages, the Industrial Revolution, the Enlightenment, the Jazz Age
DOCUMENTS	the Constitution, the Bill of Rights, the Emancipation Proclamation

Names of groups and businesses begin with capital letters. Capitalize the names of organizations, businesses, institutions, teams, and government bodies.

NAMES OF GROUPS	
ORGANIZATIONS	the United Nations (**UN**), Habitat for Humanity, the National Association for the Advancement of Colored People (**NAACP**)
BUSINESSES	Roberto & Sons, B&M Plumbing
INSTITUTIONS	University of Southern California (**USC**)
TEAMS	the Dallas Cowboys, the Oakland Raiders
GOVERNMENT BODIES	Congress, the House of Representatives, the Federal Bureau of Investigation (**FBI**)

PRACTICE YOUR SKILLS

● Check Your Understanding
Using Capital Letters

History Topic **Write correctly each word that should be capitalized.**

1. A major peacekeeping organization was created after world war II.

2. The united nations (un) was established to ensure peace.

3. It was an effort to improve on the league of nations.

4. The league of nations was formed after wwI.

5. Almost two hundred member nations support the un financially.

6. The united states senate and the house of representatives must pass the budget each year.

7. The united nations supports the world health organization and unicef.

8. The security council guides all activities of the un.

9. The general assembly includes all members of the organization.

10. The offices of the un are located in new york.

● Connect to the Writing Process: Editing
Using Capital Letters

Rewrite the following sentences, adding capital letters where needed.

11. On June 28, 1919, the allies and Germany signed a treaty to end world war I.

12. The agreement was called the treaty of versailles.

13. With the support of congress, the treaty would divide the German empire into nine nations.

14. President Wilson managed to get the league of nations included as part of the treaty.

15. This accomplishment was one of Wilson's famous fourteen points.

16. The American president hoped that the league would help lessen the impact of the treaty of versailles on Germany.

17. The republican party argued against the treaty.

18. They hoped to weaken the democratic party and President Wilson.

19. The senate foreign relations committee delayed the vote on the treaty.

20. In March 1920, the senate did not pass the treaty of versailles.

● Connect to the Writing Process: Prewriting
Using Capital Letters

In preparation for proposing a peer-group organization to improve communication at your school, jot down answers to the following questions. Use capital letters where needed.

21. What will be the formal name of the organization?

22. Which school official will sponsor the organization?

23. What officers will the organization have?

24. Where will the organization meet?

25. What state or national organization will this peer group be like?

26. How will this organization improve communication?

APPLY TO WRITING

Editorial: *Capital Letters*

Write an editorial for your school newspaper in which you call for the formation of a peer-group organization to improve the communication among groups in your school. Using your ideas from the preceding exercise, briefly describe a need for improved communication and call for specific actions. Use capital letters where needed to name the group, to identify the officers, and to ask for the support of school leaders and students.

Specific time periods and events begin with capital letters. Capitalize the days of the week, the months of the year, civil and religious holidays, and special events. Also capitalize the abbreviations A.D., B.C., A.M., and P.M.

TIME PERIODS AND EVENTS	
DAYS, MONTHS	Sunday (Sun.), Saturday (Sat.), January (Jan.), May
HOLIDAYS	Fourth of July, Presidents' Day
SPECIAL EVENTS	Rose Bowl Parade, Olympics
TIME ABBREVIATIONS	A.D. B.C. A.M. P.M. Confucius lived during the years 551 to 487 B.C.

Do not capitalize the seasons of the year unless they are part of a specific name.

My favorite spring event is the Spring Jamboree.

You can learn more about the punctuation of abbreviations on pages L525–L527.

Names of nationalities and races should be capitalized.

NATIONALITIES AND RACES	
NATIONALITIES	an **A**frican, a **S**eminole, a **C**anadian
RACES	**C**aucasian, **A**sian, **H**ispanic

Religions, religious references, and religious holidays begin with capital letters.

RELIGIOUS NAMES	
RELIGIONS	**C**hristianity, **J**udaism, **B**uddhism, **I**slam
RELIGIOUS HOLIDAYS	**H**anukkah, **C**hristmas, **R**amadan, **E**piphany, **P**urim, **E**aster, **P**assover
RELIGIOUS REFERENCES	**G**od, the **L**ord, the **C**reator, the **B**ible, the **T**orah, the **K**oran, the **N**ew **T**estament

The word *god* is not capitalized when it refers to gods in polytheistic religions. Do capitalize their names, however.

> The Vikings said that **T**hor was the **g**od of thunder.

PRACTICE YOUR SKILLS

● Check Your Understanding
Using Capital Letters

Contemporary Life **Write correctly each word that should be capitalized. If the sentence is correct, write C.**

1. The fall of the school year is full of both religious and secular holidays.

2. Just as september begins, there is labor day.

3. Also in september, jews celebrate rosh hashanah.
4. The second monday of october is columbus day.
5. United nations Day is october 24.
6. By late october halloween is upon us.
7. November 11 is celebration of veterans day.
8. On a thursday in november is thanksgiving.
9. December brings the christian season of christmas.
10. In some years during the same period, muslims begin observing ramadan.

● **Connect to the Writing Process:** Editing
Using Capital Letters

Rewrite the following paragraph, adding capital letters.

After christmas, new years' day, and martin luther king, jr., day, what is there to look forward to in february? What the winter needs is another holiday! It should be a holiday that appeals to many groups— Chinese, West Indian, Latino, and Pakistani—to name a few. Perhaps we should celebrate it on a tuesday or a thursday. It should not conflict with the days of worship for christianity, judaism, islam, and other faiths. Could it be a mixture of a fiesta and the fourth of july? The activities would start at four p.m. There would be tasty food, fun, and games. Let's have it on february 4. We'll call it february's festival day!

In preparation for proposing a new holiday, answer the following questions. Use capital letters where needed.

11. In what month would you have the new holiday?

12. On what day of the week would you have it?

13. At what time will the holiday begin and end?

14. Why did you pick that month, day, and time?

15. What is the reason for the holiday?

16. How will you celebrate the holiday?

Communicate Your Ideas

APPLY TO WRITING
Letter: *Capital Letters*

Using your answers to the questions in the preceding
Prewriting activity, write a letter to the leaders of
your community. Propose a new holiday. Explain what
the holiday will celebrate. Then pick a day, a date,

and a name for your new holiday. Suggest where and how the holiday might be celebrated. Be sure to explain how this holiday will be sensitive to the various nationalities, races, religious preferences, and values in your community. Use capital letters where needed.

Names of planets, stars, and constellations are capitalized.

ASTRONOMICAL NAMES	
PLANETS	Jupiter, Venus, Mars, Pluto
STARS	the North Star, Sirius, Vega
CONSTELLATIONS	Little Dipper, Taurus, Ursa Minor

Do not capitalize *sun* or *moon*. Do not capitalize *earth* if the word *the* comes in front of it.

CAPITAL	Is it rare that Venus lines up with Earth?
NO CAPITAL	It depends on how many times the earth travels around the sun in a given time.

Languages and specific school courses followed by a number are capitalized.

LANGUAGES AND SCHOOL COURSES	
LANGUAGES	English, Latin, Russian, Spanish
COMPUTER LANGUAGES	Java, Cobol, Visual Basic
NUMBERED COURSES	Art II, Typing I, Chorus II

Except for language courses, course names without a number—such as *history, math, science,* and *physical education*—are not capitalized.

Other proper nouns should also begin with capital letters.

OTHER PROPER NOUNS	
AWARDS	Academy Awards®, Heisman Trophy
BRAND NAMES	Klean soap, Kone cheese, Verdon chicken (The product itself—such as *soap, cheese,* and *chicken*—is not capitalized.)
BRIDGES AND BUILDINGS	Fargo Building, Tower of London
MONUMENTS AND MEMORIALS	Washington Monument, Jefferson Memorial, Statue of Liberty
TECHNOLOGICAL TERMS	Internet, Web, World Wide Web, Website, Web page
VEHICLES	*Apollo 17, Columbia, Old Ironsides*

PRACTICE YOUR SKILLS

● Check Your Understanding
Using Capital Letters

Science Topic **Write correctly each word that should be capitalized.**

1. Can you imagine what the public thought in the old days about traveling to mars or other planets?

2. Was the spaceship the size and the shape of the washington monument?

3. Did the crew fill up the tank with pell gasoline?

4. Who besides nasa could try space travel?

5. How does a person get a road map to saturn?

6. You can't exactly go north and turn right at the planet mercury.

7. Did the astronauts travel in the *voyager* spacecraft?

8. Would the astronauts have to be able to speak russian, spanish, and computer languages?

9. They would need to have passed more science courses than physics IV and chemistry IV.

10. Do you think that the astronauts should be given the congressional medal of honor?

Connect to the Writing Process: Editing
Using Capital Letters

Rewrite the following paragraph, adding capital letters where needed.

Plu is from pluto. His eyes are the size of the pancakes from the tasty maple brand of pancakes. His skin is as smooth as the ice at the metro skating rink. Toothless, he stands as tall and as bony as the eiffel tower in Paris. Plu from pluto has no arms or legs. Rapid german-like sounds come out of his toothless mouth. Through an instant translation machine borrowed from nasa, Plu asked me if I owned a fire-engine red automobile. When I told him I was too young to drive a car, he said he would settle for a ride in the *discovery* space shuttle. From what I could tell, I would have to take german I, II, and III to understand his language and physics IV to figure out how he got to earth. Unfortunately, Plu broke my computer when he tried to put his own web page on the internet.

● Connect to the Writing Process: Prewriting
Using Capital Letters

In preparation for writing an original story about an alien, answer the following questions. Use capital letters where needed.

21. What planet or constellation is your alien from?

22. What building, bridge, or monument in the world is about the same size as your alien?

23. What product in a grocery store most resembles the color of your alien?

24. What language on earth does its language sound like?

25. What kind of car does it prefer?

26. What kind of soft drink does it like?

27. What courses in school would you have to take to understand the alien's culture?

Communicate Your Ideas

APPLY TO WRITING
Story: *Capital Letters*

You have been awakened in the middle of the night by a space traveler from another planet. You have a talk with the alien traveler, but before you get a chance to take a picture, he or she or it vanishes. Using the sentences you wrote for the prewriting exercise, write a story about the alien to share with your classmates. Describe the alien and tell about the places the alien has visited. Use capital letters as needed.

 **QuickCheck** Mixed Practice

General Interest **Write each sentence, adding capital letters where needed. Then answer each question—if you can!**

1. who was the first person to sign the declaration of independence?

2. who used a middle initial that did not stand for a middle name—ulysses s. grant or harry s. truman?

3. who built their empire first, the mayas or the aztecs?

4. who was raised in the midwest, jefferson or lincoln?

5. who, little orphan annie or mickey mouse, owned a dog named pluto?

6. who was the first person to walk on the moon, michael collins or neil armstrong?

7. who sold louisiana to the americans in 1803, the english or the french?

8. who was the captain of the starship *enterprise,* james kirk or alan shepherd?

9. who warned the colonists that the british were coming by land?

10. who was the mythological god who held the world on his shoulders, zeus or atlas?

Other Uses of Capital Letters

You have learned the most common uses for capital letters. There are, however, a few other uses that you need to know.

▶ Proper Adjectives

You just finished reviewing proper nouns, words that name specific people, places, and things. Like proper nouns, most proper adjectives begin with a capital letter.

Capitalize most proper adjectives.

PROPER NOUNS	PROPER ADJECTIVES
Europe	European history
North America	North American countries
The South	Southern states
Africa	an African company
France	French dressing

PRACTICE YOUR SKILLS

● Check Your Understanding
Capitalizing Proper Adjectives

Contemporary Life **Write correctly each word that should be capitalized.**

1. Political candidates collect different experiences during a tour of the north american continent.

2. They travel north to the canadian border.

3. They go south as far as the mexican border.

4. They might collect swedish recipes from chefs in Minnesota.

5. They dine on chinese food in San Francisco.

6. Cheeses are given to them by the pennsylvania dutch population.

7. Samples of texas barbecue sauce are plentiful.

8. In the Empire State, they can feast on italian food.

9. In the South, they get bags of georgia peanuts.

10. They can sample irish stew on St. Patrick's Day.

● Connect to the Writing Process: Editing
Capitalizing Proper Adjectives

Rewrite the following paragraph, adding capital letters where needed.

The european railway system is vital to the economy. An american traveler can see all of Europe from the trains. One day an american tourist can join in the scottish dances. The next day he or she can zip south to english soil and take in a Shakespearean play. However, a real shopper will use the railroad to find goods in other countries. With a longer journey, the traveler can buy the products of spanish merchants. Many seek french fashions and italian shoes. Others want german automobiles. No one wants to miss the european sights. The buildings themselves are evidence of events from roman history.

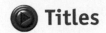 Titles

Capital letters are used in the titles of people, of written works, and of other works of art.

Capitalize the titles of people and works of art.

Titles Used with Names of Persons

Capitalize a title showing office, rank, or profession when it comes before a person's name. The same title is usually not capitalized when it follows a name.

BEFORE A NAME	Have you met **Senator C**leland? (capital letter)
AFTER A NAME	Is Max Cleland a **s**enator from your state? (no capital letter)
BEFORE A NAME	Did you consult **Chairperson B**rooks? (capital letter)
AFTER A NAME	Adam Brooks is **c**hairperson of the special committee on education. (no capital letter)

Other titles or their abbreviations—such as *Ms., Dr., and Lt.*— should be capitalized when they come before a person's name.

This message is for **Mr. J**ordan.

An official letter from the committee has arrived for **Sgt. S**haw.

Titles Used in Direct Address

A noun of direct address is used to call someone by name. Capitalize a title used instead of a name in direct address.

| DIRECT ADDRESS | When will you be free, **S**enator? |
| | I think, **G**overnor, the bill will pass. |

You can learn more about using commas with direct address on page L547.

Titles Showing Family Relationships

Capitalize titles showing family relationships when the titles come before people's names. Capitalize the titles also when they are used instead of names or in direct address.

BEFORE A NAME	Is **U**ncle Jeb running for Congress?
USED AS A NAME	Tell **M**om that he's leaving soon.
IN DIRECT ADDRESS	Are you leaving, **S**is?

Do not capitalize a title showing a family relationship when it is preceded by a possessive noun or pronoun—unless it is considered part of a person's name.

| NO CAPITAL | My dad works at the legislature. (The word *dad* is preceded by a possessive pronoun, *my*.) |
| CAPITAL | The press interviewed **U**ncle Jeb. (*Uncle* is part of the person's name.) |

You can learn about using apostrophes with possessive nouns and pronouns on pages L597–L602.

PRACTICE YOUR SKILLS

● Check Your Understanding
Capitalizing Titles of People

Science Topic **Write correctly each word that should be capitalized. If the sentence is correct, write C.**

1. Have you been to mr. Brook's new chemistry laboratory?

2. Yes, mr. Brook is my sister's chemistry teacher this year.

3. He is the nephew of principal Balinger.

4. There is a huge chart hanging on the wall in the chemistry lab.

5. In the late 1800s, dr. Dimitri Mendeleev did important work.

6. Indeed, doctor, you made the study of chemistry much easier.

7. The doctor from Russia created a table for the elements.

8. dr. Mendeleev's table arranged the elements according to atomic mass.

9. In 1913, professor Henry G. J. Moseley improved on the table.

10. The professor improved on the doctor's analysis of elements.

● Connect to the Writing Process: Editing
Using Capital Letters

Rewrite the following paragraph, adding capital letters where needed.

After many medical tests on governor salem, Dr. Harry Rose found a tumor in his patient's thyroid.

The doctor told the governor immediately. medical chief of staff Rose decided to treat the tumor with a radioactive isotope. Our governor asked about the treatment. As expected, dr. Rose was very informative. The doctor explained that she had used the isotope on her aunt last week. The isotope is called iodine-131 and is very unstable. Last week that instability helped aunt Mildred because it released radiation into her tumor. As it did for the doctor's aunt, the isotope will help shrink or kill governor salem's tumor. The isotope of iodine, according to dr. Rose, is a doctor's friend.

Titles of Written Works and Other Works of Art

Capitalize the first word, the last word, and all important words in titles of books, newspapers, magazines, stories, poems, movies, plays, musical compositions, and other works of art. Do not capitalize a preposition, a coordinating conjunction, or an article (*a, an,* or *the*) unless it is the first or last word in a title.

BOOKS AND CHAPTER TITLES	I looked up some information in *History of Russia* and found a good quotation in "The Growth of Russia."
SHORT STORIES	Have you read the story "The Stone Boy"?
POEMS	My favorite poem is "Who Has Seen the Wind?"

NEWSPAPERS AND NEWSPAPER ARTICLES	Today the *New York Daily News* published the article "Turntable of Tunes."
	(Generally the word *the* before the first word of a newspaper or magazine title is not capitalized.)
MAGAZINES AND MAGAZINE ARTICLES	*Sports Illustrated* did an article "The Spurs Win, the Spurs Win!"
MUSICAL COMPOSITIONS	I like the song "Leaving the Promised Land" from George Gershwin's *Porgy and Bess*.

You can learn about punctuating titles on pages L567–L571.

PRACTICE YOUR SKILLS

● Check Your Understanding
Capitalizing Titles

Write correctly each word that should be capitalized.

1. Helen is an old-fashioned teenager right out of Thorton Wilder's play *our town*.

2. Her favorite song is Katherine Lee Bates's "america the beautiful."

3. She enjoys reading articles like "essentials of good citizenship" in *reader's digest*.

4. She prefers animated films such as *the lion king* and *bambi*.

5. The fable "the tortoise and the hare" is a good example of how she leads her life.

6. She subscribes to *the new york times*.

7. It is a newspaper without comics like *for better or worse.*

8. Her idea of a romantic song is "moon river."

9. Her favorite book is *the summer of My german soldier.*

10. She wants to play Juliet in Shakespeare's *romeo and juliet.*

● Connect to the Writing Process: Editing
Using Capital Letters

Rewrite the following paragraphs, adding capital letters where needed.

More than 350 years ago, the inca indians of south america controlled an empire of almost 2,500 miles, from colombia to chile. In approximately a.d. 1400, this tribe conquered some 10 million people living in present-day peru, ecuador, bolivia, western argentina, and the northern part of chile.

Across the many miles of the empire, the incas built a network of roads. The roads, however, had to run through and around the andes mountains. This feat would be difficult even for modern engineers.

Often the incas tunneled through the mountain cliffs, but they also built bridges. The longest of the inca bridges was made famous in the novel *the bridge of san luis rey.* This 148-foot suspension bridge crossed a deep ravine of the apurimac river. Until the bridge fell early in the twentieth century, it had been in use longer than any other bridge in south america.

Because of an internal civil war in their empire, these mighty indians were conquered by a handful of spaniards led by francisco pizarro. Information about their art, culture, and village life is contained in spanish chronicles.

APPLY TO WRITING

E-mail: *Capitalizing Titles*

Write an E-mail to your principal about what should be included in a time capsule to represent your generation. You can suggest books, magazines, movies, TV programs, music, or other forms of art that represent the community's young people. Propose five items and explain why you chose each one. Be sure to use capital letters where needed.

 QuickCheck Mixed Practice

General Interest — **Write each sentence, adding capital letters where needed. Then answer each question—if you can!**

1. which is closer to the sun, mercury or venus?

2. what is the name of clark kent's newspaper, the *daily news* or the *daily planet?*

3. what river begins in new hampshire but is named for another state—the connecticut or the delaware?

4. what famous indian princess rescued john smith from death?

5. in what year did columbus sight land in what is now the bahamas?

6. what group first recorded the song "with a little help from my friends"?

7. what is the first monday in september called?

8. what is another name for cape canaveral in florida?

9. what state is directly north of oregon?

10. what city is sacred to jews, christians, and muslims?

11. what is the name of the girl who hid from the nazis in an attic in amsterdam?

12. what is the name of the world's highest mountain, mount everest or mount rainier?

13. what is the name of the author of *alice's adventures in wonderland,* lewis carroll or carol lewis?

14. what president issued the emancipation proclamation on january 1, 1863?

15. in 1959, alaska and what other state were admitted to the united states?

16. what award does the best actor in a movie get, an oscar® or an emmy?

17. what is the name of a south american country that starts with the letter *e*?

18. in what state is mt. rainier, utah or washington?

19. what holiday besides veterans day falls in november?

20. what city in florida has more theme parks, tampa or orlando?

Using Capital Letters

Correctly write each word that should begin with a capital letter.

1. five states border the gulf of mexico.
2. for more than 150 years, american colonists lived under british rule.
3. i love the poem "the road not taken."
4. the capital of arkansas is little rock.
5. a painting titled *lady musician and young girl* was painted in the first century b.c.
6. which is larger, jupiter or earth?
7. after moving to the east from oregon, my brother settled in connecticut.
8. get on venton road and go north for two miles.
9. my favorite aunt and uncle will visit us soon.
10. lyndon b. johnson, who was president in the mid-1960s, signed a document called the education bill.
11. is the sun farther from earth in summer or in winter?
12. is your computer connected to the internet?
13. every morning my mom reads the *washington post.*
14. the last of the thirteen english colonies to be settled was georgia.
15. uncle david is president of the ridley golf league.
16. one american signed the declaration of independence in very large letters.
17. tell us, officer, were there any witnesses?
18. which do you enjoy more, science or european history?

19. the name of the first space shuttle was *columbia.*

20. have you ever been to walker lake in nevada?

Editing for Proper Capitalization

Read the following paragraphs. Find the twenty-four words that should begin with a capital letter. Then rewrite the paragraphs correctly.

the battle of new orleans was one of the greatest victories in united states history. leading a force of frontiersmen, general andrew jackson of tennessee confronted troops of british soldiers who had just defeated napoleon's great french army.

the battle took place on january 8, 1815—just fifteen days after a treaty ending the war of 1812 had been signed in europe. unfortunately, the news of the treaty had not reached andrew jackson or the british. in fact, jackson's superiors in washington were unaware of either the battle or the treaty.

Writing Sentences

Write sentences that follow the directions.

Write a sentence that includes . . .

1. the name of your city and state.

2. today's date with the day, month, and year.

3. the name of a South American country.

4. the brand name of a product you use.

5. a proper adjective.

Language and *Self-Expression*

Sonia Terk Delaunay used her art to help others understand something about life in Portugal. For example, in *Study for Portugal* (detail), the artist used shapes with little outlining or detail to convey feeling and imply relationships among the people, animals, and structures in this scene.

Imagine that you have been asked to write a letter to a pen pal that explains what life is like in the neighborhood, city, or town where you live. Write sentences that express your ideas clearly. Be sure to use capitalization for proper names and write abbreviations correctly.

Prewriting You may want to use a word web showing your subject—people, setting, structures, activities—and their relationships to one another.

Drafting Use the ideas and relationships in your web to write about your subject. Introduce your subject in the first sentence, give details in the middle sentences, and then summarize your ideas in the closing sentence.

Revising Read your first and last sentence to a partner. Ask him or her how they relate to each other. Then let your partner read the letter and give feedback. Answer your partner's questions and revise as needed.

Editing Read your letter again, checking that you have capitalized the first word in the greeting and the closing. Be sure you have capitalized the proper names of people and places as needed.

Publishing Prepare a final copy of your letter and place it in a scrapbook about your community.

Another Look

Capital Letters for First Words
Capitalize the first word in a sentence. *(page L483)*
Capitalize the first word in a line of poetry. *(pages L483–L484)*
Capitalize the first word in the greeting of a letter and the first word in the closing of a letter. *(page L484)*
Capitalize the first word of each item in an outline and the letters that begin major subsections of the outline. *(page L485)*

The Pronoun *I*
Capitalize the pronoun *I*, both alone and in contractions. *(page L485)*

Proper Nouns
Capitalize proper nouns and their abbreviations. *(pages L488–L500)*
Capitalize the names of particular persons and animals. Also capitalize the initials that stand for people's names. *(page L488)*
Capitalize geographical names. *(page L490)*
Capitalize the names of historical events, periods, and documents. *(page L492)*
Capitalize the names of organizations, businesses, institutions, teams, and government bodies. *(page L492)*
Capitalize specific time periods and events. *(page L495)*
Capitalize the names of nationalities and races. *(page L496)*
Capitalize religions and religious references and holidays. *(page L496)*
Capitalize the names of planets, stars, and constellations. *(page L499)*
Capitalize the names of languages and specific school courses. *(page L499)*

Proper Adjectives
Capitalize most proper adjectives. *(page L504)*

Titles
Capitalize the titles used with names of persons. *(pages L506–L507)*
Capitalize a title used instead of a name in direct address. *(page L507)*
Capitalize titles showing family relationships. *(page L507)*
Capitalize titles of written works and works of art. *(pages L509–L510)*

Directions

Read the passage and decide which underlined word or words should be capitalized. Write the letter of the correct answer. If the underlined word or words contain no error, write *D*.

EXAMPLE

Golfer Ben Hogan won the 1953 U.S. <u>open, the masters, and the british open.</u>
(1)

     1 A Open, the Masters, and the British open.

        B Open, the Masters, and the british Open.

        C Open, the Masters, and the British Open.

        D No error

ANSWER   **1 C**

The decades of the 1950s and 1960s brought innovations and new milestones. In 1952, the first automatic pinsetter was installed in a <u>bowling alley in Brooklyn, NY.</u> The following
(1)
year James Baldwin published his first novel <u>*Go tell it on the*</u>
(2)
<u>*mountain*</u>. Soviet cosmonaut <u>Yuri gagarin orbited earth</u> in
(3)
1961. That same year, astronaut John Glenn became the first <u>American to orbit Earth</u>. The U.S. <u>civil rights act</u> of 1965
(4)   (5)
prohibited discrimination in employment.

1   **A**   Bowling Alley in Brooklyn, NY.

      B   Bowling alley in Brooklyn, NY.

      C   bowling alley in Brooklyn, Ny.

      D   No error

2   **A**   *Go Tell It on The Mountain*

      B   *Go Tell It on the Mountain*

      C   *Go Tell it on the Mountain*

      D   No error

3   **A**   yuri gagarin orbited earth

      B   Yuri Gagarin orbited Earth

      C   Yuri Gagarin orbited earth

      D   No error

4   **A**   American To Orbit Earth

      B   american to orbit earth

      C   American to orbit earth

      D   No error

5   **A**   civil Rights act

      B   Civil rights act

      C   Civil Rights Act

      D   No error

CHAPTER 16

End Marks and Commas

 **Pretest**

Directions
Read the passage and choose the punctuation mark that belongs in each underlined space. Write the letter of the correct answer. If no punctuation is needed, write *D*.

EXAMPLE **1.** Marin County _(1)_ California, is the place where the first mountain bike race was held.
    1 **A** colon
       B comma
       C period
       D No punctuation needed

ANSWER   1 **B**

Dear Mom _(1)_

    I am having a lot of fun with Aunt Jo. We rented mountain bikes _(2)_ and went to Mt _(3)_ Shasta. Did you know that Aunt Jo used to compete in downhill races _(4)_ Wow _(5)_ That sounds really scary to me.
    After an hour or so _(6)_ Aunt Jo and I were hungry. We ate dinner at Ms _(7)_ Jenny's Cafe. We met Ms. Jenny and her brother _(8)_ Slim. They cook yummy food! We had appetizers, dinner _(9)_ and dessert. It was getting late _(10)_ and we decided to go home.

Love,

Miguel

1 A colon
   B comma
   C period
   D No punctuation needed

2 A exclamation point
   B comma
   C period
   D No punctuation needed

3 A question mark
   B comma
   C period
   D No punctuation needed

4 A question mark
   B comma
   C period
   D No punctuation needed

5 A exclamation mark
   B comma
   C period
   D No punctuation needed

6 A question mark
   B comma
   C period
   D No punctuation needed

7 A colon
   B comma
   C period
   D No punctuation needed

8 A exclamation point
   B comma
   C period
   D No punctuation needed

9 A question mark
   B comma
   C period
   D No punctuation needed

10 A exclamation point
   B comma
   C period
   D No punctuation needed

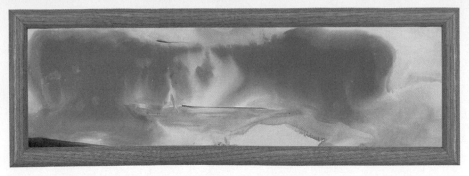

Helen Frankenthaler. *Moveable Blue,* 1973.
Acrylic on canvas, 70 by 243¼ inches. Courtesy of SBC Communications Inc. © Helen Frankenthaler.

Describe What colors do you see in this painting? What do you think the title of the painting means?

Analyze Notice the dimensions of this composition. What is the center of interest of this painting? How does the artist draw attention to this focus through the use of color?

Interpret What mood is conveyed by the painting? How does the artist use color to help create this mood? How does she use color to create space?

Judge Do you think this mood could be conveyed more or less effectively by a more realistic painting with distinct, recognizable shapes and objects? Why?

At the end of this chapter, you will use the artwork to stimulate ideas for writing.

End marks and capital letters signal to a reader that one sentence has ended and another has started. Different kinds of sentences end with different end marks.

Place a **period** after a statement, after an opinion, and after a command or request made in a normal tone of voice.

PERIODS   I have a Russian heritage.

(statement)

Russians have a different culture.

(opinion)

Give all cultures your respect.

(command)

Place a **question mark** after a sentence that asks a question.

QUESTION MARK   What is your heritage?

Place an **exclamation point** after a sentence that states strong feeling and after a command or request that expresses great excitement.

EXCLAMATION   My Italian aunt won the blue ribbon!
POINTS   Applaud so that she can hear you!

(command with great excitement)

An exclamation point also follows an interjection.

Wow! Did you taste that Italian pasta?

You can learn about end marks and quotations on pages L579–L580.

PRACTICE YOUR SKILLS

● Check Your Understanding
Using End Marks

History Topic **Read each sentence and then write the correct end mark.**

1. Who were the first people to settle in North America

2. The Europeans found Native Americans already there in the 1400s

3. Wow, that must have been an exciting first meeting

4. Where had the Native Americans come from

5. Some thought the first Americans came from Asia

6. Others said that they came from Atlantis, an island that sank into the ocean

7. Science has another theory

8. Look at a current map of the world

9. The shapes of the continents point to a missing link between America and Asia

10. Do you think the land between the two sank into the ocean

● Connect to the Writing Process: Editing
Using End Marks

Rewrite the following paragraph, adding or changing end marks where needed.

Have you ever heard of Beringia. According to scientists, that is the stretch of land that once was between Asia and America Can you imagine that. Our Earth has passed through many Ice Ages! Do you know when the last Ice Age was About twelve thousand years ago, the frozen period lowered the sea levels? When the ice melted, land was exposed! Does that theory seem likely to you.

Communicate Your Ideas

APPLY TO WRITING

Journal: *End Marks*

It is thousands of years ago. You have discovered land that stretches east out into the ocean. For a travel journal for future historians, write a series of sentences describing your thoughts as you decide whether or not to explore this land bridge. Use a variety of sentences that will require periods, question marks, and exclamation points.

Other Uses of Periods

Periods are used in places other than at the ends of sentences.

With Abbreviations

Abbreviations are brief ways of writing words. Most abbreviations, however, do not belong in formal writing such as business letters or research reports.

Use a period with most abbreviations.

The following box contains some common abbreviations. For the spelling and punctuation of other abbreviations, look in a dictionary. Most dictionaries have a special section that lists all abbreviations. This special section often appears in the back of the dictionary.

COMMON ABBREVIATIONS					
DAYS	Sun.	Mon.	Tues.	Wed.	
	Thurs.	Fri.	Sat.		
MONTHS	Jan.	Feb.	Mar.	Apr.	Aug.
	Sept.	Oct.	Nov.	Dec.	
	(The other months—May, June, July—should not be abbreviated.)				
ADDRESSES	Ave.	Blvd.	Hwy.	Pl.	
	Rd.	Rt.	St.	Apt.	
TITLES WITH NAMES	Mr.	Ms.	Rev.	Sgt.	Jr.
	Mrs.	Dr.	Gen.	Sen.	Sr.
	(All of these titles appear before a person's name except for Jr. and Sr.)				
INITIALS FOR NAMES	R. L. Rosen		Karen A. Breen		
	T. S. Eliot		H. L. March		
	R. Eric Madison		M. Ellen Zink		
TIMES WITH NUMBERS	2:30 A.M. 7:00 P.M. 47 B.C. A.D. 200				
	(A colon [:] goes between the hours and the minutes when time is written in numbers.)				
COMPANIES	Assoc.	Co.	Corp.	Dept.	Inc.

Some organizations and companies are known by abbreviations that stand for their full names. The majority of these abbreviations do not use periods. A few other common abbreviations also do not include periods.

ABBREVIATIONS WITHOUT PERIODS

JDF = Juvenile Diabetes Foundation
UN = United Nations
CIA = Central Intelligence Agency
FBI = Federal Bureau of Investigation
ATM = automatic teller machine
CD = compact disc
DVD = digital video disc
E-mail = electronic mail
Fax = facsimile
IQ = intelligence quotient
SAT = Scholastic Aptitude Test
km = kilometers

The post office's two-letter state abbreviations are used by most people today. These abbreviations do not include periods. A list of these state abbreviations can be found in the front of most telephone books. The following are a few examples.

STATE ABBREVIATIONS

AL = Alabama	MD = Maryland	OH = Ohio
CT = Connecticut	NV = Nevada	TX = Texas
HI = Hawaii	NY = New York	UT = Utah

If a sentence ends with an abbreviation that ends with a period, only one period is used. It serves both as the period for the abbreviation and as the end mark for the sentence.

The train arrives at 7:30 P.M.

With Outlines

Use a period after each number or letter that shows a division in an outline.

I. Professional Sports
   A. Baseball
      1. Minor League
      2. Major League
   B. Football
      1. Arena Football League
      2. National Football League
II. Coaching

You can learn more about using capital letters in outlines on page L485.

PRACTICE YOUR SKILLS

● Check Your Understanding
Using End Marks

Write the abbreviations that stand for the following items. Be sure to end them with a period when appropriate. Use a dictionary if you are not sure of an abbreviation.

1. pounds	**6.** Celsius	**11.** road
2. longitude	**7.** street	**12.** doctor
3. Florida	**8.** March	**13.** junior
4. meter	**9.** Friday	**14.** Tuesday
5. feet	**10.** December	**15.** Oregon

● Connect to the Writing Process: Editing
Using End Marks

Write each sentence, using periods where needed.

1. It was an emergency

2. At 8:45 AM, Dr Harriet L Sackel rushed from her car parked on 2422 Forest St

3. The patient was being given CPR by a Lt J W Snow
4. The lieutenant worked for the Orange County Sheriff's Department in CA
5. Dr Sackel asked the officer about the man's condition
6. He gave the patient's blood pressure and pulse
7. No one knew what had happened
8. Mr Gary L Martin had been found unconscious
9. His home state on his driver's license was listed as TX
10. Dr Sackel asked Sgt Barry to call for an ambulance

● Connect to the Writing Process: Prewriting
Using End Marks

An outline can come in handy when you are planning a piece of writing. Write an outline for a short narrative that tells your parents what happened to make you late for school or some other event. Be sure to provide specific details in the outline, such as what happened, when it happened, and where it happened. Use periods where needed.

Communicate Your Ideas

APPLY TO WRITING
Narrative: *End Marks*

Using your outline from the prewriting activity, write a short narrative. Tell your parents what happened to make you late for school or some other event. Provide specific details of what happened, the time when it happened, and the address where it happened. Be sure to use abbreviations and periods where needed.

Commas That Separate

Basically, a comma is used in two ways. One of these ways is to separate items. Just as an end mark keeps sentences from running together, a comma keeps items within a sentence from running together.

▶ Items in a Series

A series is three or more similar items listed one after another. When words and groups of words are written in a series, commas should separate them.

Use commas to separate items in a series.

WORDS

NOUNS	Paper, pencils, and markers were our supplies.
VERBS	We sketched, painted, and labeled our drawings of the atom.
ADJECTIVES	Our science class looked bright, colorful, and interesting.

GROUPS OF WORDS

COMPLETE SUBJECTS	My best friend, his cousin Ted, and one of his neighbors went the art store.
COMPLETE PREDICATES	They checked their list, packed their supplies, and paid with cash.
PREPOSITIONAL PHRASES	The students walked back to school, across the campus, and into science class.

If a conjunction such as *and* or *or* connects all the items in a series, no commas are needed.

> The students walked back to school **and** across the campus **and** into science class.
>
> (no commas)
>
> I will take a class in music **or** art **or** gymnastics next semester.
>
> (no commas)

You can learn about commas with direct quotations on page L578.

PRACTICE YOUR SKILLS

● Check Your Understanding
Using Commas In a Series

Science Topic **Write *C* if a sentence uses commas correctly. If a sentence uses commas incorrectly, write *I*.**

1. An atom contains electrons protons and neutrons.

2. The nucleus is the center of the atom, is positively charged, and is made of protons and neutrons.

3. A neutron is located in the nucleus has no charge, and has a relative mass of 1.

4. Electrons are negatively charged, small in mass and outside the nucleus.

5. The mass of the electron is about 1/2000 of the proton and of the neutron.

● Connect to the Writing Process: Editing
Using Commas in a Series

6.–8. Write the incorrect sentences from the preceding exercise, adding commas where needed.

Write each sentence, adding commas where needed. If a sentence is correct as written, write C.

9. The home of Thomas Edison in Fort Myers was painted in 1994 1996 and 1998.

10. White is used for the exterior walls the porch and the gables.

11. The painters wash scrape and sand the surface before painting.

12. The windows and the fixtures are more difficult to paint.

13. They require small tools delicate work and careful attention.

14. Are the windows painted a robin's egg blue a navy blue or another shade of blue?

15. The fixtures on the gables the doors and the roof are red.

▶ Adjectives Before a Noun

If you have three adjectives before a noun, you have a series. Then a comma separates each item in the series. However, if you have only two adjectives before a noun, you may or may not need a comma.

You should put a comma between two adjectives if the comma is replacing the word *and* between the two adjectives.

Shania is the tallest, most graceful person on stage.

(Shania is the tallest *and* most graceful person on stage.)

Several lovely, colorful costumes brightened the play.

(Several lovely *and* colorful costumes brightened the play.)

Use a comma to separate two adjectives that precede a noun and are not joined by a conjunction.

Occasionally, however, a comma is not needed between two adjectives. There is a test you can use to help you decide if a comma is or is not needed. Read the sentence with the word *and* between the two adjectives. If the sentence makes sense, a comma is needed. If the sentence sounds awkward, no comma is needed.

COMMA	That movie is a bright, cheerful production.
	(*A bright and cheerful production made* well.)
NO COMMA	That old movie is a dark murder mystery.
	(Since *a dark and murder mystery* sounds awkward, no comma is needed.)

Usually no comma is needed after a number or after an adjective that refers to size, shape, or age. For example, no commas are needed in the following expressions.

ADJECTIVE EXPRESSIONS	
ten E-mail messages	a small light sweater
four square boxes	a ripe green apple

PRACTICE YOUR SKILLS

● Check Your Understanding
Using Commas Before a Noun

Literature
Topic **Write the underlined words in each sentence, adding commas where needed. If no commas are needed, write C.**

1. The classic movie *Field of Dreams* is based on a short readable novel by W. P. Kinsella.

2. *Shoeless Joe* is told by a young idealistic dreamer.

3. A deep mysterious voice tells him to build a baseball field.

4. "Build it and he will come" is the vague and abstract instruction.

5. Ray plows under his fertile Iowa farmland.

6. In the novel the field first includes only a shabby left field.

7. One day the ghost of a gifted handsome outfielder appears.

8. Shoeless Joe Jackson had played for the disgraced baseball team, the 1919 Chicago White Sox.

9. Several players had taken large illegal bribes to lose the World Series.

10. Regardless of the charges, Shoeless Joe had been a great hero of Ray's dead father.

● Connect to the Writing Process: Editing
Using Commas with Adjectives

Write each sentence, adding commas where needed. If no commas are needed, write C.

11. The United States is generally thought to contain the Northeast Mid-Atlantic Midwest Southwest Southeast and Western regions.

12. The state of Florida is part of the hot sunny Southeast region.

13. The state has a low flat elevation.

14. Lake Okeechobee is one of the largest lakes in the United States and is filled with shallow fresh water.

15. Florida's delightful winter weather attracts many tourists.

● Connect to the Writing Process: Drafting
Writing Sentences with Adjectives

Write five sentences, following the instructions below. Use at least two adjectives before the noun in each sentence.

16. Describe the geography of your region.

17. Describe the geography of your state.

18. Describe the natural resources found in your area.

19. Describe the crops grown in your area.

20. Describe the climate of your area.

Communicate Your Ideas

APPLY TO WRITING
Description: *Commas*

You have a pen pal in a distant region. Read over the sentences you wrote for the preceding drafting exercise. Then use these sentences to help write a description of your region for your pen pal. Use items in a series and a series of adjectives to describe your region in specific detail. Use commas where needed.

Art Topic **Write the following paragraph, adding commas where needed.**

Andrew Wyeth, an American painter, is part of a famous family of artists. Wyeth drew sketched and painted at a very young age. He was encouraged by his father his sisters and family friends. The long difficult study of art began with his famous father at home. Andrew painted people places and experiences familiar to him. His work includes pictures of Pennsylvania and Maine. The pictures show the faces of his neighbors their houses and their land. The paintings generally are not portraits of the people but show them in their everyday ordinary surroundings.

Compound Sentences

A compound sentence is made up of two or more simple sentences. When the parts of a compound sentence are joined by a coordinating conjunction—*and, but, or,* or *yet*—a comma is usually placed before the conjunction.

Use a comma before a coordinating conjunction that joins the parts of a compound sentence.

> You can polish the saddles, and I will clean the stalls.
>
> The king's three horses jumped the fence, but we caught them within half an hour.

Do not confuse a compound sentence with a simple sentence that has a compound verb.

COMPOUND SENTENCE	Queen Kate rides well, and everyone wants her for a partner.
	(A comma is needed.)
COMPOUND VERB	Queen Kate sits straight in the saddle and holds the horse steady.
	(No comma is needed.)

You can learn more about compound sentences on pages L263–L265.

PRACTICE YOUR SKILLS

● Check Your Understanding
Using Commas with Compound Sentences

Literature Topic

Write *I* if a sentence needs a comma. Write *C* if a sentence is correct.

1. King Midas loved gold very much and a god granted him the "golden touch."

2. Midas touched his throne and turned it into gold.

3. He was very happy with his new power and soon almost everything in his palace became gold.

4. One day the king called for his dinner and a delicious meal was set before him.

5. He picked up a goblet and raised it to his lips.

6. His drink instantly hardened to gold and he could not drink it.

7. Then Midas quickly crammed a piece of bread into his mouth but it turned into a lump of hot gold.

8. Sometime later he walked through his garden and forgot about his power.

9. The beautiful roses made the air sweet and Midas loved them.

10. He gently touched one red rose and it instantly turned to gold.

11. Just then the king's daughter entered the garden and Midas drew back in horror.

12. The little girl put her hand on his arm and was turned into a golden statue!

13. Midas prayed very hard and finally the god heard his pleas.

14. The king followed the god's instructions and soon the golden touch was gone.

15. Midas happily threw his arms around his precious daughter and thanked the god for bringing her back to life.

● Connect to the Writing Process: Editing
Using Commas in Compound Sentences

16.–25. Rewrite the incorrect sentences from the preceding exercise, adding commas where needed.

● Connect to the Writing Process: Drafting
Using Commas with Compound Sentences

Write one compound sentence about each of the following topics. Make sure the clauses in each sentence are related and punctuated correctly.

26. a fantasy

27. three wishes

28. a hero

29. an important ideal

30. a fear or fears

● Introductory Elements

A comma follows certain words and groups of words when they introduce, or begin, a sentence.

Use a comma after certain introductory elements.

Usually a comma follows words such as *no, oh, well,* or *yes* when they begin a sentence.

WORDS **Oh,** that lightning was close.

Well, the weather turned cool after the storm.

Words such as *oh* and *well* can also be interjections. When they are, they are followed by an exclamation point.

Oh! Our electricity went out.

You can learn more about interjections and exclamation points on pages L140–L141.

When two or more prepositional phrases or one prepositional phrase of four words or longer comes at the beginning of a sentence, a comma should separate them from the rest of the sentence.

PREPOSITIONAL PHRASES **From the dark clouds in the east,** we heard a loud clap of thunder. (two prepositional phrases)

Throughout the long storm, the children sat quietly. (one prepositional phrase with four words)

You can learn more about prepositional phrases on pages L189–L197.

A comma follows a participial phrase that comes at the beginning of a sentence. A participial phrase is a group of words that begins with a verb form that ends in *–ing.*

PARTICIPAL PHRASES	**Hearing the wind,** the students gathered their books and went into the building.
	Sitting in the gym, the group talked quietly.

You can learn more about participial phrases on pages L221–L227.

A comma follows an adverb clause when it comes at the beginning of a sentence. An adverb clause is a subordinate clause that begins with a subordinating conjunction such as *after, because, if, since,* and *when.*

ADVERB CLAUSE	**If you can't get through the storm,** please call Megan and tell her.
	When we left, the storm was just beginning.

You can learn more about adverb clauses on pages L250–L252.

PRACTICE YOUR SKILLS

 Check Your Understanding
Using Commas with Introductory Elements

> History Topic

Write *I* if a sentence needs a comma. Write *C* if a sentence is correct.

1. To the Europeans' surprise many Native American tribes rose, flourished, and disappeared before the settlers came.

2. Adapting to the hot desert the Hohokam came to Arizona.

3. From A.D. 300 to A.D. 1200 they flourished between the Gila and Salt River valleys.

4. Their way of life depended heavily on irrigation channels.

5. In addition to miles of irrigation channels the Hohokam left behind stone pottery and shells.

6. According to historians the shells were received from coastal tribes.

7. Oh the etchings on the shells were done with a kind of acid.

8. In the area of Utah, Colorado, Arizona, and New Mexico, the Anasazi tribe lived during the same time as the Hohokam.

9. According to the Spanish conquerors they lived in great stone pueblos because of the heat.

10. Because drought threatened their large cities the Anasazi broke into small communities.

● Connect to the Writing Process: Editing
Using Commas in Compound Sentences

11.–17. Rewrite the incorrect sentences from the preceding exercise, adding commas where needed.

● Connect to the Writing Process: Drafting
Using Commas with Introductory Elements

Write five sentences, using each of the following introductory words or phrases. Add commas where needed.

18. After the long summer vacation

19. As August turned into September

20. Well

21. Fearing the worst from the new situation

22. By the first day

⊙ Commonly Used Commas

The following are examples of some other commonly used commas.

With Dates and Addresses

Commas between the parts of a date or an address are probably the most often used commas.

> Use commas to separate elements in dates and addresses.

In the following examples, notice that when a date or an address comes within a sentence another comma goes at the end to separate it from the rest of the sentence.

DATES
On July 20, 1969, Neil Armstrong took the first human step on the moon.

(No comma goes between the month and day, but a comma goes after the year to separate the date from the rest of the sentence.)

In July 1989, Annemarie's youngest brother was born.

(No comma goes between the month and the year if no day is given.)

ADDRESSES
Write to Rockland Crafts, 420 Woodbriar Drive, DeLand, Florida 32720, for a catalog.

(No comma goes between the state and the ZIP code, but a comma goes after the ZIP code to separate the address from the rest of the sentence.)

I live at 12 Richmond Street **in** Dallas, Texas.

(A preposition can take the place of a comma between parts of an address.)

In Letters

The correct punctuation in letters is important.

Use a comma after the salutation of a friendly letter and after the closing of all letters.

SALUTATIONS AND CLOSINGS	
SALUTATIONS	Dear Dad, Dearest Gram, Dear Ali,
CLOSINGS	Sincerely, Yours truly, Love, As always,

CONNECT TO SPEAKING AND WRITING

Often, deciding when to use commas makes student writers nervous. Students might decide to use one when they hesitate in speaking, take a deep breath, pause, or have not used a comma recently. Use commas only where a rule states you should. Too many commas can be confusing to a reader.

You can learn about commas with direct quotations on page L578.

PRACTICE YOUR SKILLS

● Check Your Understanding
Using Commas in Dates and Addresses

Write *a* or *b* to indicate the item that is correctly written in each of the following pairs.

1. a. Sunday, May 14 2000
   b. Sunday, May 14, 2000

2. a. Dear Maury
   b. Dear Maury,

3. a. Mary New, 129 Jones Street, Los Angeles, CA 90068
   b. Mary New, 129 Jones Street, Los Angeles, CA, 90068

4. a. Thursday August 10, 2000
   b. Thursday, August 10, 2000

5. a. Sincerely
   b. Sincerely,

6. a. Dear John,
   b. Dear John

7. a. Thursday, July 9 1946
   b. Thursday, July 9, 1946

8. a. Dr. John Jahr, Box 456 Farmington, NM 87401
   b. Dr. John Jahr, Box 456, Farmington, NM 87401

9. a. Corpus Christi Texas
   b. Corpus Christi, Texas

10. a. Very truly yours,
   b. Very truly yours

● Connect to the Writing Process: Drafting
Using Commas

Follow the directions to write sentences. Be sure to use commas correctly.

11. Write a sentence that includes the city and state in which you live.

12. Write a sentence that includes the month and year that you were born.

13. Write a sentence that includes the address of the school.

14. Write a sentence that includes the city, state, and ZIP code of someone you know.

Adding Commas to Sentences

Write each sentence, using commas correctly.

15. The United States capital city was Philadelphia Pennsylvania before the capital was moved to Washington D.C.

16. The White House is located at 1600 Pennsylvania Avenue Washington D.C. 20003.

17. John Adams and his wife hosted the first reception at the White House on January 1 1801.

18. In 1864 Abraham Lincoln sat for Vinnie Ream so that the talented 16-year-old girl could sculpt his image.

19. On July 27 1866 Ream was the first woman to receive a commission for sculpture from the United States Congress.

20. She then studied sculpture in several European cities, including Rome Italy and Paris France.

21. Ream's *Lincoln* was unveiled in the Rotunda of the Capitol Building on Wednesday January 25 1871.

22. Franklin D. Roosevelt's first Fireside Chat from the White House was broadcast by radio on Sunday March 12 1933.

23. William Howard Taft, the twenty-seventh president of the United States, was born in Cincinnati Ohio on September 15 1857.

24. On February 14 1912 3020 cherry trees were shipped from Yokohama Japan to Seattle Washington.

25. First Lady Helen Herron Taft transformed Independence Avenue Washington D.C. with these trees.

APPLY TO WRITING
Newspaper Article: *Commas*

Think about how the cherry trees in Washington,
D.C., create great beauty and generate interest in the
capital city during the spring season. This
beautification project also shows how a simple idea
can change the look and future of a community.
Imagine that you are to write an article on a
community improvement project in a town or city
near you. Choose a topic to write about. Answer the
questions *Who? What? When? Where?* and *Why?* about
your topic. Include a specific day of the week, date,
and address. Edit your article and write a final copy,
paying close attention to comma usage.

Commas That Enclose

Any group of words that interrupts a sentence can be removed without changing the meaning of the sentence. Commas are used to enclose these expressions. The word *enclose* means that a comma comes at the beginning and the end of each expression.

▶ Direct Address

Sometimes when you talk, you call another person by name. This kind of sentence interrupter is called a noun of direct address.

Use commas to set off nouns of direct address.

> Please, **Coach Curtis,** give me the signs.

In the following examples, only one comma is needed because the noun of direct address comes at the beginning or at the end of the sentence.

> **Coach Curtis,** your strategy is good.
> I would give you a sportsmanship award, **Coach Curtis.**

PRACTICE YOUR SKILLS

● Check Your Understanding
Using Commas with Direct Address

General Interest **Write *I* if commas are used incorrectly in or are missing from the following sentences. Write *C* if a sentence is correct.**

1. Quick, Coach the pitcher needs your help!

2. Christine don't you bat after, Siela?

3. On your way to first base Carla, be sure to turn toward second.

4. Do you like to steal bases, Anna?

5. Look over at the third base coach, Keisha, for the signs.

6. Josie there is only one out in the inning.

7. Yes, Karen we need to score some runs.

8. Where is your batter's helmet, Elaine?

9. Cora you bat, for Betty.

10. You're our last chance Nancy.

● **Connect to the Writing Process: Editing**
Correcting Commas with Direct Address

11.–17. Write the incorrect sentences from the preceding exercise, adding or deleting commas where needed.

▶ Parenthetical Expressions

The following is a list of common parenthetical expressions. In sentences these words usually are enclosed by commas.

COMMON PARENTHETICAL EXPRESSIONS		
after all	for instance	of course
at any rate	generally speaking	on the contrary
by the way	I believe (guess,	on the other hand
consequently	hope, know)	moreover
however	in fact	nevertheless
for example	in my opinion	to tell the truth

Use commas to set off parenthetical expressions.

A sonnet normally has fourteen lines, **for example,** not sixteen.

Only one comma is needed when a parenthetical expression comes at the beginning or at the end of a sentence.

In fact, a traditional sonnet should have fourteen lines.

A sonnet is sometimes changed, **nevertheless.**

PRACTICE YOUR SKILLS

  Check Your Understanding
Using Commas with Parenthetical Expressions

Literature Topic **Write _I_ if commas are used incorrectly in or are missing from a sentence. Write _C_ if a sentence is correct.**

1. By the way poetry offers an interesting challenge.

2. Poetry generally, speaking, is the oldest form of literature.

3. Poems, I believe, were sung or repeated around the first campfires.

4. At any rate poems require careful attention.

5. The most important part of a poem in my opinion, is the meaning of each word.

6. For example many kinds, of words, can be used.

7. The words, after all, create feelings and meaning.

8. Of course poems, also, depend on sound.

9. I, however like rhyming poems.

10. Nevertheless, many famous poems do not rhyme.

Correcting Commas in Parenthetical Expressions

11.–17. **Write the incorrect sentences from the preceding exercise, adding or deleting commas where needed.**

● Connect to the Writing Process: Drafting
Writing Sentences with Parenthetical Expressions

Write five sentences, using the following parenthetical expressions as directed. Add commas where needed.

18. *I hope* in the middle of a sentence

19. *in fact* at the beginning of a sentence

20. *to tell the truth* at the end of a sentence

21. *however* at the beginning of a sentence

22. *for example* in the middle of a sentence

▶ Appositives

Another interrupter, the **appositive,** renames or explains a noun or pronoun in the sentence. Most appositives have one or more modifiers. Usually an appositive comes immediately after the word it renames or explains and is enclosed in commas.

Use commas to set off most appositives and their modifiers.

> TWO COMMAS   Alaska, **the largest state,** was once owned by Russia.

Only one comma is needed when the appositive comes at the end of the sentence. Sometimes commas are not used if an appositive is a name.

ONE COMMA	Have you read about William H. Seward, **the secretary of state?**
NO COMMAS	Have you read the book *The History of Russia?*
	My cousin **Bill** is reading a book about the wilderness.

PRACTICE YOUR SKILLS

● Check Your Understanding
Using Commas with Appositives

Literature
Topic

Write *I* if commas are used incorrectly in or are missing from a sentence. Write *C* if a sentence is correct.

1. Over the years the legend of Paul Bunyan, the most famous lumberjack of all, grew and grew.

2. Paul Bunyan a huge man towered above the trees.

3. His voice once caused a landslide near Pikes Peak a mountain, in Colorado.

4. His mighty blue ox Babe straightened the course of the Whistling River.

5. The cook Hot Biscuit Slim, was an important member of his logging crew.

6. Cream puffs, the favorite dessert of the crew were baked by the camp cook.

7. Big Swede one of Paul's workers, was known for his accidents.

8. Johnny Inkslinger, the first bookkeeper in the legend, did all the figuring for Paul.

9. It took a bucket brigade of thirty men to fill Johnny's pen a giant rubber hose.

10. The Paul Bunyan legends stories about life in the forest are a big part of American folklore.

● Connect to the Writing Process: Editing
Correcting Commas with Appositives

11.–17. Write the incorrect sentences from the preceding exercise, adding or deleting commas where needed.

QuickCheck Mixed Practice

Literature Topic **Write each sentence, adding commas where needed. If no commas are needed, write C.**

1. Ellen does your school have a writers' workshop?

2. A writers' workshop a group of five to seven students meets regularly.

3. In fact they discuss their own writing.

4. Most workshops generally speaking focus on one type of writing.

5. This for example might be fiction or poetry or plays.

6. However some workshops can be unusual.

7. One workshop The Fourteen Liners concentrates just on sonnets.

8. That is correct Ellen.

9. Other workshops may focus on science fiction, horror, or mysteries.

10. Joyce Carol Oates a famous modern writer wrote a book about writers' workshops.

▶ Nonessential Elements

Entire phrases and clauses can interrupt a sentence the same way a parenthetical expression does. Moreover, some of these phrases and clauses are not essential, or necessary, to the sentence.

A **nonessential** phrase or clause could actually be removed from a sentence, and the sentence will still make complete sense. A comma goes before and after a nonessential phrase or clause to show that the words in between the commas could be removed from the sentence.

Use commas to set off nonessential participial phrases and nonessential clauses.

If a participial phrase provides extra, unnecessary information, it is a **nonessential phrase.**

NONESSENTIAL PARTICIPIAL PHRASES	Microcomputers, **used at home and at work,** provide access to the Internet.
	The Internet, **created mostly for data transfer,** is very popular.
	Chen Li, **searching the Internet day and night,** learns much about the world.

If the nonessential participial phrase were dropped, the main idea of each sentence would not be changed in any way.

Microcomputers provide access to the Internet.

The Internet is very popular.

Chen Li learns much about the world.

You can learn more about participial phrases on pages L221–L227.

An adjective clause is nonessential if it provides extra, unnecessary information.

<table>
<tr><td>NONESSENTIAL
ADJECTIVE
CLAUSES</td><td>The hard drive and a disk are the primary places of information storage in a microcomputer, **which uses a binary system.**</td></tr>
<tr><td></td><td>The hard drive, **which is less accessible than disks,** usually stores the computer's operating systems.</td></tr>
</table>

If the nonessential adjective clause were dropped, the basic meaning of each sentence would not be changed at all.

The hard drive and a disk are the primary places of information storage in a microcomputer.

The hard drive usually stores the computer's operating systems.

You can learn more about adjective clauses on pages L255–L261.

Many participial phrases and adjective clauses, of course, are essential. The information in them is necessary to fully understand the sentence in which they appear. If an essential phrase or clause is dropped, the meaning of the sentence will be incomplete. Essential phrases and clauses usually identify a person, place, or thing and answer the question *Which one?* When a phrase or clause is essential, no commas are used.

<table>
<tr><td>ESSENTIAL
PARTICIPIAL
PHRASE</td><td>We like computer games **imitating car races.**</td></tr>
<tr><td></td><td>(Without the phrase, the sentence would read, *We like computer games.* The reader would not know which games.)</td></tr>
</table>

ESSENTIAL ADJECTIVE PHRASE	The game **that has the best car race** is on Tom's computer.
	(Without the clause, the sentence would read, *The game is on Tom's computer.* No one would know which game.)
	Tom is the student **who has red hair.**
	(Without the clause, the sentence would read, *Tom is the student.* No would know which student Tom is.)

Notice that since the phrase and the clauses in these examples are essential, no commas are used.

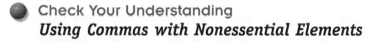

PRACTICE YOUR SKILLS

● Check Your Understanding
Using Commas with Nonessential Elements

Contemporary Life   **Write C if a sentence is correctly punctuated.**
Write I if a sentence is incorrectly punctuated.

1. People who help other people are heroes.

2. Volunteer work which happens all over the world is good citizenship.

3. In fact, there is a computer database that lists willing volunteers in a community.

4. This computer program, which is easily downloaded, also keeps track of the people, being served.

5. It also does accounting which is important for state funding.

6. However, the most important work is done by people who give of their time.

7. Often volunteers work in shelters that feed homeless people.

8. These volunteers who come from all walks of life serve food.

9. Some heroes visit hospital patients who have no families.

10. These "candy stripers" who wear uniforms with stripes help the nurses.

● Connect to the Writing Process: Editing
Correcting Commas with Appositives

11.–15. Write the incorrect sentences from the preceding exercise, adding or deleting commas where needed.

● Connect to the Writing Process: Prewriting
Writing Sentences

Write five sentences, following the instructions below. Use commas where needed for nonessential phrases and clauses.

16. Write a sentence identifying your hero, and use a clause to describe him or her.

17. Write a sentence that tells where your hero serves, and use a phrase to describe the place.

18. Write a sentence that describes the people or the cause the hero helps, and use a clause to describe the people or the cause.

19. Write a sentence that tells about your hero, and use a phrase to tell about the hero.

20. Write a sentence that describes the effect of your hero's work, and use a clause to offer specific details about that effect.

Communicate Your Ideas

APPLY TO WRITING

Character Sketch: *Commas*

Using the sentences from the previous exercise, write a character sketch of a hero in your life for your classmates. Describe the hero and what he or she does. Use phrases and clauses to sketch your hero in detail. Remember to use commas where needed.

✓ QuickCheck Mixed Practice

Sports Topic **Write each sentence, adding commas where needed. If the sentence is correct, write C.**

1. Pee Wee Reese the Brooklyn Dodger shortstop was inducted into the Baseball Hall of Fame in 1984.

2. Reese who helped Jackie Robinson adjust to major league baseball was born in Kentucky.

3. Roger Kahn's book *The Boys of Summer* tells how Reese helped baseball integration.

4. Reese however was also a great baseball player.

5. The well-liked man was an eight-time All-Star hitting 126 home runs with 885 RBIs.

6. Reese the heart and soul of the Dodgers stole thirty bases in 1930.

7. In 1947, Reese who battled cancer late in life led his league in runs scored.

8. Reese a man of many nicknames was also called "The Little Colonel."

Using End Marks Correctly

Write each sentence, adding period(s), exclamation point(s), or question mark(s) where needed. If a sentence does not need any marks, write C.

1. Are we meeting at 8 AM or 8 PM?
2. Some kittens do not like catnip
3. Look out for that car
4. My big sister gave me a CD for my birthday.
5. I asked why the two countries were at war
6. T S Eliot was a poet and a literary critic.
7. I moved from Forty-fourth St to Ivy Dr
8. How dare he say that Georgia O'Keeffe could not paint
9. Tania volunteers after school every Monday.
10. Did you see that manatee

Using Commas Correctly

Write each sentence, adding a comma or commas where needed. If a sentence does not need any commas, write C.

1. My neighbor Ellen Klerman is home from college.
2. The trunk in our attic is old large and heavy.
3. Greenland the largest island on this planet is about sixteen hundred miles in length.
4. For an hour all the lights were out.
5. Your dental appointment David is on Monday.
6. The magician is good but the mime is better.
7. We walked for two miles and then took a rest.
8. The ladybird on the other hand is actually a beetle.

Using Commas Correctly

Write the following paragraphs, adding commas where needed.

> Are you interested in athletics animals or science? There are magazines about each of these subjects. *Young Athlete* for example tells you about events in the sports world. The articles will keep you up-to-date on all the latest news and each issue includes an interview with a big star.
>
> *Three-Two-One Contact* a magazine about science covers interesting topics from hiccups to *Star Trek*. Each month there is a new experiment and each issue has some regular columns. One column for instance gives helpful facts about your health.

Using Commas

Write sentences that follow the directions below. (The sentences may come in any order.) Write about your family tree, an historical event, or a topic of your own choosing.

Write a sentence that...

1. includes a series of nouns.
2. includes two adjectives before a noun.
3. has two independent clauses joined by a coordinating conjunction.
4. includes a participial phrase at the beginning.
5. includes an adverb clause at the beginning.
6. includes direct address.
7. includes a parenthetical expression.
8. includes an appositive.
9. includes a nonessential adjective clause.
10. includes your street number and name, city, state, and ZIP code.

CheckPoint **L559**

Language and *Self-Expression*

An Abstract Expressionist, Helen Frankenthaler creates meaning indirectly by using form and color for their own sake rather than as objects in order to evoke emotion from the artist and the viewer. What emotions do you feel when you look at *Moveable Blue*?

Writing can also convey emotion and meaning indirectly. Write a few paragraphs that suggest emotion through the use of color rather than words such as *happy* or *sad*.

Prewriting Choose one to three colors and write them across the top of your paper. Below each color, list objects, places, or people that you associate with the color. Next list the emotions that you associate with each color. Choose one emotion to convey in your composition.

Drafting Write several paragraphs describing a scene that contains some of the things you listed in your prewriting. Include plenty of color words to set the mood of the scene.

Revising Read your paragraphs aloud to a classmate. Ask what emotions she or he is feeling and what images she or he remembers. Discuss any images that seem out of place and revise as necessary.

Editing Check your composition for errors in spelling and grammar. Make sure that you have used commas and end marks correctly.

Publishing Prepare a final draft of your composition. Present it in a display that uses the same color(s) you used in your writing. For example, you could print your composition on colored paper.

 **Another Look**

End Marks

Place a **period** after a statement, after an opinion, and after a command or request made in a normal tone of voice. *(page L523)*

Place a **question mark** after a sentence that asks a question. *(page L523)*

Place an **exclamation point** after a sentence that states strong feeling, after a command or request that expresses great excitement, and after an interjection. *(page L523)*

Other Uses of Periods

Use a period with most abbreviations. *(pages L525–L527)*

Use a period after each number or letter that shows a division in an outline. *(pages L527–L528)*

Using Commas That Separate

Use commas to separate items in a series. *(pages L530–L531)*

Use a comma sometimes to separate two adjectives that precede a noun and are not joined by a conjunction. *(pages L532–L533)*

Use a comma before a coordinating conjunction that joins the parts of a compound sentence. *(pages L536–L537)*

Use a comma after certain introductory elements. *(pages L539–L540)*

A comma follows a prepositional phrase of four or more words that comes at the beginning of a sentence. *(page L539)*

A comma follows a participial phrase that comes at the beginning of a sentence. *(pages L539–L540)*

A comma follows an adverb clause when it comes at the beginning of a sentence. *(page L540)*

Use commas to separate elements in dates and addresses. *(pages L542–L543)*

Use a comma after the salutation of a friendly letter and after the closing of all letters. *(page L543)*

Using Commas That Enclose

Use commas to set off nouns of direct address. *(page L547)*

Use commas to set off parenthetical expressions. *(pages L548–L549)*

Use commas to set off most appositives and their modifiers. *(pages L550–L551)*

Use commas to set off nonessential participial phrases and nonessential clauses. *(pages L553–L555)*

Directions
Read the passage and write the letter of the best way to write each underlined word or words. If the underlined word or words contain no error, write D.

EXAMPLE   <u>Rachel guess</u> what I learned today.
                        (1)

    1 **A**   Rachel guess,
       B   Rachel, guess,
       C   Rachel, guess
       D   No error

ANSWER   **1 C**

In <u>science class today</u> we studied bromeliads. They are
                (1)
native to the <u>Americas and grow</u> as far <u>north as the VA</u> coast.
              (2)   (3)
They are known for <u>their large colorful stalks</u>.
                        (4)
<u>Spanish moss or</u> "old man's beard," is a common bromeliad
      (5)
in the southeastern United States. Like many other bromeliads,

it <u>grows on trees</u> The trees <u>are not harmed and such</u>
      (6)   (7)
bromeliads are called *airplants*.

<u>Bromeliads whether</u> they grow in trees or in the ground,
        (8)
usually collect water in a central cup or in their leaves. <u>Insects,</u>
                                                            (9)
<u>snakes and frogs</u> make their homes in these moist shelters.

Fertilizing the bromeliads with <u>decaying organic matter</u> the
                                      (10)
organisms provide as large a benefit as they receive.

1 A In science class, today
   B In science class today,
   C In science, class today
   D No error

2 A Americas, and grow
   B Americas and, grow
   C Americas and grow,
   D No error

3 A north, as the VA
   B north as the V.A.
   C north as the VA,
   D No error

4 A their large colorful, stalks.
   B their large, colorful stalks.
   C their, large colorful stalks.
   D No error

5 A Spanish moss, or
   B Spanish, moss or
   C Spanish moss or,
   D No error

6 A grows, on trees.
   B grows on trees!
   C grows on trees.
   D No error

7 A are not harmed, and such
   B are not harmed and such,
   C are not harmed. And such
   D No error

8 A Bromeliads, whether
   B Bromeliads! Whether
   C Bromeliads whether,
   D No error

9 A Insects, snakes and frogs,
   B Insects snakes and frogs
   C Insects, snakes, and frogs
   D No error

10 A decaying, organic matter
    B decaying organic, matter
    C decaying organic matter,
    D No error

CHAPTER 17

Italics and Quotation Marks

Directions
Read the passage and write the letter of the word or group of words that belongs in each underlined space.

EXAMPLE   Francesca said __(1)__ got a new book."
                 1 A   to Theo "I just
                    B   to Theo I just
                    C   to Theo, "I just
                    D   to Theo, I just

ANSWER   **1 C**

Francesca showed Theo a book __(1)__ She explained that the __(2)__ is taken from the word *magazine*.
  "Unlike magazines," __(3)__ are usually homemade."
Theo asked __(4)__
  __(5)__ "a lot of kids our age or in high school write zines."
  "How do they get them published?" Theo __(6)__ you have to be rich to publish something?"
  "Zines are usually short, photocopied booklets of __(7)__ "that are stapled __(8)__ usually trade them for one another's zines."
  "What are zines __(9)__ asked.
  Fran explained that zines can include poetry, comic strips, journal entries, music reviews, even articles on the latest episode __(10)__

1 A called "Zine Scene".
   B called "Zine Scene."
   C called *Zine Scene.*
   D called, *Zine Scene.*

2 A word "zine"
   B word *zine*
   C "word" zine
   D word zine

3 A Fran began "Zines
   B Fran began, "Zines
   C Fran began, "zines
   D Fran began "zines

4 A what Fran meant.
   B "What Fran meant?"
   C what Fran meant?
   D "what Fran meant."

5 A "Well, Fran said,
   B "Well" Fran said,
   C "Well," Fran said,
   D "Well," Fran said

6 A asked. "don't
   B asked. "Don't
   C asked? "Don't
   D asked? "don't

7 A paper," Fran
      explained.
   B paper," Fran
      explained,
   C paper", Fran
      explained,
   D paper". Fran
      explained,

8 A together." "Kids
   B together." Kids, "
   C together. Kids
   D together." Kids

9 A about"? Theo
   B about?", Theo
   C about," Theo
   D about?" Theo

10 A of *The X-Files.*
    B of The X-Files."
    C of "The X-Files."
    D of *The X-Files.*"

Edgar Degas. *Dancers Practicing at the Bar,* ca. 1876–1877.
Oil colors freely mixed with turpentine, on canvas, 29¾ by 32 inches. The Metropolitan Museum of Art.

Describe   What lines do you see in this painting? What colors?

Analyze   Are there any colors, lines, or textures that repeat themselves in this painting to create a sense of unity?

Interpret How would you characterize the dancers in the painting? What details make you think this?

Judge   Why do you think dancers are a popular subject in Degas's paintings? Explain.

At the end of this chapter, you will use the artwork to stimulate ideas for writing.

Italics (Underlining)

Italics is a type of print that slants to the right *like this*. You can substitute underlining for italics when you are writing certain kinds of titles. When you use a computer, you can print in italics. To do this, first highlight the words you want to italicize. Then use the command for italics. When you write by hand, underline what should be italicized.

ITALICS	Have you ever read the book *Stuart Little* by E. B. White?
UNDERLINING	Have you ever read the book <u>Stuart Little</u> by E. B. White?

Certain letters, numbers, words, and titles should be italicized or underlined.

Italicize (underline) letters, numbers, and words when they are used to represent themselves.

LETTERS	Does that word have three *t*'s?
NUMBERS	Austin's ZIP code begins with a <u>7</u>.
WORDS	The word *Mississippi* is hard to spell.

Notice in the first example only the *t* is italicized, not the apostrophe and the *s* that makes it plural.

You can learn more about using apostrophes on pages L597–L609.

Italicize (underline) the titles of long written or musical works that are published as a single unit. Also italicize (underline) titles of paintings and sculptures and the names of vehicles.

The rule on the preceding page includes books, magazines, newspapers, full-length plays, movies, and very long poems. Long musical works include operas, symphonies, ballets, albums, and CDs. Vehicles include airplanes, ships, trains, and spacecraft.

BOOKS	After I finish *Tom Sawyer,* I am definitely going to read <u>Huckleberry Finn</u>.
MAGAZINES	My uncle reads *National Geographic.*
NEWSPAPERS	Our neighbor has the <u>Wall Street Journal</u> mailed to his house every day.
	(The word *the* is not usually considered part of the title of a newspaper or magazine.)
PLAYS AND MOVIES	The play *Our Town* by Thornton Wilder is set in a small New England town.
WORKS OF ART	Andrew Wyeth's <u>Christina's World</u> shows a woman on a New Hampshire farm.
MUSICAL WORKS	We saw the opera *The Barber of Seville.*
NAMES OF VEHICLES	One of the early space shuttles was the <u>Challenger</u>.
	(The word *the* is not considered part of the title of a vehicle.)

You can learn about the capitalization of titles on pages L509–L510.

PRACTICE YOUR SKILLS

● Check Your Understanding
Using Italics (Underlining)

Write *a* or *b* to indicate the item that is correctly underlined in each of the following pairs. For the names of newspapers, magazines, and vehicles, remember that the word *the* is not part of the title.

1. **a.** the nonfiction book Profiles in Courage by John F. Kennedy

   b. the nonfiction book *Profiles in Courage* by John F. Kennedy

2. **a.** a steamboat called the *Clermont*

   b. a steamboat called the *Clermont*

3. **a.** the letters *g* and *q*

   b. the letters *g* and *q*

4. **a.** the newspaper the *Nashville Banner*

   b. the newspaper the *Nashville Banner*

5. **a.** the movie *The Iron Giant*

   b. the movie The *Iron Giant*

6. **a.** the Broadway play *Cats*

   b. the Broadway play *Cats*

7. **a.** the famous painting *The Starry Night*

   b. the famous painting The *Starry Night*

8. **a.** the space shuttle *Discovery*

   b. the space shuttle *Discovery*

9. **a.** the movie *Flubber* with Robin Williams

   b. the movie *Flubber* with Robin Williams

10. **a.** the magazine American *Girl*

    b. the magazine *American Girl*

Using Underlining Correctly

Rewrite each sentence, underlining where needed.

11. The Los Angeles Times is a big newspaper.

12. Readers can read a review of a book such as Richard Peck's A Long Way from Chicago.

13. The reviews are longer than those in Newsweek.

14. The letter i comes before e in the word review.

15. A newspaper will announce the showing of paintings such as Van Gogh's Sunflowers.

16. The theater page will review a play such as Beauty and the Beast.

17. A feature article might give the history of the space station Mir.

18. Every newspaper in the country reviewed the movie Star Wars: Episode One.

19. Music critics review operas such as Carmen.

20. Write your 7s so that they do not look like 9s.

Communicate Your Ideas

APPLY TO WRITING

Opinion Paragraph: *Italics (Underlining)*

In a newspaper or magazine, find a review of a recent movie you have seen. Explain the reviewer's opinion in a paragraph for your classmates, and then tell why you agree or disagree with it. Use italics (underlining) when you write the name of the movie and the name of the newspaper or magazine where the review appeared.

Quotation Marks

You can improve your writing if you use quotation marks (" ") correctly. Your stories, for example, will be more realistic if you include conversations among your characters. Your reports also will be read with greater interest if they include quoted statements from experts.

▶ Quotation Marks with Titles

Not all titles are underlined. The titles of smaller parts of long works are enclosed in quotation marks.

Use quotation marks to enclose the titles of chapters, articles, stories, one act plays, short poems, and songs.

BOOK CHAPTERS	After reading "Eastward," the first chapter of Blue Highways, Tom was inspired.
MAGAZINE ARTICLES	Dad read the article "Travel Trends in the New Year" in the magazine Going Places.
SHORT STORIES IN BOOKS	Harriet enjoyed the short story "The Cat That Walked by Itself" in Just So Stories.
SHORT POEMS IN BOOKS	The short poem "Color" appears in the book Make a Joyful Sound.
SONGS	Kathy sings "My Heart Will Go On" all the time.

PRACTICE YOUR SKILLS

● Check Your Understanding
Punctuating Titles Correctly

General Interest **Read the following sentences. Write C if the quotation marks and underlining in a sentence are used correctly. Write I if the quotation marks and underlining are used incorrectly.**

1. The song Guinevere is from the musical "Camelot".

2. I read the poem "Paul Revere's Ride" in speech class.

3. The Buck in the Hills is a short story about hunting.

4. We are studying the chapter "The Colonies Win Freedom" in our history book, The Heritage of America.

5. The article A Lost Son Is Found was published in Newsweek.

6. "The Ugly Duckling" is a one-act play.

7. I copied Helen Hunt Jackson's short poem "September."

8. Julie loves the song Tomorrow from the musical Annie.

9. Sponges is the name of a chapter in our textbook Life Science.

10. We read the article "India Today" in this week's Time.

● Connect to the Writing Process: Editing
Correcting Punctuation of Titles

11.–16. Rewrite the incorrect sentences from the preceding exercise, using underlining and quotation marks correctly.

Writing Sentences with Titles

Write five sentences that answer the following questions.

17. What is the title of your literature textbook?

18. What is your favorite short story in that book?

19. What is your favorite poem?

20. What is the title of your science textbook?

21. What chapter in your science textbook are you studying now?

Communicate Your Ideas

APPLY TO WRITING

Bibliography: *Titles*

Imagine that you are writing a report on either the history of the Internet or on recent discoveries in medicine. In your library, find two magazine articles and two chapters from books that you could use for your report. List the titles of the articles and the chapters, as well as the magazines and books you found them in. Be sure to use underlining and quotation marks correctly.

▶ Quotation Marks with Direct Quotations

A person's exact words are quoted in a **direct quotation.** Quotation marks are used before and after any words the person says.

Use quotation marks to enclose a person's exact words.

EXACT WORDS	Mark said, "I have practice after school."
	He added, "It will probably last until six o'clock."

A person's exact words are not directly quoted in an **indirect quotation.** Quotation marks, therefore, are not used.

INDIRECT QUOTATIONS	Mark said that he had practice after school.
	He added he would probably finish by six o'clock.

The word *that* is often used with an indirect quotation. In the preceding example, *that* is understood.

> He added (that) he would probably finish by six o'clock.

A one-sentence direct quotation can be written in several ways. It can be placed before or after a speaker tag such as *she said* or *he asked.* A direct quotation can also be interrupted by a speaker tag. In all cases quotation marks enclose only the person's exact words, not the speaker tag.

BEFORE	"A person's normal body temperature is 98.6°F," said the nurse.
AFTER	The nurse said, "A person's normal body temperature is 98.6°F."
INTERRUPTED	"A person's normal body temperature," the nurse said, "is 98.6°F."
	(Two sets of quotation marks are needed because the speaker tag interrupts the direct quotation.)

To describe exactly how someone spoke, writers often use a variety of verbs in speaker tags. Consider using the following vivid verbs when you use direct quotations:

He **mumbled.**	She **boasted.**
She **screamed.**	He **complained.**
He **stammered.**	She **pleaded.**
She **wondered.**	He **teased.**
He **agreed.**	She **demanded.**

PRACTICE YOUR SKILLS

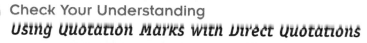

● Check Your Understanding

Using Quotation Marks with Direct Quotations

Science Topic **Read the following sentences. Write *C* if a sentence is punctuated correctly. Write *I* if a sentence is punctuated incorrectly.**

1. "I once had a temperature of 103°F, said Devon."

2. The nurse said that a temperature that high was a sign of infection.

3. "Sometimes, she added," "a lukewarm bath can bring down a temperature."

4. Kayla said, "My mom gives me medicine when I have a fever."

5. "If a fever lasts more than a few days, the nurse continued, you should probably see a doctor.

6. "The doctor may be able to tell what kind of infection you have," she explained.

7. She said "that the infection could be caused by bacteria."

8. In that case, "she went on," you might need to take antibiotics.

9. "Don't ask for antibiotics if you don't need them," the nurse urged.

10. "If you do, she explained, your body might eventually develop germs that are stronger than the antibiotics."

● Connect to the Writing Process: Editing
Punctuating Quotations Correctly

11.–16. Rewrite the incorrectly punctuated sentences in the preceding exercise, using quotation marks correctly. Be sure to place periods and commas *inside* the ending quotation marks.

Capital Letters with Direct Quotations

A capital letter begins a direct quotation.

Capitalize the first word of a direct quotation.

"**T**he meeting will be held in the gym," she said.

She said, "**T**he meeting will be held in the gym."

"**T**he meeting," she said, "will be held in the gym."

(The word *will* does not begin with a capital letter because it is in the middle of a one-sentence direct quotation.)

"**T**he meeting will be held in the gym," she said. "**I**t begins at four o'clock."

(The word *it* begins with a capital letter because it starts a new sentence.)

PRACTICE YOUR SKILLS

● Check Your Understanding
Using Capital Letters with Direct Quotations

Contemporary Life **Write C if capital letters are used correctly in a sentence. Write I if capital letters are used incorrectly in a sentence.**

1. The Boy Scout leader said, "we are here to discuss how to help our community."

2. He continued, "Our community has many different needs."

3. "We can identify these needs," he went on, "by listing the groups who have asked for our help."

4. "first, there are those who need food and shelter," he said.

5. "Among the other groups," he added, "Are the young, the elderly, and the disabled."

6. "It is important," he said, "to think of this help as community service and not as charity."

7. "Volunteers make our whole community stronger," He claimed.

8. "By helping others," he insisted, "You also help yourself."

9. "It is your community," he said. "It is your responsibility."

10. The Boy Scout leader concluded, "come join your community."

● Connect to the Writing Process: Editing
Capitalizing Direct Quotations Correctly

11.–16. Rewrite the incorrect sentences from the preceding exercise, using capital letters correctly.

Commas with Direct Quotations

A comma belongs between a direct quotation and the speaker tag.

Use a comma to separate a direct quotation from a speaker tag. Place the comma inside the closing quotation marks.

"Ms. Poe is an expert on desert animals," he said.
(The comma is *inside* the closing quotation marks.)

He said, "Ms. Poe is an expert on desert animals."
(The comma comes *before* the quotation marks.)

"Ms. Poe," he said, "is an expert on desert animals."
(Two commas are needed to separate the speaker tag from the direct quotation. The first comma goes *inside* the closing quotation marks.)

PRACTICE YOUR SKILLS

Check Your Understanding
Using Commas with Direct Quotations

Science Topic

Write C if commas are used correctly in a sentence. Write I if commas are used incorrectly.

1. "Chuckwallas are playful lizards", Ms. Poe said.

2. "They live in the desert," she added.

3. She continued ", Chuckwallas play hide-and-seek."

4. "They run to a hiding place," she explained "and then peep out to spy on the others."

5. Ms. Poe went on, "Sometimes a chuckwalla will jump out and grab another's tail just for fun."

6. "Snakes and birds" Ms. Poe added, "sometimes attack them.

7. She added, "A chuckwalla can easily protect itself."

8. "It crawls in between rocks", she explained "and blows up like a balloon."

9. She added "An enemy cannot pull it loose."

10. "When the attacker gives up," she concluded, "the chuckwalla lets out the air and scurries off."

Connect to the Writing Process: Editing
Using Commas in Direct Quotations

11.–16. Rewrite the incorrect sentences from the preceding exercise, using commas correctly.

End Marks with Direct Quotations

When a quotation ends with a period, the period goes inside the closing quotation marks.

Place a period inside the closing quotation marks when the end of the quotation comes at the end of a sentence.

The bandleader said, "The parade begins in two minutes."

"The parade begins," the bandleader said, "in two minutes."

The same is true of question marks and exclamation points that end a quotation.

She yelled, "Let's get started!"

(The exclamation point belongs inside the closing quotation marks.)

"When," he asked, "did you find time to organize this parade**?**"

(The question mark goes inside the closing quotation marks.)

When a question or an exclamation comes before a speaker tag, the question mark or the exclamation point is still placed inside the closing quotation marks, in place of the usual comma.

"Please hurry**!**" Margo pleaded.

"Do you want to bring a water bottle**?**" Peg asked.

PRACTICE YOUR SKILLS

● Check Your Understanding
Using End Marks with Direct Quotations

General Interest **Write C if the end marks in a sentence are used correctly. Write I if end marks are used incorrectly.**

1. "Have you ever hunted for pearls" asked Linda?

2. "No," Mr. Quinn answered, "but I would like to find one sometime"

3. "Is diving for pearls dangerous?" Hector asked.

4. "It can be extremely dangerous!" Mr. Quinn exclaimed.

5. Taylor asked, "Do pearl divers know which oysters contain pearls"?

6. "They can't tell," Mr. Quinn replied, "until they look inside the shell."

7. "What happens to the oyster once the pearl is removed?" she asked.

8. Mr. Quinn explained, "A diver returns the oyster to the water"

9. "The diver hopes," Mr. Quinn continued, "that the same oyster will make another pearl."

10. "What a job" Linda exclaimed "No wonder pearls are so expensive!"

● Connect to the Writing Process: Editing
Using End Marks in Quotations Correctly

11.–15. Rewrite the incorrectly punctuated quotations from the preceding exercise, using end marks correctly.

Communicate Your Ideas

APPLY TO WRITING

Interview: *Direct Quotations*

Interview a classmate about what kind of job he or she would like to have in the future. Tape-record the interview or take notes while the person talks. Then write a summary of what the person said. Use some of the speaker's exact words. Be sure to use punctuation and capital letters correctly in all direct quotations.

General Interest
Rewrite the direct quotations below, adding quotation marks, commas, end marks, and capital letters where needed.

1. many people do not realize that the crow is a very smart bird Mr. Adams said

2. he added a crow can outwit hawks and most people

3. does putting a scarecrow in a cornfield really help Andrea asked

4. that is a big mistake exclaimed Mr. Adams.

5. many crows he explained use the scarecrows as lookout posts

6. one crow he continued will act as a guard for a flock of crows in a cornfield

7. Sam asked what does the crow do if it senses danger

8. it caws a danger signal to the others Mr. Adams said and they all fly away

9. a team of three crows will also work together to get food from an animal Mr. Adams added

10. how do they do that Beth asked

11. a crow lands on each side of the animal Mr. Adams answered and pretends to steal the animal's food.

12. then the third crow he continued swoops down and snatches the food

13. that's amazing Jeff exclaimed

14. these smart birds also like to have plenty of fun Mr. Adams said

15. he explained one will quietly land next to a sleeping animal and peck it on the head

Other Uses of Quotation Marks

Now that you understand how to punctuate direct quotations, you can apply this knowledge to the following situations.

Writing Dialogue

A conversation between two or more persons is called a **dialogue.** The way a dialogue is written shows the reader who is speaking.

> When writing dialogue, begin a new paragraph each time the speaker changes.

In the following dialogue between Gina and Connie, a new paragraph begins each time the speaker changes.

> "When is your appointment with the guidance counselor?" Gina asked Connie, who was sitting on the bench outside the office.
> "I see her after lunch," Connie answered. "We are going to talk about my doing some volunteer work."

PRACTICE YOUR SKILLS

 Check Your Understanding
Using Dialogue

 Oral Expression **Read aloud the following dialogue between Gina and Connie. Point out each place where a new paragraph should begin.**

Gina exclaimed, "What a good idea! I should do that too." "I hope she has some good ideas for me,"

Connie responded. "I'm not sure what kind of work I'd like to do." "I'm sure she'll be helpful," Gina said. "Let me know what you find out," she added. "Then I can make an appointment too." "Sure," said Connie. "Maybe we can work together somewhere."

● Connect to the Writing Process: Editing
Writing Dialogue Correctly

Rewrite the preceding dialogue correctly, beginning a new paragraph each time the speaker changes.

Communicate Your Ideas

APPLY TO WRITING

Dialogue: *Punctuation*

You have many conversations each day. Some conversations are serious and others are fun. You probably talk to family members, teachers, clerks in stores, and—of course—your friends. Recall a recent conversation you had with a friend. Write a dialogue for your journal, showing each speaker's exact words. If you cannot remember the exact words, make them up. Be sure to punctuate the dialogue correctly and start a new paragraph each time the speaker changes.

Quoting Long Passages

More and more as you go through school, your teachers will want you to support your ideas in reports with quotations by experts. If any of these quotations are more than one paragraph long, there is a special way to write them.

When quoting a passage of more than one paragraph, place quotation marks at the beginning of each paragraph—but at the end of only the last paragraph.

Do not put closing quotation marks at the end of each paragraph, except the last one. By leaving out a pair of closing quotation marks at the end of a paragraph, you are telling your reader that the quotation continues.

The following is a long quotation that a student used in a report about building affordable housing in the United States.

"Here, then, is the idea to set loose in the land: *Everyone should have a simple, decent place to live.*

(no quotation marks)

"We have the know-how in the world to house everyone. We have the resources in the world to house everyone. All that's missing is the will to do it.

(no quotation marks)

"Make no small plans.

(no quotation marks)

"Can we build houses for a million people? Why not? Why not a million houses for five million people? Why not even more?"

(closing quotation marks)

—*Millard Fuller,* A Simple, Decent Place to Live

CONNECT TO WRITER'S CRAFT

Another way to quote a long passage is to set it off from the rest of the text by indenting both side margins. If you are using a computer, you also could set the passage in a smaller type size. When you use this method of quoting a long passage, no quotation marks are needed.

PRACTICE YOUR SKILLS

● Check Your Understanding

Quoting Long Passages

Oral Expression **Imagine that you are quoting the following passage in a report. Tell where you would add quotation marks.**

> In other words, how good really is a house built by volunteers?
>
> Hurricane Andrew, which destroyed thousands of houses, didn't take down a single Habitat house. *That's* how good.
>
> All twenty-seven houses built by Habitat for Humanity in south Florida were still standing with only the slightest of damage. And some were right in the hurricane's path. On Guava Street in west Perrine, all that was left of the neighborhood were splintered trees, trashed cars, headless palms, and yards full of debris, which once had been houses . . . except for four Habitat houses standing side-by-side in a sea of devastation.
>
> —*Millard Fuller,* A Simple, Decent Place to Live

✓ **QuickCheck** Mixed Practice

History Topic **Rewrite each sentence, adding underlining, quotation marks, commas, and end marks where needed. Remember that only a sentence with a speaker tag should be considered a direct quotation.**

1. Theodore H. White was a reporter for Time magazine

2. He is different from the T. H. White who wrote the book The Once and Future King

3. White wrote an article called The American Idea for The New York Times

4. In his article White wrote Americans are a nation born of an idea

5. All men are created equal Thomas Jefferson wrote in 1776

6. Theodore White said Jefferson himself could not have imagined the reach of his call across the world in times to come

7. Why did Jefferson use the word men instead of the word people

8. In 1848 Elizabeth Cady Stanton said All men and women are created equal

9. Along with Susan B. Anthony, Stanton coedited three volumes of a book called History of Woman Suffrage.

10. Anthony published a weekly journal called The Revolution

11. Charlotte Perkins Gilman also argued for women's rights in her magazine called the Forerunner.

12. The word suffragette was used to describe a woman who fought for the right to vote.

Punctuating Titles

Write each sentence, adding quotation marks or underlining to the titles. (These sentences are *not* direct quotations.)

1. The Honeymooners once was a popular TV series.
2. Catalogue is a delightful short poem about cats.
3. Ani DiFranco was featured on the covers of Spin and Ms.
4. I finished reading the short story The Pacing Goose.
5. The painting Twittering Machine is by Paul Klee.
6. I loved the movie Planet of the Apes.
7. Charles Lindbergh flew the Spirit of St. Louis on the first nonstop solo flight from New York to Paris.
8. Education in America was an article in Newsweek.
9. The American troops once marched to Yankee Doodle.
10. Read the chapter Animal Behavior in Science Today.

Punctuating Direct Quotations

Write each sentence, adding capital letters, quotation marks, and other punctuation marks where needed.

1. the Yukon is the largest river in Alaska he stated
2. why are you leaving so early Mandy asked
3. Vickie remarked fish is a good source of protein
4. the travel guide asked have you ever been to Spain
5. wow he exclaimed look at that wave
6. an earthquake can create huge sea waves she stated
7. you can't have everything Steven Wright said
8. watch out for that falling ladder she screamed

Writing Dialogue

Rewrite the following dialogue between Kenneth and Shirley. Add capital letters, quotation marks, and other punctuation marks. Begin a new paragraph each time the speaker changes.

Kenneth began our report is about the discovery of the Americas by the European world. Shirley added as everyone knows, Columbus discovered America by accident, because he was really looking for a faster route to the Far East. Why was a faster route so important Kenneth asked. A shipload of spices Shirley replied could make a person rich for life. Kenneth continued the nation that controlled the spice trade to a great extent controlled the commerce of Europe. Why were spices so important in the fifteenth and sixteenth centuries Shirley asked. They were needed for everyday life Kenneth replied. In the days before refrigeration, spices were needed to preserve food and make medicines.

Using Quotation Marks

Follow the directions below.

1. Write an imaginary dialogue between you and your great-great-grandparents. Punctuate the dialogue correctly.
2. After an introductory paragraph, quote a long passage from a nonfiction book.

Language and *Self-Expression*

French Impressionist painter Edgar Degas lived from 1834 to 1917. The Impressionists shocked their contemporaries by ignoring details, making their brush strokes visible (rather than smoothing out the texture of the painting), and leaving colors unblended.

Degas painted ordinary subjects from modern life. The ballerinas in *Dancers Practicing at the Bar* were probably just warming up when Degas saw them. What kinds of people do you see in your day-to-day life? Write a character sketch of an ordinary person.

Prewriting Interview the person about whom you have chosen to write. Note his or her physical features, occupation, and hobbies. Write down a few details about the setting in which you normally see this person.

Drafting Write a character sketch a few paragraphs long. Use a few of the details you gathered during your interview, including dialogue.

Revising Share your sketch with a classmate. Ask him or her whether the details you have provided create a consistent and believable character. Then read your partner's writing and look for details that seem out of place for the person described.

Editing Check your character sketch for errors in spelling and grammar. Make sure that you have used italics, quotation marks, capital letters, and punctuation correctly.

Publishing Read your character sketch aloud to someone who knows the person you have described. See if they can guess who the person is.

Another Look

Italics
Italicize (underline) letters, numbers, and words when they are used to represent themselves. *(page L567)*

Italicize (underline) the titles of long written or musical works that are published as a single unit. Also italicize (underline) titles of paintings and sculptures and the names of vehicles. *(pages L567–L568)*

Quotation Marks
Use quotation marks to enclose the titles of chapters, articles, stories, one-act plays, short poems, and songs. *(page L571)*

Use quotation marks to enclose a person's exact words. *(pages L573–L574)*

Punctuating Quotations Correctly
Capitalize the first word of a direct quotation. *(page L576)*

Use a comma to separate a direct quotation from a speaker tag. Place the comma inside the closing quotation marks. *(page L578)*

Place a period inside the closing quotation marks when the end of the quotation comes at the end of a sentence. *(page L579)*

Place an exclamation point or question mark inside the closing quotation marks when the end of the quotation comes at the end of a sentence. *(pages L579–L580)*

When a question or an exclamation comes before a speaker tag, the question mark or the exclamation point is still placed *inside* the closing quotation marks in place of the usual comma. *(page L580)*

Other Uses of Quotation Marks
When writing dialogue, begin a new paragraph each time the speaker changes. *(pages L583–L584)*

When quoting a passage of more than one paragraph, place quotation marks at the beginning of each paragraph—but at the end of only the last paragraph. *(pages L584–L585)*

Directions

Read the passage and write the letter of the word or group of words that belongs in each underlined space.

EXAMPLE   My friends and I made a list of favorites

from _(1)_

    1 A "A" to "Z."

       B "A" to "Z".

       C *A* to *Z.*

       D *A* to *Z*

ANSWER   **1 C**

    I started the list by saying that _(1)_ Ian agreed but said that he likes scary stories such as Edgar Allan Poe's _(2)_

    "That was so _(3)_

    Derek said that Poe was one of his favorites and asked if we knew that poem _(4)_ We all agreed that it was a very spooky poem.

    "Don't you like funny _(5)_ than scary stories?"

    Then we all laughed and talked about last week's episode of _(6)_ The word _(7)_ doesn't really do it justice.

    "Okay, who's brave enough to admit that they like sad _(8)_

    _(9)_ I confessed.

    Our short story that day in English had been _(10)_ We all looked rather glum.

1 A "I hate scary movies"
   B "I hate scary movies."
   C *I hate scary movies.*
   D I hate scary movies.

2 A *Tell-Tale Heart.*
   B "Tell-Tale Heart"."
   C "Tell-Tale Heart."
   D Tell-Tale Heart.

3 A scary," Maria piped up!
   B scary!" Maria piped up.
   C scary!", Maria piped up.
   D scary!" Maria piped up

4 A "The Raven."
   B "The Raven"?
   C *The Raven.*
   D *The Raven?*

5 A stories," I asked, "better
   B stories?" I asked, "better
   C stories," I asked "better
   D stories" I asked "better

6 A "The Simpsons".
   B "The Simpsons."
   C *The Simpsons.*
   D "the Simpsons."

7 A *hilarious*
   B "hilarious"
   C "hilarious,"
   D *hilarious,*

8 A stories?" Ian asked.
   B "stories," Ian asked?
   C stories"? Ian asked.
   D stories" Ian asked.

9 A ""Babe" made me cry"
   B *"Babe* made me cry,"
   C "Babe made me cry,
   D *"Babe* made me cry"

10 A "The Scarlet Ibis".
   B *The Scarlet Ibis.*
   C "The Scarlet Ibis."
   D *The Scarlet Ibis."*

CHAPTER 18

Other Punctuation

 **Pretest**

Directions
Read the sentences and write the letter of the correct way to write each group of underlined words. If the underlined word or words contain no error, write D.

EXAMPLE   **1.** <u>Were going</u> on a field trip, Class.
    1 A We're going
        B Were go-ing
        C Were going:
        D No error

ANSWER   **1 A**

1. This won't be your standard <u>field trip we aren't</u> going to the zoo or to a museum.
2. We're going on a <u>scientists trip</u> into the field.
3. <u>Well study the coast redwood</u> of California.
4. <u>Lets pack</u> a camera.
5. Bring the <u>textbook, a tape measure,</u> and a pen.
6. There are three kinds of <u>redwoods the coast</u> redwoods, the giant sequoias, and the dawn redwoods.
7. Your necks will <u>be sore tomorrow</u> the coast redwoods are tall!
8. In the 1930s, a 2,200-year-old coast redwood was logged, and <u>its height was</u> amazing.

1	A	field-trip we aren't	5	A	text-book, a tape measure
	B	field trip; we aren't		B	textbook, a tape-measure
	C	field trip-we aren't		C	textbook, a tape measure;
	D	No error		D	No error

1
A field-trip we aren't
B field trip; we aren't
C field trip-we aren't
D No error

2
A scientists' trip
B scientists trip:
C scientists trip;
D No error

3
A Well study the coast-redwood
B Well study: the coast redwood
C We'll study the coast redwood
D No error

4
A Lets pack:
B Lets pack;
C Let's pack
D No error

5
A text-book, a tape measure
B textbook, a tape-measure
C textbook, a tape measure;
D No error

6
A redwoods: the coast
B redwood's the coast
C redwoods; the coast
D No error

7
A be: sore tomorrow
B be sore; tomorrow
C be sore tomorrow;
D No error

8
A it's height was
B its height was:
C its' height was
D No error

Leonora Carrington. *Red Cow,* 1989. Oil on canvas, 24 by 36 inches. Private collection.

Describe What images do you recognize in this painting?

Analyze Do you notice any differences in brush strokes used in the painting? Are different brush strokes used to paint different objects?

Interpret What atmosphere do you think the artist hoped to convey? What elements of the painting help create this atmosphere? What techniques might a writer use to convey the same mood?

Judge Do you think that a red cow is a worthy subject for a painting? How do the other images in the painting influence the meaning? Do you think that a different subject would better convey these ideas?

At the end of this chapter, you will use the artwork as a visual aid for writing.

Apostrophes

Two uses of the apostrophe will be covered in this section. One use of the apostrophe is to show ownership or possession. The apostrophe is also used in contractions.

Apostrophes to Show Possession

The most common use of apostrophes is to show that someone or something owns something else.

> Rick's dinosaur book = the dinosaur book of Rick
>
> the dinosaurs' names = the names of the dinosaurs
>
> the cavemen's fossils = the fossils of the cavemen

The Possessive Form of Singular Nouns

Before writing the possessive form of a singular noun, write just the noun itself. Then add an apostrophe and an *s*.

Add 's to form the possessive of a singular noun.

> Clemens + 's = Clemens's   Samuel Clemens's pen name is Mark Twain.
>
> Seth + 's = Seth's   Is this Seth's personal copy of *Tom Sawyer?*
>
> library + 's = library's   It is the library's copy.
>
> computer + 's = computer's   The computer's database shows one shelved copy.
>
> shelf + 's = shelf's   Find the shelf's location.

A possessive and a plural noun often sound the same. So when you speak, include details that will help listeners identify possessive or plural nouns.

UNCLEAR Did you know the **authors?**

CLEAR Did you know the **author's** real name?

PRACTICE YOUR SKILLS

● Check Your Understanding
Forming Possessive Singular Nouns

Rewrite each of the following phrases, using the possessive form.

1. the fields of the farmer
2. the tires of the bus
3. the whiskers of the cat
4. the skill of the typist
5. the role of the actor
6. muffins belonging to Sue
7. end of the day
8. job of my mother
9. the lid of the box
10. the rays of the sun

● Connect to the Writing Process: Drafting
Using Apostrophes with Singular Possessive Nouns

11.–15. Write five sentences, using five of the possessive phrases you formed in the preceding exercise.

The Possessive Forms of Plural Nouns

Most plural nouns end in *s: tomatoes, papers, slippers.* A few plural nouns, such as *children* and *mice,* do not end in *s.* How the possessive form of a plural noun is written depends on the ending of the noun.

Add only an apostrophe to form the possessive of a plural noun that ends in s.

girls + ' = girls'   The girls' book reports are due.
books + ' = books'   The books' titles were similar.

Add 's to form the possessive of a plural noun that does not end in s.

men + 's = men's   The men's choice was a poem.

children + 's = children's   It was "The Children's Hour."

When you write the possessive of a plural noun, take two steps. First, write the plural of the noun. Second, look at the ending of the word. If the word ends in s, add only an apostrophe. If it does not end in s, add an apostrophe and an s.

FORMING THE PLURAL OF NOUNS

PLURAL	ENDING	ADD	POSSESSIVE
teachers	s	'	teachers' lounge
lawyers	s	'	lawyers' office
women	no s	's	women's class
children	no s	's	children's toys

Remember to use apostrophes with a noun only when you are showing possession. Do not use an apostrophe just to make a noun plural.

INCORRECT   The **boys'** were improving their grades.
CORRECT   The **boys** were improving their grades.
CORRECT   The **boys'** grades were improving.

PRACTICE YOUR SKILLS

● Check Your Understanding
Forming Possessive Plural Nouns

Rewrite each of the following phrases, using the possessive form.

1. playground of the children
2. feathers of the turkeys
3. lids of the boxes
4. mealtimes of the puppies
5. howls of the wolves
6. nest of the birds
7. migration of the geese
8. sizes of the shoes
9. suits of the women
10. claws of the tigers

● Check Your Understanding
Forming Possessive Nouns

Rewrite each of the following phrases, using the correct possessive form. Notice that some nouns are singular and some are plural.

11. the ringing of the alarm clock
12. the rising of the sun
13. the aroma of the coffee
14. the crackling of cereal
15. the sounds of appliances
16. the yawns of slow risers
17. the arrival of the newspaper
18. the schedules of the buses
19. the conversations of the children
20. the laughter of the women
21. the music of the radio
22. the riding class of the girls
23. the homework of Mercedes
24. the food selection of the pantry

25.–29. Write five sentences, using five of the possessive phrases you formed in the preceding exercise.

● Connect to the Writing Process: Revising
Replacing Phrases with Possessive Nouns

Contemporary Life **Rewrite each sentence, replacing the underlined phrases with possessive nouns.**

30. The desks of the students await their arrival.

31. The heat of the building is turned on.

32. The hands of the clock inch toward eight o'clock.

33. The coats of the girls are hung up.

34. The briefcases of the teachers are opened.

35. The music of the band floats across the room.

36. The picture of the President hangs on the wall.

37. The coffee perks in the office of the principal.

38. The pace of the day quickens.

39. The eyes of the crossing guards stare at the traffic.

Possessive Forms of Pronouns

Personal pronouns do not use an apostrophe to show possession the way nouns do. Instead, they change form.

POSSESSIVE PERSONAL PRONOUNS	
SINGULAR	my, mine, your, yours, his, her, hers, its
PLURAL	our, ours, your, yours, their, theirs

Do not add an apostrophe to form the possessive of a personal pronoun.

PERSONAL
PRONOUNS

The book bag is **hers.**
The heat cracked **its** leather.
Our new books are still in the classroom.

Indefinite pronouns, however, form the possessive by adding 's just the way singular nouns do.

COMMON INDEFINITE PRONOUNS	
SINGULAR	anybody, anyone, each, either, everybody, everyone, neither, nobody, no one, one, somebody, someone
PLURAL	both, few, many, several

Add 's to form the possessive of an indefinite pronoun.

INDEFINITE
PRONOUNS

This seems to be everyone**'s** library time.
Someone**'s** library assignment is on the floor.
Nobody**'s** books were turned in to the office.

PRACTICE YOUR SKILLS

● Check Your Understanding
Using Possessive Pronouns

Contemporary Life

Write C if the correct possessive form is used in a sentence. Write I if the incorrect form is used.

1. Everyone's report must include library research.

2. Is your's about computers?

3. Jason and I worked on our's together.

4. Its title is "Medical Miracles."

5. Does your report list all of your sources?

6. Is this library book hers'?

7. Is anyones report finished yet?

8. Hector finished his's on Monday.

9. Kayla and Erin have finished theirs, too.

10. I hope no one's grade depends on this one assignment.

● Connect to the Writing Process: Editing
Correcting Possessive Pronouns

11.–15. Rewrite the incorrect sentences from the previous exercise, using the correct forms of possessive pronouns.

● Connect to the Writing Process: Drafting
Writing Sentences

Write five sentences using possessive pronouns. Follow the directions given below.

16. Write a sentence about *the bike belonging to him.*

17. Write a sentence about *the house belonging to them.*

18. Write a question asking *if a pen belongs to anyone.*

19. Write a sentence about *the price of it.*

20. Write a sentence about *the favorite song of everyone.*

APPLY TO WRITING

Newspaper Article: *Possessive Pronouns*

Write an article for the school newspaper about one of the sports teams or musical groups at your school. Describe the accomplishments of the whole group, as well as those of individual members. Use a variety of possessive nouns and pronouns in your article.

 QuickCheck   Mixed Practice

History Topic **Write the correct form of any incorrect possessive nouns and pronouns in the following sentences. If a sentence is correct, write *C*.**

1. Eleanor Roosevelt was President Franklin Roosevelts' wife.

2. She took her job as the nation's First Lady very seriously.

3. Mrs. Roosevelt visited battlefields and raised many soldiers spirits.

4. She visited coal miners and tried to improve they're lives.

5. Mrs. Roosevelt spoke up for womens' rights.

6. She also supported African Americans' civil rights.

7. Many ideas that the President suggested were actually her's.

8. She believed that doing useful work was everyone's responsibility.

9. After World War II, she helped the United Nations with its work on human rights.

10. After she died, many presidents wives took her work as a model for their own.

Apostrophes with Contractions

A contraction is formed by combining two or more words. An apostrophe replaces one or more missing letters.

Use an apostrophe in a contraction to show where one or more letters have been omitted.

The following examples show how some contractions are formed.

CONTRACTIONS	
does not = doesn't	let us = let's
he would = he'd	that is = that's
who is = who's	of the clock = o'clock

When a contraction is written, no letters should be added or moved around. There is one common exception to this rule: *will* + *not* = *won't*.

Contraction or Possessive Pronoun?

Do not confuse a contraction with a possessive pronoun.

CONTRACTIONS | it's = it is, you're = you are
they're = they are
there's = there is or there has
who's = who is or who has

POSSESSIVES | its (belonging to it)
your/yours (belonging to you)
their/theirs (belonging to them)
whose (belonging to whom)

CONNECT TO WRITER'S CRAFT

When you are writing and you are not sure whether to add an apostrophe, ask yourself if the word could be replaced with two individual words. If the answer is yes, use an apostrophe. If the answer is no, do not use an apostrophe.

It's a lovely day. (*It's* could be replaced with *It is.* Use an apostrophe.)
Its tires were flat. (*Its* could not be replaced with *It is.* Do not use an apostrophe.)

PRACTICE YOUR SKILLS

● Check Your Understanding
Forming Contractions

Write the contractions for each pair of words.

1. there is	**5.** we have	**9.** who is	**13.** I have
2. would not	**6.** were not	**10.** are not	**14.** I am
3. they are	**7.** had not	**11.** let us	**15.** I will
4. will not	**8.** do not	**12.** you are	**16.** it is

Distinguishing Between Contractions and Possessive Pronouns

Contemporary Life **Write the correct word in parentheses.**

17. (There's, Theirs) a snake!

18. Did (your, you're) science class ever study snakes?

19. That snake was once rattling (it's, its) tail.

20. (Who's, Whose) going to touch it?

21. I think (you're, your) interested in snakes.

22. (It's, Its) going to be an interesting class.

23. Did you see (they're, their) lab manual?

24. I don't know (who's, whose) rubber gloves these are.

25. (There's, Theirs) are on the table.

26. (They're, Their) starting (they're, their) experiment.

Connect to the Writing Process: Drafting
Writing Sentences with Contractions

Make contractions from the following words. Then write five sentences, using the contractions.

27. it is	**30.** there is
28. they are	**31.** you are
29. who is	**32.** we have

Connect to the Writing Process: Editing
Using Contractions and Possessive Pronouns

Rewrite the incorrect sentences, using the correct contraction or possessive pronoun. If a sentence is correct, write C.

33. Whose picking you up after school today?

34. I hope your ready because your bus is here.

35. It's too late for them to check their lockers now.

36. Who's notebook is this?

37. There's a backpack on that desk.

38. It's zipper is broken.

39. We're going to miss the bus if we don't hurry.

40. Our bus is on time, but theirs is late.

41. Your always running late at the end of the day.

42. I'll tell your mother that you're on your way to her house.

▶ Apostrophes with Certain Plurals

To prevent confusion, certain items form their plurals by adding 's.

Add 's to form the plural of lowercase letters, some capital letters, and some words used as words that people might otherwise misread.

LOWERCASE LETTERS	Are these letters *i*'s or *e*'s? (Without the apostrophe, you might misread *i*'s as the word *is*.)
CAPITAL LETTERS	How many *U*'s did you write? (Without the apostrophe, you might misread *U's* as the word *Us*.)
WORDS USED AS WORDS	That little girl uses a lot of *no*'s when she talks to her brothers. (Without the apostrophe, you might think that *nos* was a word.)

The plurals of most other letters, symbols, numerals, dates, and words used as words can be formed by just adding *s*.

CAPITAL LETTERS	How many *C*s did you write for that exercise?
SYMBOLS	Don't use those *&*s in your report.
NUMERALS	Her *7*s look like *9*s.
DATES	The Internet became very popular in the 1990s.
WORDS USED AS WORDS	Replace some of the *but*s in your sentences.

Notice that each number, letter, symbol, and word used as a word is italicized (underlined), but the apostrophe and the *s* are not.

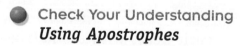
You can learn more *about italics* on pages 1567–1568.

PRACTICE YOUR SKILLS

● Check Your Understanding
Using Apostrophes

Write the plural form of each of the following letters, symbols, or words used as words.

1. a   **6.** #

2. c   **7.** 2

3. B   **8.** 1960

4. I   **9.** and

5. +   **10.** hi

● Connect to the Writing Process: Drafting

Writing Sentences Using Plurals

11.–15. Write five sentences using five of the plurals you formed in the preceding exercise.

☑ QuickCheck Mixed Practice

History Topic **Write the underlined word in each sentence correctly, adding an apostrophe where needed. If no apostrophe is needed, write C.**

1. By the <u>1700s</u>, both France and Great Britain were <u>powerful</u> nations.

2. In North America, both nations wanted to make the colonies <u>theirs</u>.

3. Each side sought the <u>Native Americans</u> help.

4. <u>Frances</u> goal was to build trade in North America.

5. <u>Great Britains</u> objective was different.

6. It wanted to add territory to <u>its</u> empire.

7. The <u>is</u> were dotted in each treaty with the Native <u>Americans</u>.

8. <u>Everyones</u> life was changed in the colonies because of both European <u>nations</u> greed.

9. The <u>mens</u> lives were changed because they became soldiers.

10. <u>Womens</u> and <u>childrens</u> lives were changed because they didn't know whether <u>their</u> husbands and fathers were coming home.

Semicolons

A semicolon (;) most often signals a pause between the parts of a compound sentence.

Semicolons with Compound Sentences

A **compound sentence** has two or more independent clauses. These clauses can be joined by a comma and a coordinating conjunction or by a semicolon.

Use a semicolon between the clauses of a compound sentence that are not joined by a coordinating conjunction. Coordinating conjunctions include *and, but, or,* and *yet.*

COMMA AND CONJUNCTION	We went to Colorado on vacation, **and** everyone enjoyed the trip.
	My mom loved Pike's Peak, **but** my favorite place was Mesa Verde National Park.
	I am going fishing on the lake, **yet** I'd prefer to go white-water rafting on the Colorado River.
SEMICOLON	We went to Colorado on vacation; everyone enjoyed the trip.
	My mom loved Pike's Peak; my favorite place was Mesa Verde National Park.
	I am going fishing on the lake; I'd prefer to go white-water rafting on the Colorado River.

You can learn more about compound sentences on pages L263–L265.

Using a semicolon is one way to correct a run-on sentence. When you edit your writing, look for sentences that are incorrectly joined by commas. Revise them by adding a semicolon or by adding a coordinating conjunction.

RUN-ON   Mesa Verde has ancient Native American cliff houses, they are at least seven hundred years old.

CORRECT   Mesa Verde has ancient Native American cliff houses, **and** they are at least seven hundred years old.

CORRECT   Mesa Verde has ancient Native American cliff houses**;** they are at least seven hundred years old.

You can learn more about run-on sentences on pages L294–L295.

PRACTICE YOUR SKILLS

● Check Your Understanding

Using Commas and Semicolons with Compound Sentences

Social Studies **Write C if a sentence is punctuated correctly.**
Write I if a sentence is punctuated incorrectly.

1. Mesa Verde is located in southwestern Colorado, it is near the city of Cortez.

2. The Anasazi people built the cliff houses; some of the buildings are four stories high.

3. The Anasazi people lived at Mesa Verde for almost one hundred years, then the people disappeared from the area.

4. Centuries later the Ute Indians moved into the area, but they stayed away from the deserted cliff houses.

5. Spanish settlers also explored the area; but they never saw the abandoned buildings.

6. Two ranchers discovered the buildings in 1888 and in the 1890s, curious visitors flocked to the ancient settlement.

7. Many visitors stole precious souvenirs from the area, then an angry newspaper reporter complained.

8. In 1906, Congress decided to protect the ancient dwellings; it passed legislation that created Mesa Verde National Park.

9. The Cliff Palace is the park's most popular attraction, and we decided to take a tour of it.

10. Visitors to the Balcony House must climb a thirty-two-foot ladder to get inside, I decided to try it.

● Connect to the Writing Process: Editing
Punctuating Compound Sentences

11.–15. **Rewrite the incorrectly punctuated sentences from the preceding exercise, using commas and semicolons correctly.**

● Connect to the Writing Process: Drafting
Writing Sentences Using Commas and Semicolons

Write sentences that follow the directions. Use commas and semicolons correctly in your sentences.

16. Write a compound sentence joined by the conjunction *and*.

17. Rewrite correctly the same compound sentence you just wrote, taking out the conjunction *and*.

18. Write a compound sentence joined by the conjunction *but*.

19. Rewrite correctly the same compound sentence you just wrote, taking out the conjunction *but*.

Communicate Your Ideas

APPLY TO WRITING
Brochure: *Commas and Semicolons*

Research facts about one of America's national parks. You can easily find a list of these parks on the Internet. Write a visitor's guide to the park for your parents. Include interesting information, based on your research, about the park's history and attractions. Use at least five compound sentences, punctuating them correctly with commas or semicolons.

▶ Semicolons to Avoid Confusion

Occasionally a semicolon will be used in place of a comma to eliminate any possible confusion in a sentence.

> Use a semicolon instead of a comma between the clauses of a compound sentence if there are already commas within one of the clauses.

In the following sentences, a semicolon takes the place of a comma between the two independent clauses of a compound sentence because the first clause already has commas in it. The semicolon is used even though a coordinating conjunction connects the clauses.

> Colombia, Brazil, and Ecuador are three nations in northern South America; and all three lie along the equator.
>
> All three countries have rain forests, lush, tropical areas crowded with tall, fast-growing trees; but Ecuador also has a cold, mountainous area.

CONNECT TO WRITER'S CRAFT

Even with the semicolons, sentences such as those above can still be confusing. Sometimes it is better to rewrite these sentences to make two or more simple sentences.

> Colombia, Brazil, and Ecuador are three nations in northern South America. All three lie along the equator.
>
> All three countries have rain forests, lush, tropical areas crowded with tall, fast-growing trees. Ecuador also has a cold, mountainous area.

When you revise your writing, check long sentences to make sure they are not confusing. If necessary, break up some long compound sentences into simple sentences. ●

A semicolon can take the place of a comma in another situation as well.

Use a **semicolon** instead of a comma between the items in a series if the items contain commas.

In the first example that follows, a comma is needed between the cities and the countries. Normally a comma would be placed between each city and country pair because they are all items in a series. If all of those commas were put in, the sentence would become very confusing to read. As a result, semicolons take the place of the commas between the items in a series.

> The capitals of these nations are Quito, Ecuador; Bogota, Colombia; and Brasilia, Brazil.
>
> Other cities in Brazil include Sao Paulo, the largest city in South America; Rio de Janeiro, a popular beach resort; and Salvador, another city on the Atlantic coast.

You can learn more about items in a series on pages L530–L531.

PRACTICE YOUR SKILLS

Check Your Understanding
Using Semicolons

Social Studies **Write _C_ if a sentence is punctuated correctly. Write _I_ if a sentence is punctuated incorrectly.**

1. Other South American nations include Chile, located on the South Pacific coast, Argentina, reaching down to the continent's tip, and Uruguay, located on the South Atlantic coast.

2. The three nations' capitals are Santiago, Chile, Buenos Aires, Argentina, and Montevideo, Uruguay.

3. Chile's population includes people of European, Indian, and other backgrounds; and its primary language is Spanish.

4. Chile's crops include wheat, corn, and grapes, but its main export is copper.

5. Argentina's major cities include Buenos Aires, with thirteen million people, Cordoba, with more than a million people, and Moron, with at least half a million people.

6. Languages spoken in Argentina include Spanish, English, Italian, German, and French; and most of the country's population is of the Roman Catholic faith.

7. Argentina exports meat, wheat, and corn, and it imports machinery, chemicals, fuel, and other industrial products.

8. Uruguay's major cities include Montevideo, Salto, and Paysandú; but Montevideo is much larger than any of the other cities.

9. In order of size, the nations are Argentina, with more than a million square miles, Chile, covering about 290,000 square miles, and Uruguay, having only 68,000 square miles.

10. In order of population, the nations are Argentina, with thirty-four million people; Chile, with fourteen million people; and Uruguay, with only three million people.

Connect to the Writing Process: Editing
Punctuating Sentences with Commas and Semicolons

11.–16. Rewrite the incorrectly punctuated sentences from the preceding exercise, using commas and semicolons correctly.

APPLY TO WRITING

Descriptive Paragraph: *Semicolons*

Jacob Lawrence. *Parade,* 1960.
Tempera with pencil underdrawing on fiberboard, 23⅞ by 30⅛ inches. Hirshhorn
Museum and Sculpture Garden. Courtesy of the artist and Francine Seders Gallery,
Seattle, Washington.

Your class took a field trip to the art museum, but
your best friend was unable to go. You thought your
friend might like this unusual painting. Write a paragraph describing the painting to your friend. Since
there is so much action in it, you will probably want
to use items in a series and compound sentences. Be
sure to use semicolons correctly.

Colons

A colon (:) is used most often before lists of items.

Use a colon before most lists of items, especially when the list comes after an expression like *the following.*

Notice that commas go between the items in each series.

> We have packed the following items: first-aid kit, sunscreen lotion, and insect repellent.
>
> The bouquet included three kinds of wild flowers: daisies, sunflowers, and lantana.

A colon is not needed between a verb and its complements or directly after a preposition.

INCORRECT	Three hiking friends of mine are: Mary, Bob, and Tad.
CORRECT	I have three hiking friends: Mary, Bob, and Tad.
INCORRECT	On our vacation we will be going to: Texas, Utah, and Idaho.
CORRECT	On our vacation we will be going to the following states: Texas, Utah, and Idaho.

There are a few other special situations that also require a colon.

COLON USAGE	
HOURS AND MINUTES	7:10 P.M.
BIBICAL CHAPTERS AND VERSES	Matthew 7:7
SALUTATIONS IN BUSINESS LETTERS	Dear Sir:

PRACTICE YOUR SKILLS

● Check Your Understanding
Using Colons

Write *C* if a sentence is punctuated correctly.
Write *I* if a sentence is punctuated incorrectly.

1. Some popular vacations include the following luxury cruises, adventure trips, and European travel.

2. Travel agencies recommend three cruise destinations: Alaska, the Caribbean, and the Mediterranean.

3. Some popular cruise ships are the *Silver Cloud,* the *Wind Song,* and the *Whisper Spirit.*

4. The great thing about a cruise is no one has to get up at 6 30 A.M.

5. Travel brochures offer the following adventures motorcycle trips in Costa Rica, polar bear viewing in Canada, or an island tour of Hawaii.

6. If you go on an adventure vacation, be sure to take: a camera, sunscreen, insect repellant, and a first-aid kit.

7. There are three popular vacation cities in Europe Paris, London, and Amsterdam.

8. Travelers' favorite American cities include New York City, Orlando, and Las Vegas.

9. A South American vacation could include adventures in: Ecuador, Venezuela, Colombia, or Peru.

10. Dear Sir
I would like information about the following vacation tours Los Angeles, Alaska, and Seattle.

Using Colons

11.–17. Rewrite the incorrectly punctuated sentences from the exercise on the preceding page, adding or taking out colons where needed.

Communicate Your Ideas

APPLY TO WRITING

Travel Diary Entry: *Colons*

Write a travel diary entry to help you recall a trip you have taken. Tell when you left, when you arrived, and when you returned. Include lists of what you took with you and what you brought back. Also include lists of the things you saw and did. Introduce each list with a sentence that explains what the list includes. You might wish to draw a chart that has several columns in your diary. It will make it easier for you to add details daily, and it will help you to remember the different things you want to list.

Date	These creatures caught my attention:	The plants and flowers were amazing:

Use colons and commas where needed.

History Topic **Rewrite each sentence, using commas, semicolons, and colons correctly. If a sentence is correct, write C.**

1. Meriwether Lewis and William Clark were important explorers, they opened up the West for expansion.

2. Their expedition set off from St. Louis, Missouri, in the spring of 1804, and they reached the Pacific Ocean in November of 1805.

3. The long trip was a success, and President Jefferson was delighted with their discoveries.

4. The two adventurers collected information on the following the people, plants, animals, and geography of the West.

5. Their crew included: soldiers, interpreters, and one slave.

6. The list of obstacles was endless: rivers, mountains, weather, and animals.

7. In a village in North Dakota, they met a Shoshone Indian woman named Sacajawea, she became their guide.

8. Sacajawea knew the land and the local tribes; and her knowledge saved the expedition.

9. Lewis and Clark explored: the Missouri River, the Columbia River, and the Snake River.

10. Afterward, they returned to the East and reported on the wonders they had seen; their reports inspired settlers to move farther westward.

Hyphens

A hyphen is used most often to divide a word at the end of a line. You should avoid dividing words whenever possible, however. Divided words slow a reader down and can cause misunderstanding. When you must divide a word at the end of a line to keep your margin even, remember to include a hyphen.

Use a hyphen to divide a word at the end of a line.

The following guidelines show how to divide a word at the end of a line. If you are not certain about where each syllable in a word ends, look the word up in a dictionary. Each entry word is divided into syllables.

GUIDELINES FOR DIVIDING WORDS

1. Divide words only between syllables.

gym·nas·tics: gym-nastics or gymnas-tics

2. Never divide a one-syllable word.

Do Not Break   stay   laugh   called

3. Do not divide a word so that one letter stands alone.

Do Not Break   around   emit   obey   sleepy

4. Divide hyphenated words only after the hyphens.

brother-in-law   maid-of-honor   face-to-face

PRACTICE YOUR SKILLS

● Check Your Understanding
Using Hyphens

Write each word, adding a hyphen or hyphens to show where it can be correctly divided. If a word should not be divided, write *no* after the word.

1. hamster	**9.** surprise	**17.** travel
2. among	**10.** strong	**18.** discover
3. galaxy	**11.** captain	**19.** magnify
4. make	**12.** build	**20.** transparent
5. about	**13.** action	**21.** illusion
6. liquid	**14.** opal	**22.** passed
7. item	**15.** trespass	**23.** commute
8. single	**16.** sister-in-law	**24.** fling

● Connect to the Writing Process: Editing
Correcting Sentences with Hyphens

Rewrite the following paragraphs, correcting the use of hyphens wherever they are misused. If a word can be hyphenated, move the hyphen to an appropriate place. If a word cannot be hyphenated, write it as one word.

Jonas Salk was a scient-
ist who studied bacteria at the U-
niversity of Pittsburgh. In 1955, he
made a discovery that changed the world. He had made a vaccine that could
protect children from a deadly disease called polio.

> In the early 1900s, polio had cri-
> ppled or killed nearly a million Americ-
> ans. Salk's vaccine was soon being give-
> n to America's children as an injec-
> tion. It was very effective, but soon an e-
> ven better polio vaccine was discovered.
> A scientist named Albert Sabin created a poli-
> o vaccine that children could take oral-
> ly. Now children can be protected from polio
> without even having a shot.

Other Uses of Hyphens

Although used most often to divide words, a hyphen has other uses.

Hyphens with Certain Numbers

When you write numbers out in a story or report, use a hyphen to spell most numbers correctly.

> Use a hyphen when writing out the numbers *twenty-one* through *ninety-nine.*

> They counted fifty-six rooms in the school.
> Twenty-one rooms in the school have computers.

If a number is the first word of a sentence, it must always be written out.

Hyphens with Certain Fractions

Fractions used as adjectives are hyphenated.

Use a hyphen when writing out a fraction used as an adjective.

HYPHEN	A **three-fourths** majority of the teachers did not have computers in school. (*Three-fourths* is an adjective that describes *majority*.)
NO HYPHEN	**Three fourths** of the class is computer literate. (The noun *three fourths* is the subject.)
HYPHEN	A **two-thirds** vote by the school board approved the purchase of new computers.
NO HYPHEN	**Two thirds** of their computers are old.

You can learn more about adjectives on pages L99–L109.

Hyphens with Some Compound Nouns

A **compound noun** is a noun made up of two or more words. The words in a compound noun may be written in one of three ways: (1) together, as one word; (2) as two separate words; or (3) as two words joined with a hyphen.

Use a hyphen to separate the parts of some compound nouns.

COMPOUND NOUNS	
ONE WORD	handbook, housewife, toothache, northeast
TWO WORDS	coffee table, home run, dream world
HYPHENATED	tractor-trailer, cross-country, drive-in

If you are unsure of the spelling of a compound noun, check it in a dictionary.

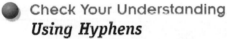

When hyphenating words at the ends of lines, writers try to avoid distracting hyphen ladders, three hyphens stacked.

DISRUPTING   I use my computer for assignments, letter writing, and researching topics. Later I hope to write professionally.

SMOOTH   I use my computer for assignments, letter writing, and researching topics. Someday, I will
write professionally.

You can learn more about compound nouns on pages L50 L51.

PRACTICE YOUR SKILLS

● Check Your Understanding
Using Hyphens

Contemporary Life   **Write C if a sentence is punctuated correctly.**
Write I if a sentence is punctuated incorrectly.

1. The student council met in the home econom-ics room yesterday afternoon.

2. Twenty two students attended the meeting.

3. Three fourths of the members answered the roll.

4. Four-teen members offered suggestions from the student body.

5. Many suggestions were about improving school lunches by offering more ham-burgers, hot-dogs, and french-fries.

6. The secretary wrote minutes in her note-book.

7. A motion was made to spend thirty-three dollars for decorations for the homecoming dance.

8. The motion passed with a three fourths majority.

9. One-fourth of the council voted against the idea.

10. At the end of the meeting, the members pose-d for their yearbook picture.

● **Connect to the Writing Process: Editing**
Punctuating with Hyphens

11.–17. Rewrite the incorrectly punctuated sentences from the preceding exercise, adding or deleting hyphens where needed.

Communicate Your Ideas

APPLY TO WRITING
Meeting Report: *Hyphens*

Write a brief report of a real or imaginary meeting for your teacher. Tell how many people attended, what was voted on, and the result of the vote. Use hyphens where needed for divided words, certain numbers, certain fractions, and compound nouns.

Contemporary Life

Rewrite each sentence, adding apostrophes, semicolons, colons, and hyphens where needed.

1. Todays school lunch includes the following turkey, green beans, mashed potatoes, apple pie, and milk.

2. Good nutrition is vital to a teenagers health and well being.

3. One third of the student body does not eat the meal offered in our schools lunchroom.

4. Everyones appetite is different, but balanced nutrition is important to success in school.

5. Some students eat only "junk food" cake, candy, and soda.

6. Other students say theyre too busy, they skip lunch completely.

7. A meal should be divided into thirds one third for protein, one third for vegetables, and one third for carbohydrates.

8. The protein offers iron and the vegetables contain fiber, minerals, and vitamins.

9. Theres no excuse for poor nutrition at school.

10. Its so easy to buy a good meal or to bring your own homemade lunch.

Punctuating Correctly

Write each sentence, adding apostrophes, semicolons, colons, and hyphens where needed.

1. Pineapples are not native to Hawaii they were first planted there in 1790.
2. A mosquitos wings can move 1,000 times a second.
3. Well meet you for lunch at 1230.
4. New York Citys population is greater than that of the following countries Denmark, Austria, and Norway.
5. Six photographers studios are on the sixth floor.
6. Thirty six members were present at the meeting.
7. I cant believe this mess is yours!
8. Texas has 154 counties Alaska has none.
9. Why isnt Mr. Browns dog inside tonight?
10. I have lived in Pittsburgh, Pennsylvania Orlando, Florida and San Francisco, California.

Using Punctuation

Write each sentence, adding apostrophes, semicolons, colons, and hyphens where needed.

1. Are there more *as* or *is* in your name?
2. Eighty four people entered the contest.
3. That brand of mens sweaters runs small.
4. There are three small eyes on top of a bees head two larger ones are in the front.
5. In 1841, the United States had three presidents Martin Van Buren, William Harrison, and John Tyler.

Punctuating Correctly

Write each sentence, adding apostrophes, semicolons, colons, and hyphens where needed. If a sentence needs no change, write C.

1. The sun is an average star it is not a huge one.
2. Because its so close to Earth, the sun seems much brighter than other stars.
3. Seventy five percent of the sun consists of hydrogen.
4. The suns interior temperature is about 27 million degrees Fahrenheit.
5. Its energy comes from nuclear reactions.
6. The following are all caused by the suns energy plant growth, ocean currents, and tides.
7. Without the sun there wouldnt be any life on Earth.
8. The sun is the center of the solar system there are nine planets orbiting the sun.
9. The planets orbits are determined by gravity.
10. The sun rotates on its axis each rotation takes a month.

Using Punctuation Marks

Write sentences that follow the directions below.

Write a sentence that ...

1. includes the possessive form of the noun *dog*.
2. includes the possessive form of the noun *friends*.
3. includes the possessive form of the noun *women*.
4. includes the possessive form of the pronoun *someone*.
5. includes the words *they're* and *their*.
6. includes the plural of *yes*.
7. includes two independent clauses joined by only a semicolon.
8. includes *two thirds* as an adjective.

Language and *Self-Expression*

British artist Leonora Carrington is often associated with surrealism, an artistic movement centered in Paris in the twenties. Surrealists attempted to tap into the subconscious, and their works of art often contain fantastic, incongruous images in dreamlike settings.

Like many surrealists, Carrington is also known for her plays, novels, and short stories. What makes a multitalented artist choose one form of expression over another? How does form affect meaning? Narrate the ideas of *Red Cow* with words rather than with paint; personify, or give human characteristics to, the figures and objects in the painting.

Prewriting Make a cluster diagram, listing characteristics for each figure in the painting. Include typically human characteristics, such as *greedy* or *solemn*, because you will be personifying them.

Drafting Write several paragraphs describing the interactions between the figures in the painting. Use the characteristics you listed above, and be sure to set the scene. Your description should create a surreal mood.

Revising Reread your story keeping characterization in mind. Would the characterization benefit by changing the person?

Editing Check your story for errors in spelling and grammar. Make sure that you have used punctuation correctly.

Publishing Prepare a final draft of your story. Submit it to your teacher. If you know any visual artists, share your story with them.

 **Another Look**

Apostrophes

Add 's to form the possessive of a singular noun. *(page L597)*

Add only an apostrophe to form the possessive of a plural noun that ends in *s*. *(page L599)*

Add 's to form the possessive of a plural noun that does not end in *s*. *(page L599)*

Do not add an apostrophe to form the possessive of a personal pronoun. *(pages L601–L602)*

Add 's to form the possessive of an indefinite pronoun. *(page L602)*

Use an apostrophe in a contraction to show where one or more letters have been omitted. *(page L605)*

Add 's to form the plural of lowercase letters, some capital letters, and some words used as words that people might otherwise misread. The plurals of most other letters, symbols, numerals, dates, and words used as words can be formed by just adding *s*. *(pages L608–L609)*

Semicolons

Use a semicolon between the clauses of a compound sentence that are not joined by a coordinating conjunction. Coordinating conjunctions include *and, but, or,* and *yet. (page L611)*

Use a semicolon instead of a comma between the clauses of a compound sentence if there are already commas within one of the clauses. *(pages L615–L616)*

Colons

Use a colon before most lists of items, especially when the list comes after an expression such as *the following. (page L619)*

A colon is not needed between a verb and its complements or directly after a preposition. *(page L619)*

Use a colon between hours and minutes, between biblical chapters and verses, and after a salutation in a business letter. *(page L619)*

Hyphens

Use a hyphen to divide a word at the end of a line. *(page L623)*

Use a hyphen when writing out the numbers *twenty-one* through *ninety-nine. (page L625)*

Use a hyphen when writing out a fraction used as an adjective. *(page L626)*

Use a hyphen to separate the parts of some compound nouns. *(pages L626–L627)*

Posttest

Directions
Read the passage and write the letter of the correct way to write each group of underlined words. If the underlined word or words need no change, write _D_.

EXAMPLE   Exercise is at the top of <u>everyones</u> list of new
                                                    (1)
                    year's resolutions.

                1 **A** everyones
                    B everyone's
                    C every-ones
                    D No error

ANSWER   **1 B**

People use many activities to <u>stay healthy</u> jogging, aerobics,
                                                    (1)
or rollerblading. One activity predates the <u>Western worlds</u>
                                                                    (2)
<u>interest</u> in <u>fitness and</u> is referred to as an _art_—the martial arts.
                            (3)
    <u>Peoples misconceptions</u> about the martial arts are
                    (4)
surprising to me. For people <u>who devote a lifetime</u> to a martial
                                                    (5)
art, it's not about <u>violence the goal is</u> not to hurt others. <u>The</u>
                                    (6)
<u>dos at the end</u> of judo and aikido mean "the way" <u>to the</u>
    (7)
<u>following goals</u> enlightenment, self-realization, and
    (8)
understanding. <u>Students goals should be</u> to train their minds
                                    (9)
and energize their bodies. This focus <u>lets students connect</u>
                                                            (10)
with the true spirit of martial arts.

1 **A** stay: healthy
   B stay healthy:
   C stay healthy;
   D No error

2 **A** Western world's interest
   B Western worlds' interest
   C Western-worlds interest
   D No error

3 **A** fitness: and
   B fitness; and
   C fitness-and
   D No error

4 **A** Peoples' misconceptions
   B People's misconceptions
   C Peoples misconception's
   D No error

5 **A** who devote a lifetime:
   B who de-vote a lifetime
   C who devote a life-time
   D No error

6 **A** violence the goal is:
   B violence; the goal is
   C violence the goal is;
   D No error

7 **A** The *do*'s at the end
   B The *do*s at the end;
   C The *do*-s at the end
   D No error

8 **A** to: the following goals
   B to the following goals;
   C to the following goals:
   D No error

9 **A** Students' goals should be
   B Student's goals should be
   C Students goals should be:
   D No error

10 **A** let's students connect
   B lets student's connect
   C lets students connect:
   D No error

A Writer's Guide to Citing Sources

When you write a report, you usually research your topic by investigating other people's ideas. You may even quote an author directly. When you use the words or ideas of other people in your report, you must give them proper credit. A note that gives this credit is called a **citation.**

A **parenthetical citation** is a brief note in parentheses that is placed immediately after the words you have borrowed. Readers can then refer to the works-cited page at the end of your report for complete information about each source. Use the following examples for the correct form of parenthetical citations.

BOOK BY ONE AUTHOR	Give author's last name and page number(s): (Levine 74–75).
BOOK BY MORE THAN ONE AUTHOR	Give all of the authors' last names and page number(s): (Green and Sanford 33).
ARTICLE WITH AUTHOR NAMED	Give author's last name and page number(s): (Matthiessen 58).
ARTICLE WITH AUTHOR UNNAMED	Give a shortened form of the title of the article (unless full title is already short) and page number(s): ("Save This Species" 4).
ARTICLE IN A REFERENCE WORK; AUTHOR UNNAMED	Give title (full or shortened). No page number is necessary if the article is a single page from an encyclopedia arranged alphabetically: ("Tiger").

You should keep parenthetical citations as close as possible to the words being credited. To avoid interrupting the flow of the sentence, place them at the end of a phrase, clause, or sentence.

A **works-cited** page is a list of sources at the end of your report that you include regardless of the style of citation you use in the body of the report. The works-cited page lists complete information about each source you have used to write your paper. The sources are listed alphabetically by the author's last name or by the title if there is no author listed. Use the following examples to help you create a works-cited page.

GENERAL REFERENCE WORKS	"Tiger." Academic American Encyclopedia. 1995 ed.
BOOKS BY A SINGLE AUTHOR	Levine, Stuart P. The Tiger. San Diego: Lucent Books, 1999.
BOOKS BY MORE THAN ONE AUTHOR	Green, Carl R. and William R. Sanford. The Bengal Tiger. Mankato: Crestwood House, 1986.
ARTICLES IN MAGAZINES	Matthiessen, Peter. "The Last Wild Tigers." Audubon. Mar.–Apr. 1997: 54–67.
ARTICLES IN NEWSPAPERS	Sas-Rolfes, Michael. "How to Save the Tiger." The Wall Street Journal 17 Feb. 1998: A22.
ARTICLE FROM A CD-ROM	Encyclopedia of U.S. Endangered Species. CD-ROM. Dallas: Zane Publishing, 1998.
ARTICLE FROM AN ON-LINE DATABASE WITH A PRINT VERSION	Sunquist, Mel. "What I've Learned About Tigers." International Wildlife Nov.–Dec. 1997: 29 pars. 6 Oct. 1999 <http://www.nwf.org/nwf/intlwild/tigers.html>.
ON-LINE MATERIAL WITH NO PRINT VERSION	"Tiger, (Panthera tigris)." U.S. Fish and Wildlife Service Endangered Species Home Page: 29 pars. 6 Oct. 1999 <http://species.fws.gov/bio_tige.html>.

CHAPTER 19

Spelling Correctly

· ·

Directions
Read the passage and write the letter of the choice that correctly respells each underlined word. If the underlined word needs no change, write *D*.

EXAMPLE   The <u>begining</u> of a trip is fun.
                                (1)

  1 A   begening
     B   beginning
     C   biginning
     D   No error

ANSWER   **1 B**

Camping combines work and <u>plesure</u>. It is <u>usefull</u> to
                                       (1)   (2)
know how to pitch a tent and how to cook outdoors. It

takes teamwork to pitch a tent <u>successfully</u>. Meal
                                              (3)
<u>preperation</u> requires menu planning, cooking, and cleaning.
  (4)
<u>Divideing</u> the work leaves time for fun. Campgrounds have
  (5)
a <u>variety</u> of activities. <u>Swiming</u> pools are common. The
  (6)   (7)
nature trail provides <u>peaceful</u> scenery. A sharp eye <u>usually</u>
                                (8)   (9)
reveals insects, birds, and animals. At day's end, campers

gather with <u>egerness</u> around a roaring campfire.
                  (10)

1	**A**	pleasure	**6**	**A**	vareity
	B	pleasyre		**B**	veriety
	C	pleassure		**C**	varietie
	D	No error		**D**	No error
2	**A**	yousful	**7**	**A**	Swimming
	B	usful		**B**	Sweming
	C	useful		**C**	Swimmin
	D	No error		**D**	No error
3	**A**	sucessfully	**8**	**A**	peacefull
	B	sucesfully		**B**	peaseful
	C	successfuly		**C**	peacful
	D	No error		**D**	No error
4	**A**	preparation	**9**	**A**	usualy
	B	preperration		**B**	usualie
	C	preparashun		**C**	useally
	D	No error		**D**	No error
5	**A**	Deviding	**10**	**A**	eagrness
	B	Dividing		**B**	eagernes
	C	Dividding		**C**	eagerness
	D	No error		**D**	No error

Strategies for Learning to Spell

Your senses of hearing, sight, and touch help you learn to spell words correctly. Many people successfully spell unfamiliar words by using the following five-step strategy.

1   Auditory
Say the word aloud. Answer these questions.
- Where have I heard or read the word before?
- What was the context in which I heard or read the word?

2   Visual
Look at the word. Answer these questions.
- Does this word divide into parts? Is it a compound word? Does it have a prefix or a suffix?
- Does this word look like any other word I know? Could it be part of a word family I would recognize?

3   Auditory
Spell the word to yourself. Answer these questions.
- How is each sound spelled?
- Are there any surprises? Does the word follow spelling rules I know, or does it break the rules?

4   Visual/Kinesthetic
Write the word as you look at it. Answer these questions.
- Have I written the word clearly?
- Are my letters formed correctly?

5   Visual/Kinesthetic
Cover up the word. Visualize it. Write it. Answer this question.
- Did I write the word correctly?
- If the answer is no, return to step 1.

Spelling Strategies

When you write, you want readers to concentrate on what you are saying. You don't want them to be distracted or confused by spelling errors. Making sure that your writing is free of spelling errors takes just a few extra minutes and makes a world of difference. Use these strategies to check for spelling mistakes.

STRATEGY **Use a dictionary.** If you are not sure how to spell a word, check its spelling in a dictionary. If good spelling doesn't come easily to you, you can make up for it by keeping a dictionary close at hand and using it automatically.

STRATEGY **Proofread your writing carefully.** It may be easiest to look for one kind of error at a time. Do not rely on your computer to catch these errors. It cannot read your mind and will not know that you meant to type *proceed* or *recede* instead of *precede*.

PRACTICE YOUR SKILLS

● Check Your Understanding
Recognizing Misspelled Words

Write the letter of the misspelled word in each set. Then write the word correctly.

1. (a) disease   (b) benifits   (c) height

2. (a) vegetable   (b) grammar   (c) exsercise

3. (a) seize   (b) allready   (c) similar

4. (a) scenrey   (b) acquire   (c) visible

5. (a) lovable   (b) interrupt   (c) embarass

6. (a) pursue	(b) excape	(c) fascinate
7. (a) reccommend	(b) emigrate	(c) heroes
8. (a) opinion	(b) existance	(c) license
9. (a) occassion	(b) debtor	(c) sincerely
10. (a) seperate	(b) eighth	(c) definite

STRATEGY **Be sure you are pronouncing words correctly.**
"Swallowing" syllables or adding extra syllables can
cause you to misspell a word.

PRACTICE YOUR SKILLS

● Check Your Understanding
Pronouncing Words

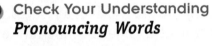 **Practice saying each syllable in the following
words to help you spell the words correctly.**

1. pos•si•bil•i•ty
2. ab•bre•vi•ate
3. a•lu•mi•num
4. per•spire
5. in•ter•est•ing

6. co•in•ci•dence
7. soph•o•more
8. jew•el•ry
9. car•a•mel
10. par•tic•u•lar

STRATEGY **Make up mnemonic devices.** A sentence like
"**Je**nnie **wel**comed **Ry**an's ring" can help you remember
how to spell *jewelry*. (Using a dictionary or word list
makes it easier to create your own mnemonics.) Also,
look for memorable spelling patterns: "It's a *coincidence*
that three *c* + *vowel* combinations appear in **coincidence**
and that the vowels are in reverse alphabetical order—*o*,
i, and *e!*"

STRATEGY **Keep a spelling journal.** Use it to record the words you have had trouble spelling. Here are some suggestions for organizing your spelling journal.

- Write the word correctly.
- Write the word again, underlining or circling the part of the word that gave you trouble.
- Write a tip that will help you remember how to spell the word in the future.

geography	geo*graphy*	George *Evans's* *old* grandfather *rode* *a* *pig* home *yesterday.*
dessert	de*ss*ert	The de*ss*ert you eat has 2 *s's* in it—just like strawberry *shortcake!*
knowledge	knowl*edge*	If I want to gain an *edge* in the job market, I need to invest in knowl*edge.*
gnaw	*gn*aw	The *gn*u at the zoo likes to *gn*aw on the fence

Spelling Generalizations

The English language contains at least 500,000 words. If you tried to memorize the spellings of 10 words a day, it would take you more than 130 years! A far easier way to become a good speller is to learn spelling generalizations and to look for patterns in the words you use most often.

▶ Spelling Patterns

Some spelling generalizations are based on the patterns of letters in words. You can find certain common patterns in words spelled with *ie* or *ei* and in words that end with the *seed* sound.

Words with *ie* and *ei*

Many generations of students have used the following rhyme to help them spell words with *ie* and *ei*.

> Write *i* before *e*
> Except after *c*
> Or when the sound is long *a*
> As in *neighbor* and *weigh*.

When you spell words with *ie* or *ei*, *i* comes before *e* except when the letters follow *c* or when they stand for the long *a* sound.

IE AND EI			
I BEFORE E	believe	mischief	niece
	piece	thief	brief

EXCEPT AFTER *C*	ceiling	conceit	deceive
	perceive	receipt	receive
SOUNDS LIKE *A*	eight	freight	sleigh
	veil	weight	neighbor

These words do not follow the pattern.

EXCEPTIONS			
either	foreign	height	ancient
leisure	protein	their	conscience
neither	seize	weird	species

Unfortunately, sometimes there are a lot of exceptions to a generalization. To make them easier to remember, create a mnemonic sentence using words with the same spelling. For example, if you know how to spell *their,* you can spell every word in this sentence.

The foreign heirs must seize the sheikdom or forfeit their claims.

Words Ending in *–cede, –ceed,* and *–sede*

Some other words that cause problems are those that end with a "seed" sound. This sound can be spelled *–cede, –ceed,* or *–sede.* By far the greatest number of words that end with this sound are spelled with *–cede.*

In all but four words that end with the "seed" sound, this sound is spelled *–cede.*

–CEDE			
EXAMPLES	precede	recede	concede	intercede

You'll have no trouble spelling these words if you memorize the four exceptions.

EXCEPTIONS			
exceed	proceed	succeed	supersede

PRACTICE YOUR SKILLS

● Check Your Understanding
Using Spelling Patterns

Write each word correctly, adding *ie* or *ei*.

1. r ■ ndeer
2. ach ■ ve
3. rel ■ ve
4. anc ■ nt
5. n ■ ghbor
6. v ■ n
7. w ■ rd
8. th ■ r
9. f ■ ld
10. w ■ gh
11. f ■ rce
12. conc ■ t
13. s ■ ve
14. l ■ sure
15. n ■ ther
16. h ■ ght
17. dec ■ t
18. ■ ther
19. p ■ ce
20. s ■ ze
21. th ■ f
22. bel ■ f
23. ■ ghteen
24. s ■ smic
25. fr ■ nd
26. v ■ l

Write each word correctly, adding –sede, –ceed, or –cede.

27. re ■
28. ex ■
29. ac ■
30. se ■
31. suc ■
32. con ■
33. pre ■
34. pro ■
35. super ■
36. inter ■

● Connect to the Writing Process: Editing
Using Spelling Patterns

History Topic **Find and rewrite the eight words that have been spelled incorrectly.**

In medeval times, wealthy lords often made war against one another over small greivances or to acquire their nieghbor's property. Outright theivery did not bother some if they thought they could succede in adding to their wealth. Most nobles had so few trained soldiers that they did not wage war on the battlefield. Instead, the attacker proceded to surround the castle with the knights and peasants who owed allegiance to him. They shot arrows and lobbed rocks over the wall to persuade their enemies to yeild. However, what usually caused one side to conceed defeat was a lack of food.

 Plurals

The following generalizations will help you spell the plurals of nouns correctly. When you're in doubt about an exception, look up the word in a dictionary.

Regular Nouns

To form the plural of most nouns, simply add *s*.

MOST NOUNS				
SINGULAR	computer	book	bath	plane
PLURAL	computers	books	baths	planes

If a noun ends in *s, ch, sh, x,* or *z,* add *es* to form the plural.

	S, CH, SH, X, OR Z				
SINGULAR	boss	match	dash	box	quartz
PLURAL	bosses	matches	dashes	boxes	quartzes

Follow the same generalizations when you write the plural forms of proper nouns.

the Lynch family = the Lynch**es**
the Martinez family = the Martinez**es**

The apostrophe is never used to make the plural form of proper nouns. It is used only to show possession.

You can learn about using the apostrophe with proper nouns on pages L597–L599.

Nouns Ending in y

Add *s* to form the plural of a noun ending in a vowel and *y.*

	VOWELS AND Y			
SINGULAR	boy	tray	buoy	valley
PLURAL	boys	trays	buoys	valleys

Change the *y* to *i* and add *es* to a noun ending in a consonant and *y.*

	CONSONANTS AND Y			
SINGULAR	lily	hobby	diary	courtesy
PLURAL	lilies	hobbies	diaries	courtesies

PRACTICE YOUR SKILLS

● Check Your Understanding
Forming Plurals

Write the plural form of each noun.

1. berry
2. radish
3. fox
4. day
5. kiss
6. maze
7. topaz
8. ash
9. cross
10. company
11. tax
12. anxiety
13. stick
14. stitch
15. volley
16. discovery
17. whisper
18. century
19. speech
20. Harris

● Connect to the Writing Process: Editing
Spelling Plural Nouns

 Science Topic **Rewrite this paragraph, changing the underlined nouns from singular to plural.**

From rolling <u>field</u> to woodland <u>valley</u>, red fox make their homes in most parts of North America. These shy creatures have <u>body</u> that are about thirty-six <u>inch</u> long and weigh ten to fifteen <u>pound</u>. All red <u>fox</u> have white-tipped <u>brush</u>, or tails, and black <u>leg</u>, but their <u>coat</u> may be different <u>color</u>. There are yellowish-red <u>fox</u> with white <u>belly</u>, black <u>one</u> with white-tipped fur, and red <u>one</u> with black <u>cross</u> on their <u>back</u>. All three <u>variation</u> may be seen among the <u>baby</u> in a single litter.

Nouns Ending in *o*

Add *s* to form the plural of a noun ending with a vowel and *o*.

VOWELS AND *O*				
SINGULAR	ratio	video	shampoo	igloo
PLURAL	ratios	videos	shampoos	igloos

Add *s* to form the plural of musical terms ending in *o*.

MUSICAL TERMS ENDING WITH *O*				
SINGULAR	alto	cello	piano	crescendos
PLURAL	altos	cellos	pianos	crescendos

Add *s* to form the plural of words that were borrowed from the Spanish language.

SPANISH WORDS WITH *O*				
SINGULAR	burro	burrito	pueblo	patio
PLURAL	burros	burritos	pueblos	patios

The plurals of nouns ending in a consonant and *o* do not follow a regular pattern.

CONSONANTS AND *O*				
SINGULAR	auto	rhino	tomato	motto
PLURAL	autos	rhinos	tomatoes	mottoes

When you are not sure how to form the plural of a word that ends in *o*, consult a dictionary. Sometimes you will find that either spelling is acceptable. In these cases, use the first form given. If the dictionary does not give a plural form, the plural is usually formed by adding *s*.

Nouns Ending in *f* or *fe*

To form the plural of some nouns ending in *f* or *fe*, just add *s*.

	F AND FE			
SINGULAR	chief	gulf	safe	giraffe
PLURAL	chiefs	gulfs	safes	giraffes

For some nouns ending in *f* or *fe*, change the *f* to *v* and add *es*.

	F AND FE TO V			
SINGULAR	half	self	life	knife
PLURAL	halves	selves	lives	knives

Because there is no way to tell which generalization applies, consult a dictionary for plural forms of words that end in *f* or *fe*.

 Watch out! Your computer spell-check will not inform you that you have misspelled the plurals of some nouns. That's because they can also be used as verbs. For example, someone *loafs* around or bakes *loaves* of bread.

PRACTICE YOUR SKILLS

● Check Your Understanding
Forming Plurals

Write the plural form of each noun. Check a dictionary to be sure you have formed the plural correctly.

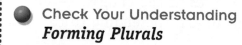

1. potato   **3.** echo   **5.** hero   **7.** cameo

2. café   **4.** whiff   **6.** leaf   **8.** scruff

9. studio	12. wolf	15. bronco	18. radio
10. belief	13. wife	16. tattoo	19. hoof
11. cello	14. sheriff	17. handkerchief	20. soprano

● **Connect to the Writing Process: Editing**
Spelling Plural Nouns

General Interest **Rewrite this paragraph, changing the underlined nouns to plural from singular.**

Have you seen any of the video of the State Championship Cook-off? I watched the one in which the chef had to create main courses using local produce like tomato and avocado. They had many shelf full of fresh vegetables and other foodstuff to work with. One creatively made some hen-shaped meatloaf surrounded by potato puff in a nest of cabbage leaf. Another made delicious-looking taco that had chopped-up potato in them.

Compound Words

Most compound nouns are made plural in the same way as other nouns, by adding an *s* or *es* at the end. However, sometimes it makes more sense to add the ending to the first word in the compound.

The letter *s* or *es* is added to the end of most compound nouns to make them plural.

MOST COMPOUND NOUNS		
SINGULAR	classmate wristwatch	headaddress flare-up
PLURAL	classmate**s** wristwatch**es**	headaddress**es** flare-up**s**

When the main word in a compound noun appears first, that word is made plural.

COMPOUND NOUN EXCEPTIONS		
SINGULAR	sister-in-law secretary general	runner-up standard of living
PLURAL	sister**s**-in-law secretar**ies** general	runner**s**-up standard**s** of living

Numerals, Letters, Symbols, and Words as Words

To form the plurals of many numerals, letters, symbols, and words used as words, add an *s*.

> Are those *G***s** or *6***s**?
> The Great Depression occurred during the early 1930**s**.
> Good writers use *!***s** very seldom.
> She wanted to know the *why***s** and *wherefore***s**.

To prevent confusion, it's best to use an apostrophe and s with lowercase letters, some capital letters, and some words used as words. When you use this method to create the plural of italicized letters or words, you do not italicize the apostrophe and *s*.

> The *y*'**s** in old English writing stand for the *th* sound.
> The arches were like upside-down *U*'**s**.
> There are too many *so*'**s** in this paragraph.

You can learn about the use of italics on pages L567–L568.

PRACTICE YOUR SKILLS

● Check Your Understanding
Forming Plurals

Write the plural form of each noun.

1. 9
2. 1900
3. take-off
4. *o*
5. right-of-way
6. cost of living
7. bowling alley
8. G
9. '20
10. lookout

11. *!*
12. *yes* and *no*
13. brother-in-law
14. Ooo and ah
15. prisoner of war
16. hand-me-down
17. queen of hearts
18. commander in chief
19. boot camp
20. coat of arms

● Connect to the Writing Process: Editing
Spelling Plural Nouns

General Interest **Rewrite each sentence, changing the underlined items from singular to plural.**

21. Chiffoniers are chest of drawers.
22. Don't forget to dot your *i*.
23. The Enlightenment refers to the 1600 and 1700.
24. We prefer the word *menu* to *bill of fare*.
25. When the British make *naught*, they are making *0*.
26. *Man-of-war* are ships, not soldiers.
27. Some lily-of-the-valley are known as *convallaria*.
28. Do you have any brother-in-law?
29. Curtain-raiser are short plays.
30. Who are your first cousin once removed?

Other Plural Forms

Irregular plurals are not formed by adding *s* or *es*.

IRREGULAR PLURALS		
tooth, t**ee**th	man, m**e**n	ox, ox**en**
foot, f**ee**t	woman, wom**e**n	child, child**ren**
goose, g**ee**se	mouse, m**ice**	person, pe**ople**

Some nouns have the same form for singular and plural.

SAME SINGULAR AND PLURAL			
Chinese	sheep	scissors	Portuguese
moose	headquarters	politics	surf
Swiss	salmon	series	corps

PRACTICE YOUR SKILLS

 Check Your Understanding

Forming Plurals

Write the plural form of each noun.

1. clergywoman
2. webfoot
3. field mouse
4. Japanese
5. shorts
6. Canada goose
7. countryman
8. news
9. catfish
10. mail
11. childhood
12. clothing
13. ox
14. rabies
15. moose
16. knowledge
17. canine tooth
18. pliers
19. child
20. Canadian

Rewrite each sentence, changing the underlined items to plurals whenever appropriate.

21. New England blue plate specials often feature <u>shrimp</u> or <u>codfish</u>.

22. Blue-collar <u>worker</u> got that name because <u>man</u> who did hard labor often wore blue shirts.

23. The <u>child</u> of <u>royalty</u> were "born to the purple."

24. Family <u>member</u> who don't conform may be called black <u>sheep</u>.

25. Blue <u>doe</u> are not <u>deer</u> but female <u>kangaroo</u>.

26. Indigo <u>snake</u> are black and may grow to nearly nine <u>foot</u> long.

Communicate Your Ideas

APPLY TO WRITING
Letter to the Editor: *Plurals*

Blizzards, hurricanes, and tropical storms are three major storms that meteorologists can predict. School is sometimes canceled because of these storms. The editor of the local newspaper has asked readers this question: *If a storm is predicted to hit on Tuesday, should the superintendent announce on Monday that there will be no school on Tuesday—or should the superintendent wait until Tuesday morning?* Consider the photograph on the previous page and write a response to the editor of the newspaper. Include reasons that support your opinion. Be sure to use at least ten plural nouns in your letter.

QuickCheck Mixed Practice

Write *a* or *b* to indicate the letter of the word that is spelled correctly in each of the following pairs.

1. **a.** cieling
   b. ceiling

2. **a.** height
   b. hieght

3. **a.** weird
   b. wierd

4. **a.** dishs
   b. dishes

5. **a.** canarys
   b. canaries

6. **a.** radioes
   b. radios

7. **a.** knives
   b. knifes

8. **a.** mouses
   b. mice

9. **a.** teeth
   b. teeths

10. **a.** sheeps
    b. sheep

Prefixes and Suffixes

A **prefix** is one or more syllables placed in front of a base word to form a new word. When you add a prefix, the spelling of the base word does not change.

PREFIXES

in + complete = **in**complete	**im** + possible = **im**possible
pre + judge = **pre**judge	**over** + rule = **over**rule
dis + obey = **dis**obey	**mis** + step = **mis**step
re + appear = **re**appear	**un** + natural = **un**natural
ir + regular = **ir**regular	**il** + literate = **il**literate

In a few cases, you must add a hyphen after a prefix to avoid confusing your reader. Check a dictionary if you are in doubt.

HYPHENATED PREFIXES

anti-intellectual	**semi**-independent	**re**-evaluate

You will never misspell *misspell* if you do not change the base word when you add a prefix. Words like ***mis**shapen, **dis**satisfy, **il**logical, **over**ripe,* and ***ir**responsible* should be easier to spell, too.

A **suffix** is one or more syllables placed after a base word to change its part of speech and possibly also its meaning. In many cases, especially when the base word ends in a consonant, you simply add the suffix.

SUFFIXES WITH CONSONANTS

thick + **ness** = thick**ness**	mild + **ly** = mild**ly**
content + **ment** = content**ment**	pain + **ful** = pain**ful**

In other cases, however, you must change the spelling of the base word before you add the suffix.

Words Ending in *e*

Drop the final *e* before a suffix that begins with a vowel.

SUFFIXES WITH VOWELS	
struggle + **ing** = strug**gling**	like + **able** = lik**able**
locate + **ion** = locat**ion**	culture + **al** = cultur**al**

Keep the final *e* in words that end in *ce* or *ge* if the suffix begins with an *a* or *o*. The *e* keeps the sound of the *c* or *g* soft before these vowels.

CE AND *GE*
knowledge + **able** = knowledge**able**
outrage + **ous** = outrage**ous**
replace + **able** = replace**able**
notice + **able** = notice**able**

Keep the final *e* when adding a suffix that begins with a consonant.

SUFFIXES WITH FINAL *E*	
EXAMPLES	peace + **ful** = peace**ful**
	amuse + **ment** = amuse**ment**
	hope + **less** = hope**less**
	wise + **ly** = wise**ly**
EXCEPTIONS	wise + **dom** = wis**dom**
	judge + **ment** = judg**ment**
	true + **ly** = tru**ly**
	argue + **ment** = argu**ment**

 Word Alert Remind yourself that you're likely to remember the *e* in *likely* but that *truly* has a truly unusual spelling.

PRACTICE YOUR SKILLS

● Check Your Understanding
Adding Suffixes

Combine the base words and suffixes. Remember to make any necessary spelling changes.

1. erase + er		**11.** continue + al
2. nature + al		**12.** pale + ness
3. move + able		**13.** operate + ion
4. grace + ful		**14.** grave + ly
5. imitate + ion		**15.** mule + ish
6. value + able		**16.** resemble + ance
7. agree + ment		**17.** judge + ment
8. confuse + ion		**18.** peace + able
9. true + ly		**19.** confuse + ion
10. secure + ity		**20.** notice + ing

● Connect to the Writing Process: Editing
Spelling Words with Prefixes and Suffixes

Art Topic **Rewrite the underlined words in the following paragraphs, correctly spelling those that are incorrect.**

Artist Clayton Turner's <u>drawings</u> of the Old West show <u>truely</u> <u>remarkable</u> <u>creativeity</u> and <u>sensitiveity</u>. Turner has had little formal art <u>educateion</u>, but he has been <u>refining</u> his skills for decades. His Western scenes show such things as cowboys <u>batheing</u> in a river or <u>couragous</u> pioneers <u>traveling</u> westward. He shows cowboys <u>angling</u> out their knees as they ride, so he is clearly a <u>knowledgable</u> horseman himself.

However, his pictures are based on his recollections of a distant past. Since an unfortuneate water skiing accident in his teens, his hands and legs have been unuseable. He paints by clamping a brush between his teeth and moving his head. His perseverance has made him not only an noteable artist but a valuable political spokesperson. He has tirelessly lobbied for architectureal reforms to make public places more accessible to anyone with a disability.

Words Ending with *y*

To add a suffix to most words ending in a vowel and *y*, keep the *y*.

	VOWELS AND Y
EXAMPLES	employ + **able** = employ**able**
	prey + **ing** = prey**ing**
	annoy + **ance** = annoy**ance**
	fray + **ed** = fray**ed**
EXCEPTIONS	day + **ly** = dai**ly**
	gay + **ly** = gai**ly**

Word Alert

Use mnemonic devices, such as phrases or short poems, to help remember how to spell exceptions.

Jay changes the *y* daily
And adds the *i* gaily.

To add certain suffixes to most words ending in a consonant and *y*, change the *y* to *i* before adding the suffix. However, do not drop the *y* when adding the suffix *–ing*.

CONSONANTS AND *Y*

EXAMPLES   rely + **able** = reli**able**   duty + **ful** = duti**ful**
clumsy + **ly** = clumsi**ly**   dry + **ing** = dry**ing**
ready + **ness** = readi**ness**

EXCEPTIONS shy + **ness** = shy**ness**
dry + **ness** = dry**ness**

Doubling the Final Consonant

Sometimes the final consonant in a word is doubled before a suffix is added.

Double the final consonant in a word before adding a suffix when *all three* of the following are true:

(1) The suffix begins with a vowel.
(2) The base word has only one syllable or is stressed on the last syllable.
(3) The base word ends in one consonant preceded by a vowel.

DOUBLE CONSONANTS

ONE-SYLLABLE WORDS win + **ing** = wi**nn**ing   drum + **er** = dru**mm**er
shop + **ed** = sho**pp**ed   hot + **est** = ho**tt**est

FINAL SYLLABLE STRESSED   begin + **ing** = begi**nn**ing
allot + **ed** = allo**tt**ed
refer + **al** = refe**rr**al
occur + **ence** = occu**rr**ence

You do not double the final *r* in words that end in *fer* when you add the suffix *–ence* or *–able*. You can recognize these words because the pronunciation of the base word changes when the suffix is added.

FINAL *R*	
refer + ence = reference	infer + ence = inference
defer + ence = deference	transfer + able = transferable

Be sure *not* to double the final letter if it is preceded by *two* vowels.

TWO VOWELS	
float + **ing** = floating	shout + **ed** = shouted
speak + **er** = speaker	neat + **est** = neatest

PRACTICE YOUR SKILLS

● Check Your Understanding

Adding Suffixes

Combine the base words and suffixes. Remember to make any necessary spelling changes.

1. mislay + ing
2. whip + ed
3. enjoy + ed
4. survey + ing
5. occur + ing
6. transfer + ed
7. heat + er
8. day + ly
9. read + able
10. knit + ing
11. mad + est
12. defy + ance
13. red + en
14. pity + ful
15. shy + ly
16. prefer + ed
17. rely + able
18. soap + y
19. journey + ed
20. unlucky + ly

General Interest **Rewrite the underlined words in the following paragraph, correctly spelling those that are incorrect.**

I visited Waitomo Cave when I was staying in New Zealand. It was one of the most enjoiable things I did on my trip. Accompanyed by other tourists, I stepped into the murkyness of the cave. The limestone decorateions in the forms of stalactites, stalagmites, and sculptures made the cave look like a natureal cathedral. We followed our guide to a demonstration platform. There she identified some colonys of glowworms on the walls of a small grotto. She also explainned how they live. Next we were taken to a woodden dock and loaded into a flat-bottomed boat. The boat carryied us down a gloomy underground river to a large grotto. Overhead and reflected in the water, stary blue-green lights were shining eerily. The otherwise black cavern was occupyed by tens of thousands of glowworms. I would have prefered to study them dreamily for hours. I regreted being ferryed back to the dock and leaving that stuning spectacle behind. That cavern was easly one of the most beautiful sights I have ever seen.

APPLY TO WRITING
Friendly Letter: *Suffixes*

Some sights make you think you must be on another planet. Have you visited or seen pictures of a place that seemed otherworldly? Write a letter to a friend, describing this place as if you have just paid a visit to it. Use five of the following words with suffixes in your narrative.

- un + believe + able
- change + able
- un + earth + ly + ness
- un + forget + able
- ordinary + ly
- plan + ed *or* ing

- serene + ity
- opportune + ity
- memory + able
- un + deny + able
- locate + ion
- trek + ed *or* ing

Add the prefix or suffix to each base word and write the new word.

1. raid + ers
2. icy + ness
3. prefer + able
4. over + ripe
5. crafty + ly
6. judge + ment
7. unfit + ed
8. pay + able
9. false + ity
10. confuse + ion
11. deter + ed
12. regret + able
13. fly + er
14. destroy + ing
15. active + ity
16. love + able
17. pronounce + able
18. soap + y
19. slim + est
20. move + ing
21. occur + ence
22. annoy + ance
23. clumsy + ly
24. ready + ness
25. study + ing
26. under + estimate
27. un + event + ful
28. excel + ence
29. anti + inflate + ion
30. balance + ing
31. fatigue + ing
32. taste + less
33. dedicate + ion
34. persuasive + ly
35. opposite + ness
36. re + assure + ance
37. dis + loyal
38. courage + ous
39. empty + ness
40. magnify + ing

Make it your goal to learn to spell these fifty words this year. Use them in your writing and practice writing them until spelling them comes automatically.

accompany	environment	pursuit
acquaint	fascinate	receipt
altogether	fiery	reference
argument	foreign	referral
assistance	heiress	regrettable
bargain	immigrant	reign
boulevard	inference	remembrance
campaign	irregular	responsibility
chauffeur	jealous	scenery
condemn	lieutenant	separation
convenient	mileage	sufficient
cooperate	occasion	supersede
courtesy	opponent	undeniable
deceive	pamphlet	unique
definition	preferred	unmanageable
dependent	professional	weight
drought	pronounceable	

Applying Spelling Generalizations

Write the letter of the misspelled word in each group. Then write the word, spelling it correctly.

1. (A) piece   (B) radioes   (C) merriment
2. (A) supersede   (B) weight   (C) inconsistant
3. (A) harass   (B) niether   (C) entertainment
4. (A) suffered   (B) harmonize   (C) mathmatics
5. (A) deceit   (B) churchs   (C) conscientious
6. (A) practicaly   (B) thickness   (C) rights-of-way
7. (A) pridefull   (B) wisely   (C) misbehave
8. (A) thirtieth   (B) sideing   (C) amusement
9. (A) companes   (B) trained   (C) exceed
10. (A) strapped   (B) knaves   (C) alloted
11. (A) mistake   (B) believe   (C) sombreroes
12. (A) imoveable   (B) curing   (C) portrayal
13. (A) indelable   (B) frying   (C) judgment
14. (A) amused   (B) sovereign   (C) courteus
15. (A) chilly   (B) triping   (C) galleys
16. (A) runners-up   (B) reefs   (C) *yeses*
17. (A) carving   (B) releive   (C) partying
18. (A) leisure   (B) chiefs   (C) noisyly
19 (A) cameos   (B) tooths   (C) mispronounce
20. (A) playful   (B) seprate   (C) king

Another Look

Spelling Patterns

In words with *ie* or *ei, i* frequently comes before *e* except when the
letters follow *c* or when they stand for the long *a* sound.
(pages L644–L645)

The "seed" sound at the end of a word is spelled *cede* except for four
words: exceed, proceed, succeed, supersede. *(pages L645–L646)*

Plurals

To form the plural of most nouns, simply add *s.* If a noun ends with *s,
ch, sh, x,* or *z,* add *es* to form the plural. *(pages L647–L648)*

Add *s* to form the plural of a noun ending in a vowel and *y.* Change the *y*
to *i* and add *es* to a noun ending in a consonant and *y. (page L648)*

Add *s* to form the plural of a noun ending with a vowel and *o,* to form
the plural of musical terms ending in *o,* and to form the plural of
words borrowed from the Spanish language that end in *o.*
(pages L649–L650)

Add *s* or *es* to the end of most compound nouns to make them plural.
When the main word in a compound noun appears first, that word is
made plural. *(pages L652–L653)*

To form the plurals of many numerals, letters, symbols, and words used
as words, add an *s. (page L653)*

Prefixes and Suffixes

When you add a prefix, the spelling of the base word does not change. In
many cases, when you place a suffix after a base word, especially
when the base word ends in a consonant, you simply add the suffix.
(pages L657–L658)

Drop the final *e* before a suffix that begins with a vowel. Keep the final *e*
when a suffix begins with a consonant. Keep the final *e* in words that
end in *ce* or *ge* if the suffix begins with an *a* or *o. (page L659)*

To add a suffix to most words ending in a vowel and *y,* keep the *y.* To
add certain suffixes to most words ending in a consonant and *y,*
change the *y* to *i* before adding the suffix. However, do not drop the *y*
when adding the suffix *ing. (pages L661–L662)*

Other Information About Spelling

Doubling the final consonant *(pages L662–L663)*

Directions
Read the passage and write the letter of the choice that correctly respells each underlined word. If the underlined word needs no change, write *D*.

EXAMPLE   Traveling to a <u>foreign</u> country increases a
                                                    (1)
                         person's knowledge of the world.
                         1 A foriegn
                            B foring
                            C fareign
                            D No error

ANSWER   **1 D**

Bangkok, the capital of Thailand, offers a <u>mickture</u> of the
                                                                (1)
old and the new. Tall skyscrapers dot the <u>horizen</u>. In contrast
                                                             (2)
lie hundreds of <u>beautiful</u>, aged Buddhist temples. Large <u>factorys</u>
                        (3)   (4)
and small family-owned shops operate side by side. Individual

vendors <u>peddling</u> their goods compete with modern department
                (5)
stores. Broad streets have <u>reeplaced</u> many narrow roads.
                                         (6)
<u>Espressways</u> have been constructed over some filled-in canals.
    (7)
Bicycles and carts are no competition for cars, trucks, and

three-wheeled <u>taxies</u>. The bicyclists and cart-pushers are a <u>daily</u>
                        (8)   (9)
reminder of the past. <u>Hopefulley</u>, the old ways will never be
                                     (10)
completely lost.

1	A	mixshur	6	A	replaced
	B	micksure		B	replased
	C	mixture		C	reeplased
	D	No error		D	No error

2	A	herizen	7	A	Expresways
	B	horizon		B	Expressweighs
	C	herizon		C	Expressways
	D	No error		D	No error

3	A	beutiful	8	A	taxees
	B	beautifull		B	tackcees
	C	beauteeful		C	taxis
	D	No error		D	No error

4	A	factories	9	A	daylee
	B	factorees		B	dailey
	C	facteries		C	dayly
	D	No error		D	No error

5	A	peddeling	10	A	Hopefuly
	B	pedaling		B	Hopefully
	C	peddleing		C	Hopfully
	D	No error		D	No error

A Study Guide for Academic Success

Academic success depends a great deal on preparation. You must be familiar with the material presented in textbooks and in the classroom; you must also be aware of various test-taking strategies. In some ways, preparing for a test is like learning to play football. You can't simply grab the ball and run with it. You must first learn the rules of the game and strategies for offense and defense. If you apply the strategies and heed helpful pointers, for example, you can become both a better football player and a better test taker. Also, the more practice you have, the better prepared you are to play a difficult game or take an important test.

In the following chapter you will become familiar with the different kinds of questions asked on standardized tests. Pay close attention to the "rules" for each type of question and the strategies used to master them. These lessons and practice exercises will help you develop your test-taking muscles.

Keep in mind that the abilities you acquire in this chapter will carry over into homework and daily classroom assignments—and even into areas outside of school. Learning how to read for various information and how to approach different kinds of questions and problems will sharpen the critical thinking skills you use when you participate in classroom discussions, play sports, and make important life decisions.

Learning Study Skills

Applying good study habits helps you in taking tests as well as in completing daily classroom assignments. Begin to improve your study habits by using the following strategies.

> **Strategies for Effective Studying**
> - Choose an area that is well lighted and quiet.
> - Equip your study area with everything you need for reading and writing, including a dictionary and a thesaurus.
> - Keep an assignment book for recording assignments and due dates.
> - Allow plenty of time for studying. Begin your reading and writing assignments early.
> - Adjust your reading rate to suit your purpose.

Adjusting Reading Rate to Purpose

Your reading rate is the speed with which you read. Depending on your purpose in reading, you may choose to read certain materials quickly.

If your purpose is to get a quick impression of the contents of a newspaper, you should scan the headlines. If you want to learn the main ideas of a certain article, you should skim it. If your purpose is to learn new facts or understand details, you should read the article closely.

Whether you are reading a newspaper, an article in a periodical, or a textbook, you can read with greater effectiveness and efficiency if you adjust your reading rate to suit your purpose in reading the material.

Scanning

Scanning is reading to get a general impression and to prepare for learning about a subject. To scan, you should read the title, headings, subheadings, picture captions, words and phrases in boldface or italics, and any focus questions. Using this method, you can quickly determine what the passage is about and what questions to keep in mind. Scanning is also a way to familiarize yourself with everything a book has to offer. Scan the table of contents, appendix, glossary, and index of a book before reading.

Skimming

After scanning a chapter, section, or article, you should quickly read or skim the introduction, the topic sentence of each paragraph, and the conclusion. **Skimming** is reading quickly to identify the purpose, thesis, main ideas, and supporting ideas of a selection.

Close Reading

Close reading means reading to locate specific information, follow the logic of an argument, or comprehend the meaning or significance of information. After scanning the selection or chapter, read it more slowly, word for word.

Reading a Textbook

The techniques of scanning, skimming, and close reading are combined in the **SQ3R study strategy.** This method helps you to understand and remember what you read. The *S* in *SQ3R* stands for *Survey,* the *Q* for *Question,* and the *3R* for *Read, Recite,* and *Review.*

▶ Taking Notes

Taking notes when reading a textbook or listening to a lecture will help you identify and remember important points. Three methods of taking notes are the informal outline, the graphic organizer, and the summary.

In an **informal outline,** you use words and phrases to record main ideas and significant details. Notes in this form are helpful in studying for an objective test because they emphasize specific facts.

In a **graphic organizer,** words and phrases are arranged in a visual pattern to indicate the relationships between main ideas and supporting details. This is an excellent tool for studying information for an objective test, for an open-ended assessment, or for writing an essay. The visual organizer allows you instantly to see important information and its relationship to other ideas.

In a **summary** you use sentences to express important ideas in your own words. A summary should not simply restate the ideas presented in the textbook or lecture. Instead, a good summary should express relationships between ideas and draw conclusions. For this reason, summaries are useful in preparing for an essay test.

In the following passage from a textbook, the essential information for understanding the snow leopard is underlined. Following the passage are examples of notes in an informal outline, in a graphic organizer, and in summary form.

MODEL: Essential Information

The harsh Himalaya Mountains are home to the snow leopard. Beautiful and rare, this creature lives and hunts alone. Its beautiful, thick winter coat has rows of charcoal gray spots on a light gray to white background. Large paws thickly padded with hair and powerful back legs give the snow leopard protection and great hunting ability. Unfortunately, it has been hunted almost to extinction.

Despite laws against either owning or selling its fur, the snow leopard is still a target for poachers.

INFORMAL
OUTLINE:

1. Snow leopards live in the Himalaya Mountains.
2. The snow leopard has large paws and powerful back legs.
3. Poachers have hunted the leopard almost to extinction.
4. The snow leopard lives and hunts alone.
5. The snow leopard has a white or light gray coat with gray spots.

GRAPHIC
ORGANIZER:

The Snow Leopard

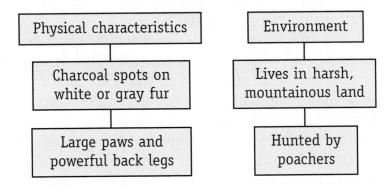

SUMMARY:

The Snow Leopard

The snow leopard is a beautiful animal living in the Himalaya Mountains. The snow leopard, with its large paws and powerful back legs, is an excellent hunter. Its gray spots and white or light gray fur provide protection against predators. Unfortunately, poachers have been able to hunt the snow leopard almost to extinction.

Whichever note-taking method you use, the following strategies will help you make those notes clear and well organized.

Strategies for Taking Notes

- Label your notes with the title and page numbers of the chapter or the topic and date of the lecture.
- Record only the main ideas and important details.
- Use the titles, subtitles, and words in special type to help you select the most important information.
- Use your own words; do not copy word for word.
- Use as few words as possible.

Taking Standardized Tests

A **standardized test** measures your academic progress, skills, and achievement in such a way that results can be compared with those of other students who have taken the same test. Standardized tests that assess your ability to use language—or verbal—skills include vocabulary tests, analogy tests, sentence-completion tests, reading tests, and tests of standard written English.

The best way to do well on standardized tests is to work consistently on your school subjects throughout the year, to read widely, and to learn the strategies of test taking.

> ### Strategies for Taking Standardized Tests
>
> - Read the test directions carefully. Answer the sample questions to be sure you understand what the test requires.
> - Relax. Although you can expect to be a little nervous, concentrate on doing the best you can.
> - Preview the whole test quickly by skimming to get an overview of the kinds of questions on the test.
> - Plan your time carefully, allotting a certain amount of time to each part of the test.
> - Answer first the questions you find easiest. Skip hard questions, coming back to them later if you have time.
> - Read and reread all choices before you choose an answer. If you are not sure of the answer, try to eliminate choices that are obviously wrong. Educated guessing often helps.
> - If you have time, check your answers. Be sure you have not made a mistake in marking your answer sheet.

Vocabulary Tests

One kind of vocabulary test asks you to find **antonyms**—words most nearly opposite in meaning. For instance, in the following test item, you must find the antonym for *weary* among the four choices.

> WEARY: (A) tired   (B) energetic   (C) sleepy
>   (D) worn   (E) exhausted
>
> (The answer is *(B)* because *energetic* is an antonym for *weary*. The other choices are wrong because they each have a meaning similar to *weary*.

Synonym items have the same format as antonym items, but instead of choosing the answer that means the opposite of the word in capital letters, you choose the word that means the same. For example, in the following item, the answer is *(A) gleam,* which means the same as *shimmer.*

> SHIMMER: (A) gleam   (B) shake   (C) dance
>   (D) blink   (E) dull

Always consider every choice carefully. You can often figure out the meaning of a word by using a prefix, a root, or a suffix as a clue.

PRACTICE YOUR SKILLS

 Check Your Understanding
Recognizing Antonyms

Write the letter of the word that is most nearly opposite in meaning to the word in capital letters.

1. PERISHABLE:
       (A) everlasting   (B) dislike   (C) thin
       (D) tasty   (E) decayed

2. ORDINARY:
       (A) uncommon   (B) usual   (C) funny
       (D) noble   (E) regular

3. CHOPPY:
    (A) calm   (B) rough   (C) fine
    (D) short   (E) loose

4. PROLONG:
    (A) shorten   (B) lengthen   (C) close
    (D) disturb   (E) run

5. COARSE:
    (A) stupid   (B) strong   (C) grainy
    (D) fine   (E) rough

Check Your Understanding
Recognizing Synonyms

Write the letter of the word that is most nearly the same in meaning as the word in capital letters.

6. VESSEL:
    (A) blood   (B) slave   (C) container
    (D) stop   (E) tomb

7. EMOTIONAL:
    (A) fierce   (B) funny   (C) violent
    (D) excitable   (E) happy

8. INTRODUCTORY:
    (A) final   (B) social   (C) immediate
    (D) beginning   (E) end

9. EMBRACE:
    (A) learn   (B) hug   (C) fear
    (D) batter   (E) fight

10. HARDY:
    (A) strong   (B) boyish   (C) steep
    (D) ugly   (E) delicate

▶ Analogies

Analogy questions test your skill at figuring out relationships between words. Your first step is to decide how the given words—the first, capitalized pair of words—are related to each other. The next step is to decide which other pair has the same kind of relationship as the given pair.

The single colon in an analogy question stands for the words *is to,* and the double colon stands for the word *as.*

> FURNACE : FIRE : : reservoir : water
>
> FURNACE *is to* FIRE *as* reservoir *is to* water.

The above example reads, "A furnace *is to* fire *as* a reservoir *is* to water." That is, a furnace has the same relationship to fire as a reservoir has to water. A furnace and a reservoir are both containers for natural elements—fire and water. Explaining an analogy to yourself in one sentence can help you to figure out the answer. In the following example, you might say, "One kind of flower is a tulip."

> FLOWER : TULIP ::
> (A) deer : buffalo   (B) fever : virus
> (C) automobile : station wagon   (D) plumber : wrench
> (E) oak : tree
>
> (The answer, *(C) automobile : station wagon,* expresses the same category-to-item relationship.)

Keep in mind that the word order in an analogy is very important. If the given pair of words in the analogy expresses a part-to-whole order, for example, the words in the correct answer should also be taken in order of part to whole.

Some analogies are written in sentence form.

> *Urbane* is to *polite* as *verbose* is to ■.
> (A) outstanding   (B) bitter   (C) wordy
> (D) brief   (E) calm
>
> (The first two italicized words are synonyms. Therefore, the correct answer is *(C) wordy*, a synonym for *verbose*.)

Knowing some of the common types of analogies, like those in the following chart, will help you figure out word relationships.

COMMON TYPES OF ANALOGIES	
Analogy	**Example**
word : synonym	slim : slender
word : antonym	exciting : dull
part : whole	wing : airplane
cause : effect	drought : famine
worker : tool	carpenter : hammer
worker : product	baker : bread
item : purpose	ruler : measure
item : category	robin : bird

PRACTICE YOUR SKILLS

● Check Your Understanding
Recognizing Analogies

Write the letter of the word pair that has the same relationship as the word pair in capital letters.

1. WHISPER : SHOUT : :
   (A) foretell : predict   (B) lessen : increase
   (C) wish : desire   (D) decay : organism
   (E) hug : embrace

2. SHIMMER : SHINE : :
   (A) smile : grin   (B) cry : laugh   (C) walk : ride
   (D) needle : thread   (E) dull : exciting

3. CUNNING : SLYNESS : :
   (A) beauty : ugliness   (B) bravery : courage
   (C) emptiness : fullness   (D) game : tennis
   (E) smart : dumb

4. FLEXIBLE : RIGID : :
   (A) black : white   (B) similar : alike
   (C) reliable : trustworthy   (D) doctor : profession
   (E) pencil : paper

5. CONFIDENTIAL : SECRET : :
   (A) nervous : calm   (B) rainy : dry
   (C) lifeless : dead   (D) telephone : message
   (E) scared : brave

● Check Your Understanding
Completing Analogies

Use the chart on page L682 to determine the relationship of the first pair of words. Then complete the analogy with the choice that correctly completes the second pair.

6. *Maximum* is to *minimum* as *mature* is to ■.
   (A) far   (B) stout   (C) childish
   (D) ill   (E) old

7. *Inquiry* is to *question* as *cup* is to ■.
   (A) mug   (B) saucer   (C) plate
   (D) drink   (E) table

8. *Jubilant* is to *sad* as *tall* is to ■.
   (A) gruff   (B) large   (C) fat
   (D) short   (E) high

9. *Consumer* is to *seller* as *student* is to ■.
   (A) boy   (B) school   (C) teacher
   (D) bicycle   (E) desk

10. *Phase* is to *stage* as *photograph* is to ■.
   (A) camera   (B) picture   (C) album
   (D) flash   (E) color

Sentence-Completion Tests

Sentence-completion tests measure your ability to comprehend what you read and to use context correctly. Each item consists of a sentence with one or more words missing. First read the entire sentence. Then read the answer choices and select the one that completes the sentence in a way that makes sense. For example, in the following item, read the sentence and then find the word that most appropriately completes the sentence.

The new cars are very ■; they burn no more fuel than they absolutely need.
(A) small   (B) expensive   (C) efficient
(D) reliable   (E) colorful

(The answer is *(C) efficient,* which means they only use the fuel they need.)

Some sentence-completion questions have two blanks in the same sentence, with each answer choice including two words. Find the correct answer in this example.

Her long illness left Maria ■ and ■.
(A) happy . . . rested   (B) scarred . . . smiling
(C) cheery . . . homesick   (D) thin . . . tired
(E) sleepy . . . careful

(The answer is *(D) thin . . . tired.* The other choices do not make sense.)

PRACTICE YOUR SKILLS

● Check Your Understanding
Completing Sentences

Write the letter of the word that best completes each of the following sentences.

1. The cloud ■ itself around the mountain like a shawl around giant shoulders.
(A) wrapped   (B) opened   (C) left
(D) pounded   (E) tickled

2. The twins were ■ in every way, from the dimples in their cheeks to the color of their hair.
(A) annoyed   (B) identical   (C) young
(D) sisters   (E) happy

3. The doctor was pleased to announce that the patient had made a complete ■ and showed no sign of illness.
(A) recovery   (B) sickness   (C) mistake
(D) operation   (E) coma

4. Something is missing in the egg salad; I must have ■ an ingredient.
(A) doubled   (B) omitted   (C) chopped
(D) mixed   (E) bought

5. The ■ of the house was run-down, but the interior of the house was beautifully kept up.

(A) outside   (B) roof   (C) basement

(D) paint   (E) kitchen

● **Check Your Understanding**

Completing Sentences with Two Blanks

Write the letter of the words that best complete each of the following sentences.

6. Deep-sea ■ keep warm by wearing suits that water cannot ■.

(A) skiers . . . immerse   (B) boats . . . freeze

(C) divers . . . penetrate   (D) boaters . . . wrinkle

(E) fishers . . . drink

7. To avoid being ■ while taking a shower, always use your hand to ■ the water before entering the shower to make sure it is not too hot.

(A) scalded . . . test   (B) wet . . . drink

(C) cleaned . . . touch   (D) cold . . . freeze

(E) sleepy . . . splash

8. Sheryl was ■ and shy, while her sister was proud and ■.

(A) boisterous . . . meek   (B) quiet . . . outgoing

(C) loud . . . boisterous   (D) timid . . . shy

(E) lonely . . . scared

9. After paying all our expenses, our club has a ■ of $45, which we are going to donate to ■.

(A) wallet . . . ourselves   (B) surplus. . . charity

(C) bowl . . . spend   (D) wish . . . families

(E) purse . . . groceries

10. Jason became ■ and gave up quickly, but Ben was
■ and, after hours of work, finally solved the
brainteaser.

(A) happy . . . angry   (B) wonderful . . . talented

(C) frustrated . . . persistent

(D) eager . . . confused   (E) cheerful . . . lost

Reading Comprehension Tests

Reading tests assess your ability to understand and
analyze written passages. The information you need to answer
the test questions may be either directly stated or implied in
the passage. You must study, analyze, and interpret a passage
in order to answer the questions that follow it. The following
strategies will help you answer questions on reading tests.

> **Strategies for Reading Comprehension Questions**
> - Begin by skimming the questions that follow the passage.
> - Read the passage carefully and closely. Notice the main
>   ideas, organization, style, and key words.
> - Study all possible answers. Avoid choosing one answer the
>   moment you think it is a reasonable choice.
> - Use only the information in the passage when you answer
>   the questions. Do not rely on your own knowledge or ideas
>   on this kind of test.

Most reading questions will focus on one or more of the
following characteristics of a written passage.

- **Main idea** At least one question will usually
  focus on the central idea of the passage.
  Remember that the main idea of a passage covers
  all sections of the passage—not just one section
  or paragraph.

- **Supporting details** Questions about supporting details test your ability to identify the statements in the passage that back up the main idea.

- **Implied meanings** In some passages not all information is directly stated. Some questions ask you to interpret information that is merely implied.

- **Purpose and Tone** Questions on purpose and tone require that you interpret or analyze the author's attitude toward his or her subject and the author's purpose for writing.

PRACTICE YOUR SKILLS

● Check Your Understanding
Reading for Comprehension

Read the following passage and write the letter of each correct answer.

The amount of the sun's energy a place receives varies because of the way the earth moves in space. In many places, including most of the United States, winters are colder than summers. Other places may have hot or cold weather all year round. The differences are caused by changes in the earth's position in relation to the sun. That position changes in two ways—rotation and revolution.

As it travels through space, the earth spins like a top. This spinning motion is called rotation. The earth rotates on its axis. The axis is an imaginary line through the center of the earth from one pole to the other. It takes twenty-four hours for the earth to make one complete turn on its axis. When your part of the earth turns toward the sun, it is daytime. As the earth continues to rotate, your part of the earth turns away from the sun. Then it becomes dark. The earth's rotation is the reason for day and night.

In addition to spinning on its axis, the earth travels around the sun. In this motion, called revolution, the earth follows a nearly circular path, or orbit, around the sun. The earth takes about 365 days to make one complete revolution around the sun.

1. The best title for this passage is
   (A) Earth's Movement and the Sun.
   (B) Earth and Its Moon.
   (C) Our Incredible Solar System.
   (D) The History of the Sun.
   (E) My Trip to the Moon.

2. Changes in temperature on the earth's surface are due to
   (A) the temperature of the sun.
   (B) the movement of the earth.
   (C) the distance of the moon from the earth.
   (D) earth's position in the galaxy.
   (E) the position of people on earth.

3. The passage indicates that the United States
  (A) is not the only country to have differences in temperature.
  (B) is warm all year.
  (C) has hot winters and cold summers.
  (D) has the same temperatures as the countries at the equator.
  (E) has many ski resorts.

4. This passage would most likely appear in
  (A) a science textbook.
  (B) a fashion magazine.
  (C) an article on the White House Website.
  (D) a textbook on the history of space travel.
  (E) the classified ads in the newspaper.

The Double Passage

You may also be asked to read two paired passages, called the **double passage**; then you will be asked to answer questions about each passage individually and about how the two passages relate to each other. The two passages may present similar or opposing views, or they may complement each other in various ways. A brief introduction preceding the passages may help you anticipate the relationship between them.

All the questions follow the second passage. The first few questions relate to Passage 1, the next few questions relate to Passage 2, and the final questions relate to both passages. You may find it helpful to read Passage 1 first and then immediately find and answer those questions related only to Passage 1. Then read Passage 2 and answer the remaining questions.

PRACTICE YOUR SKILLS

● Check Your Understanding
Reading for Double Passage Comprehension

The following passages are about uniforms for schoolchildren in the United States. Read each passage and answer the questions that follow.

Passage 1

The recent increase in school violence has led teachers, parents, and students to consider uniforms for public-school children in America. In doing so, these proponents of similar fashion are squashing our schoolchildren's self-esteem. As children mature, they seek their individuality—they want to know *who* they are. Wearing a uniform to a school in which every other student is wearing the same outfit limits a student's self-expression. If students can't express themselves, they cannot possibly understand who they are. Although they might believe they are protecting children from school violence, those who force students to wear uniforms are stifling the individual personalities, creativity, and freedom of America's children.

Passage 2

Peer pressure for America's schoolchildren is overwhelming. Most children today are caught between pleasing their friends and following the rules. As unusual as it may seem, much peer pressure involves clothing. Children are harassed, berated, and attacked because of their choice of clothing. One solution to the problem is to require all schoolchildren to wear uniforms. If all the students in a school are wearing the same clothes, no one will be singled out for their choices. Wearing uniforms will give students relief from the pressures of deciding what to wear and the fear of wearing the "wrong" outfit. It's a simple solution with a valuable result.

1. According to the author of Passage 1, which of the following best explains the reason why schoolchildren should not wear uniforms?
   (A) Wearing uniforms stifles a student's individuality.
   (B) Students like to wear expensive clothes.
   (C) Students need to spend more time studying.
   (D) Students need to look the same.
   (E) Uniforms are cost effective.

2. The purpose of Passage 1 is to
   (A) inform readers about self-esteem.
   (B) persuade people to require uniforms.
   (C) entertain readers with humorous stories about uniforms.
   (D) persuade people not to require uniforms.
   (E) inform the reader of the cost of uniforms.

3. According to the author of Passage 2, which of the following is a result of wearing uniforms?
   (A) relief from peer pressure
   (B) an increase in violence against students
   (C) a decrease in students' self-esteem
   (D) an increase in choices of clothing
   (E) an increased laundry bill

4. The tone of Passage 2 is
   (A) lighthearted.
   (B) emphatic.
   (C) mean-spirited.
   (D) humorous.
   (E) optimistic.

5. Which of the following is not mentioned by either author?

   (A) School uniforms can decrease the amount of peer pressure faced by children.

   (B) Wearing uniforms will not eliminate all problems faced by children.

   (C) School uniforms might be a solution to many problems faced by children in school.

   (D) Expressing individual tastes in clothing can increase self-esteem.

   (E) Students who wear uniforms will not be singled out for their choices.

▶ Tests of Standard Written English

   Objective tests of standard written English assess your knowledge of the language skills used for writing. They contain sentences with underlined words, phrases, and punctuation. The underlined parts will contain errors in grammar, usage, mechanics, vocabulary, and spelling. You are asked to find the error in each sentence, or, on some tests, to identify the best way to revise a sentence or passage.

Finding Errors

The most familiar way to test a student's grasp of grammar, usage, capitalization, punctuation, word choice, and spelling is by finding errors in a sentence. A typical test item of this kind is a sentence with five underlined choices. Four of the choices suggest possible errors in the sentence. The fifth states that there is no error. Read the following sentence and identify the error, if there is one.

> The <u>bay</u> of Fundy, between Nova Scotia and New
>   **A**
>
> Brunswick, <u>has</u> the highest tides in the <u>world</u>. <u>No error.</u>
>   **B** **C**   **D**   **E**
>
> *(The answer is A. The word bay should be capitalized as part of the proper name, the Bay of Fundy.)*

The following list identifies some of the errors you should look for on a test of standard written English.

- lack of agreement between subject and verb
- lack of agreement between pronoun and antecedent
- incorrect spelling or use of a word
- missing, misplaced, or unnecessary punctuation
- missing or unnecessary capitalization
- misused or misplaced italics or quotation marks

Sometimes you will find a sentence that contains no error. Be careful, however, before you choose *(E)* as the answer. It is easy to overlook a mistake, since common errors are the kind generally included on this type of test.

Remember that the parts of a sentence that are not underlined are presumed to be correct. You can use clues in the correct parts of the sentence to help you search for errors in the underlined parts.

PRACTICE YOUR SKILLS

● Check Your Understanding
   Recognizing Errors in Writing

Write the letter of the underlined item that is incorrect. If the sentence contains no error, write E.

(1) Volcanoes <u>occur</u> when pressure <u>builds up</u>
                    A   B
<u>under neath</u> the <u>earth's</u> surface. (2) <u>Usually</u> a volcano
     C   D   A
<u>warns</u> that <u>its</u> going to <u>erupt</u> by rumbling. (3) The
    B   C   D
eruption can take <u>two</u> <u>forms</u> <u>both</u> <u>impressive.</u> (4) Either
                      A   B   C   D
<u>it shoots</u> out chunks of burning <u>debris,</u> or it sends out
     A   B
a flow of <u>liquid</u> <u>rock,</u> called lava. (5) Lava may seem
             C   D
<u>scaryer,</u> <u>but</u> the <u>flying</u> debris can be more <u>dangerous.</u>
     A   B   C   D
(6) Because lava <u>move</u> slowly, it is not <u>impossible</u> to
                    A   C
<u>avoid.</u> (7) Flying chunks of rock <u>on the other hand,</u>
   D   A   B
can travel far and <u>ignite</u> <u>roofs</u> instantly.
                       C   D

Sentence-Correction Questions

Sentence-correction questions assess your ability to recognize appropriate phrasing. Instead of locating an error in a sentence, you must select the most appropriate and effective way to write the sentence.

In this kind of question, a part of the sentence is underlined. The sentence is then followed by five different ways of writing the underlined part. The first way shown, *(A)*, simply repeats the original underlined portion. The other four give alternative ways of writing the underlined part. The choices may involve grammar, usage, capitalization,

punctuation, or word choice. Be sure that the answer you choose does not change the meaning of the original sentence.
   Look at the following example.

> Maria <u>seen that movie at the theater</u> last night.
> (A) seen that movie at the theater
> (B) seen that movie, at the theater
> (C) saw that movie, at the theater
> (D) saw that movie at the theater
> (E) saw that movie. At the theater

PRACTICE YOUR SKILLS

● Check Your Understanding
Correcting Sentences

Write the letter of the correct way, or the best way, of phrasing the underlined part of each sentence.

1. Harry <u>hasn't said nothing</u> since breakfast.
   (A) hasn't said nothing
   (B) hasnt said nothing
   (C) hasn't said, nothing
   (D) hasn't said anything
   (E) has not said nothing

2. The first person off <u>the plane was aunt bea.</u>
   (A) the plane was aunt bea.
   (B) the plane was Aunt bea.
   (C) the Plane was Aunt Bea.
   (D) the plane was Ant Bea.
   (E) the plane was Aunt Bea.

3. The weather forecast <u>called for sleet snow and rain.</u>
   (A) called for sleet snow and rain.
   (B) called for sleet, snow, and rain.
   (C) call for sleet, snow, and rain.
   (D) called for sleet snow, and, rain.
   (E) called for sleet snow. And rain.

4. Last night I finished <u>reading the story Today.</u>
   (A) reading the story Today.
   (B) reading the, story Today.
   (C) reading the story *Today.*
   (D) reading the story "Today."
   (E) read the story Today.

5. All the boys <u>carried theirs own suitcases.</u>
   (A) carried theirs own suitcases.
   (B) carried his own suitcases.
   (C) carried their own suitcases.
   (D) carried him own suitcases.
   (E) carried its own suitcases.

Revision-in-Context

Another type of multiple-choice question that appears on some standardized tests is called **revision-in-context**. These questions are based on a short passage that is meant to represent an early draft of student writing. The questions following the passage ask you to choose the best revision of a sentence, a group of sentences, or the essay as a whole or to clearly identify the writer's intention. This type of test assesses your reading ability, your writing skills, and your understanding of standard written English.

MODEL: Correcting Sentences

(1) The explorers found themselves in a barren land. **(2)** No signs of life were nowhere. **(3)** The sun parched the earth. **(4)** Water was nowhere to be found. **(5)** Suddenly they heard the rattle of a snake. **(6)** The explorers fled for safety. **(7)** Snakes were not the only kind of hazard these newcomers would have to face.

1. In relation to the rest of the passage, which of the following best describes the writer's intention in sentence 7?
 (A) to restate the opening sentence
 (B) to interest the reader in the story
 (C) to persuade the reader to buy a snake
 (D) to summarize the paragraph

2. Which of the following is the best revision of sentence 2?
 (A) There were no signs of life anywhere.
 (B) Signs of life were anywhere.
 (C) Nowhere is signs of life.
 (D) Signs of life wasn't anywhere to be found.

3. Which of the following is the best way to combine sentences 3 and 4?
 (A) The sun parched the earth, and water was nowhere to be found.
 (B) The sun parched the earth and found water nowhere.
 (C) The sun parching the earth and finding water nowhere.
 (D) The sun was parching the earth and water was nowhere to be found.

PRACTICE YOUR SKILLS

● Check Your Understanding
Correcting Sentences

Carefully read the following passage, which is an early draft of an essay about the rain forest. Write the letter of the correct answer next to each number.

> **(1)** With so many species of plants many thousands are still not studied. **(2)** The rain forests hold secrets

of many more possible cures for illnesses that need medical attention. **(3)** Scientists believe that the cure for many illnesses including cancer, may come from plants. **(4)** This cure might be from a plant that is not yet discovered. **(5)** That's why scientists argue to protect the rain forest and its natives, the people.

1. What is the purpose of sentence 2?
   - (A) to state the main idea of the essay
   - (B) to entertain the reader with unusual facts
   - (C) to persuade the reader to move to the rain forest
   - (D) to provide supporting details for the main idea
   - (E) to entertain readers with humor

2. The best revision of sentence 2 is
   - (A) The rain forests hold secrets of many more possible cures for medical illnesses.
   - (B) The rain forests, holding secrets of many more possible cures, can cure illnesses.
   - (C) The rain forests hold secrets of many more possible cures.
   - (D) The rain forests—hold secrets of many more possible cures—can cure illnesses.
   - (E) The rain forests, holding secrets, need medical attention for possible cures.

3. The best revision of sentence 3 is—
   - (A) Scientists believe that the cure for cancer may well come from a plant.
   - (B) Scientists believe, that the cure for, cancer, may well come from a plant.
   - (C) Scientists, believing that the cure for cancer, may well come from a plant.
   - (D) Scientists believe that cancer may well come from a plant with a cure.
   - (E) Scientists believe, coming from a plant with a cure, is leukemia or cancer.

4. What is the best way to combine sentences 3 and 4?

   (A) Scientists believe that cures come from plants.

   (B) Scientists believe that the cure for cancer may well come from some undiscovered plant.

   (C) Scientists believe that the cure for cancer; may well come from an undiscovered plant.

   (D) Although the plant has not yet been discovered, the scientists believe that the cure for cancer might come from the undiscovered plant.

   (E) The undiscovered plant might hold the cure to diseases like cancer, scientists believe.

5. What is the best revision for sentence 5?

   (A) This is reason enough, scientists argue, to protect the rain forest and its people.

   (B) This reason is to protect the rainforest and its native people.

   (C) Scientists argue to protect the rain forest's native people.

   (D) This reason, scientists argue, protects the rain forests, its natives, and its people.

   (E) This is reason to protect the rain forest, its native people.

Taking Essay Tests

Essay tests are designed to assess both your understanding of important ideas and your ability to see connections, or relationships, between these ideas. To do well, you must be able to organize your thoughts quickly and express them logically and clearly.

Kinds of Essay Questions

Always begin an essay test by carefully reading the instructions for all the questions on the test. Then, as you reread the instructions for your first question, look for key words, such as those listed in the following box. Such key words will tell you precisely what kind of question you are being asked to answer.

KINDS OF ESSAY QUESTIONS	
ANALYZE	Separate into parts and examine each part.
COMPARE	Point out similarities.
CONTRAST	Point out differences.
DEFINE	Clarify meaning.
DISCUSS	Examine in detail.
EVALUATE	Give your opinion.
EXPLAIN	Tell how, what, or why.
ILLUSTRATE	Give examples.
SUMMARIZE	Briefly review main points.
TRACE	Show development or progress.

As you read the instructions, jot down everything that is required in your answer or circle key words and underline key phrases in the instructions as in the following example.

(Explain) the destruction of the rain forest, the history behind the destruction and the effects experienced by people around the world. Write three paragraphs, giving (specific examples) or illustrations.

PRACTICE YOUR SKILLS

● Check Your Understanding
Interpreting Essay Test Items

Write the key direction word in each item. Then write one sentence explaining what the question asks you to do.

EXAMPLE   Trace the life cycle of a frog.

POSSIBLE ANSWER   *Trace*—Show the development, in order, of the stages in the life of a frog.

1. In your own words, define *precipitation*.

2. How does the appearance of a wolf compare with that of a coyote?

3. Briefly summarize the novel *Where the Red Fern Grows*.

4. John F. Kennedy said, "Mankind must put an end to war or war will put an end to mankind." Discuss his meaning.

5. Evaluate one of Ray Bradbury's short stories.

▶ Writing an Effective Essay Answer

The steps in writing a well-constructed essay are the same for an essay test as they are for a written assignment. The only difference is that in a test situation you have a strict time limit for writing. As a result, you need to plan how much time you will spend writing each answer and how much time you will devote to each step in the writing process. As a rule of thumb, for every five minutes of writing, allow two minutes for planning and organizing and one minute for revising and editing.

Prewriting Writing Process

Begin planning your answer by brainstorming for main ideas and supporting details. Then organize your main ideas into a simple informal outline. Your outline will help you to present your ideas in a logical order, cover all your main points, and avoid omitting important details.

INFORMAL
OUTLINE:

Destruction of the Rain Forest

1. explanation of the history

2. reasons for destruction

3. effects of destruction

GRAPHIC
ORGANIZER:

Your next step is to write a main idea statement that states your main idea and covers all of your supporting ideas. Often you can write a suitable main idea statement by rewording the test question.

ESSAY QUESTION:	Explain the destruction of the rain forest, the history behind the destruction and the effects experienced by people around the world. Write three paragraphs, giving specific examples or illustrations.
MAIN IDEA STATEMENT:	The destruction of the rain forest in recent history will have lasting effects on humanity.

Drafting   Writing Process

As you write your essay answer, keep the following strategies in mind.

> ### Strategies for Writing an Essay Answer
>
> - Write an introduction that includes the main idea statement.
> - Follow the order of your outline. Write one paragraph for each main point, beginning with a topic sentence.
> - Be specific. Support each main point by using supporting details such as facts and examples.
> - Use transitions to connect your ideas and examples.
> - End with a strong concluding statement that summarizes your main idea.
> - Write clearly and legibly because you will not have time to copy your work.

MODEL: Essay Test Answer

MAIN IDEA STATEMENT:	The destruction of the rain forest in recent history will have a lasting effect on humanity. The riches of the rain forest are invested in its plants, trees, and living creatures. Beneath them, the soil is thin and poor for growing crops. Nonetheless, for centuries, the few people living in the forests

have cleared patches of land and farmed. After a few years, the land would harden and grow nothing, so the people would move on and start again. Then the forest could start to heal the old, wounded clearing, sending up new plants to restore the growth.

Then things began to change. Cities strained at the seams with poor people. Industries grew. Suddenly, like a plague, the rain forests were filling up with humans. They came not to live from its wealth of fruits and plants and animals, but to wipe them from the land. They cleared spaces for homes, farms, ranches, and mines. They cut trees for lumber. Millions of acres were destroyed each year. The smoke from hundreds of thousands of fires lifted into the sky.

More time passed. No one seemed to understand what was being lost. Thousands of species of plants and animals were disappearing. Life-giving oxygen was being replaced by carbon dioxide from fires. Even the ashes of the burned trees, rich with nutrients, were washed away. Today, perhaps the world is beginning to understand and act to preserve remaining rain forests. Areas have been set aside where no one may harm the forest. World summits have been convened to consider the problem. Has the world acted in time to save the rain forests?

CONCLUDING STATEMENT:

Revising ▸ Writing Process

Leave time to revise and edit your essay answer. To keep your paper as neat as possible, mark any corrections or revisions clearly and write additional material in the margins. As you revise, think of the following questions.

- Did you follow the instructions completely?

- Did you interpret the question accurately?

- Did you begin with a main idea statement?

- Did you include facts, examples, or other supporting details?

- Did you sequence your ideas and examples logically in paragraphs, according to your informal outline?

- Did you use transitions to connect ideas and examples?

- Did you end with a strong concluding statement that summarizes your main idea statement?

Editing   Writing Process

After you have made any necessary revisions, quickly read your essay to check for mistakes in spelling, usage, or punctuation. As you edit, check your work for accuracy in the following areas:

- agreement between subjects and verbs *(pages L393–L429)*

- forms of comparative and superlative adjectives and adverbs *(pages L435–L457)*

- capitalization of proper nouns and proper adjectives *(pages L488–L504)*

- use of commas *(pages L530–L555)*

- use of apostrophes *(pages L597–L609)*

- division of words at the end of a line *(page L623)*

APPLY TO WRITING

Prewriting: *Essay Test Question*

Conferencing

Select any subject area such as English, science, or social studies. With your teacher's permission, form a small group with other students who are interested in the same subject. Brainstorm together a list of essay test questions related to a topic you are currently studying in the course.

EXAMPLE   Some students and parents are complaining that athletics programs in public schools have teams with only male members. The students and parents think that more girls should be allowed to play sports alongside boys on the same team. What do you think about coed teams? Use the organizer below to think about both sides of the argument.

GRAPHIC
ORGANIZER:

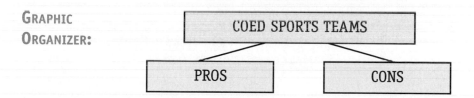

Timed Writing

Throughout your school years, you will be tested on your ability to organize your thoughts quickly and to express them in a limited time. Your teacher may ask you to write a twenty-minute, two-hundred-word essay that will then be judged on how thoroughly you covered the topic and organized your essay. To complete such an assignment, you should consider organizing your time in the following way.

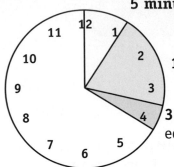

5 minutes: Brainstorm and organize ideas.

12 minutes: Write a draft.

3 minutes: Revise your work and edit it for mistakes.

The more you practice writing under time constraints, the better you will be able to apply these effective writing strategies during timed tests.

> **Strategies for Timed Tests**
> - Listen carefully to instructions. Find out if you may write notes or an outline on your paper or in the examination book.
> - Find out if you should erase mistakes or cross them out by neatly drawing a line through them.
> - Plan your time, keeping in mind your time limit.

Communicate Your Ideas

APPLY TO WRITING

Prewriting, Drafting, Revising, Editing: *Timed Writing*

Choose one side of the coed sports teams argument. Then give yourself twenty minutes to write a response. Begin by writing an informal outline and a main idea statement. As you draft your essay, follow the Strategies for Writing an Essay Answer on page L704. Be sure to revise and edit your essay answer.

A   **Abbreviation** shortened form of a word.

Action verb word that tells what action a subject is performing.

Adjective word that modifies a noun or a pronoun.

Adverb word that modifies a verb, an adjective, or another adverb.

Analogy logical relationship between a pair of words.

Antecedent word to which a pronoun refers.

Antonym word that means the opposite of another word.

Appositive noun or pronoun that identifies or explains another noun or pronoun in a sentence.

Audience person or persons who will read your work or hear your speech.

B   **Body** one or more paragraphs composed of details, facts, and examples that support the main idea.

Brainstorming prewriting technique of writing down ideas that come to mind about a given subject.

Business letter formal letter that asks for action on the part of the receiver and includes an inside address, heading, salutation, body, closing, and signature.

C   **Case** form of a noun or a pronoun that indicates its use in a sentence. In English there are three cases: the nominative case, the objective case, and the possessive case.

Chronological order the order in which events occur.

Clarity the quality of being clear.

Clause group of words that has a subject and verb and is used as part of a sentence.

Close reading reading carefully to locate specific information, follow an argument's logic, or comprehend the meaning of information.

Coherence logical and smooth flow of ideas connected with clear transitions.

Collective noun noun that names a group of people or things.

Colloquialism informal phrase or colorful expression that is not taken literally, but is understood to have a particular meaning.

Complement word or group of words used to complete a predicate.

Complex sentence sentence that consists of a dependent and an independent clause.

Composition writing form that presents and develops one main idea.

Compound sentence sentence made up of two simple sentences, usually joined by a comma and the coordinating conjunction *and*, *but*, *or*, or *yet*.

Compound subject two or more subjects in a sentence that have the same verb and are joined by a conjunction.

Compound verb two or more verbs in one sentence that have the same subject and are joined by a conjunction.

Concluding sentence a strong ending added to a paragraph that summarizes the major points, refers to the main idea, or adds an insight.

Conclusion paragraph that completes an essay and reinforces the main idea.

Conjunction word that connects words or groups of words.

Connotation meaning that comes from attitudes attached to a word.

Contraction word that combines two words into one. It uses an apostrophe to replace one or more missing letters.

Coordinating conjunction single connecting word used to join words or groups of words.

Creative writing writing style in which the writer creates characters, events, and images within stories, plays, or poems to express feelings, perceptions, and points of view.

D | **Declarative sentence** statement or expression of an opinion. It ends with a period.

Demonstrative pronoun word that substitutes for a noun and points out a person or thing.

Denotation literal meaning of a word.

Descriptive writing writing that creates a vivid picture of a person, an object, or a scene by stimulating the reader's senses.

Dialogue conversation between two or more persons.

Direct object noun or a pronoun that answers the question *What?* or *Whom?* after an action verb.

Direct quotation passage, sentence, or words stated exactly as a person wrote or said them.

Documentary images, interviews, and narration put together to create a powerful report.

Double negative use of two negative words to express an idea when only one is needed.

Drafting stage of the writing process in which the writer draws ideas together on paper forming a beginning, a middle, and an ending in a composition.

E | **Editing** stage of a writer's process in which the writer polishes his or her work by correcting errors in grammar, usage, mechanics, and spelling.

Elaboration addition of explanatory or descriptive information to a piece of writing, such as supporting details, examples, facts, and descriptions.

Electronic publishing various ways to present information through the use of technology. It includes desktop publishing (creating printed documents on a computer), audio and video recordings, and online publishing (creating a Website).

E-mail electronic mail that can be sent from one computer to another.

Essay composition of three or more paragraphs that presents and develops one main idea.

Exclamatory sentence expression of strong feeling that ends with an exclamation point.

F | **Fact** statement that can be proven.

Fiction prose work that is partly or totally imaginary.

Freewriting prewriting technique of writing freely about ideas as they come to mind.

Friendly letter writing form that may use informal English and includes six parts: heading, salutation, body, closing, and signature.

G | **Generalizing** forming an overall idea that explains something specific.

Glittering generality word or phrase that most people associate with virtue and goodness that is used to trick people into feeling positively about a subject.

H | **Helping verb** auxiliary verb that combines with the main verb to make up a verb phrase.

I | **Imperative sentence** a request or command that ends with either a period or an exclamation point.

Indefinite pronoun word that substitutes for an unnamed person or thing.

Indirect object noun or a pronoun that answers the question *To or for whom?* or *To or for what?* after an action verb.

Infinitive verb form that usually begins with *to* and is used as a noun, adjective, or adverb.

Informative writing writing that explains with facts and examples, gives directions, or lists steps in a process.

Interjection word that expresses strong feeling.

Internet global network of computers that are connected to one another with high speed data lines and telephone lines. (See also *Basic Internet Terminology* in *A Writer's Guide to Using the Internet*.)

Interrogative pronoun pronoun used to ask a question.

Interrogative sentence a question. It ends with a question mark.

Introduction first paragraph of a composition that catches the reader's attention and states the main idea.

Irregular verb verb that does not form its past and past participle by adding *-ed* to the present participle.

L | **Linking verb** verb that links the subject with another word that renames or describes the subject.

M | **Modifier** word that makes the meaning of another word more precise.

N | **Narrative writing** writing that tells a real or an imaginary story with a clear beginning, middle, and ending.

Network a system of interconnected computers.

Nonessential phrase phrase or clause that can be removed from a sentence and the sentence will still make sense.

Nonfiction prose work that contains facts about real people or events.

Nonstandard English less formal language used by people of varying regions and dialects. Not appropriate for use in writing.

Noun word that names a person, place, thing, or idea. A common noun gives a general name. A proper noun names a specific person, place, or thing and always begins with a capital letter. Concrete nouns can be seen or touched; abstract nouns can not.

O **Occasion** cause or purpose for writing; an event which prompts a writer to take action.

Online connected to the Internet via a line modem connection.

Opinion judgment or belief that cannot be absolutely proven.

Order of importance or size way of organizing information by arranging details in the order of least to most (or most to least) pertinent.

Outline information about a subject organized into main topics and subtopics.

P **Paragraph** group of related sentences that present and develop one main idea.

Participle verb form used as an adjective.

Parts of speech eight categories into which all words can be placed: noun, pronoun, verb, adjective, adverb, preposition, conjunction, and interjection.

Personal writing writing that tells a real or imaginary story from the writer's point of view.

Persuasive writing writing that expresses an opinion and uses facts, examples, and reasons in order to convince the reader of the writer's viewpoint.

Play piece of writing to be performed on a stage by actors.

Plot sequence of events leading to the outcome or point of the story; contains a climax or high point, a resolution, and an outcome or ending.

Plural form of a noun used to indicate two or more.

Poetry form of writing that uses rhythm, rhyme, and vivid imagery to express feelings and ideas.

Possessive pronouns pronouns used to show ownership or possession.

Predicate part of a sentence that tells what a subject is or does.

Predicate adjective adjective that follows a linking verb and modifies the subject.

Predicate nominative noun or a pronoun that follows a linking verb and identifies, renames, or explains the subject.

Prefix one or more syllables placed in front of a base word to form a new word.

Preposition word that shows the relationship between a noun or a pronoun and another word in the sentence.

Prepositional phrase group of words made up of a preposition, its object, and its modifiers.

Prewriting stage of the writing process in which the writer plans for drafting based on the subject, occasion, audience, and purpose for writing.

Principal parts of a verb the *present*, the *past*, and the *past participle*. The principal parts are used to form the tenses of verbs.

Proofreading carefully rereading and making corrections in grammar, usage, spelling, and mechanics in a piece of writing.

Pronoun word that takes the place of one or more nouns. Three types of pronouns are personal, reflexive, and intensive.

Publishing stage of writing process in which the writer may choose to share the work with an audience.

Purpose reason for writing or speaking on a given subject.

R **Regular verb** verb that forms the past and past participle by adding –ed or –d to the present.

Relative pronoun pronoun that begins most adjective clauses and relates the adjective clause to the noun or pronoun it describes.

Report composition that documents specific information from books, magazines, and other sources to support the thesis of the report.

Revising stage of the writing process in which the writer rethinks what is written and reworks it to increase its clarity, smoothness and power.

Root part of a word that carries the basic meaning.

Run-on sentence two or more sentences that are written as one sentence and are separated by a comma or have no mark of punctuation at all.

S **Sentence** group of words that expresses a complete thought.

Sentence fragment group of words that does not express a complete thought.

Sequential order the order in which details are arranged according to when they take place or where they are done.

Setting environment (location and time) in which the action takes place.

Short story well-developed story about characters facing a conflict or problem.

Simple sentence sentence that has one subject and one verb.

Slang nonstandard English expressions that are developed and used by particular groups.

Spatial order the order in which details are arranged according to their physical location.

Standard English proper form of the language that follows a set pattern of rules and conventions.

Style visual or verbal expression that is distinctive to an artist or writer.

Subject names the person, place, thing or idea that a sentence is about; the topic of a composition or essay.

Subordinating conjunction single connecting word used to introduce a dependent clause.

Suffix one or more syllables placed after a base word to change its part of speech and possibly its meaning.

Supporting sentences specific details, facts, examples, or reasons that explain or prove a topic sentence.

Synonym word that has nearly the same meaning as another word.

T | **Tense** form a verb takes to show time. The six tenses are the *present, past, future, present perfect, past perfect,* and *future perfect.*

Thesaurus online or print reference that gives synonyms for words.

Topic sentence sentence that states the main idea of the paragraph.

Transitions words and phrases that show how ideas are related

U | **Understood subject** unstated subject that is understood.

Unity combination or ordering of parts in a composition so that all the sentences or paragraphs work together as a whole to support one main idea.

V | **Verb** word used to express an action or state of being.

Verb phrase main verb plus one or more helping verbs.

Voice the particular sound and rhythm of the language the writer uses (closely related to *tone*).

W | **World Wide Web** network of computers within the Internet capable of delivering multimedia content and text over communication lines into personal computers all over the globe.

Writing process recursive stages that a writer proceeds through in his or her own way when developing ideas and discovering the best way to express them.

Note: Italic page numbers indicate skill sets.

Note: Italic page numbers indicate skill sets.

Note: Italic page numbers indicate skill sets.

L

Lake, capitalizing, L490–*L491*

Languages, capitalizing, L499–*L502*

Lay, lie, L469–L470, *L472–L473*

Learn, teach, L322–*L324,* L469, *L472–L473*

Leave, let, L324–*L326,* L469, *L472–L473*

Less, fewer, L465, *L467*

Letters, *See also* Business letter
capitalizing parts of, L484, *L487*
commas in, L543–*L546*
to the editor, L410

Letters of the alphabet
forming plurals of, L608–*L610,* L653–*L654*
italicizing (underlining), L567

Lie, lay, L470, *L472–L473*

Linking verb, *L86, L93,* L166
defined, L83
distinguishing from action verb, *L87–L89*
other then *be, L85*
subject complements and, L183

Little, L440–*L442*

Long passages, quoting
indent inside margins, L585
quotation marks for, L584–*L586*

-ly, adverbs ending in, L113

M

Magazines
article titles, quotation marks with, L571–*L573*
capitalizing parts of, L509–*L512*
citing articles as sources, L636–L637
italicizing titles of, L568

Main clauses. *See* independent clauses

Main idea, L687

May, can, L465, *L467–L468*

Meanings, implied, L688

Misplaced adjective clause, L260–*L262*

Misplaced adjective phrases, L194–*L195*

Misplaced modifiers, L194, L211, L227–*L228,* L260–*L262*

Misspelled words, recognizing, L641–*L642*

Mnemonic devices, L642
with spelling exceptions, L645

Modifier. *See also* adjective; adverb; comparison of modifiers
definition, L99
finding sentence patterns and, L174, *L175*

irregular, L440–*L443*

misplaced, L194–*L195,* L211, L227–*L228,* L260–*L262*

one-syllable, regular, L437

three-syllable, regular, L438

two-syllable, regular, L437

More
double comparisons with, L447–*L449*
forming comparative/superlative degrees with, L437–*L440*

Most
double comparisons with, L447–*L449*
forming comparative/superlative degrees with, L437–*L440*

Much, many, L440

Multimedia. *See* Media center

Musical terms, ending with *o,* spelling, L650

Musical works/compositions
capitalizing parts of, L509–*L512*
italicizing titles of, L568
song titles, quotation marks with, L571–*L573*

N

Negative, double, *L449–L450,* L465, L467–*L468*

Neither, nor, agreement, subject-verb with compound subjects and, L411–*L414*

Newspapers
articles, citing as sources, L636
capitalizing parts of, L509–*L512*
titles, italicizing, L568

Nominative case, L349, L387
defined, L351
pronoun as predicate nominative, L354–*L358*

Nonessential adjective clause, L256
commas with, L553

Nonessential appositive, L202

Nonessential participial phrase, L222
commas with, L553

Nonessential phrase, using commas with, L553–*L557*

Nonstandard English, L460

North, east, west, south, capitalizing, L490–*L491*

Not
as adverb, L114
verb phrase and, L18–*L19*

Note taking, L675–L677

Noun, *L47–L50,* L151
abstract, L47, L69
adjective, distinguishing from, L107–*L108,* L123

collective, L414–*L417,* L429

common, L52, *L53–L54,* L69

compound, L50–*L52,* L69
hyphenated, L626–*L628*
spelling, L652–*L654*

concrete, L47, L69

defined, L47, L69

ending in *f, fe,* spelling plural, L651–*L652*

ending in *o,* spelling plural, L649–*L650*

ending in *s, ch, sh, x,* or *z,* spelling plural, L648–*L649*

ending in *y,* spelling plural, L648–*L649*

irregular plurals, L655–*L656*

number, L376, L393–*L394*

plural, forming, *L651–L652*

plural, spelling, L647–*L652, L656–L657,* L669

possessive, *L604–L605*

possessive plural, forming, L598–*L601*

possessive singular, forming, L597–*L598*

proper, L52–*L54,* L69
capitalizing, L488–*L489, L500–L502,* L517

regular, spelling plural, L647

review, L143

spelling, same singular and plural, L655–*L656*

Nowhere, anywhere, everywhere, somewhere, L462, *L464*

Number, L376. *See also* agreement
defined, L429
of noun and pronoun, L393–*L394*
of verbs, L394–*L395*

Number, amount, L462, *L464*

Numbers
forming plurals of, L609–*L610,* L653–*L654*
italicizing (underlining), L567
spelled out, using hyphens with, L625, L626, *L627–L628*

O

Objective case, L349. *See also* Direct object; Indirect object; Pronoun
defined, L359

Object of preposition
compound, L133
pronoun as, L362–*L366*

Objects, transitive verbs and, L78–L79. *See also* Direct object; Indirect object

Of, have, L466, *L467–L468*

Other, else, L445–*L447*

Outlines

Note: Italic page numbers indicate skill sets.

Note: Italic page numbers indicate skill sets.

INDEX

INDEX

Repetition
  parts of speech and, L47
Request, understood subject in,
  L23
Revising, L40
  for essay tests, L705–L706
Revision-in context, *L698–L700*
Rise, raise, L471, *L472–L473*
Run-on sentence, *L294–L296*
  correcting, L295
  defined, L294, L301

S Salutations. See Greetings
  Scanning, L674
Script, L142
-sede, -ceed, and *-cede,* spelling
  words ending with, L645–*L647*
Semicolon, L633
  to avoid confusion, *L615–L617*
  in compound sentences,
    L611–*L614*
Sentence, *L6*
  capitalizing first word, L483
  classifying, *L33–L34*
  complex, L268–*L270*, L277
  compound, L263–*L267*, L269,
    L275, L277, L536–*L538*,
    L611–*L618*
  correcting, *L696–L697*
  declarative, L32, *L33–L35*, L41
  defined, L5, L41, L301
  diagraming, *L237, L272–L273*
  exclamatory, *L33–L35*, L41
  imperative, L32, *L33–L35*, L41
  interrogative, L32, *L33–L35*, L41
  inverted order of, L22–L23,
    L407–L409, L429
  kinds of, L32–*L35*, L39,
    L263–L265
  natural order of, L22–L23
  revising, *L15*
  run-on, *L294–L296*, L301
  simple, L263, *L264–L265*, L269,
    L277
  simple, compound, and complex,
    L269–L270
  simple and compound,
    L264–L265, L266–L267
  write in complete, L283
Sentence base, L176
Sentence-completion tests,
  L684–*L687*
Sentence diagram, defined, L36
Sentence diagraming. *See*
  Diagraming sentences
Sentence fragment, L283–*L284*
  defined, L5, L41, L283, L301
Sentence patterns, L174, *L175*
Sentence structure, L275

  variety in, L23
Set, sit, L471, *L472–L473*
Shall, will, L471, *L472–L473*
Short stories
  titles of
    capitalizing, L509–*L512*
    quotation marks with,
      L571–L573
Simple predicate. *See* verb
Simple sentence, *L264–L265*, L269,
  L277
  defined, L263
Simple subject, *L9–L11, L42–L43*
  defined, L8, L41
Singular subject, L396
Skimming, L674
Slang, colloquialisms, C470
Software. *See* computer software
Somewhere, anywhere, everywhere,
  nowhere, L462, *L467*
Spanish language, spelling plural
  words borrowed from, L650
Speaker tags
  exclamation points and question
    marks with, L580–*L581*
  quotation marks with, L574–*L576*
Spell-check programs,
  limits of, L641, L651
Spelling, *L638–L639*, L657, L668,
  L670–L671
  affixes, L657–L658, *L663–L666*,
    L669
  affixes, L669
  bases, L657–*L666*, L669
  compound noun, *L652–L654*
  irregular plural noun, *L655–L656*
  letters of the alphabet, plural
    forms of, *L653–L654*
  numerals, plural forms of,
    L653–L654
  plural noun, L647–*L652*,
    L656–L657, L669
  prefixes, L657–L658, *L663–L666*,
    L669
  strategies
    five-step, L640
  suffixes, L669
  words as words, plural forms of,
    L653–L654
  words to master, L667
Spelling exceptions
  compound noun, L653
  words ending in *-cede, -ceed,* and
    -sede, L646
  words with *ie* and *ei,* L645
Spelling journals, L643
Spelling patterns, L669
  words ending in *-cede, -ceed,* and
    -sede, L645–*L647*

  words with *ie* and *ei,* L644–L645,
    L646–L647
Spelling patterns, *L646–L647*
Spelling strategies
  five-step, L640
  mnemonic devices, L642, L645
  proof reading, L641–*L642*
  spelling journals, L643
  using dictionaries, L641–*L642*
  word pronunciation, L642
SQ3R study strategy, reading
  textbooks, L674
Standard English, L460
Standardized tests, L678
  double passage comprehension,
    L691–L693
  essay tests, L701–*L708*
  reading tests, L687–*L693*
  sentence-completion, *L685–L687*
  sentence-completion tests,
    L684–*L687*
  standard written English tests,
    L693–L700
  strategies for taking, L678
  vocabulary tests, L678–*L684*
Standard written English tests,
  L693
  identifying errors in writing,
    L694–*L695*
  revision-in-context, L697–*L700*
  sentence-correction questions,
    L695–*L697*
States, abbreviations for, L527
Study skills. *See also* standardized
  tests
  reading rate, L673–L674
strategies
  for effective studying, L673
  for reading test, L687
  for taking notes, L675–L677
  for taking standardized tests,
    L678
  for timed essay tests, L708
  for writing an essay answer, L704
Subject
  compound, L411–*L414*, L429
  pronoun as, L351–*L353*
Subject, of a sentence, *L24–L25.*
  See also agreement, subject-
  verb
  complete, L7, *L8–L11*, L41
  complete and simple, *L9–L11*
  compound, *L27–L28*, L41,
    L42–L43
  defined, L5
  diagraming, *L37*
  diagrammed, L36–*L37*
  placement of, L22–L23, *L25*
  plural, L396

Note: Italic page numbers indicate skill sets.

Note: Italic page numbers indicate skill sets.

INDEX

ACKNOWLEDGMENTS

Every effort has been made to trace the ownership of all copyrighted selections in this book and to make full acknowledgment of their use. Grateful acknowledgment is made to the following authors, publishers, agents, and individuals for their permission to reprint copyrighted material.

L372: From *New and Selected Poems* by Gary Soto © 1995. Published by Chronicle Books, San Francisco. Used with permission. **L484:** The lines from "who knows if the moon's." Copyright 1923, 1925, 1951, 1953, © 1991 by the Trustees for the E.E. Cummings Trust. Copyright © 1976 by George James Firmage, from *Complete Poems: 1904–1962* by E.E. Cummings, edited by George J. Firmage. Used by permission of Liveright Publishing Corporation. **L484:** From *The Poetry of Robert Frost,* edited by Edward Connery Lathem. Copyright 1939, 1939 by Henry Holt & Company. Copyright © 1958 by Robert Frost. Copyright © 1967 by Lesley Frost Ballantine. Reprinted by permission of Henry Holt and Company, LLC.

PHOTO CREDITS

Key: (t) top, (c) center, (b) bottom, (l) left, (r) right.

L4, L40: Erich Lessing/Art Resource, NY. **L11:** Anna Mary Robertson (Grandma) Moses, the most popular American folk artist of this century, began painting while in her seventies; her works celebrate rural traditions and community life. **L46, L68:** The Detroit Institute of Arts, Gift of Robert H. Tannahill. Photograph © 1996 The Detroit Institute of Arts. **L98, L124:** The Metropolitan Museum of Art, Alfred Stieglitz Collection, 1952. (52.203). © 2001 The Georgia O'Keeffe Foundation/Artists Rights Society (ARS), New York. **L104:** Art Resource, New York. © 2001 The Georgia O'Keeffe Foundation/Artists Rights Society (ARS), New York. **L130, L150:** Photograph by Cal Kowal. **L156, L182:** © Fiduciario en el Fideicomiso relativo a los Museos Diego Rivera y Frida Kahlo. Reproduction authorized by the Bank of Mexico, Mexico City. Av. 5 de Mayo No. 2, Col. Centro 06059, Mexico, D.F. Reproduction authorized by the National Institute of Fine Arts and Literature, Mexico City, Mexico. **L188, L210:** The Nelson-Atkins Museum of Art, Kansas City, Missouri. Purchase: acquired through the generosity of an anonymous donor. **L216, L240:** Fratelli Alinari/SuperStock. **L246, L276:** © Charles E. Burchfield Foundation, courtesy of Kennedy Galleries, New York. **L342:** Photo by George Holmes, © 1998 Blanton Museum of Art, University of Texas. **L348, L386:** Erich Lessing/Art Resource, NY. **L392, L428:** Courtesy of the Freer Gallery of Art, Smithsonian Institution, Washington, D.C. 04.232. **L434, L456:** The Baltimore Museum of Art, The Cone Collection, formed by Dr. Claribel Cone and Miss Etta Cone of Baltimore, Maryland BMA 1950.196. **L452: (t)** The Art Institute of Chicago. Gift of Elizabeth R. Vaughan. Photograph © 1996, The Art Institute of Chicago. 1950.1846. All rights reserved; **(b)** © 2001 Estate of Pablo Picasso/Artists Rights Society (ARS), New York. Photograph by Giraudon/Art Resource, New York. **L482, L516:** The National Museum of Women in the Arts, Gift of Wallace and Wilhelmina Holladay. © L & M Services B.V. Amsterdam 200109. **L566, L590:** The Metropolitan Museum of Art, H.O. Havemeyer Collection. Bequest of Mrs. H.O. Havemeyer, 1929. (29.100.34). Photograph © 1986 The Metropolitan Museum of Art. **L596, L632:** Courtesy Brewster Arts Ltd. © 2001 Leonora Carrington/Artists Rights Society (ARS), New York. **L618:** Photograph by Lee Stalsworth.